A GUIDE TO
BALTIMORE ARCHITECTURE

A GUIDE TO
BALTIMORE ARCHITECTURE

Third Edition
Revised and Enlarged

By John Dorsey and James D. Dilts

Introduction by John Dos Passos
Essays by Wilbur Harvey Hunter
and Phoebe B. Stanton

TIDEWATER PUBLISHERS
Centreville, Maryland

Library of Congress Cataloging-in-Publication Data

Dorsey, John R.
    A guide to Baltimore architecture / by John Dorsey and James D. Dilts ; foreword by John Dos Passos ; introductions by Wilbur Harvey Hunter and Phoebe B. Stanton. —3rd ed., rev. and enl.
        p.   cm.
    Includes bibliographical references and index.
    ISBN 0-87033-477-8 (pbk.)
    1. Architecture—Maryland—Baltimore—Guidebooks. 2. Baltimore (Md.)—Buildings, structures, etc.—Guidebooks. I. Dilts, James D.   II. Title.
NA735.B3D67   1997
720′.9752′6—dc20   96-31928

Manufactured in the United States of America
First edition, 1973; third edition, 1997

Contents

Preface

Since we began work on the first edition of this book thirty years ago, much has changed and much has remained the same. For this, the third edition, our essential purposes have remained constant: to gather in one place Baltimore's works of architectural significance, to organize them into useful walking and driving tours, and to produce a book that both the visitor and the resident, the layman and the expert might find of some use. Our overriding criterion in selecting the buildings has been architectural interest, rather than prominence of location or historical importance (though some of the buildings herein combine all of those qualities). To include every building on Mount Vernon Place or around the Inner Harbor, or to include a building solely for what took place there or who lived there (such as the Poe House or the Mencken House) would, we felt, weaken the focus of the book.

Since the second edition appeared in 1981, there has been no vast new renovation project such as the Inner Harbor redevelopment then under way. But there as elsewhere there have been prominent additions to the architectural landscape, from the Columbus Center, 250 West Pratt Street, and the Visionary Art Museum downtown to the Fidelity and Guaranty Life Insurance Company in Mount Washington. In addition, we have discovered older buildings of note overlooked in previous editions, from St. James and St. John's Church in East Baltimore and Temora near Columbia to the Enoch Pratt House in the heart of Baltimore and the Baltimore County Courthouse in Towson. There are twenty-four additional buildings in this edition and one added tour, Tour H: Fort McHenry–BWI Airport.

A few buildings have, unfortunately, been lost to the wrecker's ball and thus dropped from this compendium of extant architecture, including the Tower Building, the Safe Deposit and Trust Company Building, and the Marburg Tobacco Warehouse, the last a building of outstanding integrity, the destruction of which was a particularly nonsensical act of vandalism. Nevertheless, much of our architectural heritage has been preserved, thanks in no small part to such groups as Baltimore Heritage and the Commission for Historical and Architectural Preservation. We also dropped a few still-extant buildings from the present edition for various reasons: we thought them less significant than we had before, they were too out-of-the-way to be readily accessible, or they were houses whose owners did not want their addresses given.

For this edition, however, we did not simply add and subtract buildings. With but one or two exceptions, we visited anew, re-researched, and rewrote every entry in the book and every tour introduction. There is a new introductory essay, by architectural historian Phoebe B. Stanton, on twentieth-century Baltimore, taking into account the developments of the last quarter-century. The vast majority of the buildings have been rephotographed, most of them by professional photographers Bruce Savadow and Aaron T. Levin. (We made a few exceptions, such as the Battle Monument, where a new photograph would not have yielded as unobstructed a view as the earlier one.) Architect William C. Riggs painstakingly redrew and renumbered for the present book the maps he created for the first two editions. In short, we feel this volume can lay legitimate claim to being a new and completely revised edition.

We are indebted to many people for their contributions to this effort. The late John Dos Passos graciously contributed an introduction to the first edition which, though by now in a few respects out of date, is reprinted here as written. To tamper with it would have risked violating the tone Mr. Dos Passos so happily achieved. The late Wilbur Hunter's introductory essay, which deals with the history of the city's architecture down to about 1900, also stands.

For each edition, the authors had the benefit of informed advice from an advisory board of architects, scholars, and experts. For this edition the members were architects Warren Peterson, Walter Schamu, Michael F. Trostel, and James Wollon; architectural historians Carlos P. Avery, Randolph W. Chalfant, Phoebe B. Stanton, and Christopher Weeks; preservationist John McGrain; and architecture critic Edward Gunts.

We made use of and are extremely grateful for substantial recent research conducted by architects, architectural historians, and other professionals, especially those connected with the Historic Architects Round Table, informally known as the Dead Architects Society.

Others who helped with the collection of materials and with advice included the staff of the Commission for Historical and Architectural Preservation, in particular executive director Kathleen Kotarba and Birgitta Fessenden; the staff of the Maryland Historical Trust; the staff of the Maryland Room of the Enoch Pratt Free Library; architectural historians Robert Alexander and Charles E. Brownell; architect David Wright; preservationist Catharine F. Black; and photographer Gretchen Redden.

We wish to thank the Baltimore Architecture Foundation and the Baltimore chapter of the American Institute of Architects for grants that helped underwrite the cost of photography.

Finally, we are most grateful to Richard Parsons, of the Baltimore County Public Library, who not only gave us his enthusiastic encouragement but also introduced us to our publisher.

The authors selected the buildings which are included in this guide and, needless to say, are solely responsible for any errors or omissions.

A User's Guide to This Book

This guide to the architecture of Baltimore, Maryland, is divided geographically into fifteen walking and driving tours beginning downtown and ending with outlying areas. A few are also organized around themes, such as Tour H, on railroads (but not restricted to railroad buildings), and Tour M, on mill towns and planned communities. The maps on pages xi-xiii indicate where the various tours are located around the city. The first five are walking tours in and near the city center, the following ten are driving tours, covering areas from near the city's center to its outskirts. We have not set arbitrary geographical limits for the book but, rather, were governed by the vaguer idea of what can be seen on a comfortable ride, not straying too far outside the Baltimore Beltway.

Each tour begins with a map on which locations of the buildings are indicated by the tour letter and number of the building within the tour (example: K12). Following the map is a list of the buildings on the tour, giving the address, date of completion, and architect. A tour introduction, usually brief, is followed by an entry on each of the buildings, which contains the tour letter, building number, and name of the building.

D11 • CITY HALL
(BCL, NR)
100 Holliday Street
1875—George A. Frederick; 1975—Architectural Heritage; Meyers and D'Aleo, renovation architect

This is sometimes followed by either BCL (Baltimore City Landmark) and/or NR (listed on the National Register of Historic Places). The address is given on the next line, and the last line contains the date and architect, or the designation "architect unknown." The date given for a building is, so far as we can determine, the date of its completion or the date when it began to be used (in cases where originally designed parts of the structure were completed much later). When a building has had a major renovation or restoration, that date and the architectural firm are given; where there has been less work on the building, the architect may instead be mentioned in the body of the text that follows the header.

If the reader wishes to learn more about an architect of a particular building, there is a Brief Biographies of Architects section, which begins on page 395. The entries in this section are limited to architects who are no longer living and who worked in Baltimore. A glossary, beginning on page 420, defines architectural terms used in the text.

Finally, we hope our readers will not be content merely to glance at the small photographic reproductions of the buildings contained herein, but will make the effort to get around and see the buildings. To get a grasp of a work of architecture, there is no adequate substitute for seeing it firsthand.

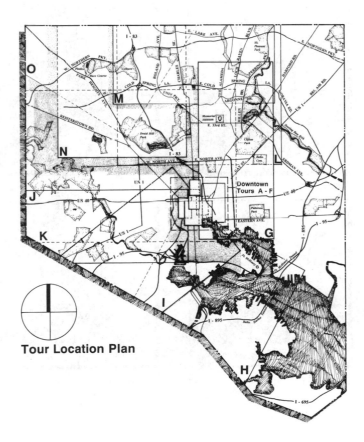

Tour Location Plan

Tours A - F

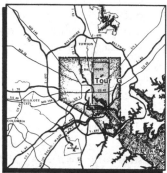

Tour G

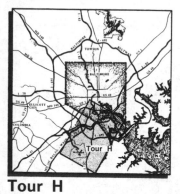

Tour H

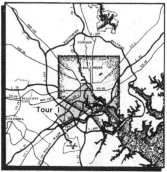

Tour I

Tour J

Tour K

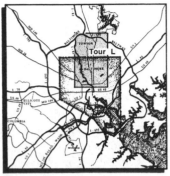

Tour L

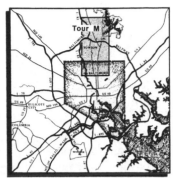

Tour M

Tour N

Tour O

Introduction

The Streets of Baltimore

John Dos Passos, December 1968

When I was a child, Baltimore held special eminence among the cities I knew. Baltimore, much
more than Richmond or Norfolk, was the capital of the
Northern Neck of Virginia, where I was more or less
brought up. At our Potomac River wharf at Lynch's
Point, or Cintra as my father liked to have it called, in
deference to his Portuguese ancestors, we had most days
a steamboat out of Baltimore and another bound for
Baltimore from Washington. The stately *Three Rivers*
made the round trip in two nights and a day. On the way
she nosed into incredibly small creeks and tied up at a
great variety of little wharves. You'd wake up in the night
to hear the roustabouts laughing and singing as they
unloaded guano, as we always called fertilizer in those
days, or rolled bags of wheat or barley up the gangplank.

All our stores came from Baltimore and all our
produce was shipped up there. It was the center of the
tall tales the watermen told. To tell the truth I never saw
much of the city except the dockside section as a child,
because when I went through I was usually on my way to
boarding school or college and was taken straight to the
B & O depot. One odd little scene has stuck in my mind.
My father, who was full of all sorts of curiosity, had
discovered a cobbled street that still had an open sewer
running down the middle of it. He exhibited it to me
with some pride as an example of how people lived
when he was a boy.

Up to very recent years Baltimore city was full of
survivals. There was a wealth of public markets, each
one with its peculiar population and lingo. Neighborhoods had a special flavor. Somehow the houses and
people of Hampden didn't look the same as the houses
and people around Union Square where the Mencken
brothers lived. The modest calm of Govans was entirely
different from the faded nineteenth-century elegance
of Mount Washington with its enormous groves of trees.
There was the old-time German section of Patterson
Park that specialized in scrubbed white marble steps

and a sort of bead curtain that I've never seen before or since in this country. These bead curtains were hung in the front doors to help keep out the flies in summer. The gaudy colored beads were strung so as to make pictures of castles on the Rhine or Niagara Falls or a lighthouse or a clipper ship in a stormy sea. Haussner's restaurant with its magnificent collection of pompier paintings and bronzes set the key for a whole region of East Baltimore. You may not think this sort of thing is "art" but it certainly manifests a cheering exuberance of spirit.

To this day there is still Dickeyville, a New England village encysted in a Baltimore suburb, and Castle Street where the colored hucksters stable their ponies and their spring wagons with the polished brass trim. And Little Italy. That corner of South Baltimore, in spite of the hideous false fronts that have been plastered over many of the old brick houses, still has a character of its own. Maybe it's the smell of tomato paste and garlic and parmesan cheese that filters out of the Italian restaurants. There's something special, too, about the docks in South Baltimore, particularly if there are a couple of freighters tied up with their loading lights on—vistas of the harbor through cables and anchor chains. That old-time maritime feeling is focused for me in a little restaurant on the harbor side of Pratt Street where my wife and I occasionally stop for a plate of oysters on the way to eat manicotti at Sabatino's. There are chromos of old steamships on the walls. The moment I step out of the car and sniff the sludgy harbor I feel again, just for an instant, the chill down the spine I felt as a small boy at the sight and smell of seagoing ships, the desperate urge to sail blue water.

Dundalk, way off east, with its higgledy-piggledy shacks and marinas and boatyards has a special Chesapeake Bay character—it might be Crisfield—but the culmination of the port of Baltimore, from the point of view of drama and visual excitement, is the foot of South Broadway. If you are so lucky as to see it when the bow of a large freighter towers above the street you immediately feel, as you do in some of the squares in Venice, that the stage is set for a play. Between the old market, and the Acropolis Restaurant with its bellydancers, and the steamers and the gold splattered black lacquer of the nighttime harbor beyond, you get a concentrated impression of a seaport town. The Block might be any-where but South Broadway is pure Baltimore.

This guide to the city won't come out a day too soon. There'll barely be time to get a look at the last vestiges of the old seaport before they are obliterated, as old-time mercantile Boston was, under concrete and speeding automobiles.

Some day the prime movers who decide our desti-nies may come to understand that the character of a city as a fit place for men and women to live depends on the survival of intriguing vestiges of the past. They give a city the historic dimension that, whether people are entirely conscious of it or not, imbues the inhabitants with a certain dignity they would not otherwise attain.

The ideal city would be one where, as in so many cities in Europe, samples have been preserved of all the different phases of architecture and decoration the place has gone through since the beginning. It isn't enough to do a Williamsburg on a few choice mansions. It is the modest buildings, adapted and readapted to a thousand uses, showing the special tricks of local brick-layers, peculiarities in stonework, some unusual way of setting chimneypots, that give the color of history. In the old architecture intimations of the kind of lives the citizens lived linger on.

Local and neighborhood idiosyncracies tend to cluster about old buildings. Survivals and traditions en-rich the city's life and make up somewhat for the disad-vantages of overcrowding and bad air. Up to a few years ago there used to be street criers in Baltimore. Some-body probably made a recording of them but folk arts without the folk are a dreary business. Baltimore will be poorer again, when the Negro hucksters give up their spring wagons, put aside the gay harness they dress up their ponies with, and take to driving trucks.

I don't mean that Baltimore doesn't still have indi-viduality. It has. A few years ago I drove a sharp-eyed friend around who could not ever remember having looked at the town carefully before. "Why it's a city of domes," he cried out, "a city of domes and spires."

We were looking up Mount Royal at the hand-somely proportioned dome of the old synagogue of Eutaw Place. A few minutes later we stopped to look east across the Fallsway at the odd cityscape which then included the old jail at one end, the dome of Johns Hopkins Hospital in the center, and odd masses of indeterminate brick buildings, topped by an unexpected little cupola, along the ridge to the southward. The noblest of Baltimore's domes is undoubtedly Latrobe's dome which caps the original Catholic Cathedral. You see it best from a distance when you are headed west across the viaduct.

One really unique building is the Shot Tower, further south down the Jones Falls valley. Besides being an interesting reminder of an outmoded technology it is an elegant piece of brick construction. Anyone who enjoys good brickwork can study it for some time. Looking down the hill from St. Paul Street there is a marvelous view of the Shot Tower and the sparkling white semi-Palladian tower of the church of St. Vincent de Paul, framed by tall dark walls. It's the sort of thing tourists go to Bologna or San Gimignano to see. Nearby is Godefroy's Battle Monument, one of the most satisfactory pieces of urban decoration I know anywhere. From the Shot Tower, Gay Street runs obliquely towards the northeast across a dilapidated part of town. Even in decay there are inklings of the fine old mercantile street it must once have been. Up towards North Avenue on Gay Street is the American Brewery, a thoroughly entertaining example of what could be called the nineteenth-century circus style.

Mills's Washington column, given a handsome setting by the distinguished landscaping of Mount Vernon Place a good many years later, is much more than a period piece. In my opinion the combined design of the monument and the garden ranks with some of the well-planned public squares of Europe.

Roaming around Baltimore, as in most of the older American cities, you keep coming across traces of often brilliant essays at city planning. Usually the plans have been left incomplete or destroyed by the irresistible march of the commercial banal. The latest effort and the most ambitious is, of course, Charles Center. Perhaps it is too early to gauge the final effect. Hamburger's and the Mechanic Theatre seem to me all to the good, and the amusing overhead walks that take the pedestrian across the streams of traffic. There's an accomplished little square with a fountain in it near the theater; but I'm afraid the final ensemble will be irrevocably marred by a hideous new hotel and by the stolid bureaucratic bulk of the Federal Building which looks as if it had been designed by a particularly uninspired computer. "That's what you think," I hear someone saying.

Let me hasten to add that any zany notions or architecturally off-color ideas expressed in the foregoing notes are purely my own. The gentlemen who compiled this guide are in no way responsible for them. My aim was merely to whet the visitor's appetite before placing him in the hands of more competent cicerones.

Part I
Essays

Baltimore Architecture in History

Wilbur Harvey Hunter, Director, Peale Museum, 1973

A lthough "Baltimore Town" was officially created by an act of the Colonial Assembly in 1729 and the original 60 acres surveyed in 1730, it was a long time before substantial buildings were erected within its precincts. In fact, the oldest surviving pre–Revolutionary War structure within the city's present boundaries is the country house Mount Clare [I5], which was built without reference to the town.

In the midst of a large tobacco and wheat plantation, and facing southeast toward the Middle Branch of the Patapsco River where the farm's own wharf was situated, Mount Clare was what the Maryland country gentleman considered elegant and necessary in the 1750s. Charles Carroll the Barrister, as he was called to distinguish him from other Carrolls, was familiar with the current fashions in Annapolis and undoubtedly had access to some of the many English architectural style books. We can assume that he designed the house himself, as did many another plantation owner, and it is certainly a personal variation on the standard English Georgian themes.

It is a miracle that Mount Clare should have survived two centuries when its few contemporaries in the town have vanished. After the Revolutionary War, however, Baltimore Town became an important mercantile center, specializing in the export of wheat and flour and in the kindred industries of shipbuilding and ropemaking. The population grew rapidly and the building trades prospered. Thousands of small, simple houses were put up to accommodate the artisans and merchants, and a dozen new churches were built.

Very little remains of this pre-1800 town. Architecturally we see the culmination of the earlier English Georgian, already old-fashioned in England, in such houses as St. Paul's Rectory of 1789 [B4] and the somewhat earlier "Captain John Steele House" [G1] at 731 Fell Street. The former is located on a substantial lot, as if it were a country house, and the latter was originally the end of an attached row of houses.

The old Otterbein United Methodist Church of 1785 [H2] and the 1783 Old Town Meeting House [F9] stand alone as the survivors of such churches as the Christ Protestant Episcopal (1785), First Presbyterian (1791), and German Reformed (1796)—all of which might have been designed out of James Gibbs's *A Book of Architecture* (1728) or similar British building guides.

At the turn of the century a new elegance appears in the country houses of the wealthy merchant princes. Homewood [L8], built in 1801–3 by Charles Carroll (son of the famous Charles Carroll of Carrollton), is the perfect example of the fashion. Sadly, it is also the last example in existence. Others were Thoroughgood Smith's Willowbrook, whose oval parlor was salvaged for display in the Baltimore Museum of Art; General Samuel Smith's remarkable Montebello; Henry Thompson's Clifton; Robert Oliver's Greenmount; John Eager Howard's Belvidere. Their names alone remain current, although the houses have long been demolished—or, in the case of Clifton, grossly altered.

Once again, the style of these country houses was old-fashioned, being a Baltimore variation of the manner of Robert Adam, introduced to England in the 1760s. It offered a new delicacy of ornamentation, based on the decorative style shown in the wall paintings and mosaics found in the ruins of Pompeii and in Diocletian's palace at Spalato [the Italian name for Split, now in Croatia]. It compared to the earlier Georgian as the severe delicacy of the furniture designs of Hepplewhite compared to the voluptuous curves of Chippendale. In this country it is described as the Federal style because it became popular about the time of the creation of the new Constitution and federal government (1789).

If this first flowering of architectural quality in Baltimore was old-fashioned by European standards, the very newest fashion followed quickly with a force that has marked the city ever since. The avant-garde architectural style of the later eighteenth century came from a new awareness of the essential forms of Greek and Roman buildings. In England, Sir John Soane, S. P. Cockerell, and others were experimenting with the ancient motifs to express volume and scale without fussy detail. In France, Claude-Nicolas Ledoux and others went even further toward geometrical simplicity; after Napoleon's 1798 expedition to Egypt they added ancient Egyptian mannerisms to the repertoire.

It was Baltimore's fortune that highly original representatives of both the English and French schools came to practice here: Benjamin Henry Latrobe, a self-styled refugee from an England whose politics he could no longer accept; and Maximilian Godefroy, a real political refugee from Napoleonic France. Their great works, and those of their students and followers, have indelibly marked the city. They gave Baltimore its first truly creative period.

Latrobe, a pupil of S. P. Cockerell, immigrated in 1795. He became a friend of Thomas Jefferson, who soon employed him as architect of the United States Capitol. Since that project moved fitfully, Latrobe worked in Virginia, Philadelphia, and particularly Baltimore. His great opportunity came when John Carroll, Archbishop of Baltimore, desiring an appropriate Cathedral for the first Roman Catholic Diocese of the United States, was sophisticated enough to employ the best architect available. Latrobe submitted alternative designs for the Cathedral in 1805. One was Gothic, the other classical.

To Archbishop Carroll and most other Baltimoreans of the day, Gothic was too radical and too unfamiliar for such an important building; he chose the classical design. It is a lesson in the changing fashions in architectural style that forty years later a Presbyterian building committee would make precisely the opposite choice for a church on Franklin Street across from the Cathedral.

The Baltimore Cathedral [B9] is Latrobe's masterpiece. The design is a precise and powerful arrangement of form, space, and mass in a manner reminiscent of the best classical architecture, but entirely original as an ensemble. One of America's greatest buildings, it has even been ranked with the best European buildings of its period by such historians as Henry-Russell Hitchcock and Sir Nikolaus Pevsner.

Meanwhile, Godefroy arrived from France in 1805 and was employed as the professor of civil and military architecture at St. Mary's College. The college was operated by the Sulpician Order, who also conducted St. Mary's Roman Catholic Seminary, founded in 1795. It was natural that the Sulpician fathers would ask Godefroy to design a new chapel building. Dedicated in 1808, and Godefroy's first work in Baltimore, St. Mary's Seminary Chapel [J3] is an anomaly for its time and place: it

ST. MARY'S SEMINARY CHAPEL

is in the Gothic manner, the first church of this architectural style to be built in America. Godefroy did not really understand Gothic architecture; the chapel is a pastiche of Gothic detail mixed with some classical motifs. The effect is pleasant, nevertheless, and the oddity of the style adds to its considerable charm.

The architect's Commercial and Farmers' Bank of 1810 showed his knowledge of the current French geometrical classicism. Although this has been destroyed, Godefroy's mastery of the style is preserved in the largest and most important of his buildings, the Unitarian Church of 1818 [B12]. The interior has been greatly altered but the overall composition—literally a cube surmounted by a hemisphere and a simple arcaded porch capped with a pediment framing a sculpture of "The Angel of Truth"—is a pure expression of the architectural theories of C. N. Ledoux. It would have seemed very up-to-date had it been built in Paris instead of Baltimore.

Godefroy's third surviving production was the Battle Monument [D1], built in memory of those who fell in the British attack on Baltimore in September 1814. The symbolism of the Roman fasces, the Egyptian tomb, and mythical griffons reflects the architect's background in Revolutionary France, where patriotic holidays and military victories were marked by great civic celebrations featuring elaborate symbolic stage settings, floats, and temporary monuments. The unique aspect of the Battle Monument is that it was a democratic monument commemorating only those who died in action—not, as was the custom, the surviving politicians and generals. Appropriately, it was adopted as the official symbol of the city of Baltimore in 1827 and appears on the city seal and flag.

Godefroy returned to France in 1819, and Latrobe left for Pittsburgh about that time, going on to New Orleans, where he died in 1820. Although the prime movers of the classical movement had left the scene, their followers continued the influence for another decade. It was one of Latrobe's students, Robert Mills, who created Baltimore's primary landmark, the Washington Monument [C1]. Mills, who liked to call himself the first American-born trained architect, also worked in Philadelphia, Washington, Richmond, and Charleston.

When it was decided to erect a monument to George Washington in Baltimore, the committee advertised for designs. Three or four were rejected, including one by Godefroy, and Mills's scheme for a giant column won the prize in 1813, with a solution almost as novel as Godefroy's Battle Monument.

It was an ancient Roman conceit to use a tall column as the base for a statue, as for example Trajan's Column in the Forum. The earliest post-Roman use seems to have been the London Monument of 1677, commemorating the Great Fire of 1666. The two other pre-Mills examples were the Colonne de La Grande Armée in Paris (1801), which was demolished in 1870 for political reasons and rebuilt later, and the Nelson Column in Dublin (1808), which was blown up in 1966. Dozens of columnar monuments of this type have been built since Baltimore's and may be found from Leningrad [St. Petersburg] to London in all sizes and styles. Mills's column is easily the largest of the genre, as well as the second oldest, and it is the best proportioned.

Both begun in 1815, the Battle Monument and the Washington Monument gave Baltimore its most famous sobriquet. In 1827, when both of them were nearly finished, President John Quincy Adams at a big public dinner in Baltimore gave as his toast, "Baltimore, the monumental city." It was more than an idle comment: no other large city in America had even one substantial monument to show. And the Monumental City we have been ever since.

A local architect, Robert Cary Long, Sr., carried forward the romantic classicism of Latrobe and Godefroy with considerable versatility. Long began as a carpenter but learned quickly from association with the masters. His first major building was the Assembly Rooms of 1797, essentially in the Georgian manner. The break into classicism came with his Union Bank of 1807, which seems to have been derived from plates in Sir John Soane's *Sketches in Architecture* (1798).

The example of Latrobe is clear in Long's Medical School building for the University of Maryland (1812). Now called Davidge Hall [E10] after one of the founding physicians, it is an exercise in the Pantheon design—a circular domed structure with a pedimented portico. In this case the plan provided instructional theaters, one above the other. In 1817 Robert Mills used the same plan for the First Baptist Church, now demolished.

Long's other major works were the St. Paul's Protestant Episcopal Church (1812), the Holliday Street Theater (1813) where the "Star-Spangled Banner" was first sung, and, up the street, Peale's Baltimore Museum (1814) [D13]. Only the last of these survives, but it has a special interest: it is the oldest museum building in this country and one of the oldest in the world.

One of the few features of Long's St. Paul's Church that survived its fire in 1854 was a pair of sculptured marble reliefs of Christ and Moses, now on the façade of the present church [B1]. A unique aspect of Baltimore architecture in this period was the extensive use of sculptured ornament. Some sculptors came from France, while President Jefferson imported Italian sculptors to work on the Capitol; some of these had time to spare for Baltimore. Antonio Capellano did the work on the Battle Monument, the Unitarian Church, and St. Paul's Church. Enrico Causici did Washington's statue for Mills's great monument. Others who worked here were Giuseppe Cerracchi, Andrei, Franzoni, and Chevalier.

Latrobe's direct influence was continued in Baltimore in the 1820s by a young man named William F. Small, who had trained in the great architect's office for two years. He produced such important buildings as Barnum's City Hotel, the Athenaeum, several churches, and a number of town houses—all now gone. Remaining are the 1829 Archbishop's Residence [B8] on Charles Street, the great country house Folly Quarter in

Howard County, and, in collaboration with William Howard, the little McKim Free School [F8].

The first two are derivative of Latrobe's "stripped classicism," with their flat wall surfaces relieved by shallow recesses for the windows, and the simple decorative moldings and capitals. However, the school is quite another page in architecture.

Small died in 1832, before the building was completed; the records of the Baltimore Library Company show that Howard had borrowed a volume of the 1762 *Antiquities of Athens*, by James Stuart and Nicholas Revett, in which there are accurate plates of the Temple of Haephaestus in Athens. The McKim School is a good three-fifths scale model of one end of that building.

Robert Cary Long, Sr., died a year after the younger Small; by then, Robert Mills had finished the Washington Monument and left for Washington and other places. The direct influence of Latrobe and Godefroy was gone. The field was left open to a new generation—the next phase of Baltimore's architectural development was led by Robert Cary Long, Jr.

The young Long was not content to follow his father's practice, but went to New York for professional training in the office of architect Martin Euclid Thompson. Here he found in the midst of the continuing classical fashion a countertrend toward Gothic and even more exotic styles. It is probable that he first saw in New York *Specimens of Gothic Architecture* (1821), by A. C. Pugin and E. J. Wilson, whose handsome illustrations of English buildings were later to be his guides in Baltimore.

Long had the opportunity to learn about the latest work of Ithiel Town and A. J. Davis, pioneers in the revival of the Gothic mode in America. In 1832 Davis had designed the Tudor Gothic country villa Glen Ellen for Baltimore's wealthy and sophisticated Robert Gilmor, Jr.

When his father died, young Long hurried back to Baltimore, but despite Gilmor's example there was no widespread demand for Gothic. Long designed the Patapsco Female Institute and the nearby house Mount Ida in Ellicott City about 1837 in a severely simple classical manner. About this time he submitted a design for the gates to Green Mount Cemetery in the Egyptian style; it was not accepted, although seemingly appropriate for the purpose. In 1836 he designed an even more elaborate Egyptian scheme for the Baltimore City and County Record Office. This was approved, but built in a very much simplified style. The new ideas were afloat.

Long's opportunity came with the sudden increase in Baltimore's population toward the end of the 1830s, largely because of the massive wave of immigration from Ireland and Germany. A good many of the Irish and some of the Germans were Roman Catholic, and some of the Germans were Jewish. There was an immediate need for more churches, and it was Long's fortune to design five churches for four different denominations within the space of two or three years. More important, he established a taste in Baltimore for the Gothic style in church building that lasted for a generation.

His first accepted design in the Gothic manner was for the gates to Green Mount Cemetery [K1]—a design that was published as a lithograph in about 1837, although not built for a few years. The next was more significant—St. Alphonsus' Roman Catholic Church [B5] begun in 1842.

St. Alphonsus' Church

Long's own drawing calls it the German Catholic Church, for it was built for a congregation of Bavarian immigrants. While this was under construction, he was called upon to design a church for a congregation of predominantly Irish Catholics settled near the Mount Clare shops of the Baltimore and Ohio Railroad. A Greek Doric temple scheme was adopted for this new St. Peter's Church [J6].

The ambivalence of choice was voiced formally in 1844, when Long submitted two designs to the building committee for a new Presbyterian congregation on Franklin Street. As the minutes of the committee state, he offered both a "Greek" and a "Gothic" scheme. Long argued for the latter, and the committee voted "in favor of the Gothic." This seemed to decide the issue for Baltimore—with only one or two exceptions, the numerous churches that sprang up in the next two decades were Gothic.

FRANKLIN STREET PRESBYTERIAN CHURCH

Long provided one of the exceptions immediately. Just after the decision of the Franklin Street Presbyterian Church [B11], the Baltimore Hebrew Congregation chose a classical design for its first synagogue on Lloyd Street [F7]. Was this the alternate Presbyterian design? In any case, it was much less specifically Greek than St. Peter's. The Doric portico is a true porch, jutting forward from the middle of the façade, and the wing walls are pierced by round windows. Inside, Long provided the usual Orthodox arrangement of a balcony for the women and ranks of pews on the main floor facing the ark at the east end.

The Lloyd Street Synagogue, for all of its classicism, is more original than the Franklin Street Church. The latter's Tudor Gothic details can be traced precisely to *Specimens of Gothic Architecture*, particularly the plates showing Hampton Court. Long's arrangement of the familiar details is skillful, however, and the general effect cannot be faulted. It must be noted that the Franklin Street Church, the synagogue, and St. Alphonsus' Church were originally painted in a color to imitate stone. The modern fondness for the natural brick is not that of the church builders.

Long decided to move to New York in the midst of this flurry of commissions, but he died suddenly; and so in the end his fame rests on his local production covering a period of only a dozen years. His experiments in eclecticism were bookish and tentative, and beneath the ornamental detail is a simple classical plan. Since he had no direct followers, it cannot be said that he was an important influence on the course of Baltimore architecture. But at least he introduced the city to the picturesque architectural ideas that supplanted the classicism of his father's generation.

The next three decades witnessed Baltimore architectural production on a scale and over a range greater than the city had ever before experienced. Immigration and economic growth in both mercantilism and manufacturing doubled the city's population and multiplied its wealth. This is the period in which Baltimore got its first comprehensive water system, its first public parks, its first public "rapid transit" system, built its first city hall, and received its first great philanthropic institutions from George Peabody and Johns Hopkins. What had been little more than an overgrown port town achieved the status of a true city.

The key factor in this era was the railroad. When Charles Carroll of Carrollton laid the first stone of the Baltimore and Ohio Railroad in a field southwest of Baltimore in 1828, he is reported to have said that it was the second most important public act of his life, the first being the signing of the Declaration of Independence.

The railroad commenced an economic revolution with results to American life every bit as far-reaching as the political revolution in 1776, and nowhere was the effect felt more deeply than in Baltimore. The B & O and the other railroads that followed linked the Baltimore port with the rich farming country of the Frederick valley and the York and Lancaster regions in Pennsylvania, and in 1852 tapped the Ohio River valley.

They also brought about the development of industrial satellite towns such as Woodberry [N4] on the Jones Falls, Avalon, Oella, and Ellicott City [J12] along the Patapsco River; industrial plants such as Cooper's Iron Works in Canton; and Winans' car and locomotive works in southwest Baltimore. The railroads were far more than transportation arteries: they ushered Baltimore into the industrial age.

Early industrialism produced little significant architecture arising out of its own needs. The development of the railroads themselves was a story of constant invention and improvisation to solve new problems, not the least of which were those relating to the right-of-way. The first sizable stream that the B & O had to cross was Baltimore's Gwynns Falls. Here was built in 1829 the first railroad bridge in this country, a simple masonry arch called the Carrollton Viaduct [I6]. Much more impressive is the great Thomas Viaduct [I7] over the Patapsco River at Relay, which was in use by 1835. Two other fine masonry bridges served the early railroad: the Patterson Viaduct near Ilchester, now mostly destroyed, and the Oliver Viaduct at Ellicott City, one arch of which still supports the track and is dated 1829.

The masonry bridges were throwbacks to classical Rome, and technically obsolete when they were built. No one could fault them for permanence—the Patterson Viaduct was abandoned because the line was changed at that point, the Oliver Viaduct was altered to accommodate the highway under it, and the other two still carry the line's trains—or for the beauty of timeless design, but they were expensive and took too long to build. Construction of the railroad moved too fast to wait for stone bridges, and the age of iron was at hand.

The Baltimore and Ohio Railroad was the school for two important American iron-bridge builders, Albert Fink and Wendel Bollman. Both joined the engineering department of the railroad as young men, grew up with the industry, and then went into bridge building themselves, Bollman remaining in Baltimore. His firm in Canton made bridges for Cuba, Chile, and other distant places, as well as several across Jones Falls in Baltimore, and he designed and constructed the iron City Hall dome. Unfortunately, most of his bridges have been replaced.

CARROLLTON VIADUCT

Another architectural by-product of the railroad was the planned industrial suburb on a large scale. The concept of a company-owned mill town was a century old in Europe and had been implemented on a small scale in early Baltimore. The Ellicotts, in developing their large flour-milling business on the Patapsco River in the late eighteenth century, had built houses for themselves and for some of their employees nearby, but the town grew in a haphazard manner. The Washington Cotton Manufactory, established in 1808 on the Jones Falls, provided some employee housing in the vicinity, although it is all gone today. The first of the new wave of industries was the Ashland Manufacturing Company, a cotton-weaving mill, which replaced an older flour mill in the vicinity of Wetheredsville (now Dickeyville [K26]), and the company built some houses for employees to supplement the existing supply.

The railroads opened up stretches of the Patapsco River and Jones Falls which were eminently suitable for mills but had no prior settlements; company-built housing was essential. The Union Manufacturing Company, located at what is now Oella, is an example. Two rows of stone houses along the hillside above the mill were built for its employees. Downstream, near the Thomas Viaduct, the Avalon Rolling Mill Company was established in 1845 with a long row of company houses, of which only one house survives today.

The Jones Falls valley was the site of the most ambitious industrial suburban development. It began with the purchase of the Woodberry flour mill by Horatio N. Gambrill in 1842 and its replacement—a large cotton mill requiring many more employees. Within the next thirty years four more cotton factories went up, as well as the Poole and Hunt machinery works, and hundreds of houses were built nearby by the mill owners. The best-planned unit is on a hill above Mount Vernon Mill [N1], built of stone about 1850 and now known as Stone Hill. The mill owners proudly pointed out that each had a side yard so the mill operatives could grow vegetables and supplement their incomes. It was paternalism, of course, but far better than the abysmal horrors of the English mill town of the same time.

Because of the needs of the railroads, and nearby supplies of ore and fuel which the railroads could easily reach, Baltimore became a major iron-production center. The ease with which iron could be cast in complicated shapes led to its extensive manufacture in the 1850s as architectural decoration. Hayward, Bartlett and Company and others turned out large quantities of iron window cornices, roof fences, grillwork for porches and balconies, and other ornamental detail.

It was James Bogardus of New York who gave Baltimore its first all-iron building in 1850, the Sun Iron building at Baltimore and South streets. It was built entirely of cast iron and wrought iron pieces bolted together. His associate, architect R. G. Hatfield of New York, provided the decorative taste by styling the building like a Renaissance palazzo with columns, pilasters, arches, and cornices—an exaggeration of surface details in imitation of stone and wood. It is most unfortunate that this landmark in architectural history was destroyed in the Fire of 1904.

Most of the iron for the building had been fabricated by Baltimore firms, but there was no local demand for another such building. Instead, commercial builders preferred masonry bearing walls, liking the ornamental possibilities of cast-iron fronts. The material permitted larger windows and was considered the elegant way to finish a street façade in mid-century. Only a few examples of the hundreds of cast-iron fronts still remain to illustrate the skill of the Baltimore foundries of that time.

On the other hand, the Peabody Institute [C2] and City Hall [D11] are significant demonstrations of the first tentative uses of structural iron in conjunction with traditional building techniques.

George Peabody, merchant and financier, who had begun his business career in Baltimore but had subsequently moved to London, in 1857 proposed to give to Baltimore an endowed cultural center which would encompass art, music, and literature. It was the first philanthropy of its kind in Baltimore and among the first in the country. Peabody insisted on placing his institute on a corner of Mount Vernon Place facing the Washington Monument, even though it was one of the most expensive building sites available. To house this magnificent gift, architect Edmund George Lind, recently arrived from London where he had been trained at the Government School of Design at Somerset House, designed an Italian Renaissance palace with marble facing. The exterior is little better than an exercise in classicism, but the extensive use of structural iron is highly original. The concert hall is spanned with iron beams and braced with iron columns, although everything is covered with plaster. There is a splendid iron spiral staircase from the cellar to the top floor, but the most exciting feature is the library reading room, a great six-story room walled with balconies and book stacks and illuminated by a skylight. All of this is supported on iron members, and iron is used extensively for balconies, floors, and shelving. It is a proto-modern construction of much sophistication.

At the same time the Peabody Institute was going forward, Baltimore put up its first large City Hall, begun in 1867 and completed in 1875. A young Baltimore architect, George A. Frederick, received the commission; for style he turned to the French Second Empire of Napoleon III as illustrated in the New Louvre of the 1850s. Popular in America at the time, it was used for such contemporary buildings as the Boston City Hall of 1862–65 and the State, War, and Navy Department building (now the Executive Office Building) adjoining the White House. Frederick capped his mansard roofs with a tall, slender dome inspired by Thomas U. Walter's recently completed dome for the United States Capitol.

If the architectural style for the City Hall was derivative and uninspired, Frederick's use of iron was bold and modern. Although the building weight is carried on masonry walls, the floor joists, rafters, and four grand staircases are iron. The chief glory is the towering cast-iron dome and drum, designed and built by Wendel Bollman.

The exploration of the new technology of iron construction is interesting to us, but it was peripheral to the desires of the architects' clients of the mid-century. To them, superficial style was more important; the whole range of historical mannerisms from Orient to Occident was ransacked for ideas, with very little concern as to whether they were academically "correct" or not.

Where the monumental effect still seemed appropriate (the Peabody, City Hall) the designs came from the Renaissance. This elaborate and formal manner was used both for the iron-front office buildings downtown and for fine private town houses in the Mount Vernon Place area.

John Rudolph Niernsee, Austrian-born and trained, and his Baltimore partner, J. Crawford Neilson, designed a number of the great town houses. Their masterpiece is the 1851 mansion at 1 West Mount Vernon Place (Hackerman House [C18]). Others are the Miller House, at 700 Cathedral Street, and Asbury House [C8], next to the Mount Vernon Place Methodist Church [C9], where the Italian palazzo style is rendered in brownstone. The change in fashion in only a decade is illustrated by comparing these buildings with the restrained classicism of the Mount Vernon Club [C16].

Gothic was preferred for churches, but the trend was away from the regularity and bookish quality of Long's Franklin Street Church to the picturesque character of earlier periods such as "English Decorated" and "Norman Gothic," as contemporaries called them. Niernsee and Neilson designed three very different specimens in the early 1850s: Grace and St. Peter's Church [C15] in English country-parish Gothic; Emmanuel Church [C11] (originally Norman in style but remodeled in 1919 to appear more academically Gothic); and the elaborate mortuary chapel for Green Mount Cemetery [K2].

Another dimension of the Gothic, figuratively and literally, was provided by Norris G. Starkweather in the vertical lines and soaring tower of the First Presbyterian Church [C13], begun in 1853 and completed in 1874. The interior is a flamboyant display of intricate plasterwork.

FIRST PRESBYTERIAN CHURCH

The freest expression of the high Victorian version of Gothic is the Mount Vernon Place Methodist Church [C9] of 1870–72 by architects Thomas Dixon and Charles L. Carson. The use of green stone from the Bare Hills quarry and contrasting red sandstone trim is quite original.

Another picturesque theme competing with the Gothic in popularity was the "Italian Villa" style used for hundreds of country houses, a few city churches, and even a railroad station in Baltimore. The source was the rustic architecture of the Tuscan countryside, particularly as interpreted by the American architect Andrew Jackson Downing and published in his *Cottage Residences* of 1842, with subsequent editions. Richard Upjohn of New York was a master of this style, as well as of Gothic, and provided the Italian basilican design for the 1854 St. Paul's Protestant Episcopal Church [B1], replacing the burned-out classical church of

Robert Cary Long, Sr., and the elegant Wyman villa, unfortunately demolished.

Local architects followed the fashion: Niernsee and Neilson used the Italianate style for St. John the Evangelist Roman Catholic Church [F12] and for the Calvert Street railroad station and the great Winans country house, Alexandroffsky. The last two are no longer standing.

Johns Hopkins "modernized" his early-nineteenth-century house Clifton [G10] in 1852 by adding a great tower, a broad veranda, and other features considered to be Italian. Many another villa rose through the countryside and in villages such as Catonsville and Reisterstown. A few remain: Crimea [K25] in Leakin Park, Anneslie, Woodbourne [M2], Dumbarton [M3]. Most of the great ones are now only names for subdivisions: Guilford, Homeland, Stoneleigh, for example.

An eccentric use of Italian ideas was the 1853 tower for the Independent Fire Company house, now Number 6 Engine House [F11], by architects William H. Reasin and Samuel Wetherald. The last appearance of this mode came after the Civil War in the new public high schools of Baltimore, of which only the old Eastern Female High School [F10] remains.

It was in "rural architecture," as Downing called it, that the greatest inventiveness is seen. Although nominally in such styles as "Rural Gothic," "Pointed," or "Tudor," "Bracketted," "Italian," or even "Elizabethan," the rural cottages of this period were really closer to an indigenous American style than almost any other buildings. They were often sheathed in wood, or at least with heavy wooden ornamental trim, scallops, and brackets, and they usually had extensive porches or verandas, features not common in similar cottages in Europe. In particular, the board-and-batten siding technique had been invented by the American architect A. J. Davis and widely popularized by Downing and others.

Baltimore's inventory of these charming cottages is still sizable. They range from the elegant Family and Children's Society House [K15] to a wide variety of wooden ornamental cottages in Mount Washington, Catonsville, Lutherville, and along the York Road corridor. The most exotic variations on the picturesque theme are the century-old pavilions in Druid Hill Park [K24] that were designed by George A. Frederick.

The appearance in the 1850s and 1860s of the "rural cottage" as an extension of the city's residential area was an early symptom of a fundamental change in the structure of Baltimore brought about by improved transportation facilities. Until 1844, the only practical means of daily transportation for almost everyone in Baltimore had been walking. Few could afford carriages, cabs, or private horses.

But in that year, franchises were granted for omnibus lines, common carriers that followed regular street routes. As the Baltimore *Sun* said: "These lines [tend] to enhance the value of property in the outskirts of the city, enabling persons to reside at a distance from their places of business, in more healthy localities, without loss of time or fatigue in walking. . . ." Similar words would be repeated after every mass transit improvement: the horse-drawn street railway in 1859, the electric streetcar in the 1890s, the automobile omnibus in the 1920s, etc.

Although land use was decidedly mixed, before 1800 speculative builders were putting up short rows of identical houses in order to get the highest economies and profits. Information about such operations is scarce, but the record of one builder in 1838 shows that he built six identical two-and-a-half-story houses, 12½ feet wide, with two rooms on each floor and attic, on Mott Street at a cost of $400 per house. He sold them for $450–$475 each, retaining ownership of the land, which he rented separately for $11 a year for each house. Then, as ever since, the builder made little construction profit but a long-term investment gain from his "ground rent." Square miles of Baltimore speculative houses were and are being built on the same system. It is not surprising that the builders sought economy rather than architectural quality and used novelties, such as white marble steps, as sales points.

As the city's population increased swiftly in the 1820s and 1830s, residential development spread slowly away from the older core. The first planned development—and Baltimore's first planned neighborhood—was John Eager Howard's Belvidere estate, stretching north of Centre Street between Howard Street and the Jones Falls to above Monument Street.

This immense tract of high-lying ground became available for development with Howard's death in 1827.

The executors of his estate decided to set it off in lots, rather than parcels. To make the most of the Washington Monument, in 1831 they established four boulevard squares about it. The north-south pair were called Washington Place, the east-west pair, Mt. Vernon Place, the name that has popularly been identified with not only the squares but an extended neighborhood.

The creation of the squares had no precedent in the United States but is an example of Baroque city planning that would not be out of place in Paris or Rome. The executors had predicted correctly: the squares around the monument became the finest residential area of Baltimore.

One or two houses had been built on Mount Vernon when the speculative building partnership of James and Samuel Canby of Wilmington, Delaware, made a proposal in 1839 for a large-scale development of middle-class housing on the outskirts of the built-up area of Baltimore. Having bought a 30-acre tract in West Baltimore, they offered the city a square of ground in the midst of the property for use as a "public square," and they pledged themselves to build substantial residences in the neighborhood for "such members of the community as may incline to retire from its more central and confined parts." The city on its part was to put up an iron fence and landscape the square.

Called Franklin Square, it was the first of the eight similar squares which encircle the heart of the city—Union, Lafayette, Harlem Park, Perkins Spring, Johnson, Madison, and Collington, to which may be added the landscaped boulevards—Eutaw Place [K18], Park Avenue, and North Broadway. The purpose behind each of them was to enhance prospective residential development; in most of them, the initiative came from the owners of the adjacent ground who then built rows of identical houses about the squares, along the boulevards, and in the vicinities.

The creation of these oases in the midst of the otherwise planless and formless march of rows of houses was in itself an architectural accomplishment. Although several have been encroached upon in the name of education and recreation, some still function as they were intended, in the words of a committee of the City Council in 1839: "Ground on which the citizens and visitors may recreate themselves on summer evenings after the toils of the day are ended."

The houses themselves had little architectural distinction; their presence was all that counted, and where rows have been demolished for schools or playgrounds, or setback apartment groups, the original architectural character of the squares and boulevards is changed. The best specimens remaining are Lafayette Square, with its exciting mixture of picturesque churches and houses; Union Square, with three sides intact and the charming cast-iron Spring House in the park; and Franklin Square, the first, with the best single row of houses of any of them, Waverly Terrace [J8]. The very name recalls the era of Sir Walter Scott and his romantic novels, and on Fayette Street nearby is a row called Ivanhoe Court.

The public-squares movement began in the age of the omnibus and gained momentum with the introduction of the horse-drawn street railway in 1859, but the real creation of the horse car was Druid Hill Park [K24]. A syndicate sought a street-railway franchise in 1858, but Mayor Thomas Swann demanded that the franchise carry with it a tax on the railway's gross receipts which was to be applied to the establishment of "one or more large parks." By 1860, the money was rolling in, and the newly appointed Park Commission purchased the estate of Lloyd Rogers, called Druid Hill, and began the long process of landscaping and developing to achieve a properly picturesque setting for the appreciation of nature and for passive exercise.

The land was manipulated to provide scenic views, romantic pathways, lakes with swans and boats, picnic groves, rustic bridges, formal promenades, and a grand entrance gateway at Madison Avenue. Under the general superintendence of Augustus Faul, engineer, the design of the park was by Howard Daniels, "landscape gardener and engineer," and the original buildings were designed by George A. Frederick. As a specimen of romantic nineteenth-century landscape art, Druid Hill Park ranks with the best in America, as well as the oldest—New York's Central Park is only a few years older.

Howard's *Monumental City* said in 1882, "The influence of the park upon adjacent property has been wonderful. Its value has been greatly enhanced, streets have been opened, avenues created, and long lines of elegant and costly residences have been built. . . ." Yet the instrument responsible for the park, the horse-drawn street railway, was also setting in motion a major change in the living habits of Baltimoreans: the garden suburb, where every house owner might have his miniature park, his own trees, garden, lawns of grass, and recreational space.

The improved transportation facilities placed a very large area within acceptable commuting distance. Speculators bought large tracts and planned subdivisions with such romantic names as Eden Terrace, Oak Forest Park, Monumental Heights, and Highland Park. The names have long since been forgotten.

The common factor of these developments was the detached house on a lot, usually rectangular and as small as the developer felt he could successfully merchandise. Streets were usually ruled off in straight lines and conventional blocks created. Although the houses were rather varied in appearance, this was mainly a matter of gables and porches—there is little of architecture and less of site planning in the late-nineteenth-century subdivisions that grew out beyond the row-house core.

The first subdivision with both architectural and planning merit was Dixon's Hill [N15], in Mount Washington. The wooded hills west of Jones Falls and the old Washington Cotton Factory had all the ingredients for the setting of a picturesque cottage, and the Northern Central Railroad running along the stream valley offered fast, reliable service to Baltimore, four miles away.

Before the Civil War some substantial wooden villas had been built on the hills, and in 1856 Thomas Dixon, architect, bought Clover Hill Farm on top of one of the hills and built his own villa. After the war, he subdivided the property, laid out irregular lots and curving roads, and built about thirty-five large villas in a variety of the popular picturesque styles. Even Downing's favorite board-and-batten style is used for the Mount Washington Presbyterian Church [N14] of 1878, which is the single most interesting building in the development.

Dixon's Hill was a true "bedroom community" from inception. By 1880, several families were in residence, and within five years almost all the houses were owned by men employed in downtown Baltimore, who had no other residential address.

The site plan was simple: a winding ring road circling the top of the hill, with several radial roads giving access to the country highway at the foot of the hill.

Because of the steep terrain and exceptionally large, irregular lots, the houses are distributed freely at different elevations.

In sharp contrast to this thoughtful plan, the conventional subdivisions such as that of the Walbrook Land Company in West Baltimore or the Peabody Heights project in the vicinity of what is now Wyman Park offer nothing but a gridiron street pattern and narrow rectangular lots. No doubt the superior quality of the plan for Dixon's Hill was due to the fact that the developer was also a resident and an architect.

By the 1880s this kind of planned community was being called a garden suburb, a name coined in England, and the most distinguished designer in the new field was the landscape architect Frederick Law Olmsted, Sr. Baltimore has only one project by this pioneer city planner, the 1887 summer colony Sudbrook, near Pikesville [O10]. The completion of the Western Maryland Railroad sparked the idea. A syndicate purchased an old estate to develop a family summer resort that would rely on the village of Pikesville for stores and the railroad for daily commuting by the breadwinners.

The land was essentially flat and featureless, and Olmsted laid out the development with the railroad station as the center of focus. At that place a bridge went over the tracks toward Pikesville, and space was allocated for a hotel intended to accommodate weekend guests. Gently twisting ring roads circled around the property, and large irregular lots were laid out. One large lot was set aside as Cliveden Green, a kind of common land. A number of the houses were designed by the Boston architectural firm of Langdon and Company, and the rest by local builders; there is little remarkable about the architecture.

Although the houses were originally without central heat and were later adapted to year-round living, Sudbrook has survived very well and retains its identity among acres of modern ranch houses—proof of the soundness of the original plan. The hotel is reputed to have had an interesting career during the Prohibition era; unfortunately, it burned soon after.

The plateau rising to the north of the mill town Hampden, bounded on the west by the Jones Falls valley and on the east by the valley of Stony Run, was the site of the greatest of the nineteenth-century garden suburbs, Roland Park [N10]. William Edmunds owned about a hundred acres of this land, and in 1890, seeing the possibilities of a large-scale subdivision, looked for capital.

Charles H. Grasty, a newspaper publisher, put him in touch with Jarvis and Conklin of Kansas City, the agents for the Lands Trust Company of England, a syndicate of capitalists. In mid-1891 a company was formed with Samuel R. Jarvis as president, young Edward H. Bouton of Kansas City as general manager, $1 million from the Lands Trust, and a name taken from a nearby reservoir, Lake Roland.

The Roland Park Company put together a number of tracts of land aggregating 550 acres and hired George E. Kessler, a topographical and landscape engineer from Kansas City, to lay out the first plat. This was the section north of Cold Spring Lane and east of Roland Avenue, probably chosen because it was the most level part of the property, and closest to the new Baltimore and Lehigh Railroad along Stony Run (later the "Ma & Pa" of commuter fame). In June 1892, Mr. Louis Lewis bought the first lot, but sales went so poorly at first that Edward H. Bouton decided it would be wise to build some houses for ready sale. Mme. Jeanne Bret, the city's most prominent dressmaker, bought one of them and became the first resident of Roland Park.

In 1897, when less than half of the lots in Plat Number One had been sold and a dozen or more of the company-built houses were not inhabited, Bouton contracted with Olmsted, Olmsted, and Eliot of Boston to plan Plat Number Two for property on the west side of Roland Avenue. Thereafter, the Olmsted firm was consistently involved in planning for the company, and Frederick Law Olmsted, Jr., was personally engaged.

In contrast with the dull uniformity and indeterminate character of most speculative real estate developments before or since, Roland Park is unusually complex in style and aspect, while also being one of the few genuine neighborhoods in Baltimore. To say that Roland Park is a state of mind is to underline the reality of the success of its planners. It has achieved in a bare seventy years the kind of historical identity we associate with much older areas in Baltimore, such as the Mount Vernon Place section or Fells Point.

Roland Park resulted from intensive planning of a sort almost unknown at that time and rarely applied today. It involved site design, land-use and architectural control, creation of common amenities, provision for transportation facilities, and, it must be said, selection of inhabitants.

By all accounts, one man was responsible for the formulation of the master plan: Edward H. Bouton, resident manager of the Roland Park Company from its inception until his retirement in 1935. His great contribution was the inclusion of land-use restrictions in each property deed—the so-called restrictive covenant by which the owner agreed to abide by certain regulations established by the Roland Park Company and which was intended to run permanently with the land.

The 1892 deed to Louis Lewis spelled out the basic restrictions: first, the premises could be used only for a single residence; second, the house must be set back from the street 30 feet; third, no stable, outbuilding, or private sewage plant was allowed; fourth, the owner agreed to pay a proportionate share of the cost of maintaining the streets, water supply, lighting and sewer systems, supplementary fire and public service; and fifth, it must cost more than $3,000.

The first three categories are no less than land-use zoning, the first such effective restrictions to be applied in Maryland until state legislation was passed twenty years later. The fourth item reveals Bouton's equally advanced conception of providing the most modern public utilities as part of the broad plan for development, using the company's initial capital and recovering the costs out of property assessments.

Bouton's most important innovation along these lines was the founding of the Lake Roland Elevated Railway in 1893, an electric streetcar line that ran from the City Hall to Roland Park and within a few years boasted of scheduled trips every four minutes running twenty-four hours a day. To round out community facilities, he built a "shopping center" on Roland Avenue and founded the Baltimore Country Club for recreational purposes; his wife helped to found the Roland Park Women's Club.

The section of the Lewis deed stipulating the minimum cost was soon transformed into a requirement that property holders must obtain the company's approval of their architectural plans. While this implies conservatism, the prevailing architectural fashion for suburban houses was quite eclectic within narrow limits.

H. H. Richardson and McKim, Mead, and White had popularized a highly picturesque version of the New England shingled cottage of the Colonial period. Most of the houses in Plat Number One, on the east side of Roland Avenue, and more than a few on the west side, belong to this genre.

No architect has been connected with these houses, but it is plain that they were built under excellent supervision and with a great deal of thought for siting. The company-built houses were deliberately scattered over Plat Number One and made an obvious standard by which to judge the "harmonious" quality of new proposals.

When the second plat, on the west side, was opened for development in 1901, Roland Park had arrived as a desirable residential neighborhood. People of considerable means and social standing bought lots and employed architects to build more impressive houses than the original cottages.

J. B. Noel Wyatt and William G. Nolting, partners in one of Baltimore's most talented architectural firms, built themselves houses in Roland Park and designed the Country Club and a good many houses for clients. The firm Ellicott and Emmart did much work, and Ellicott took up residence, too. Palmer and Lamdin were quite active in the later stages of building. The New York architect Charles A. Platt designed an entire street of houses, Goodwood Gardens.

In this phase of development can be found all the contemporary fashions in suburban architecture. Wyatt was particularly fond of the half-timbered English Tudor style which had been revived in England by Richard Norman Shaw; the shopping block is an example. Revived versions of the Georgian and the Regency styles are found, although the styles are handled quite freely and not in the later spirit of rigid copying, as seen in the "Colonial" houses in Guilford.

The steep hillsides and curious irregular lots found in the northern part of the west side called forth highly original designs which more closely identify with the British Arts and Crafts movement of William Morris, who preached the virtues of strength, sturdiness, and simplicity. Here, this was often interpreted in a new kind of Picturesque reminiscent of medieval farmhouses.

Besides these styles, we also find tile-roofed Spanish villas, Gothic churches, and, in recent years, the commonplace red brick "Colonial" exemplified by the Country Club which replaced Wyatt's shingled building. It might seem that this variety would be inharmonious, but the prodigious tree cover, extensive lawns, and shrubbery unify the landscape so that even the shingle houses which have been painted white and a few white-painted clapboard houses are scarcely noticeable. Green and brown are the colors of Roland Park.

While the new suburban lifestyle was luring middle-class people out of the city, there was a great spurt of downtown private and institutional building on a scale and lavishness not seen before. It is ironic that most of these costly buildings put up in the 1870–1900 period are considered obsolete, while many have been demolished or greatly altered, since the same period saw the practice of architecture achieve a fully professional status.

The American Institute of Architects had been formed in 1857 with Richard Upjohn as president and E. G. Lind and J. R. Niernsee representing Baltimore. The Baltimore chapter of the Institute was founded in December 1870 by fifteen architects and three engineers, most of whom had been trained in the offices of such men as Lind, Frederick, and Niernsee. Within a few years there was a new influence from such men as J. B. Noel Wyatt, who studied for a year at the new course in architecture at the Massachusetts Institute of Technology and four years at the Ecole des Beaux-Arts in Paris. This kind of scholastic training became the normal preparation for an architectural career.

The appearance of the *American Architect and Building News* in 1876 was most important in spreading knowledge of what the leading architects were doing, and similar English periodicals were easily available. New Baltimore architects were in close touch with the mainstream; on the other hand, these factors led to a great degree of uniformity and academicism.

The stylistic retreat from the exuberant revivalism of the Gothic First Presbyterian Church and the Mount Vernon Place Methodist Church begins in the 1870s with a group of new churches in what was often called Norman Gothic. The Eutaw Place Baptist Church, by Thomas Ustick Walter [K19]; Christ Church, by Baldwin and Price; and the Brown Memorial Church, by Hutton and Murdoch—all designed in 1869 and 1870—are severely restrained as to ornamental detail, and their character arises from the rugged walls laid up in courses of rough-hewn or quarry-faced stone. Otherwise the pointed windows, steeples, and other details are academic exercises in early Gothic.

At this point the genius of Henry Hobson Richardson began to influence architectural development. Following the trends set in England by Richard Norman Shaw, he pursued an architectural style that Professor Carroll L. V. Meeks called "creative eclecticism," in which the reminiscent forms and details are employed with great freedom rather than literally, so as to embellish the building without disguising its purpose.

A counter academic reaction was led by two of Richardson's pupils, Charles Follen McKim and Stanford White. Both architectural attitudes are well represented by Baltimore buildings, from the Richardsonian St. Michael and All Angels Church designed in 1877 by J. B. Noel Wyatt and Joseph Evans Sperry to a spate of "Colonial," "Gothic," and "classical" buildings of the 1930s and even later.

Wyatt and Sperry's Mercantile Trust and Deposit Company Building [D7] of 1885 is Baltimore's finest example of one mode of "creative eclecticism." Meanwhile, in 1882, Stanford White had introduced Richardson's second major theme, the early Romanesque, in the monumental Lovely Lane Methodist Church [L1] for Dr. John F. Goucher. Although by this time White was already moving away from Richardson's ideas, this church is in the master's spirit of powerful simplicity, with great rough stone walls, dramatic massing of the tower and circular auditorium, and a minimum of Romanesque detail.

Baltimore architects and their clients welcomed this manner, and over the next dozen years it was the predominant style for large institutional buildings. It was not surprising that the 1886 main building for Dr. Goucher's new Woman's College of Baltimore [L2], adjoining the church, was an echo of White's manner by the Baltimore architect Charles L. Carson. Thereafter it was commonplace, as for example in such disparate structures as the Associated Reformed Church (now Greek Orthodox), by Charles E. Cassell, 1889 [K10]; Baldwin and Pennington's Maryland Club, 1892 [K6]; Joseph Evans Sperry's Oheb Shalom Temple of 1893

[K17]; and the Maryland Penitentiary of 1893 by Jackson C. Gott.

The most original evocation of Richardson's stone style was the 1895 Mount Royal Station of the Baltimore and Ohio Railroad [K11]. Here Baldwin and Pennington married the Romanesque character to the needs of the railroad age as well as it could be done.

At the time Stanford White designed the Lovely Lane Church, the firm of McKim, Mead, and White had already begun the transition from Richardson's free eclecticism toward academicism. Their grand house for Ross Winans on St. Paul Street [K3], begun in the same year as the church, is in the French Renaissance chateau manner, with very tightly controlled brick and stone decoration. The same tendency shows in the house built on Mount Vernon Place [C17] for the Robert Garretts, with which Stanford White was closely associated. The addition in 1905 was by John Russell Pope, one of the principal continuators of the "academic reaction."

The new academicism quickly replaced free eclecticism in Baltimore as it did everywhere in the country. The tide seemed to turn just after 1900 with such formal examples as the Greek temple designed by Parker and Thomas in 1907 for the Savings Bank of Baltimore [A9]; the same firm's competition-winning neo-Georgian plan for the proposed Homewood campus of the Johns Hopkins University in 1904 [L9]; and Sperry's 1910 Emerson Tower [E7], a hulking office building tricked out to look like the tower of the Palazzo Vecchio in Florence.

The Walters Art Gallery of 1905–9 [C19] was intended as a copy of a Genoese palazzo by architects Delano and Aldrich in New York. By the 1920s Italian Baroque appears in the Ss. Philip and James Roman Catholic Church by Theodore W. Pietsch, and Gothic in the big City College [G11] by Buckler and Fenhagen. These re-revivals were all far more precise in historical accuracy than the first time around, although under the carefully contrived surface they were steel and concrete, the materials of the new age.

Baltimore in the Twentieth Century

Phoebe B. Stanton, Professor Emerita, History of Art,
The Johns Hopkins University, 1996

Baltimore was still a nineteenth-century city when, in the twentieth, who its people were, how they moved about, and where they lived and worked began to change. Suburbs developed that would over the years become larger in land and population than the city itself.

The reshaping of Baltimore was to be a classic example of what took place in many American cities. What happened here in the mid-twentieth century differed only in local particulars from the experience of other places in such things as the quality and character of the housing stock, the quantity of the migration from the city, and the valiant attempt to manage and, through aggressive urban planning, to enhance the positive and qualify the undesirable results of these changes. Architectural design would play a part in this defensive process. Although it was visible it would be a secondary rather than a formative element in the creation of the city as it is today.

At the end of the nineteenth century the shore of the Inner Harbor was lined with piers and warehouses. Like most nineteenth-century cities, Baltimore had turned its back on its industrial and maritime activities. The governmental and commercial districts of central Baltimore were located along east-west streets parallel to but insulated from the north shore of the Inner Harbor. Lombard Street, which, incidentally, lay roughly on what had been the shoreline before land was created for the piers, was the boundary that separated the commercial center from the activities at the water's edge. At the western end of the harbor a cluster of older houses—some were remnants of the original town—lay between the harborside industrial buildings and the Baltimore and Ohio Railroad yards and the shops and satellite industries that had grown up around them to the west. Industry bordered the middle and northwest branches of the Patapsco River, and in the east it had expanded to Canton and beyond. On the south side of the Inner Harbor at Federal Hill, industry adjoined another neighborhood of old houses. In the valley of the Jones Falls there were mills and dwellings occupied by those who worked in them.

A city of row houses had developed in the nineteenth century. In character the houses ranged from the elegant terraces of large houses surrounding the Washington Monument and on Charles, Cathedral, St. Paul, and Calvert streets and Park Avenue, to communities of modest working-class dwellings. Clusters of older buildings—for example, the dwellings in Tyson Street and those between Eutaw and Paca streets near St. Mary's Seminary—survived, although they had been engulfed by the growing city. As it expanded, the city would absorb other such remnants of the past that lay in its path.

A singularly effective formula for urban development, the row house was used in many cities on the East Coast, but it was a particular favorite in Baltimore, where, because it allowed as much building as possible on each lot, it was suited to the system of ground rents that prevailed. Whether the units of which they were composed were grand or modest, the continuous façades of house fronts, set immediately adjacent to the footway and related in their style, delivered an urbane totality, an understated monumentality, that established and became the visual character of Baltimore.

The pattern of two-, three-, and four-story continuous dwellings did not obliterate but emphasized the grace of the contour on which the city was set. The land descended gently from the north to the harbor in a series of slopes and it also reflected the shallow valley of the Jones Falls. These changes were magnified by the rows of houses and they, in turn, were saved from monotony and made elegant by the way in which the contour reappeared in the cornice lines and the horizontals of the windows in the façades. But these relationships between land and structures were fragile; taller buildings on lower ground could destroy the pattern by making the height of all the buildings appear to be uniform.

Also, and important for what was to come as the city grew, the traditional row house permitted development of a compact city with relatively high population densities that could be served by travel on foot or by carriage and, later, by streetcar.

In the mid-nineteenth century, as Baltimore expanded west, northwest, and east of downtown, wealthier citizens, because they owned carriages and could make the journey to and fro, began to leave the city center, foreshadowing the flight to the suburbs that was to come. The Garrett family, for example, moved from the inner city to Franklin Square when it was developed. Gradually, new streets lined with rows of houses absorbed large and small estates and farms adjacent to the city; their names, or the names of their owners—Bolton, Upton, Patterson, Tyson—survived in the sections of the town that grew where they had been.

Baltimore entrepreneurs realized building lots around a square would attract residents. English practice provided a precedent for enterprise of this kind, for some families—Grosvenor, Bedford, Cavendish, Leicester, Westminster, Cadogan—so fortunate as to own London property, had broken their estates into precincts that they made attractive by the provision of common parks and squares with graceful arrangements of terraces of houses around them. In Baltimore, Mount Vernon would be marketed in this way and so would the eight squares that distinguished nineteenth-century Baltimore.

As Baltimore entered the twentieth century it possessed a type of land use and an architectural legacy of houses that worked well together, that could be adapted to the needs and purchasing power of various classes, that was tailored to meet the financial arrangements to which Baltimore was accustomed, that exploited local building materials (bricks, marble, cast iron), that achieved a reasonable density without the construction of tall buildings filled with dwellings which, in cities such as Chicago and New York, would become tenements when they were inhabited by the less prosperous who came to settle in the inner city.

Baltimore resembled many American cities. It had a distinct city center, a "downtown," which could be reached from residential areas on foot, by easy carriage ride, or by public transport. As population changed, a new measurement, the journey to work, would define where people lived and their social status, and the place and extent of commercial and residential development. This was particularly the case with working-class residential settlement, for these people did not have the means for a long journey. Workers in the Winans locomotive shops and for the Baltimore and Ohio Railroad lived in Poppleton, those employed in the industries on and around Federal Hill and South Baltimore lived nearby,

East Baltimore would rise to serve Canton, and Hampden was home to the people who worked in the mills in the Jones Falls Valley. People who could afford to do so moved out and away from the inner city with its workplaces.

In the twentieth century the means of transport would define where and when Baltimore grew. In 1937, Steen Eiler Rasmussen, in his astute book on the history and characteristics of London, demonstrated how the growth of the underground system gave rise to suburban expansion. Theoreticians realized that the size of a city should be calculated on the distance that can be traveled in an hour; according to this measurement, as we have grown to suspect, Baltimore and Washington are one. Changes in many American cities, including Baltimore, had a special meaning, for, in the twentieth century, as the perimeter of the city was expanded by the automobile, inner-city neighborhoods were emptied and then filled by migrants from the agricultural south.

Baltimore differed from other cities in its architectural preferences. In 1887 a local critic could announce that Baltimore did not hold "quite the architectural rank she should, and that perhaps she once did, among neighboring sisters nearest her equal in size." Among Baltimore buildings he found none that "made them objects of more than local interest or place them in the front ranks with the best work that is now being done throughout the country." But he said Baltimore possessed character. It had become a city of "individual homes" that relied for their effect on "a certain amount of simplicity, where plain surfaces and natural construction are allowed to take care of themselves. . . . It may be the traditional spirit of conservatism in this old city that tempts us even in architecture to linger . . . among the good things of the past rather than to deal with the more practical things of the present or the prospects of the future."

The movers and shakers, the class that commissioned buildings, remained loyal to the taste of their forebears. In 1855, when the trustees of the Peabody Institute [C2] sought a design for their new building in Mount Vernon, they specified that they wanted a style they dubbed "Greco-Italian." Although Baltimore did not lack architectural talent, its community of architects was not large enough to produce innovative designs, its support for architecture was too limited to attract out-standing architects to establish offices, nor did Balti-more patrons seek out foreign talent. So, while in the late nineteenth century inventive architectural design developed in Chicago, Philadelphia, Boston, and New York, and while Pittsburgh commissioned major Ameri-can architects to design its public buildings, Baltimore continued to build in the Neo-Classical manner with which it had been identified in the nineteenth century. No local architect emerged around whom a Baltimore school could coalesce. Caught between Washington, a thriving city with federal patronage and a preference for the Classical style, and Philadelphia, an artistically inno-vative and sophisticated community where a school of talented designers flourished, Baltimore chose Wash-ington as its model.

Baltimore's unwillingness to experiment is illus-trated by the many buildings, in various historic styles, that Parker, Thomas, and Rice of Boston and Balti-more would add to the city in the twentieth century. The Ionic temple form of the Savings Bank of Balti-more [A9] and the Baltic style of Hansa Haus [A8] next door (two more different buildings one cannot imag-ine), the Baltimore Gas and Electric Building [A13], the Belvedere Hotel [K7], and Gilman Hall [L9] at Johns Hopkins University represent the stylistic terrain on which the firm was willing and able to perform grace-fully.

This situation would persist, as Baltimore clients found architects to satisfy their taste. In the twentieth century Laurence Hall Fowler, Baltimorean, scholar of architectural history, meticulous and exceptional designer, filled Homeland and Guilford with houses of a restrained and elegant demeanor, designed the War Memorial on City Hall Plaza and the perfectly proportioned evocation of English Regency design in the Wolman House on Charles Street [L7]. His work represented Baltimore public and private taste at its best. Mr. Fowler's reputation is only now recovering from the eclipse it suffered when radical modernism condemned eclecticism. John Russell Pope, the leader of the Neo-Classical school, who worked extensively in Washington, would be a favorite with those who com-missioned buildings on upper Charles Street. He would design the Baltimore Museum of Art [L6], University Baptist Church [L10], and the Frick mansion, Charlcote

House, with which Charles Street visually terminates; add final touches, which certainly included the Pantheon portico, to the Temple of Freemasonry [L13] at Charles and 39th streets; and prepare a scheme for the development of the Johns Hopkins University campus.

These preferences persist; in 1995 the federal judges here would say that they did not feel comfortable in a courthouse that had no columns and other classical appurtenances.

In the twentieth century the character of Baltimore and the architecture it was to acquire would respond to pressures from within and without. These stimuli emerged from Baltimore's existing buildings, the 1904 fire, the city's geographical expansion, the influx of a new population, and the arrival of a new type of design.

First of all, there was the massive legacy of earlier buildings, many of them houses, described here, that were being left behind as the city enlarged its boundaries. They were structurally sturdy, they could sustain reuse and some abuse, and their size and character meant that Baltimore would not become a slum of high-density tenements.

Then, the fire of 1904 effectively destroyed much of what had been the commercial district, from the Jones Falls to Liberty Street and south of Fayette Street to the harbor's edge, leaving the land free for rebuilding. After the fire, the mercantile and retail center was reconstituted west and north along Howard Street, which had been, particularly at its northern end, residential; the nineteenth-century houses that survive on Howard Street are proof that it once was a street where people lived. The burnt district would become the governmental (City Hall, the courthouse, and the post office bounded by Lexington, St. Paul, Fayette, and Gay streets were spared) and financial center.

The third cause of change was the geographical expansion of the city as its population grew, altering its living patterns and increasing its physical size. People who earlier would have settled in the inner city moved out along roads and by public transport and later by car to suburbs, leaving much of the housing in the center of the city to its fate. This exodus followed the old roads that bore the names of their original destinations—Belair, Frederick, York, Harford, Reisterstown—and as it progressed it absorbed earlier settlements. Parts of the old city—Hampden, Fells Point, Federal Hill, Otterbein—would survive, artifacts of what had been.

In the years between 1900 and 1929, the city expanded in all directions at the expense of inner Baltimore. In the east the neighborhood of rows of houses south and north of Patterson Park began to take shape before World War I. During and after the war, as people arrived to work in Canton and in industries to the east of the city, this area would develop an astonishing display of neat, uniform dwellings, the quintessential Baltimore row house community, and its own shopping street—a primitive mall or a second downtown—for local residents.

Above North Avenue and surrounding Druid Hill Park on the west, rows of a new kind of house appeared; rejecting the Baltimore row house pattern, many were set back from the street allowing a small dooryard, and many had front porches.

Roland Park [N10] was one of several in-town suburbs, Mount Washington was another, that grew at the end of the nineteenth century. When it took over the investment and planning policies of a European consortium that backed out of entanglement with Baltimore development, the Roland Park Company enlarged its sphere of influence and continued the benign and successful policies acquired from the Olmsted office. The earliest houses in Roland Park, especially those along Roland Avenue, were inspired by houses Stanford White and his peers were designing for Newport; others were modest efforts in the Shingle style, and a few demonstrated the desire for grandeur and stylistic variety that was infecting the American suburbs everywhere. All the houses came with some or ample grounds. Whatever their style they and their designed community were part of a retreat from the kind of dense urban living that characterized the old city.

After 1908, the extension of Roland Park above Deepdene Road would underscore these characteristics, add others, and illustrate what had been a source for the design of Roland Park. This development was notable because, set on hilly ground with interesting features that included the shallow valley of a stream, it was clearly inspired by the design of what was then a recent addition to Hampstead Garden suburb in London. The plan of the area and its houses resemble closely those that had been designed for the suburb by the English architect Baillie Scott. As in London, some of the blocks have inner block parks.

To the south of its original holdings the company moved on to develop the land on either side of University Parkway as far as 40th Street. It is a beautiful and successful plan which retains and exploits the contour of the ground with a park in the median of the street. On its west side there are some notable row houses of poured concrete [N9] and large half-timbered dwellings set far back from the street. On the north, in groups developed somewhat later, there are freestanding and semidetached Georgian Revival houses.

Inspired by its success, the Roland Park Company would undertake the development of Guilford and Homeland, retaining as much as possible of the contour and many great trees on the site. The houses display a radical departure from Baltimore's tradition of uniformity and a new preference for exotic styles; Queen Anne and Neo-Georgian predominate, but they stand beside what in England is called "stockbroker Tudor." There are a few houses in vaguely Spanish and French Provincial styles, others are reminiscent of English "Arts and Crafts" cottages. A few are Art Deco. Ultimately, the company would undertake, with less success, because the economy and the population of the city were changing, to build what is called Old Northwood, between The Alameda and Loch Raven Boulevard.

Despite the fact that it originally imposed stringent deed restrictions—they have now been lifted—the Roland Park Company and the inspiration of the Olmsted office must be credited with the creation of areas of housing that have kept their quality over the years, saved valuable residential sections of the city, and encouraged people of means to stay within the city limits.

Others were encouraged to profit from the flight from the inner city. Until the First World War the Christian Science Church in the 100 block of West University Parkway stood alone in a forest of old trees. After the war, the land bounded by University Parkway, St. Paul Street, 40th Street, and Highfield Road began to sprout apartment houses; it would become and it has remained the area of highest residential density in the city. Many of the people who settled in this area had grown up in the central city.

100 West University Parkway (1927) was designed by John H. Scarff, partner in the firm of Wyatt and Nolt-

ing, shortly after he returned to Baltimore from his training in Paris; although there are suggestions of Elizabethan detail on the exterior of this building, the influence of Sharff's French experience is revealed in the building materials and the ingenious plan of the apartments, many of which have internal sun porches that are distant relatives of those Le Corbusier used in his exhibition dwellings in the 1920s. The Ambassador (1929), across the street, is pseudo-Tudor; the lobby, restaurant, and shops are fortunately intact and perfectly reflect the prevailing taste at the time they were installed. Just as the Depression struck, the Warrington (1930) and the Northway (1931) were completed. A number of smaller apartment buildings and houses in Georgian Revival style, and particularly a fine house, now unfortunately demolished, by Laurence Hall Fowler filled the gaps between these larger buildings. Eight other apartment houses in this area were to come in the years after the Second World War; of these, Highfield House [L14] by Mies van der Rohe is one of the finest buildings in the city. The other new apartment houses are of no design consequence.

Institutional architecture both followed and encouraged the movement north along Charles Street. The Episcopal Cathedral [L12], the churches at 29th and at 39th streets and Charles, and the Second Presbyterian Church on St. Paul Street, although grand, are, predictably, stylistically unadventurous. Until it commissioned Donald Sickler, who had worked with Mies van der Rohe, to design its student union in the 1970s, Johns Hopkins University continued its solemn iteration of the stylistic manner of the Homewood House [L8] and the University of Virginia.

Charles Street had become the ceremonial residential and institutional avenue; it displayed, in chronological order, the variety of styles that were popular as it developed. The Roman Catholic church had, years earlier, received a bequest designated for a new cathedral, but the war years had intervened between the gift and building. When the decision to build was finally made the gift had multiplied, and the "modern Gothic"—the term is here used advisedly—Cathedral of Mary Our Queen [L18] was built. Its ornament suggests the Art Deco of the 1930s. Although its size is impressive, the new cathedral does not as architecture hold a position in its time in any way comparable to that held in the early nineteenth century, and today, by the magnificent basilica [B9] by Latrobe.

Simultaneously, illustrating the confusion that reigned about the meaning of architectural style for churches, a Neo-Georgian church rose at the corner of Charles Street and Northern Parkway. A short distance farther to the north, the Church of the Redeemer [L19] by Pietro Belluschi presents a tasteful modern evocation of Gothic stained glass and the beauty of exposed structure. They are united with expensive good taste.

The Embryology Laboratory at University Parkway and 39th Street [L11] is a fine representative of conservative modern design. It is carefully placed on the land it occupies, its proportions, particularly its height in relation to its breadth, are excellent, its manner is recessive, and its materials have survived the thirty years since it was built.

When, just before the Second World War, Goucher College decided to leave its campus below 25th Street [L2] and migrate to Towson [M8], it profited from the move, for land it acquired and subsequently sold would increase in value as Towson grew. But the city suffered. When the college left, it dealt Baltimore a blow from which it has not yet recovered. The part of town that was its campus remains in limbo; the college buildings, some by distinguished architects, remain; old dwellings have been demolished to make way for parking lots and car dealerships. For its part, on its new site, the college missed an opportunity to create a campus of distinction; it acquired a good landscape design but its new buildings, while pleasantly suburban, are far from exciting. Goucher College is now embedded in Towson.

In the years immediately after the war, Loch Raven Boulevard, as the result of the energy of speculative developers, became a middle-class Charles Street. Garden apartments, houses, and churches rose to accommodate people moving out of the city. To the west, the Jewish community fled north to settle on Park Heights Avenue and in Baltimore County. New synagogues replaced those that had been left behind. Noble houses on Eutaw Place [K18] above and below North Avenue would become apartments and, one after another, fall into disrepair; some burned, others were pulled down, some survive—but barely. The Marlborough apartment house, which had been a luxurious building, is still there, but it sits among new garden apartments and next to a small shopping center. The parts of Linden Avenue that in the war years had become slums, were closed, the street was obliterated, and its houses were replaced by common open space and new town houses in a variety of chic modern idioms.

The fourth and a major cause of change was the influx of a new population that occupied the old houses left behind as people moved out of the city. Between 1940 and 1970 black and white Americans in search of better jobs and living conditions moved, *en masse*, from the rural south to the urban north. In his excellent book, *City Life* (1996), Witold Rybczynski says of this migration that it "changed the nature of black America. In 1940, three quarters lived in the South, and about half were rural; by 1970, only half were Southerners and less than a quarter were rural. It also had a profound effect on American cities; after 1940, urban problems increasingly revolved around the question of black poverty and flawed race relations." The stage was set for a further dramatic modification of Baltimore, which Rybczynski singles out as a city whose experience was typical of these changes.

The fifth cause of change was the appearance of a new kind and style of architecture and its body of theory about what architecture could and should accomplish and about the history of cities and the value of planned urbanism.

In advance of the arrival of a new modern architectural style, a fashionable decorative manner, Art Deco, had appeared in the 1930s as its precursor. Baltimore, as always slow to accept new ideas, hesitated, but in the end accepted Art Deco for a few of its new buildings. The NationsBank Building [D4] is the major survivor in this style, but Art Deco can also be found hidden away in unexpected places, such as details on an occasional office building or a shop built in the 1930s, and on and in buildings different from one another as the exquisite lobby decorations at the Baltimore Country Club in Roland Park, old Dunbar High School, and the entrance to the former Hutzler's store [E2] on Howard Street.

Most of the ideas behind modern architecture came from Europe and, in the 1930s, when members of its leadership arrived as emigrés to the United States, they invaded this country's architecture schools. The principles of this new style challenged the borrowing from the past of architectural styles and decorative details that was then common. In its place an aesthetic of a new kind of architectural design came into being. It was founded upon the revelation of building materials and the means of construction. From these ideas, supposedly expressive of honesty and integrity, it was but a short step to a feeling that architecture possessed some responsibility for the reformation of society, a notion that had lurked in the background of many nineteenth-century theories. From this preoccupation came respect for the history of cities and the development of a new humane urbanism mindful of the past and reforming of the future.

Although this new kind of design, entitled the International Style, would emigrate to the United States in the 1930s, it would not have an impact in Baltimore until after the Second World War. Both Le Corbusier and Frank Lloyd Wright—representatives of two very different schools of modern design—had lectured in Baltimore in the 1930s, but their audiences thought of their ideas as art rather than sources for practical solutions for local problems that were then emerging.

Alexander Cochran, a Baltimorean and an architect who returned home after education at Princeton, Yale, and Harvard and service in the war, was the emissary of these new ideas. He built, to the astonishment of Baltimore, a home for his family in the modern idiom [O1]. He established his own architectural office and throughout the rest of his life he worked as a missionary in the cause of the new kind of design and the social ideals upon which it was founded. Conforming to the respect for older architecture of good design that was part of the doctrine of the modern movement, his office would adapt the old Mount Royal Station [K11] for use by the Maryland Institute and rehabilitate St. Mary's Chapel [J3] on Paca Street.

The handwriting was on the wall. In 1953 Hutzler's built a luxurious store in Towson, a small town which was well on its way to becoming Baltimore's second central business district. A shopping mall rose at Mondawmin—it was first built as an open courtyard surrounded by two stories of shops and it was later roofed-in to become a true "mall." Northwood appeared and so did commercial developments on the western edge of the city. They included branches of the major downtown department stores and acres of new housing. There was talk of need for a road that would encircle the city, circumvent its complications, and provide access to areas that could be or were already developed as suburban housing. The Beltway was the result and, although it eased the situation, it was itself a generator of traffic. In 1996 the news is out that it will be widened.

In the vocabulary of commerce and consumers the word *mall* has supplanted *downtown*. Air-conditioned, adorned with potted palms and fountains, with movie houses and other recreational and social activities, even exercise such as "mall walking" for the elderly, this new kind of marketplace, equipped with acres of parking, has replaced the traditional center city that had for centuries been a part of urban life. The United States no longer offered the kind of pleasure that, ironically, Americans most enjoyed and remembered about Florence and Verona and other European cities. It became possible to live and work in Baltimore and never enter its downtown. The automobile was all-consuming, conditioning everything in its path. Central Baltimore would become something one drove around or hurried through or into. Early on, Robert Moses had been imported from New York to deliver an opinion on highways to improve the Baltimore situation; it was his plan that turned Franklin and Mulberry into one-way streets across downtown and created the depressed and depressing expressway that splits the old residential section of West Baltimore into two parts. Whole neighborhoods were lost when hundreds of small houses that had been part of the original city were destroyed in the course of this so-called improvement. Henry Barnes, an expert on traffic, was brought in; it is he who, in the 1950s, made many streets one-way and coordinated the traffic signals to allow for an uninterrupted journey by car. The sight and sound and vibration of fast one-way automobile traffic would destroy the fragile peace and scale of old residential neighborhoods.

In spite of attempts to remedy their destructive influence, over the years highways overwhelmed Baltimore. They relieved the strain on some inner-city streets but they also swallowed up land and made the parking garage a necessity, for cars had to be stored somewhere while their owners were at work. No matter how much one tries to disguise them, garages on the lower floors of office buildings are inert and unsatisfactory and their sloping ramps cannot be hidden. A road that would connect the Beltway and downtown was inevitable; in the 1960s the Jones Falls Expressway was laid in the valley of the Jones Falls. Unlike Washington and Philadelphia, which had preserved streambeds in their midst, Baltimore filled its with an elevated highway. The coup de grace was the construction of the Martin Luther King, Jr. Boulevard, which ploughed through older residential settlements and circled the inner city on the west. On one hand it could be said that roads such as this and the Jones Falls Expressway siphoned automobile traffic off the city streets. On the other, they helped to create a situation in which the downtown became just one of Baltimore's many nodes of settlement and commercial life.

Concern for what was happening to Baltimore and its people had inspired the foundation of the Citizens Planning and Housing Association, a national pioneer among those addressing the problem of inner-city housing. The Municipal Art Society had also begun to worry. In 1954, the Committee for Downtown, a group of retail merchants and property owners, was founded to explore how the inner city could be rescued. In 1955, the Greater Baltimore Committee, of which James Rouse was a leading member, was formed, and in 1956 its Planning Council was convened, uniting a will to improve the city and the means to do so. At the same time the city government convened an Urban Renewal Study Board, a group composed of experts from outside of Baltimore. It presented a scheme for reformation of government and planning that included creation of a Baltimore Urban Renewal and Housing Agency, an extraordinary arm of government to work in tandem with the private sector to rescue the business district and halt the deterioration of residential Baltimore.

In January 1957, David Wallace was called from Philadelphia to be the Director of the Planning Council. In 1959, Richard Steiner returned to Baltimore from employment with the federal government in Washington to head the new agency created by the Urban Renewal Study Board. The private interest and public administration needed to make Charles Center a reality was at hand. Together, these agencies could exploit financial assistance offered by the federal government, the state of Maryland, and local sources to replan and rebuild part of downtown. The plan the council designed would include the best in current ideas on city form. The ideals of urbanism that were part of the modern movement in architecture had come to Baltimore.

Thanks to Mr. Wallace and his staff, the participation of business interests, an enlightened city administration, and the financial assistance of the federal government, Charles Center was to be, perhaps, the most successful of the city centers rebuilt in the United States in the 1950s. Its plan was presented and bonds for the city's part in its construction and procurement of money from the state of Maryland and the federal government were in place in 1958 and 1959.

Charles Center was unusual in that it was to be woven around some existing buildings of good design that were occupied by businesses: those of the Baltimore and Ohio Railroad and the Baltimore Gas and Electric Company [A13] (to which a new building was added when Charles Center was built), the Fidelity Building [A15], and structures on the east side of Charles Street. It was to include mixed uses: a federal building, office and retail space, a theater, housing, hotels—one preexisting and others to be built—recreational and dining facilities, a sports arena, and ample parking underground and out of sight. It was also designed to relate to and bridge the gap between adjacent business districts on Howard Street and the financial and governmental center to the east.

Prior to offering parcels of land to developers, sites for new buildings were carefully defined. There were to be a few bumps in the road. When his proposal for the site of the first building in Charles Center did not observe the requirements set by the plan and Metropolitan Structures was invited to have Mies van der Rohe design One Charles Center [A12], Jacob Blaustein purchased a site at Charles and Fayette streets adjacent to Charles Center and constructed an office building by Vincent Kling of Philadelphia. When it opened in 1964 it disturbed but did no irreparable damage to the plan for office space availability that underlay the program for Charles Center. Later, the block where the Blaustein building stood would be filled to the south when the Grace Building at Charles and Baltimore streets, a careful and understated design, was built.

Many of the buildings of Charles Center and the character and quality of its details were notable. An Architectural Review Board of advisors on design was established to examine proposals for buildings and for designs required for service structures, such as parking garages, the treatment of open spaces, the plazas, and provision for pedestrian movement via overhead walkways that were integral to the scheme. In his agency, Mr. Steiner established the Design Advisory Panel to perform comparable tasks. Both boards were advisory only; their effectiveness would depend on the willingness of the city to accept their decisions. Both panels have continued to exist. Two members of the Design Advisory Panel also sit on the Architectural Review Board.

One Charles Center [A12] was opened in 1962. It would be the only building in the inner city by one of the original masters of modern architecture. Although the requirements of the site meant that Mies had to devise a T-shaped structure and provide for steps down from one plaza to another, things he would not normally have condoned, he conformed to the overall design requirement. The use of the building has changed, the flight of steps Mies designed from his building to the plaza below has been removed and another substituted, and the travertine paving at ground level has been altered because it did not survive Baltimore winters, but One Charles Center continues to reign as the keynote statement of the optimism with which Baltimore undertook renovation and rebuilding of its downtown.

The buildings, plazas, and system of walkways that followed were designed by architects whose work was chosen for its quality and the way it fitted into the design of the whole. Some of these architects had been trained by the leaders of the modern movement who had come to the United States from abroad. For example, New York's John Johansen, architect of the American Embassy in Ireland and of the Mechanic Theater [A10], had studied at Harvard with Walter Gropius and Marcel Breuer. At the time he worked in Baltimore, Johansen was experimenting with the use of concrete. Like the South Bank theaters in London, the Mechanic has no cream and gold Baroque ornament traditional to theaters. Borrowing from and adapting the handling of concrete by Le Corbusier, the surfaces of the theater are rough inside and out, and their color and texture are that of the concrete. The external forms of the building are massive, legible expressions of the volumes and arrangement of the interior spaces. The entrance from the plaza typifies the aesthetic of the whole; there is no formal lobby or antechamber; instead, the audience mounts an unostentatious staircase directly from plaza level to a major interior lobby of which one wall is the exterior of the auditorium.

Many of the buildings in Charles Center were the work of local firms: Warren Peterson and Charles Brickbauer designed buildings in 1966 and 1969, and RTKL Associates, a distinguished local firm, would, in 1975, design Charles Center South [A6], one of the best of the new structures. The plan suggested that the Hamburgers clothing store, which had been displaced by the construction of Charles Center, be rehoused in a dramatic bridge building over Fayette Street that would connect the plaza beneath One Charles Center with the pedestrian walkway.

With the exception of One Charles Center, the new buildings in Charles Center display the beginning of a stylistic revision, a movement away from the stringent standards set by the first or classical phase of the modern movement. Although all are in a compromised modern idiom, there is little uniformity among them save that they all demonstrate a concern for the decorative. They emphasize rich materials, granite of various colors and textures, travertine, black glass, glass-enclosed lobbies that contain no offices (the Sun Life Building [A7] is an example), exposed polished metal, concrete treated in exotic ways.

It was inevitable that a discordant note would be struck somewhere in so extensive a planned rebuilding; the new federal office building, over which the Planning Council and the administration of Charles Center had slight control, is in no way the equal of the Mercantile Safe Deposit [A11] (by Peterson and Brickbauer) or the Mechanic Theater that face it across Hopkins Plaza. The Civic Center, even with its recent renovation, is hardly a thing of beauty.

Every attempt was made to improve areas adjacent to Charles Center. The street to the east of the Civic Center has been widened and planted. Lexington Street between Cathedral and Eutaw streets was carefully redesigned into a pedestrian space; improvements in the

Lexington Market helped, but the decay of Howard and Eutaw streets would progress unchecked. Today Howard Street is virtually derelict—only its upper end exhibits some vitality. Some buildings have been demolished and more will be. The movie houses are gone. There are few pedestrians. It is sad to recall that not very long ago there were so many pedestrians that Henry Barnes (the traffic expert consulted in the fifties) arranged the traffic lights at Howard and Lexington to give them free access to walk diagonally with impunity; and that at the corner of Howard and Lexington streets, one could shop in four major department stores. None are now there. But improvements have taken place. The old Western High School at Howard and Centre streets has been converted to housing and other new housing has begun to appear. South of Lexington Street on Lombard and Pratt streets are new hotels; and a handsome new office building, one of the best additions to downtown in a very long time, has been built at Howard and Baltimore streets. They promise that improvement may come from that direction.

When negotiations for the building of Charles Center and the establishment of the principles that would be followed in its development were complete, David Wallace left Baltimore in 1961 to establish a planning firm in Philadelphia.

Two years later, when Mayor McKeldin announced that the redevelopment of the Inner Harbor, which was an unsightly collection of piers, warehouses, and parking lots, was to follow on the heels of the success of Charles Center, Mr. Wallace was called in to prepare its master plan, which was accepted in 1967. Money would be provided for acquisition and clearance of the existing buildings, and an arm of government, entitled Charles Center–Inner Harbor Management, was established to provide continuity of oversight and design. The city began to build the public walkways along the harbor, part of its share of the improvement. The Architectural Review Board would function under its aegis.

Primary considerations of design in this new area would be to try to prevent the old downtown from being cut off from the harbor by a range of new tall buildings, and to see to it that Lombard Street did not become a service street addressed by the entrances to parking garages and truck access to the new office buildings and hotels. As at Charles Center, the Wallace plan for the Inner Harbor called for inclusion of older buildings. It also proposed a wide pedestrian walkway along the north side of Pratt Street and a uniform and, most importantly, a relatively low height of the new buildings along it. Mr. Wallace perceived that tall buildings would alter the relationship between architecture and contour that characterized Baltimore and separated the old downtown from the harbor.

The United States Fidelity and Guaranty tower (1973), a luxurious corporate headquarters, was the first building in the new development. It broke the height line Wallace had suggested. From then on this fundamental principle of the plan was under siege and there was nothing the Architectural Review Board could do to defend it; desire to have new buildings overwhelmed principles of urban design.

One by one, new buildings along the edge of the harbor followed. Christ Church apartments for the elderly (1974), at the southwest corner, sits on one of the finest housing sites in the city. It is a subdued design in the manner of Le Corbusier. Pietro Belluschi designed the original IBM Building (1974), the low building that faces Pratt Street. In 1991 a tall addition with a fanciful decoration on its summit and a new parking garage would be added. This addition violates two of the principles of the Wallace design: the building contradicts the height limit and the entrances and north façade of the garage do threaten to turn Lombard Street into a service road for Pratt Street.

The intimations of change in architectural design that had appeared in some of the buildings in Charles Center had been significant. Although it had not yet been defined as "post modern," the rebellion was under way and by 1976 it was in full swing. The Science Center by Edward D. Stone (1976) was an exotic addition to the architectural scene; against the backdrop of Federal Hill it is an aggressive stranger. The Harbor campus of the Community College of Baltimore (1976) bore a distinct resemblance to the building for the history faculty at Cambridge University by James Sterling, a rebel hero of the new kind of design. The World Trade Center [A1] by Henry Cobb, a partner of I. M. Pei, departs, albeit elegantly, in its shape and materials from the modern idiom. Its concrete exterior is its structure. It was a graceful version of the tower concept that had been first announced by the bulky U. S. F. & G. building. Amid a cloud of protest about its design and a sculpture supplied by the General Services Administration, both felt by the judges to be too "modern," a new federal courthouse (1976) materialized between Pratt and Lombard streets behind the Federal Building. It was white and conventionally modern. The C. & P. Telephone Company headquarters by RTKL Associates (1977) was constructed at Pratt and Light streets on land on which it had once been hoped there would be a building by Louis Kahn. It is what can be called "utilitarian traditional modern" and it is not a masterpiece. Along the way, other buildings, urban improvements, and rehabilitation areas joined the Inner Harbor effort. The two Harborplace pavilions opened in 1980; they offered recreation and recreational shopping, casual food and dining adjacent to the water, a promenade and views of the boats and ships drawn up to the shore, and, in the near distance, Federal Hill. When Harborplace began to operate, a new facet of Baltimore life came into being; the city had its own, very special, mall possessed of features that nothing along or around the Beltway could offer.

With these buildings in place, others and other architectural events followed. Like the telephone company headquarters, the Equitable Financial Corporation Building at Charles and Lombard streets (1980) is in a routine business style. The National Aquarium [A2] and its addition are really too special a response to a unique purpose to be compared with other buildings. They can, for lack of a better term, be called "expressionist." The power plant, a noble reminder of the harbor's industrial past, opened in 1985 as an "urban family entertainment center." In 1996 it is about to reopen as something else, still undetermined. The Gallery (1988), a mixed-use building, although it breaks the height limitation, is significant for many reasons: first, its construction was a statement of confidence in the longevity of the Baltimore renaissance; second, it incorporates a hotel, a shopping mall, and an office building; third, the office tower does not turn its back on Lombard Street but enters from it; fourth, but not least, it is a handsome design, which, because it unites a number of parts and because of its reflective skin, appears less large than it is.

Two buildings, the Baltimore Convention Center [A4] and 250 West Pratt Street [A5], exhibit quality that reflects the high hopes expressed in the rebuilding of downtown Baltimore. As architecture and as functional spaces for exhibitions and meetings, the Convention Center is an unqualified success. The addition, designed by the same people who prepared the original building, will continue its forms. 250 West Pratt Street is a clean tower, beautiful to look at, and an elegant and fitting reminder of the principles that inspired the modern movement.

At the east end of the Inner Harbor a variety of buildings have appeared. The isolation of the south side of Pratt Street from the north side and the presence of the unusual buildings of the Aquarium suggested that fanciful architecture might take root on what had been the piers. The Columbus Center [A3] is such a building. To its east Scarlett Place (1988), an apartment house that incorporates an existing warehouse from which it derives its name, concludes the Inner Harbor. Further development, called Inner Harbor East, is under way along the shore in this direction. Turning north, new construction at the water's edge encouraged rehabilitation and development: the Candler Building, a dignified structure that had housed light industry, was totally renovated and renewal marched north to join the rehabilitated fish market and other old and new buildings.

On the west end of the Inner Harbor and effectively concluding it, the new ballpark, Oriole Park at Camden Yards [I3], beyond the warehouse to which it is related, is nationally recognized for its design, as a sports facility, the way it relates to and enhances the city, and the pleasant and humane pedestrian precinct in which it is embedded.

The section of older houses, many of them ruined, that lay between the impressive B & O Railroad warehouse and the harbor contained the only extant eighteenth-century church in Baltimore. In 1975, as part of the Inner Harbor project, the buildings in this area that could be rehabilitated were auctioned with the proviso that they would be restored. New dwellings were built to fill in the gaps. The result is Otterbein, one of the most appealing residential areas in the city.

Restoration and rehabilitation have extended to Federal Hill, where new houses have been built, many old ones have been restored, and the park on the crest of the hill has been improved. Below, on Key Highway, on land once used for ship repair yards, a new residential development has been begun. One apartment tower, a community building, and a pier have been built.

Architectural preservation and the rehabilitation of fine older buildings are as much an architectural act as the design of new buildings. Occasionally, a fragment has survived, as in the use of the cast-iron front in the façade of the Marsh and McLennan Building [H1] on Pratt Street. As always, more could be done and too often quality buildings are lost to fire, abuse, and demolition; but Baltimore deserves credit for the way in which it attempts to preserve its heritage. Not only Otterbein and Federal Hill but Bolton Hill and Reservoir Hill and Patterson Park survive and are constantly improving. The city's Commission for Historical and Architectural Preservation (CHAP) keeps track of and tries to protect, sometimes against great odds, what is old, characteristic, or valuable.

For too long the University of Maryland hospital and medical, dental, pharmacy, and law schools, to the west of the center of the city, remained dormant, their buildings standing in the midst of temporary parking lots. Finally, in the 1980s, after much planning and study, the institution began an astonishing building program that will, ultimately, fill all the land between Greene Street and the Martin Luther King, Jr., Boulevard with new buildings or refurbished old ones. The state of Maryland and its design review panel, rather than the panels convened by the city, has primary authority over design.

In 1996 some new buildings are already in place. The vitality of this development in the form of new construction, additions to the hospital and its schools, and the adoption and improvement of older buildings is entirely positive. A spectacular major addition to the hospital and improvement of its entrance, and the construction of a Veterans Administration hospital warrant optimism for what is to come.

The neighborhoods near the hospital have profited from this development. The university has tastefully converted to student residences a terrace of early-nineteenth-century houses, Pascault Row [J4]. Satellite facilities, such as doctors' offices and clinics, have been located in renovated older buildings. Temporary housing for the families of children being treated in the hospital have been built. As a result of these changes, some of the brick warehouses and manufacturing buildings that distinguish the neighborhood have, in recent years, become attractive market rate apartments and offices.

In the eastern part of the city, Johns Hopkins Hospital [G6] has continued to develop. It is in the nature of medical facilities to become obsolete and at this time the institution plans to keep the oldest building with its dome but demolish and rebuild many of its more recent structures, even those that date from the 1960s and 1970s. It proposes to expand along both Broadway and Orleans Street. The design currently favored recapitulates the High Victorian of the Dome building; this is to be regretted, for it can only reduce the impact of the original and at the same time appear what it will be, a modern replication.

Meanwhile, the hospital has recently built a new outpatient facility, parking garage, pedestrian walkway, and a connection with the new Baltimore Metro station and with the old hospital across Broadway. The outpatient building is one of the best modern designs to embellish Baltimore in recent years. It functions well as a building both for patients and staff; its materials are rich but not overwhelming.

To the north, two new in-town villages, Cross Keys [N16] and Coldspring [N17], have appeared to attract those who might move away to remain within the city limits. Cross Keys has its own discreet shopping center, a tall apartment building, a hotel, clusters of town houses and small apartment houses, recreation facilities, well-managed and -maintained open spaces, and an office building. Its architecture, which tends to be cozy rather than aggressive, is pleasantly domestic in scale and materials.

Coldspring is different. Moshe Safdie, now of Harvard University but at the time he came to work in Baltimore fresh from his much discussed design for Habitat '67 in Montreal, was asked to devise an in-town residential village. His design was stylistically adventurous, an expression of ideas that contradict the starchy design formula approved by the modern movement. The principles of urban excellence ratified by the modernists are there: the separation of pedestrian and vehicular movements, village scale, and intimacy combined with planned access to roads. To these attributes the design of Coldspring adds a slight flavor of the instinctive feeling of architecture without architects, as it can be seen in Italian and Near Eastern villages. But the houses at Coldspring were structurally sophisticated and difficult to build, and the many special features of the community, such as the decks with parking beneath them, added to the cost of the whole. Only a part of Coldspring was built as Safdie designed it; additions to it, most of which do not reflect its style, have been made, but the principles of its design and its wayward attractiveness warrant the fame it has attained.

Housing for people who do not have much to spend has always been an inner-city problem. Subsidized public housing raises many questions, not the least of which is the inevitable segregation of the less prosperous that is a result. In the 1950s, in part because the federal government was parsimonious in its per-unit grants for new housing, and in part because the leaders of the modern movement recommended high-rises, apartments in residential towers replaced neighborhoods of old houses on either side of downtown Baltimore. Here, as was the case elsewhere in the United States and in England, this solution did not work. Social problems seemed to be intensified by tower dwellings—for example, for a reason that no one understands, people who reside in this kind of building tend to be sickly and visit the doctor more often than those who do not. In 1995, after they had degenerated beyond repair and the social problems associated with them had reached catastrophic proportions, many of these public housing high-rises east of downtown were demolished. They will be replaced by planned neighborhoods of houses—both subsidized and owner occupied—and buildings to contain a variety of social amenities. The same process has taken place on the western side of the city. Planning and architectural design are fundamental to these projects and this time it is hoped, given the knowledge of what has happened, that the new communities will survive to serve the people who dwell in them.

Baltimore is distinguished for the way its administration, developers, and institutions, such as churches, have exploited federal money available for subsidized housing for the elderly. Most housing of this kind is in apartment towers; older people have no difficulty with quarters of this kind; indeed, they feel more secure than in houses, and they appreciate the medical supervision and the social opportunities they offer. If you go to the top of the World Trade Center and look across the city it will be immediately apparent how many of these apartment houses there are. The towers at the corner of Maryland and North avenues, at Cathedral Street near the Waxter Center, and on 29th Street overlooking the Dell in front of the Baltimore Museum of Art are typical. What you will not see as you look across the city are the older buildings that have been rehabilitated for this purpose. An exact count of apartment units of this kind in Baltimore is not available, but it is surely in the thousands. It can be argued that many of the new buildings for this purpose are functional rather than great architecture, but it cannot be said that the purpose they serve is of little social significance.

So Baltimore goes on. Like other American cities, it is confronted with social and planning problems which it attempts to solve, it is surrounded by suburbs that have drained its population, and it is afflicted with responsibilities that the suburbs do not share. Economic forces have tended to limit the amount of control the city can exercise over its present development.

But there are signs that a combination of the very qualities that have set Baltimore apart in the past and that characterize its urban scene today will make possible the city's survival in the future. It will not be Baltimore as it once was, it may not have a centralized downtown, old Baltimore may exist only in memory, but from the past has come an inheritance of a stock of houses and intimate neighborhoods that have potential. The quality of life that Baltimore's traditional housing patterns and its old dwellings provide has become a resource rather than a liability. The conservatism of taste in design and a stubborn resistance to change that have characterized Baltimore will bring whole neighborhoods virtually intact or even improved into the twenty-first century. Models for survival can be found in Mount Vernon, Otterbein, Bolton Hill, Fells Point, Washington Hill, Hampden, Patterson Park, development along Boston Street, and in the prosperous settlements in Mount Washington, Roland Park, Guilford, and Charles Village. As speed of transportation accelerates with the inevitable development of rapid transit, the distance between Washington and Baltimore will be reduced and the suburbs to the north of the city will draw closer to these inner-city neighborhoods.

As Baltimore waits for these changes it is imperative that no further losses be allowed in its fabric. What remains of downtown should be protected; possibly no further demolition should occur between the Inner Harbor and North Avenue and from Broadway to Carey Street without exhaustive analysis and review by a special panel protected from political interference. Baltimore is an unspectacular treasure that should be carefully guarded.

PART II
THE TOURS

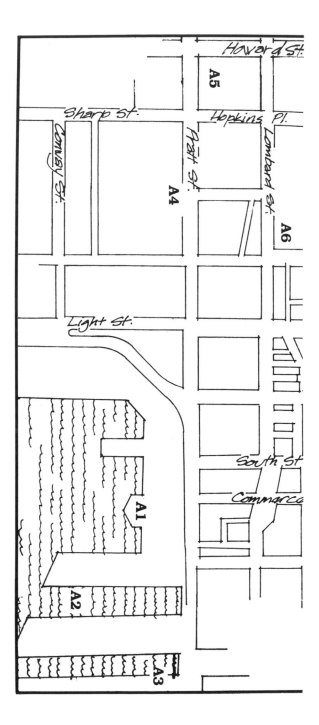

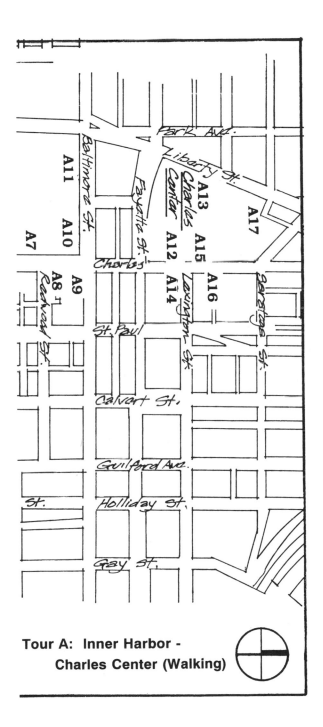

**Tour A: Inner Harbor -
Charles Center (Walking)**

Tour A

Inner Harbor–Charles Center (Walking)

A1   WORLD TRADE CENTER
401 East Pratt Street
1968–77—I. M. Pei and Partners

A2   NATIONAL AQUARIUM IN BALTIMORE
501 East Pratt Street
*1981—Cambridge Seven; 1990—Grieves, Worrall,
Wright, and O'Hatnick*

A3   COLUMBUS CENTER
701 East Pratt Street
1995—Zeidler, Roberts Partnership

A4   BALTIMORE CONVENTION CENTER
One West Pratt Street
*1979—Naramore, Bain, Brady, and Johanson;
Cochran, Stephenson, and Donkervoet, Inc.
1996—Loschky, Marquardt, and Nesholm;
Cochran, Stephenson, and Donkervoet, Inc.*

A5   250 WEST PRATT STREET
1986—Skidmore, Owings, and Merrill

A6   CHARLES CENTER SOUTH
Charles and Lombard streets
1975—RTKL Associates, Inc.

A7   SUN LIFE BUILDING
South Charles and Redwood streets
1966—Peterson and Brickbauer; Emery Roth and Sons

A8   HANSA HAUS
South Charles and Redwood streets
1912—Parker, Thomas, and Rice

A9   FIRST UNION NATIONAL BANK OF MARYLAND
Baltimore and Charles streets
1907—Parker and Thomas

A10 MECHANIC THEATER
Baltimore and Charles streets
1967—John M. Johansen

A11   MERCANTILE SAFE DEPOSIT AND TRUST
        COMPANY BUILDING
        2 Hopkins Plaza
        1969—Peterson and Brickbauer; Emery Roth and Sons

A12   ONE CHARLES CENTER
        100 North Charles Street
        1962—Mies van der Rohe

A13   BALTIMORE GAS AND ELECTRIC COMPANY
        BUILDING
        39 West Lexington Street
        *1916—Parker, Thomas, and Rice; 1966—Fisher,
        Nes, Campbell, and Partners*

A14   ONE EAST LEXINGTON STREET
        1890—Charles L. Carson

A15   FIDELITY BUILDING
        210 North Charles Street
        1894—Baldwin and Pennington

A16   MASONIC TEMPLE (former)
        223–225 North Charles Street
        *1869—Edmund G. Lind; 1893—Carson and Sperry;
        1909—Joseph E. Sperry*

A17   TWO CHARLES CENTER
        Charles and Saratoga streets
        1969—Conklin and Rossant

The city's transformation of its Inner Harbor from a
moribund warehouse and industrial area to a radiant tourist attraction has refocused civic attention on
the place where Baltimore began, and has inspired national and international praise and imitation.

The plan to redevelop 100 or so acres around the
Inner Harbor at a cost of $260 million over 30 years
was announced in 1964 by the same City Hall–downtown business group partnership that had inaugu-
rated the Charles Center renewal project during the
previous decade. Several mayors of Baltimore, developer James W. Rouse with the Greater Baltimore Committee, and planner David A. Wallace of Philadelphia
were key members.

Demolition began in the blocks to the north, west,
and south of the Inner Harbor in 1969. Only four buildings in the plan's first phase were spared. Two of them,
the News American building and the McCormick's

Spice Plant, have since come down. The third was the Christ Lutheran Church at the area's southwest corner; the church developed the first new building in the Inner Harbor, a medical center completed in 1972. The last was the former Baltimore Copper Paint Company's building on Key Highway, now a part of the 1995 American Visionary Art Museum. Among the losses were some fine iron-fronted warehouses on South Charles Street.

The proud symbols of the renewed Inner Harbor began to rise in the early 1970s as new bulkheading was completed, providing for the creation of 30 new acres of land on three sides. One of the earliest was I. M. Pei's World Trade Center. At the end of the 1970s, the Rouse Company announced plans to build a festival marketplace at the harbor's northwest corner. In 1980, one hundred thousand people attended the opening of Harborplace, designed by Benjamin Thompson and Associates of Cambridge, Massachusetts. Since then, the influence of the Inner Harbor's redevelopment has spread east to the Columbus Center and west to 250 West Pratt Street. (Pratt Street itself was widened into a boulevard during the process.)

The Inner Harbor West project was established in the early 1970s between the Inner Harbor and Charles Center districts, centering on the Otterbein Church; it now features a successful mix of restored residences and new office buildings. The latest adjunct is an office and apartment development located between the Inner Harbor and Fells Point: Inner Harbor East, currently under construction.

Some of the individual buildings first planned for the Inner Harbor have evolved into interesting new forms and only one completed project—the Harrison's Pier 5 hotel—was a commercial failure, partly due to its remoteness and inaccessibility. However, less than half the projected housing was built and, in the mid-1980s, officials substituted more waterfront public attractions. The various Inner Harbor development programs now total about 250 acres and represent some $4 billion in new construction. Both the Inner Harbor and Inner Harbor East projects have received urban design awards from the American Institute of Architects.

The inspiration for the Inner Harbor was Charles Center, which grew out of an earlier attempt to counter the decline of the downtown area and the migration of capital and population to the suburbs. The idea began in 1954 when the Committee for Downtown, a merchants' group, organized and raised money to pay for a master plan. The Greater Baltimore Committee, made up of leaders in finance, industry, and the professions (with James W. Rouse as one of its most active members), aided the effort and set up an independent planning council headed by David A. Wallace.

The planners located a promising area for redevelopment, "an area of economic instability lying between the financial center on the east and the shopping district—which was economically weakened, but still a strong anchor—on the west," wrote Wallace. In 1958, the voters approved a $25 million bond issue for Charles Center, and the following year the City Council adopted the urban renewal plan.

Its main principles were to incorporate public open space, to separate pedestrian and vehicular traffic, and to create a new focus for the downtown. Rather than bulldoze the 33 acres and build an island of commercial towers surrounded by a moat of traffic, as some cities have done, Baltimore retained five buildings and incorporated a felicitous mixture of new ones. Some of these are outstanding, notably Mies van der Rohe's One Charles Center.

The project is organized around three parks, all constructed atop underground parking garages: Charles Plaza in the north, Center Plaza in the middle, and Hopkins Plaza at the south end. One can experience a pleasantly scaled succession of urban spaces interspersed with frequent views of the surrounding skyline without encountering a car (at least on the same level), via a system of walkways, bridges, and stairways. (The stairways are necessary because of a north-south decline in elevation of 68 feet.) In fact, it is possible to travel on the "Skyway" system all the way to the Inner Harbor.

An apartment tower was constructed at the north end in the 1980s on the last remaining vacant parcel in Charles Center, and improvements were made to Center Plaza at that time. They included a new stairway at the northeast corner connecting to Charles Street (and to Charles Plaza up above), designed by Schamu, Machowski, Doo, and Associates. Charles Center still serves as a downtown anchor, has aged well, and continues to look, as a *Fortune* writer prophetically observed in 1958, "as if it were designed by people who like the city." ❖

A1 • WORLD TRADE CENTER

401 East Pratt Street
1968–77—I. M. Pei and Partners

Several elements contribute to the success of this distinguished design: its pentagonal shape, which keeps it from looking like a bulky, upended box and which allows two sides to come to a point at the water's edge, suggesting the prow of a ship; the proportions of the long, uninterrupted windows and the notches in the concrete between them, which provide elegant horizontals to balance the verticality of the building; the five structural piers at the building's angles (a sixth supports the core), with their deep recesses, which are lighted at night. These features work functionally as well as visually. The 65-foot-long windows define the interior spaces on each floor around the service core and provide remarkable views for the office workers inside. The pentagonal shape allows "more usable office space in less visible mass to interrupt the view of the harbor," as architectural historian Phoebe Stanton has noted. The corner piers allow long uninterrupted interior spaces for flexible design of offices.

The building, of reinforced concrete construction, was completed at a cost of $22 million and is owned by the state of Maryland and operated by the Port Administration. The twenty-eight-story tower has a public observation deck at the twenty-seventh level, which provides good views and has exhibits on the city and the port. The principal architects were Henry Cobb and Pershing Wong of the Pei firm; the local affiliated firm was Richter, Cornbrooks, Matthai, Hopkins, Inc., with H. P. Matthai the principal and Ronald A. Gribble project manager. ❖

A2 • NATIONAL AQUARIUM IN BALTIMORE

501 East Pratt Street
1981—Cambridge Seven; 1990—Grieves, Worrall, Wright, and O'Hatnick

Peter Chermayeff, architect-in-charge of the aquarium's first and principal building, has said that "architecture is not the issue" in terms of the design. The form resulted, in other words, from the kinds of exhibit spaces the building would enclose rather than the other way around. The visitor first encounters a variety of exhibits on a succession of levels, and these are suggested by the multicolored painted wall on the west façade. The glass pyramid at the top encloses the tropical rain forest, and the drum tanks are indicated by the rounded concrete wall at the south end of the complex.

But it's also true that "form follows function" has created a notable architectural success here. The building's lumpy form is not beautiful by any standards; nevertheless, as an architectural object the aquarium is one of the most admired—and enjoyed—buildings in the whole Inner Harbor area. Its echoing pyramids have been compared to sails, quite fitting for a site on the water. Overall, the form can be thought to suggest a huge abstract sculpture, part high tech and part brutalist. Its endearingly awkward body can also make you think of some great sea creature heaving up out of the water—or perhaps of a not quite so huge creature with one of its young following after. Then, too, with its multiple interior levels, many indicated on the outside, it can suggest an updated Piranesian fantasy. Its success, in fact, depends partly on its ability to say so many different things to people.

As a functioning building, it has also largely been a success despite the problems it has presented for both people and fish. Many ridiculed as hopelessly inflated early projections of 650,000 visitors a year. As soon as it opened, however, the Aquarium immediately and repeatedly drew more than a million visitors a year, resulting in crowded, sometimes claustrophobic conditions. The first inhabitants of the dolphin tank, because of the crowds and other unfavorable conditions, had nervous breakdowns, and one even died. Mercifully, the rest were removed and have been replaced, most recently with a ray exhibit. The addition of an annex building has meant more spaces in which the crowds can circulate.

The interior of the building eschews traditional floors in favor of a series of levels determined by the exhibits. From the lobby, where the ray tank greets visitors, ascending levels offer exhibits in which instruction mingles with fun. At the top one emerges into the light of the rain forest, with a background view of the harbor area. Then one descends through the middle of the ring tanks, surrounded by water and fish, first to a coral reef exhibit, and below to an open ocean exhibit with sharks. The progression from dark to light to dark again gives one the feeling of emerging from and resubmerging in the water.

In 1990 the Marine Mammal Pavilion, primarily devoted to an amphitheater for dolphin shows, opened on the adjacent pier, connected to the main building by an over-water bridge. It was hailed by *Washington Post* architecture critic Benjamin Forgey as "an ideal architectural companion piece to the aquarium, a splendid fraternal twin." Baltimore *Sun* architecture critic Edward Gunts, after some initial reservations, came to a similarly positive but slightly different conclusion. He noted that the architects had repeated certain motifs of the original building, particularly the pyramidal roof, but had treated details such as windows and colors differently, and had created a bright airy space in contrast to the dark interior of the original building. It is "more like the original's cousin than its twin," he stated. ❖

A3 • COLUMBUS CENTER
701 East Pratt Street
1995 — Zeidler, Roberts Partnership

The architects of a new national center for research and education in marine biotechnology were charged with designing a signature building wherein science could meet the public. They produced a high-tech big top that resembles both an oceangoing vessel and a large sea creature.

These somewhat contradictory aims and aspects conjoin in an unorthodox but striking techno-modern building with a free-form awning. The prominent 8-acre site is located at the northeast corner of the inner harbor on piers that fan out like spread fingers toward Fells Point. The Columbus Center parallels the Jones Falls and is angled to Pratt Street, leaving a wedge of pierside space in front for a public plaza.

The center's two major components are the metal-clad laboratory wing and a more organic structure with a sail-like roof housing the public exhibits. Their juncture is the common meeting ground for laboratory scientists and the public.

The Columbus Center's structure is reinforced concrete. The research building has a precast concrete base and five upper floors finished with tan and white, plain and corrugated aluminum panels separated by green-tinted ribbon windows and topped by a two-story mechanical penthouse. The four stacks are connected (via a heat-extracting manifold in the mechanical penthouse) to the exhaust ducts from the laboratory fume hoods, expressed on the east side as curved vertical elements with translucent sides and zigzag pipes.

A glass wall and a billowing fabric roof with scalloped edges enclose the public exhibit space. Eberhard H. Zeidler, the partner-in-charge, describes this section as "an amorphous sea form." The fiberglass-reinforced Teflon roof is topped by four elliptical skylights of faceted green-tinted glass. The steel tension rings that form the skylights anchor the support cables connected to the perimeter columns. Under the skylights are steel masts with hydraulic lifts; after the inner and outer layers of fabric were hung in segments and their seams field-welded, the columns were raised, tensioning the roof. Peter Sheffield and Associates, Toronto, were the structural engineers.

The Hall of Exploration inside is a soaring open space with two large balconies, the first for Disney-type exhibits, such as a 20-foot-long rockfish, a working waterfall, a walk-through cell, and a forty-seat horsehoe-crab theater; the second for a food court where visitors will have a chance to meet and talk with marine scientists who descend in glass-enclosed elevators (or on cantilevered, DNA-inspired helical staircases), from their laboratories next door. The exhibit center is scheduled to open in 1997.

A handsomely detailed lobby with an L-shaped balcony that continues the nautical theme is located under the awning at the front of the building. This leads to the Science and Technology Education Center, which includes an auditorium, a computer-equipped classroom, and two custom-designed laboratories for training groups of students or teachers.

The research structure houses the Center of Marine Biotechnology, a division of the University of Maryland and the last of the institution's three elements. There are three floors of instrument-equipped laboratories and a ground-floor Aquaculture Research Center. The Columbus Center cost $160 million in federal, state, city, and private funds. ❖

A4 • BALTIMORE CONVENTION CENTER

One West Pratt Street
1979—Naramore, Bain, Brady, and Johanson;
Cochran, Stephenson, and Donkervoet, Inc.
1996—Loschky, Marquardt, and Nesholm;
Cochran, Stephenson, and Donkervoet, Inc.

The opposite of the box type of exhibit hall, the Baltimore Convention Center is notable for being open and spacious. Site conditions and difficult project requirements, combined with the talents of the architects and engineers, resulted in the building's highly sophisticated design.

Constructed with a low profile to reduce its impact on the surrounding structures, the center's three levels step back in successive tiers from the main entrance on Pratt Street and enclose an impressive amount of space. The first level contains a two-story lobby, four large exhibit halls, kitchens, truck docks, and other service facilities. The main lobby is connected at the mezzanine level to a secondary one facing Sharp Street (made possible by the site's upward slope to the west), with a windowed walkway that allows visitors to see down on either side into the exhibit halls. The third level has twenty-three meeting rooms (the largest with a seating capacity of two thousand), indoor lounges, and an outdoor plaza.

The roofs of the various levels, supported by 90-foot steel trusses, are linked by sloping skylights, most of which run the entire length of the building. These, held in place by steel beams set at an angle, allow at the eastern end a well-lighted, unobstructed view from the top level down to the fountains in the main lobby. From the outside at night, the skylights appear as narrow bands of light. The lobby, enclosed by 8-foot-square panels of suspended glass, is also highly visible from the street. The base of the building is covered with gray granite.

The major difficulty overcome by the designers was in the four 140-by-180-foot exhibit halls. Each was to have a 35-foot ceiling, be column-free, yet able to support meeting rooms or plazas on its roof. To maintain the building's low profile, the normal deep roof trusses could not be used.

Instead, the architects and structural engineers (Skilling, Helle, Christiansen, Robertson, Inc., of Seattle) produced a radical post-tensioned reinforced concrete system, the outlines of which are clearly visible both inside and outside the building. The structure of each exhibit hall might be likened to four suspension bridges, inclined toward one another at 37 degrees, with a roof on top. The system, developed with the aid of models and computer diagrams, consists essentially of steel cables 4 inches in diameter (one-quarter the size of those supporting the Brooklyn Bridge), slung between the corner posts and embedded in concrete.

The load, instead of being suspended from the cable, as in a bridge, descends from above, transmitted by steel beams. The cable structure picks up the roof load and transfers it to four corner columns, each 3½ feet in diameter. These columns rest on concrete caissons, extended to bedrock. The largest caisson is 9 feet in diameter, spreads to 16 feet at its base, and is about 70 feet deep. The corner columns, subject to centrifugal pressure like that exerted by a masonry dome, are tied together at the bend with heavy reinforced concrete

beams, also post-tensioned. Local architects and engineers were skeptical as to whether the system would work, but it has stood the test of time. The builder was the Whiting-Turner Contracting Company.

When it opened, the $50 million Convention Center was capable of accommodating all but the largest conventions and trade shows. It was, however, quickly upstaged by newer and even larger facilities in other cities.

A $151 million addition to the Convention Center was completed in the fall of 1996. Taking up two and a half blocks to the west of the existing structure, it is vastly overscaled compared to the rest of downtown. (The entire complex now covers the equivalent of five city blocks.)

The expansion continues the structural pioneering of the initial Convention Center, but more, in this case, turns out to be less. The new building adds (to the 115,000 square feet in the first one) 185,000 square feet of exhibit space in four halls. It does so, due to the exhibitors' requirements for column-free space, with just four major steel-reinforced concrete support columns. (The largest of these, 4 feet in diameter, rests on a caisson 13 feet in diameter that reaches down 60 feet to bedrock.) This engineering feat is made possible by a custom-designed, two-way steel truss system, 27 feet deep, that extends, in 60-foot spans, 180 feet in each direction. Jack Christiansen of Seattle, affiliated with Leslie E. Robertson Associates of New York, structural engineers, developed the concept. (Christiansen and Robertson were partners in the firm that engineered the original Convention Center.) Structurally efficient it may be, but the truss system is less satisfying esthetically: its elements protrude defensively from the expansion's exterior and interfere visually inside, particularly in the main entrance lobby.

The new structure has four levels. The first, below grade, houses the new exhibit space, connected by tunnel below Sharp Street to the exhibit area in the older building. (There are thirty new loading docks; a tractor trailer can drive from Conway Street through a new tunnel directly onto the exhibit floor.) The second, at street level, is the main reception area with a major entrance from Pratt Street under a cantilevered space frame canopy and another entrance in the rear facing Sharp Street. Handsome views of Camden Station and the Old Otterbein Church are a feature of the third level, which holds the football field–sized registration area and fifty meeting rooms sandwiched in among the truss members; a bridge across Sharp Street also links this level to the existing center. The fourth level includes a ballroom, the largest in the state, with kitchen facilities, and a capacity of 2,500. The combined facilities can accommodate conventions of 10,000 and more. ❖

A5 • 250 WEST PRATT STREET

1986—Skidmore, Owings, and Merrill

No addition to Baltimore's downtown skyline over the past fifteen years has distinguished it as much as the landmark twenty-six-story Skidmore, Owings, and Merrill (SOM) office tower. Like a finely sculptured, shimmering block of ice, it radiates its presence for blocks and even miles around.

The architects took advantage of an oddly shaped site to create a vertical slab at a prominent corner with a stepped roofline and an angled (at 45 degrees) eastern end to maximize office views of the Inner Harbor. They clothed the structure in cool, elegant materials arrayed in gray pinstripes. Cabot, Cabot, and Forbes was the original developer.

The Sullivanesque notion that the modern office building should have an obvious base, shaft, and capital like a classical column, and Mies van der Rohe's concept of an exquisitely proportioned structural grid, are here creatively abstracted. Alternating horizontal bands of

polished gray Vermont granite and silver-coated reflective glass are intersected by vertical V-shaped indentations. These divide the building's broad façade into bays and mark the descending rooflines of each. The horizontal bars of stone and glass, precisely matched in width, seem to change color and even orientation depending on the angle of view and time of day.

The granite bands bridge the indentations at the fifth, sixth, and seventh floors and in a staggered fashion on the higher levels. This sophisticated device visually establishes a horizontal base for the building, binds together the upper divisions, and creates from a distance the impression of a series of faceted glass towers of diminishing height connected by bridges. The Pratt Street façade houses a four-story lobby, fronted with suspended plate glass and finished with Andes black granite. Inside, a bank and a store occupy the wings of the open lobby, and angled balconies look down from above.

The top of the building is defined by a multistory, granite-faced cap enclosing mechanical space. Each stepped-down bay was designed to contain a rooftop garden terrace. The use of long-span structural steel (the columns are located at the indentations) allowed for unusually wide bay spacing and made the upper floors virtually column-free. David Childs was the architect-in-charge.

SOM also designed the structurally aggressive highrise addition to the existing ten-story IBM Building at 150 East Pratt Street. The addition is crowned with a helmetlike steel truss that helps to support its foremost section, cantilevered above the older structure. Dramatically lit at night, the "hat truss" accomplishes esthetically what iron roof cresting did in the Victorian age—it gives the 1992 twenty-eight-story addition an "agitated silhouette." The attractive lobby, entered from Light Street, echoes artistically—with struts, cables, and suspended glass—the building's most obvious external feature. ❖

A6 • CHARLES CENTER SOUTH

Charles and Lombard streets
1975—RTKL Associates, Inc.

This building's unusual hexagonal shape and its skin of glass are the most obvious elements in its felicitous design by RTKL (the official title of the firm, a successor to Rogers, Taliaferro, Kostritsky, and Lamb). Poised at the southeast corner of Charles Center, the building acts, as architectural historian Phoebe Stanton has pointed out, as a kind of hinge between the city's first major downtown renewal effort (Charles Center) and the newer Inner Harbor development. There are other opinions. It has been remarked that this building "turns Charles Center's back on the Inner Harbor." But its shape encourages the eye to move gently around the building from the harbor to the Charles Center side, as a pair of squared off blank walls meeting at the corner would not.

Dr. Stanton has noted that the shape of the building acts as a foil for the cubical Sun Life Building to the north and the slablike Federal Building to the west. The curtain walls of dark gray glass panels achieve the effect of lightness, their almost watery surfaces making a visually apt statement, given the harbor's proximity. The overall effect of the building is refreshing, not quite like anything else in the area but not self-consciously different enough to be jarring. Its only drawback is its lack of height. The architect's original rendering suggested a taller building, which would have had a more slender and elegant appearance. ❖

A7 • SUN LIFE BUILDING
South Charles and Redwood streets
1966—Peterson and Brickbauer; Emery Roth and Sons

This, the earliest of Peterson and Brickbauer's major Baltimore buildings, is less dynamic and imaginative than the others, but it combines solidity, grace, and handsome proportions. Faced with nonreflective black Canadian granite, the twelve-story building with two sublevels has a concrete substructure and a separate steel superstructure carried on four large steel columns anchored in bedrock. The columns are visible on the east and west sides.

According to the architects' descriptions, "These four columns, in turn, support two welded steel trusses 143 feet long and 14½ feet deep. The mechanical equipment in the penthouse is supported by another system of trusses, which is carried again by the four major columns. This permits the remainder of the columns around the periphery and in the core to be reduced to a minimum dimension," thereby providing wide open

areas inside, flexibility of office space, and floor-to-ceiling windows.

The first-floor plaza is devoted to an open terrace and lobby whose materials—stone floors, red marble–encased elevator cores, glass, and steel—are complemented by the Dimitri Hadzi sculpture, "Helios," that hangs from the ceiling. ❖

A8 • HANSA HAUS

South Charles and Redwood streets
1912—Parker, Thomas, and Rice

Built as the offices of the North German Lloyd Steamship Company, Hansa Haus's name is derived from the Hanseatic League, a confederation of northern European towns formed to protect trade and commerce. The half-timbered architecture is German Renaissance in style, and the building at the time it opened was said to be based on the Zwicken, a courthouse in Halberstadt, Germany. The Charles Street gable houses a representation of a Viking ship in full sail executed in tile, and the coats of arms of the members of the Hanseatic

League are painted under the second-story windows.
When Hansa Haus first opened it housed the consulates
of Germany and Sweden in addition to offices of the
steamship line. Later it housed offices of the bank directly to its north. ❖

A9 • FIRST UNION NATIONAL BANK OF MARYLAND

Baltimore and Charles streets
1907—Parker and Thomas

The architects of this "Temple of Thrift," as it was called
when it opened as the Savings Bank of Baltimore, were
inspired by the Erechtheum on the Acropolis in Athens.
They set their two-story building of white Beaver Dam
marble on a low platform approached by steps. Four
massive but graceful Ionic columns support the pediment in front; six similar columns line the Charles
Street side of the building. The ornamentation around

the bases of the columns and the lions' heads that decorate the cornice were reproduced from casts that came from Athens.

The interior was originally a single, large, open banking space with Italian marble wainscoting, huge windows covered with bronze gratings, and a high, coffered ceiling. This was drastically altered in 1953 with the addition of a second floor, which doubled the usable banking area but sacrificed some of the grandeur. Even so, the present banking room, with its handsome appointments, is still impressive. The office space on the second floor was recently renovated. In the early 1980s, the bank added an administrative office tower to the east, connected on two levels to the older structure, whose timeless, classic design it helps to set off. ❖

A10 • MECHANIC THEATER
Baltimore and Charles streets
1967—John M. Johansen

"Functional expressionism" is the architect's term for the style of this theater, whose outside form reflects its interior functions. The concept is most easily understood after a visit inside the building. The stage is at the east end below a tower capable of supporting 34 tons of scenery, two stair towers are at the west end, and balcony seating is in the projecting compartments.

The theater was envisioned in the plan for Charles Center as a relatively small sculptural form in a setting of tall, neutral façades, such as the Fallon Federal Building across Hopkins Plaza to the south. The theater rests on a platform containing stores and restaurants; two levels of parking and delivery docks lie below the plaza.

The lobby is carried up two stories behind a glass wall. There is a street-level entrance and also entrances at the level of the pedestrian walkways. Some sixteen hundred seats, none of them obstructed by columns, fan out from the stage.

The roof is supported by steel trusses. The exterior surfaces are of poured-in-place concrete, cast in forms of rough-sawn oak boards. ❖

A11 • MERCANTILE SAFE DEPOSIT AND TRUST COMPANY BUILDING

2 Hopkins Plaza
1969—Peterson and Brickbauer; Emery Roth and Sons

"The structure of the building is the architecture of the building," according to the designers of this twenty-four-story office tower. The structure, in reinforced concrete, is simply yet forcefully expressed by the exterior load-bearing columns. They divide each long façade into seven bays; the bays, in turn, are divided visually by vertical stainless-steel tracks for window-washing equipment. The exterior concrete finish is continued inside the lobby, which has a granite floor and coffered ceiling. The building has three levels below the lobby, two for parking and the third for vaults. ❖

A12 • ONE CHARLES CENTER

100 North Charles Street
1962—Mies van der Rohe

This somber, elegantly proportioned twenty-four-story tower, designed by one of the giants of twentieth-century architecture, was the first new office building in Charles Center.

The architect was chosen as the result of a design competition that included an entry by Marcel Breuer. The unusual, eight-sided, T-shaped form of One Charles Center follows the building zone established by the Baltimore Urban Renewal and Housing Agency.

The tower rises from a landscaped plaza, which extends underneath the building to the relatively small lobby surrounding the elevator cores. Below the plaza lie three levels for parking, servicing, and retail stores. To the west the tower overhangs Center Plaza. The handsome but not very functional stairway and platform leading down to the plaza, designed by the architect, were removed around 1990 and replaced by a stairway offering more direct access.

The structure of the building is reinforced concrete. The exterior curtain wall is of aluminum with a dark brown finish and gray-tinted plate glass. One Charles Center took just thirteen months to complete and cost $10,350,000—fairly economical for a Mies van der Rohe office building.

In a $2 million renovation program over the past decade, the travertine marble paving of the plaza has been replaced with granite composition stone. The lobby was given a new limestone floor, its green Tinos marble walls were repolished, and there have been improvements to the upper floors. ❖

A13 • BALTIMORE GAS AND ELECTRIC COMPANY BUILDING

39 West Lexington Street
1916—Parker, Thomas, and Rice; 1966—Fisher, Nes, Campbell, and Partners

Directly across Center Plaza from One Charles Center are this utility's buildings. The older is a twenty-story, steel-frame structure faced with granite and terra-cotta and decorated at the fourth-floor level with a row of 8-foot figures representing knowledge, light, heat, and power. At night its strong crown, brightly illuminated, resembles a Greek temple. The lower, plainer addition makes an effective foil. ❖

A14 • ONE EAST LEXINGTON STREET
1890—Charles L. Carson

Built as the Central Savings Bank, One East Lexington Street is a small gem of an office building. Moreover, since the pointless destruction in the 1980s of Carson's Marburg Brothers warehouse on South Charles Street, it is one of just three remaining commercial structures in Baltimore by one of the city's finest architects. (The others are the Eutaw Savings Bank Building [E5] and Marlboro Square [E8].)

The massive strength of the Romanesque Revival is forcefully invoked here in Carson's Commercial Style building with its expansive windows. The exterior is faced with red granite, brownstone, and brick laid in red mortar. The original entrance has been widened.

The main attraction of the interior is a central light court that extends through the four office floors above the former ground-level banking room. A 1981 restoration of the building, during which modern mechanical systems were installed, highlighted many of its original features: decorative metal railings, oak wainscoting and molding, and stained-glass windows. Each suite of offices has a safe and some have fireplaces. ❖

A15 • FIDELITY BUILDING

210 North Charles Street
1894—Baldwin and Pennington

The Fidelity and Deposit Company of Maryland built their headquarters at this location just over a century

ago, and the company remains there under the same name. Meanwhile, the building has changed drastically. As first constructed, it consisted of eight floors of solid granite in the Commercial-Romanesque Style, with a red-tiled mansard roof, high pointed dormers, and a turret in the center. This roofline was substantially altered when seven more stories were added, between 1912 and 1915, framed with steel and faced with terra-cotta to match the stone.

The lobby, visible from the street, has marble wainscoting, brass grilles, and a barrel-vaulted ceiling with decorative, brightly painted coffers. The huge former banking and office space adjacent to it, also handsomely appointed, is now used for storage. This room contains a wrought-iron and bronze stairway (there are others throughout the building), a mezzanine level, and a large metal-clad vault that was used to store the valuables from nearby banks whose buildings burned during the Baltimore Fire of 1904.

The architecture of the Fidelity Building successfully conveys the stability of the bonding and insurance company that has occupied it for more than one hundred years. ❖

A16 • MASONIC TEMPLE (former)

223–225 North Charles Street
*1869—Edmund G. Lind; 1893—Carson and Sperry;
1909—Joseph E. Sperry*

Two fires, the first on Christmas Day, 1890, and the
second in January 1908, destroyed the interior of this
building, but pictorial evidence reveals that the façade,
up to the lower cornice, remains from Lind's 1869 structure. In the last rebuilding, Sperry added the new roof
in the Second Empire style and doubtless the new entrance.

He was also responsible for the interior, one of the
more remarkable in the city. There are ten major meeting rooms, including the Grand Lodge on the second
floor, which has walls of Italian marble; the fourth floor
Asylum, a Tudor Gothic room modeled on Edinburgh's
Roslyn Chapel, with walls paneled in oak; and a columned hall that resembles an Egyptian temple. There
are also two large kitchens, banquet and reception
halls, lobbies on each level, a marble staircase with cast-
bronze railings and grilles; and stained-glass windows,
Rococo chandeliers, and pipe organs throughout the
building.

In 1994, the Masons, after one hundred twenty-five years on the site, decided to move to a new headquarters on property they own near Hunt Valley in Baltimore County and put their former temple up for sale. ❖

A17 • TWO CHARLES CENTER

Charles and Saratoga streets
1969—Conklin and Rossant

The Two Charles Center complex, consisting of the north and south apartment towers (twenty-seven and thirty stories respectively) and adjoining stores and offices, occupies a 1.9-acre plot at the northern tip of Charles Center. The plan originally called for square apartment towers and a third, lower building, which was to house a department store. But the New York architectural firm of Conklin and Rossant, the master planners for Reston, Virginia, altered the plan somewhat.

Their changes were for the better. The architects divided what was to have been the third commercial building into a pair of well-scaled groups of two-story offices, stores, restaurants, and a movie theater (now the

Berman Auditorium of the Johns Hopkins University School of Continuing Studies).

These structures are surrounded by Charles Plaza, the northernmost of the three open spaces in Charles Center. A small park has been installed in the lower half of the plaza. It is pleasantly secluded, but only partially and rather awkwardly fulfills its intended function as the termination of the major north-south pedestrian route through Charles Center. In the upper half, the space fans out into a broad stairway, opening onto Charles Street and creating a vista of St. Paul's Church.

The structure of the apartment towers and the adjacent buildings is reinforced concrete faced with a specially made dark brown brick. The exterior columns dividing the bays are structural and give the towers a strong feeling of verticality.

The towers are basically square, but their corners have been indented and the resultant façades broken into vertical planes that advance and recede. The design of the entire complex is clean, simple, and forceful. ❖

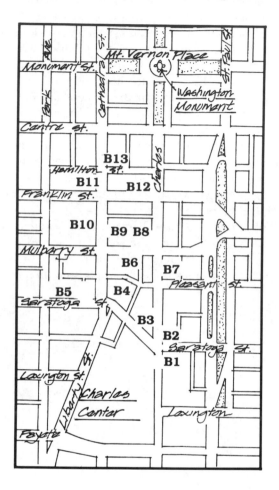

**Tour B: Between Downtown
and Mt. Vernon Place (Walking)**

Tour B

Between Downtown and Mount Vernon Place (Walking)

B1   ST. PAUL'S EPISCOPAL CHURCH
Charles and Saratoga streets
1856—Richard Upjohn

B2   301 NORTH CHARLES STREET
1930—Mottu and White

B3   YMCA BUILDING (former)
Charles and Saratoga streets
1873—Niernsee and Neilson

B4   ST. PAUL'S RECTORY (former)
Cathedral and Saratoga streets
1791, with later alterations—architect unknown

B5   ST. ALPHONSUS' CHURCH
Park Avenue and Saratoga Street
1841–45—Robert Cary Long, Jr.

B6   7–9 WEST MULBERRY STREET
1834 and after—architect unknown

B7   LOGGIA STORES
343 and 345 North Charles Street
façades ca. 1925

B8   ARCHBISHOP'S RESIDENCE
408 North Charles Street
1829—William F. Small

B9   BASILICA OF THE ASSUMPTION
Cathedral Street between Franklin and
Mulberry streets
*1805–21—Benjamin H. Latrobe; later additions
and alterations*

B10 ENOCH PRATT FREE LIBRARY
400 Cathedral Street
1933—Clyde N. Friz, with Tilton and Githens

B11 FRANKLIN STREET PRESBYTERIAN CHURCH
(former)
Franklin and Cathedral streets
1847—Robert Cary Long, Jr.

B12 FIRST UNITARIAN CHURCH
Charles and Franklin streets
1818—Maximilian Godefroy

B13 HAMILTON STREET ROW HOUSES
Hamilton Street between Charles and
Cathedral streets
ca. 1815—Robert Cary Long, Sr.?

Curiously, Centre Street seems to have become a sort of unofficial boundary in central Baltimore. South of Centre is the downtown commercial, office, government, and financial section of town. North of Centre, the city has remained basically residential, for all the changes that have taken place.

But it was not always so. The area bounded by Centre, Lexington, Howard, and Calvert streets was largely residential through most of the nineteenth century. When it began to change toward the end of the century, Baltimore was in a period when growth was more important than beauty. As a result, the commercial buildings that replaced the residential ones are, with a few exceptions, of little note. But much of what has survived from the precommercial age is significant, and that is almost exclusively ecclesiastical in nature.

This area contains some of the most important architecture in the city. Three of the most famous architects to work in Baltimore—Maximilian Godefroy, Benjamin H. Latrobe, and Robert Cary Long, Jr.—are represented by their most important local work. One of the few surviving eighteenth-century houses in the city is here, as is the only Richard Upjohn building in Baltimore. Much of what Baltimore is proudest of is contained in these few blocks. Also located here is what is left of the Charles Street shopping district, at one time the most fashionable in town and still the home of shops and galleries. ❖

B1 • ST. PAUL'S EPISCOPAL CHURCH
(BCL, NR)
Charles and Saratoga streets
1856—Richard Upjohn

In 1854, St. Paul's Church burned. It was the third church on this venerable site, had been designed by

Robert Cary Long, Sr., and opened in 1817. (The first St. Paul's was built here in 1729.) Upjohn, whose most famous work is the Gothic Trinity Church in New York, was commissioned to design a new St. Paul's. His building incorporated the foundation and the surviving brick walls (25 to 35 feet high) of Long's church.

Upjohn designed an Italian Romanesque basilica with a six-story tower (never completed) on the northwest corner. The building is constructed of red brick with light and dark sandstone trim. The well-proportioned west front is distinguished by three large arches and a portico. In the upper façade are two relief sculptures, representing Moses and Christ, carved by Antonio Capellano for the 1817 church and salvaged from the 1854 fire.

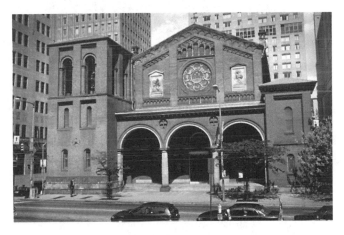

Inside, the same sense of proportion and restraint is evident. Four arches on each side divide the church into nave and side aisles, but the plan is so open that it creates the feeling of a single large, rectangular space. Above the nave is a clerestory with stained-glass windows, and over these are timber trusses supporting the roof. Some windows are by Louis Comfort Tiffany. The great east window, recently restored, located under the coffered barrel vault of the chancel, was designed by New York's Maitland, Armstrong & Co., a Tiffany protégé.

In recent years, the church building itself has undergone extensive restoration, including the reinforcement of chancel foundations, plaster repairs, and the re-laying of the original marble floor in the portico. The top floor windows of the truncated tower have also been opened up, coinciding with the installation of a carillon. ❖

B2 • 301 NORTH CHARLES STREET
1930—Mottu and White

The Baltimore Life Insurance Company built its eleven-story downtown headquarters, a steel-frame structure with a granite and brick exterior, in the then-popular Modernistic style. Restrained Art Deco ornamentation is visible in the cast- and wrought-iron balconies, the inset marble and bronze panels, the piers, and the parapets. One of the lower roofs (designated "roof garden" on the original drawings) contains shrubbery and a pond; the other does not.

More spirited Art Deco devices appear at ground level: fans, chevrons, and zigzags; reed, cable, and leaf moldings; as well as bronze gates, doors, and screens with a vine motif. The lobby is more lavish still, with bronze and marble decor, grilles, and chandeliers.

The Baltimore Life Insurance Company left its former headquarters for a Howard Street location in 1961 and recently moved to Owings Mills. The Commercial Credit Company bought the building and renovated it for expansion purposes in 1971. That company has also since sold and vacated the building, which now has an out-of-town owner and new tenants. ❖

B3 • YMCA BUILDING (former)

Charles and Saratoga streets
1873—Niernsee and Neilson

Diagonally across the street from St. Paul's is the former
Morris Building, originally the YMCA. As designed in
1873, it was a heavily ornamented Victorian pile with
stone columns and arches decorating the windows and
dormered mansard roof sprouting towers and turrets.
The latter were removed and the entrance changed in a
1907 alteration by Joseph E. Sperry. The building has
passed through several hands and undergone more than
one renovation. ❖

B4 • ST. PAUL'S RECTORY (former)

(BCL, NR)
Cathedral and Saratoga streets
1791, with later alterations—architect unknown

This Federal-period house was for almost two hundred
years home to the rectors of St. Paul's Church a block
away, but recently it has been put to other uses.

The symmetrical façade of the central building has a slightly projected center section with a Palladian window over a pedimented doorway that echoes the gable above. The front windows are surmounted by pink, flat-arch headers. The string course across the front above the first story and the water table below show a restrained but careful attention to detail.

The original kitchen wing was torn off in about 1829 and a new kitchen hyphen of two and a half stories added to the east end of the building. It has been suggested that the 1829 changes might have been made by Robert Cary Long, Sr., as there are touches similar to ones at his Davidge Hall and the Hamilton Street houses thought to be by him. The west addition was added between 1833 and 1837, and the back porch also dates from the 1830s.

The interior of the house has well-proportioned rooms and a generous stair hall with a staircase that ascends at several gentle angles rather than with the continuous curve of a circular staircase.

In recent years the rectors of St. Paul's have lived elsewhere. The church still owns the building but leases it out. In 1990 the house received a rehabilitation, with Michael F. Trostel as the consulting architect and Stiles T. Colwill as interior design consultant. The first-floor rooms were restored with grain painted doors and decorated in the classical revival style of the 1820–30 period. Since then the house has been occupied by Preservation Maryland.

Behind the rectory at 309 Cathedral Street is St. Paul's House, an 1886 building designed by T. Buckler

Ghequier, a pupil of Niernsee and Neilson who may have been influenced here by the heavily decorated buildings of Frank Furness. The building has a tower at the north end, decorative brickwork and terra-cotta work, and screens over entrance door and windows. The iron stair railings are distinctive and echoed on the interior stairway. One of three second-floor fireplaces is similar to a Furness design. The building was originally used for church offices and functions, with upper floors providing rooms for working women. Today, it still houses church offices, with other parts of the building rented out for office and other use. ❖

B5 • ST. ALPHONSUS' CHURCH

(NR)
Park Avenue and Saratoga Street
1841–45—Robert Cary Long, Jr.

In 1841 a group of German and American Roman Catholic Redemptorist fathers who had settled in Baltimore to help minister to the city's large Catholic population commissioned Robert Cary Long, Jr., to design a church for them. The result, St. Alphonsus', was the first major Gothic Revival church in Baltimore. It was also the first important commission for its designer, who was to become nationally known during a brief career that ended with his sudden death in 1849.

The plan is simple: a rectangular room, divided into nave and side aisles, with a rounded apse at one end and a vestibule at the other. Over the latter rises a tiered tower 200 feet tall (50 feet taller than the length of the church), whose stages rise from one another "like the joints of a telescope," as Long described them. The church is of brick, but iron was used in the spire, the interior columns, and the window tracery.

The building has a simple, sedate, somewhat severe exterior, with minimal buttresses (indicating that the vaulting inside is plaster, not stone) set flat against the walls, pointed-arch windows, and battlemented walls and tower sections. A rendering of the church (see Essays, p. 10) indicates that more ornamentation was originally planned than finally built, a frequent outcome.

For its first century and a quarter the church was painted in imitation of stone—a frequent practice, especially on more important buildings. In 1968, following an unfortunate trend, the paint was stripped off, and the brick now appears au naturel with the stonework gray. It is less expensive not to have to paint the building every few years, but most unfortunate; not only is a painted exterior more authentic, as intended by the architect—it's also vastly better looking.

The delightfully ornate interior has brown marbleized columns with sixteen ribs rising from each pier toward the ridge ribs down the central and side aisles. The ceiling is painted in delicate colors, and the altar and pulpit add to the richness of the overall impression.

While the Redemptorist fathers desired a church designed after German models and were apparently satisfied with Long's work, the architect described St. Alphonsus' as English Perpendicular. In truth, both influences are present: German, for the most part, in the overall pattern; English in much of the detail and decoration.

The residence and office building adjacent to the church on the east and St. Alphonsus' "Halle" across the street were added later. Both are in harmony with, but subordinate to, the church itself. ❖

B6 • 7–9 WEST MULBERRY STREET
(BCL)
1834 and after — architect unknown

Number 9, the western part of this structure, is the much older part and known to some as the Partridge-Morris House. Eaton R. Partridge, a successful merchant, built the house but died before he could occupy it, so the first and major nineteenth-century occupant was politician and businessman John B. Morris.

A handsome and unusual bow-front form, it boasts a fine portico with Corinthian columns, window lintels ending in rosettes, and string courses, with more carving under the windows. Pilasters extend to the height of the building on this handsome Greek Revival façade.

In 1891 the Catholic diocese bought the building from a Morris descendant and added Number 7, on what had been a side yard, to house the Cathedral School. The façade treatment is the same on the upper floors, but an open three-arch loggia was used as the first-floor treatment, with modern windows added later behind the arches. The cupola was also an 1890s addition, and wrought-iron balconies across the second-floor windows add another unifying touch.

After its school years the building was used by the Maryland Academy of Sciences and then by the architectural firm of Gaudreau, Inc. It is now devoted to offices occupied by various tenants. ❖

B7 • LOGGIA STORES

343 and 345 North Charles Street
façades ca. 1925

In the 1920s there was a movement by Charles Street merchants to add marble façades to their buildings. The effect is especially successful here, where the arches of the second-floor "loggia" of 343 complement the Palladian window of 345 and give the two an Italian look. There are also some notable fronts in the 400 block, opposite the archbishop's residence. ❖

B8 • ARCHBISHOP'S RESIDENCE

408 North Charles Street
1829—William F. Small

Built to house the Archbishop of Baltimore and connected to Latrobe's cathedral [B9], this Greek Revival house now resembles the five-part plan often seen in country houses. That, however, is due to later additions.

The original house was the central section, two stories high and minus the bay window over the entrance. The windows in blind arches echo those on the cathedral, and there is a beautiful entrance treatment with arched entrance and fanlight, now obscured by the bay window above.

This bay window, the two wings with their bay windows, and the third floor of the main building were added in 1865. Originally faced with stucco scored to resemble cut stone, the house was covered with a concrete veneer, also resembling stone, in the 1950s.

Other changes include a link established between the house and the cathedral building in 1919, at which time the house's stair was moved from a side hall to the center hall. Frank J. Baldwin was the architect of those changes. David L. Guth, recent architect of the basilica and the archbishop's residence, oversaw other changes: a gate added to the main entrance, enclosing the vestibule; window grilles on the ground floor; restoration of the main floor's double parlor; and the kitchen's move from the basement to the first floor. ❖

B9 • BASILICA OF THE ASSUMPTION

(BCL, NR)
Cathedral Street between
Franklin and Mulberry streets
1805–21—Benjamin H. Latrobe;
later additions and alterations

This is Baltimore's greatest work of architecture and the extant masterpiece of one of the foremost architects to work in America.

In the first years of the nineteenth century, Archbishop John Carroll sought a design for the first Roman Catholic cathedral in the United States. The initial submission was by William Thornton, first architect of the Capitol in Washington, D.C.; but his cathedral design proved impractical, and Latrobe was invited to submit one. On April 13, 1805, he presented two designs, "the one in Gothic, the other in Roman style," declaring "an equal desire to see the first or the second erected, my habits rather inclining me to the latter, while my reasonings prefer the first." Had the Gothic design been chosen, it would have been the first major Gothic church building in this country. Instead, Latrobe's romantic classical design was preferred. It is somewhat similar to that of the Pantheon in Paris, but with a lower Roman dome rather than a taller Renaissance one, and the Greek cross lengthened to become a Latin one.

The design underwent several variations by Latrobe, partly to satisfy a not always perfectly agreeable board of trustees, and building proceeded slowly with a hiatus caused by the War of 1812. But by 1818, when Latrobe left for New Orleans, the building was under roof. In 1821, the year after the architect's death, the basilica was dedicated without the portico and with the towers unfinished.

The south tower was complete by 1831 and the north one by 1837. There has long been doubt about the author of the design of the towers' onion domes, a source of much mystery and controversy. Latrobe's extant design shows small rounded domes quite different from those eventually erected. The design of the present domes, termed Saracenic (or Islamic), has never been documented. It has been credited to Latrobe, to his son (sometime architect John H. B. Latrobe), and to another, unknown hand.

In his 1917–18 articles on the building, architectural historian Fiske Kimball declared the domes inappropriate and not by Latrobe, and that opinion has dominated most twentieth-century discussion. However, in the 1995 publication *The Drawings of Benjamin Henry Latrobe*, architectural historian Charles E. Brownell refutes Kimball's opinion and declares the domes to be Latrobe's.

Essentially, his arguments are that: (1) an 1831 newspaper account describes the towers, including the Saracenic domes, and credits them to "the original design of the distinguished artist, the late B. H. Latrobe, by whom [the cathedral] was planned;" (2) while there is

no specific Latrobe drawing for these domes, late in his career Latrobe designed bell-like domes somewhat similar to the Saracenic ones for two other churches; (3) Latrobe was a constant innovator, quite likely to change a design when he came up with one he liked better; (4) Latrobe's son, John H. B., who oversaw completion of the first (south) tower, was a "faithful guardian of his father's artistic legacy" who would not independently have introduced such a major change; and (5) far from being inappropriate, the Saracenic domes with their long finials are a light, dynamic foil for the "rotund gravity" of the main dome.

These arguments are convincing. In the absence of documentary proof there can be no definitive answer. Unless evidence to the contrary should present itself, however, it should now be presumed that the domes are by Latrobe.

John H. B. Latrobe was responsible for the portico foundation in 1841; the portico, a part of the original design, was completed in 1863 under the direction of Eben Faxon, but even then the building was not complete. The sacristy wing was added to the north in 1879, with John R. Niernsee as architect, and in 1888 the sanctuary was lengthened to the east, with E. Francis Baldwin as architect. Latrobe had originally proposed the longer version and had been denied it.

In the 1940s there were other major changes, including construction of an interior wall inside the west entrance to create a vestibule, closing of windows in the dome and the apse, and the installation of stained-glass windows by the Conrad Schmidt studios of New York. Each of these windows contains a scene from the Old

Testament at the top, the New Testament in the middle, and the history of the Catholic church in Maryland at the bottom.

At present the Basilica Historic Trust, Inc., has an ongoing plan to preserve and restore the church and to update it with such improvements as a recently finished ramp for the disabled and a new lighting design.

Despite all the hands that have worked on it and all the changes it has undergone, it is undeniably Latrobe's church and his surviving masterpiece. The exterior's massive granite walls are relieved by a few judiciously placed windows set in recessed arched panels with plaques above. Parts of the building project or recede slightly, ". . . so that," writes architectural historian Henry-Russell Hitchcock, "one is conscious of a well-proportioned group of geometric shapes that are carefully interrelated." The dome, sitting on an octagonal drum, cannot be seen well from the immediate street level. The best view is from the Orleans Street viaduct several blocks to the east.

The highest praise, however, has been reserved for the interior. The central dome, supported on segmental vaults, dominates the whole fluid space and is echoed by low saucer domes to east and west. The rotunda's width encompasses both nave and side aisles, so that the aisles lead into it diagonally. Thus all the parts flow into the center and it in turn flows out to them, giving the whole an extraordinary unity. At the same time, there is a marvelous balance of mass and space, so that the eye is never presented with the dominance of one over the other, or inclined to come to a full stop. Where it might do so, as at the apse or the transepts, rows of columns urge it back toward the complex of interconnected spaces. The whole interior presents one with a sense of quiet movement that only enhances its mystique and its beauty.

While the cathedral's founding trustees had not always been in agreement with Latrobe, when he left Baltimore for the last time in 1820 with the building nearing its dedication, they sent him a letter in which they acknowledged his great gift to their church and to Baltimore. It read in part:

> . . . this magnificent building, the design and plan of which are entirely yours, is fast approaching completion,

and bids fair to stand for ages as a monument, not only to the piety of those who have contributed to its construction, but likewise to your genius and architectural skill and taste, for having availed themselves of which, the Trustees consider themselves singularly fortunate . . . . Rest assured, Sir, that the Trustees will ever cherish the memory of your distinguished services, and in taking leave of you, which they do with the utmost regret, they will indulge the hope that your great abilities will meet with the encouragement to which they are so eminently entitled, and they fervently pray the Almighty Being, to whom you have erected the most splendid temple, on this side of the Atlantic, to take you under his special protection.

Latrobe died before the year was out, but the building remains. Architectural historian Nikolaus Pevsner called it "North America's most beautiful church." ❖

B10 • ENOCH PRATT FREE LIBRARY

400 Cathedral Street
1933—Clyde N. Friz, with Tilton and Githens

In the late nineteenth century Enoch Pratt, who had made a fortune in mule shoes and dry goods, believed that what Baltimore needed most was a library where the people could educate themselves. Accordingly, in 1886 he gave the city the Enoch Pratt Free Library, which was to be—and always has been—in his words, "for all, rich and poor, without distinction of race or color, who, when properly accredited, can take out the books, if they will handle them carefully and return them." At the time it was a radical idea and one of the first free public libraries in the country.

The library's first home was a building that faced Mulberry Street, where the side of the present building is now. When that building was to be replaced, those in charge of the library were quite specific in ordering a building in keeping with the spirit of the donor's original gift. A 1933 publication on the library reads:

> The memorandum of instructions to the architects . . . called for a building that should depart from the traditional institutionalism of the past. It asked for a dignity befitting such an institution, but a dignity characterized by friendliness rather than aloofness. Long stairways of approach, small ground floor windows, giving the appearance of a fortress or mausoleum, were ruled out. Instead, one enters the new Baltimore Library on its main service floor at sidewalk level . . . . The building itself, with its series of twelve great windows, extends directly along the sidewalk line. The lower portions of these twelve windows were especially designed for exhibitions, of a constantly changing variety, definitely planned to show how books connect with each and all the interests of the community.

In other words, the library got exactly what it asked for from the architect, and it has been a remarkably successful and influential library building for more than sixty years, inspiring other library buildings in Toledo, Ohio; Rochester, New York; and elsewhere.

In a 1980s renovation, leading up to the library's centennial, Ayers, Saint, Gross, with Adam Gross as principal, added mezzanines above the reading rooms in the four corners of the main floor. Plans have been announced for the construction of an annex that will connect the existing building with the Library for the Blind and Physically Handicapped at the corner of Franklin Street and Park Avenue. ❖

B11 • FRANKLIN STREET
PRESBYTERIAN CHURCH (former)
(BCL, NR)
Franklin and Cathedral streets
1847—Robert Cary Long, Jr.

One of Long's fine buildings of the 1840s, this is English Tudor in exterior style, essentially a simple rectangle inside. The façade, which probably came to Long via A. C. Pugin, consists of five nicely balanced masses, with twin towers flanking a central door. This is surmounted by a Gothic window filled with Perpendicular tracery. Stone is used functionally in the crenellated towers and buttress offsets of the brick building and aesthetically around the door.

The building was originally painted to resemble stone. In most cases where paint has been removed to reveal the brick, as at Long's St. Alphonsus' [B5], the result is not only not authentic but unfortunate. Here, however, the effect is more pleasing.

The interior consists of a small vestibule and an almost square hall six bays long, with a gallery at the rear over the vestibule. There is no chancel. The walls are ashlared (painted to resemble stone blocks), the paneled wooden ceiling is supported on corbels, and the stained-glass windows and the pews' ornamental finials add touches of decoration to an otherwise austere but refreshingly serene interior. The church was lengthened in 1865, and the present screen is an addition of about 1915.

Since Franklin Street merged with First Presbyterian Church [C13] and its congregation moved there in 1973, this building has changed hands twice. It is now owned by the Bread of Life church and known as Bread of Life at the Cathedral. The present owners plan no major interior or exterior changes.

Not long after designing this church, the Lloyd Street Synagogue [F7], and St. Alphonsus', Long moved to New York to pursue his career. He died of cholera in 1849, leaving his most significant architectural contributions in Baltimore. ❖

B12 • FIRST UNITARIAN CHURCH
(BCL, NR)
Charles and Franklin streets
1818—Maximilian Godefroy

The geometry of Godefroy's major structure in Baltimore is eminently simple—a cube surmounted by a hemisphere. So is its design: the exterior of the church is an excellent example of romantic classicism.

The building is fronted by a beautiful wrought-iron fence, designed by the architect. An arcade encloses a vaulted porch and five doors. Above it is a plain frieze and cornice that extends around the building, and above that is an attic story. The pediment contains a terra-cotta sculpture representing the angel of truth. The original sculpture, by Antonio Capellano, sculptor for the Battle Monument, deteriorated; in 1954, it was

replaced with a replica by Henry Berge. The sides and back of the church have arched recesses, some containing windows. Its structure is brick covered with stucco.

Originally, the church nave was formed by four semicircular arches, each 53½ feet in diameter, supporting a dome of equal diameter and 80 feet above the floor at its center. The acoustics, however, were never good and, in 1893, the church was remodeled by Joseph E. Sperry, who added the barrel vault in classic Roman style.

As it stands now, the interior consists of a large, square nave and shallow side aisles, separated by three arches on each side. The eight 12-inch-square posts carry four timber Howe trusses, each 8 feet deep, that support the vault. The sanctuary in front contains Godefroy's original pulpit, but a new organ, replacing the one he had designed in the shape of a lyre, was added during the renovations. The original dome, patterned on the Roman Pantheon, remains overhead. ❖

B13 • HAMILTON STREET ROW HOUSES

Hamilton Street between Charles and Cathedral streets
ca. 1815—Robert Cary Long, Sr.?

Of the seven houses in this Federal-style row, three—numbers 12, 16, and 18—are basically unaltered. They have unusual and wide single tripartite windows on the second and third floors. Architect Robert Cary Long, Sr., owned the entire row in about 1815 and lived in one of the houses himself. He is thought to have designed them as well.

Their interiors have the main reception rooms on the second floors, with the first floors given to smaller spaces, some for service. The houses are not large, but surprisingly commodious, with extremely well proportioned spaces, especially on the main reception floor. Number 16 West, one of the unaltered houses, is still a single-family dwelling with nine rooms and four and a half baths on four floors. Its five fireplaces are all in working condition and were the house's only source of heat until 1940. ❖

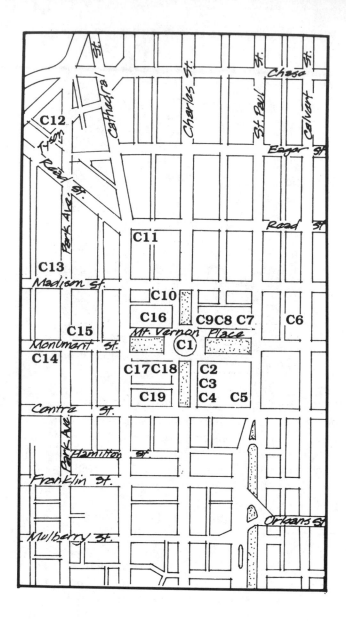

Tour C: Mt. Vernon Place (Walking)

Tour C

Mount Vernon Place (Walking)

C1 WASHINGTON MONUMENT
Mount Vernon Place and Washington Place
1815–29—Robert Mills

C2 PEABODY INSTITUTE OF THE JOHNS
HOPKINS UNIVERSITY
One East Mount Vernon Place
*1859–66—Lind and Murdoch; 1875–78—
Edmund G. Lind*

C3 SCHAPIRO HOUSE
609 Washington Place
ca. 1850s—Michael Roche, builder

C4 PEABODY INN
601–607 Washington Place
*ca. 1850s—Michael Roche, builder;
1993—Murphy and Dittenhafer, renovation architect*

C5 PEABODY DORMITORY
St. Paul and Centre streets
1969—Edward Durrell Stone

C6 ST. IGNATIUS–CENTER STAGE BUILDING
700 North Calvert Street
*1856—Louis L. Long; 1899—James W. O'Connor and
James F. Delany; 1975—James R. Grieves Associates;
1991—Ziger, Hoopes, and Snead*

C7 BROWNSTONE ROW
22–32 East Mount Vernon Place
1853—Louis L. Long

C8 ASBURY HOUSE
10 East Mount Vernon Place
ca. 1855—Niernsee and Neilson

C9 MOUNT VERNON PLACE UNITED
METHODIST CHURCH
Mount Vernon Place and Washington Place
1872—Dixon and Carson

C10 GRAHAM-HUGHES HOUSE
718 Washington Place
ca. 1888—George Archer

C11 EMMANUEL EPISCOPAL CHURCH
811 Cathedral Street
1854—Niernsee and Neilson; 1890—J. Appleton Wilson and William T. Wilson; 1914–18—Ralph Adams Cram; 1919—Waldemar H. Ritter

C12 TYSON STREET
Off Read Street between Park Avenue and Howard Street
ca. 1830—architect unknown

C13 FIRST AND FRANKLIN STREET PRESBYTERIAN CHURCH
210 West Madison Street
1854–75—Norris G. Starkweather

C14 ENOCH PRATT HOUSE (Maryland Historical Society)
201 West Monument Street
1847—architect unknown; 1868—Edmund G. Lind, renovation architect

C15 GRACE AND ST. PETER'S EPISCOPAL CHURCH
707 Park Avenue
1852—Niernsee and Neilson

C16 MOUNT VERNON CLUB OF BALTIMORE
8 West Mount Vernon Place
1842—architect unknown

C17 ENGINEERING SOCIETY OF BALTIMORE
7–11 West Mount Vernon Place
1884–93—McKim, Mead, and White; 1905–16—John Russell Pope

C18 HACKERMAN HOUSE
One West Mount Vernon Place
1849–51—Niernsee and Neilson; 1892—Charles A. Platt, renovation architect; 1989–91—James R. Grieves Associates, renovation-restoration architect

C19 WALTERS ART GALLERY
Washington Place and Centre Street
1905–9—Delano and Aldrich; 1974—Shepley, Bulfinch, Richardson, and Abbott; Meyer, Ayers, and Saint

Even now, this is essentially a nineteenth-century city, and Mount Vernon Place is where the elite lived in the nineteenth century; they have long since moved away, but this is still thought of as the heart of Baltimore.

The several statues (to Wallis, Lafayette, Taney, etc.) in the four squares are evidence that Baltimoreans look upon this as a historic area ("our municipal Pantheon," one resident called it), as are the efforts of preservation organizations to keep things as they are. These efforts have met with success: the only twentieth-century buildings on the squares are the addition to the Garrett-Jacobs House (1905), the Washington Apartments (1906), the Walters Art Gallery (1909), and the Peabody Conservatory's Leakin Hall (1926).

Those two institutions are not only themselves significant additions to Baltimore's life, but represent the many institutions created or largely endowed by huge gifts from the rich and philanthropic—in these cases William and Henry Walters and George Peabody. Thinking of Baltimore as a whole, one could also cite in this context Johns Hopkins, Moses Sheppard, the Garretts, Mary Frick Jacobs, Enoch Pratt, and Claribel and Etta Cone.

If Henry Walters was the richest man ever to live on Mount Vernon Place, he assuredly was not the only one of that breed. Because this was the neighborhood of the rich, many of the buildings here are the work of architects prominent in their times—some of them nationally: Robert Mills, Niernsee and Neilson, Edmund G. Lind, Stanford White, Dixon and Carson, John Russell Pope.

Here, too, one can see several, though by no means all, of the successive nineteenth-century styles, including Greek Revival, Italian Renaissance, Gothic Revival, White's eclecticism, the chateauesque. And the fact that there is a building by Edward Durrell Stone just off the squares is indicative of the recent revival of interest in architecture—to the point of commissioning architects of international stature to work here—that has taken place in Baltimore.

But the variety of architects and the succession of styles cannot hide a certain uniformity of outlook that reflects a civic attitude. Henry James, who visited the city in 1904, later recorded his impression of the Baltimore character to be inferred from these squares:

There . . . were the best houses, the older, the ampler, the more blandly quadrilateral; which in spite of their still faces met one's arrest, at their commodious corners and other places of vantage, with an unmistakable manner. . . . A certain vividness of high decency seemed . . . to possess them, and this suggestion of the real Southern glow, yet with no Southern looseness, was clearly something by itself. . . .

The blandness that James detected in our grandest houses, not unrelated to what architectural historian Phoebe Stanton has called the recessive quality of our row-house architecture, reflects a quality of quiet and somewhat smug inhibition which is as close as Baltimore comes to having a tangible character. These houses, built by the wealthy as personal monuments, are imposing, but they make no effort to overwhelm. This is in part because the sizes of the squares and of the individual pieces of land on which the houses were built prohibit grand gestures. But one can also sense in the mentality of those who lived here a certain reserve, a disinclination to draw attention to oneself for fear of being thought vulgar. These houses project not only what they are, but also, and as a virtue, the quality of not being something more.

Mount Vernon Place, which tells us so much about the city and the people who live here, is actually two places. That part of Monument Street running east and west between Cathedral and St. Paul streets is Mount Vernon Place. That part of Charles Street between Centre and Madison streets is Washington Place. The distinction is worth noting, though most local residents group all four squares, and even the neighborhood around them, under the name Mount Vernon Place.

At the beginning of the nineteenth century it all belonged to John Eager Howard, Revolutionary War hero, whose equestrian statue stands in the north square. From his estate, Belvidere, he gave the land for the Washington Monument; his heirs gave land for the four parks and later sold the lots around them to private citizens who were interested in building.

In the middle decades of the nineteenth century the city was quickly expanding northward from the harbor. There were major houses on the squares by the 1840s, and from before the Civil War until the 1920s this was the most desirable place to live in Baltimore. The parks have been relandscaped several times, most recently in 1916 by Thomas Hastings of the New York firm of Carrere and Hastings. The essentials of that design remain, though some of the plantings have been changed over the years.

During the 1920s the automobile made suburban living as practical as it made urban living unpleasant; the decline of Mount Vernon Place began as old families moved out and the houses were divided into apartments and then divided again.

During the 1930s, however, Mount Vernon Place and its surrounding neighborhood acquired a champion in the person of Douglas Gordon, who formed the Mount Vernon Improvement Association and fought blight tenaciously for decades. Among his signal victories was the repeated defeat of a city bond issue which would have funded a major expansion of the Walters Art Gallery on the south side of West Mount Vernon Place, replacing all the buildings on that block except One West.

In the 1960s and since, there has been a major if sporadic renovation effort on these squares. A few buildings, notably 16 and 18 East, became single-family houses again. Others, such as 3 and 6 West, have been successfully converted to condominiums. The Peabody Institute has preserved façades on the east square and renovated buildings on the south square (see C4). Since 1985 the interior of the Washington Monument [C1] has been restored, and there has been a combined public-private effort to improve the four parks at a cost so far of more than $1 million. That effort continues, with reconstruction of the fountains in the east and south parks still to come at this writing. ❖

C1 • WASHINGTON MONUMENT
(BCL, NR)
Mount Vernon Place and Washington Place
1815–29—Robert Mills

In 1809 a group of patriotic citizens formed a committee to commission and fund a monument to George Washington. They held an architectural competition entered by well-known architects Maximilian Godefroy, Joseph Ramee, and probably Benjamin H. Latrobe, who is believed to have designed an anonymous submission. Although Robert Mills entered his design after the competition's closing date, and though it was clearly the

most expensive design, the judges chose his monumental column in 1815.

The cornerstone was laid July 4 of that year, and the Washington statue was raised, virtually completing the monument, on November 25, 1829. It was the first major monument to the first president.

Mills's original design was considerably more ornate than the present column, involving balconies at several levels, inscriptions, and other decorations. One by one these were discarded for lack of funds; as it was, the monument cost twice the budgeted $100,000. The present monument, however, is more elegant and forceful in it simplicity than the proposed design.

The monument, made of local Cockeysville marble, has a square base that contains a room surrounding the column. The latter, 20 feet in diameter at its base, tapers to the crowning statue of Washington resigning his commission as commander of the Continental Army at Annapolis in 1783. The 16-foot, 6-inch statue is by Italian sculptor Enrico Causici, who also worked on the Capitol in Washington, D.C. The total height of the monument is 178 feet.

The iron fence surrounding the base was designed by Mills and added in 1838; the design includes some of the symbolism that was dropped from the column itself.

In 1985 the interior of the monument was closed due to danger from lead paint. Over the next seven years the paint was removed, a restoration completed at a cost of $314,000, and on December 4, 1992, the monument reopened. The room surrounding the base of the column now contains an exhibition relating to Washington, the monument, and Mount Vernon Place. From there, visitors can climb the column's interior, winding staircase of 228 steps to windows in the base of the statue, from which there are fine views in all directions. ❖

C2 • PEABODY INSTITUTE OF THE JOHNS HOPKINS UNIVERSITY

(BCL)
One East Mount Vernon Place
1859–66 — Lind and Murdoch;
1875–78 — Edmund G. Lind

The Peabody Institute's formal Renaissance Revival façade gives little indication of what lies within: a high, spacious hall, completely surrounded by stacks of books that rise, supported on structural and decorative iron-work, six floors to the ceiling. It is one of the finest interiors in the city.

The library, opened to the public in 1866 with twenty thousand volumes (it now contains roughly two hundred fifty thousand), was originally on the second floor of the west wing, consisting of the three bays to the right of the present main entrance. This section was built of Beaver Dam marble as a separate building and completed in 1861; its opening was delayed by the Civil War. The west wing now incorporates a concert hall on the first floor, and on the second and third, reached by a gracefully curved iron staircase, a recital and lecture hall (the former sculpture gallery with a plaster frieze inspired by the Parthenon), and the classrooms and music studios of the conservatory.

The east wing was also faced with Beaver Dam marble; successive elevation studies by Lind show that he carefully considered the best way of integrating the two sections into a single façade topped by a unifying balustrade.

The present library was one of Baltimore's earliest examples of fireproof construction. French tile blocks were used to insulate the cast- and wrought-iron columns and beams which, anchored in the masonry walls and foundation, form the structural grid. This is covered with decorative cast iron in the Neo-Grec style, the precision and symmetry of which were particularly suited to metal construction; even the floors in the stacks are of iron.

Some of the most important elements of the building's unique structure are hidden overhead: six Pratt roof trusses, fabricated by Pennsylvania's Phoenix Iron Co., span the tops of the columns in the library and support the exterior and interior skylights. The concert hall ceiling and the floors above it are similarly supported in part by four cast-iron Pratt trusses spanning the distance between the masonry walls; their bottom chords are made up of wire cables. These trusses were produced by Baltimore's Hayward, Bartlett & Co., the firm that, with its successors, provided the grand staircase and library ironwork as well. James Crawford Neilson was the consulting architect for the west wing and his partner, John Rudolph Niernsee, for the east. Joseph F. Kemp was the superintendent for both phases of construction.

The Peabody Institute building was intended to be impressive to reflect the quality of its programs. George Peabody was America's first great philanthropist and he had a direct influence on the subsequent philanthropic work of Johns Hopkins and Enoch Pratt. Peabody's 1857 bequest called for the establishment of "an extensive Library," a lecture series, "an Academy of Music," and a "Gallery of Art." Gradually, the music program predominated.

The library was rehabilitated in the 1970s; the concert hall and the former trustees' room in the northwest corner of the building overlooking the square, in the 1980s. The Peabody Institute became a division of The Johns Hopkins University in 1986. ❖

C3 • SCHAPIRO HOUSE
609 Washington Place
ca. 1850s — Michael Roche, builder

The Schapiro House was built for John Duer and features a handsome, two-story cast-iron balcony. Its last owner, John D. Schapiro, gave it to the Peabody Institute with the stipulation that its exterior remain

unchanged. Plans call for the renovation of the façade, including the cast iron, and the interior, currently used as administrative offices and music studios. ❖

C4 • PEABODY INN
601–607 Washington Place
ca. 1850s—Michael Roche, builder;
1993—Murphy and Dittenhafer, renovation architect

Next door to the Schapiro House, a pair of double town houses, also with cast-iron balconies and also owned by the Peabody Institute, have been renovated at a cost of

$2.4 million as an inn. It provides accommodations for participants in the Elderhostel program, which enables people aged sixty and over to spend a week or so at universities and other cultural institutions at nominal expense. The town houses, after having stood derelict for several years, were almost totally rebuilt (some fireplaces and original architectural features were saved), and interconnected. They now house a fifty-room inn, two lecture-recital halls, classrooms, and top floor office space. The cast-iron balconies were taken down, repaired, and reinstalled. In the rear, later additions to the buildings were removed and replaced by a sunken garden and a glass-fronted lobby. The main entrance to the inn is from the enclosed Peabody Plaza. ❖

C5 • PEABODY DORMITORY

St. Paul and Centre streets
1969—Edward Durrell Stone

Stone's 1969 dormitory addition combined several uses and at the same time created a private and much-needed campus for the Peabody Institute. The architect took advantage of the sloping site to include a parking garage (whose walls are adorned with his characteristic grilles), turned its roof into a landscaped plaza, and, at the south end of this, placed two dormitory pavilions.

The perimeter of the terrazzo-paved plaza is defined by a row of 101 arches. Those on the southeast corner, enclosed with gray-tinted glass, make up the outside walls of the student lounge; around the rest of the building they form an arcade. The dormitory pavilions are identical twins, but one has been given a quarter turn with respect to the other. The first floor of the west building, the men's dormitory, houses a kitchen and that of the east building, a lounge. A one-story common dining room lit by skylights links the two sections.

Stone's modernism has blended in surprisingly well with the more traditional surroundings. One drawback is the formidable wall created by the parking enclosure; but the nighttime view from the plaza, with the city's lights shining through the arches, more than makes up for it. ❖

C6 • ST. IGNATIUS– CENTER STAGE BUILDING

700 North Calvert Street
1856—Louis L. Long; 1899—James W. O'Connor and James F. Delany; 1975—James R. Grieves Associates; 1991—Ziger, Hoopes, and Snead

The exterior of this block-long building, completed in two stages in the second half of the nineteenth century, reveals little of what is inside. First constructed, to a design by Louis L. Long, were the church on the northern end and the porticoed central section next to it. Finished in 1856, they would doubtless look more

Italianate than they do if two projected 180-foot towers had been completed. The rest of the complex, from the present Center Stage entrance section to the southern end, was added in 1899 and designed by architects O'Connor and Delany of New York. Aside from the church, these buildings were the home of Loyola College and High School.

The principal delights of the building are to be found inside. The elegant white Baroque interior of the church, only open during services, is a revelation. And the glass and metal Center Stage canopy only begins to reveal that the southern portion of the building has become one of the finest examples of adaptive reuse in the city.

In 1974, Center Stage's previous home on North Avenue burned. A little over a year later came the announcement that the Jesuits, who owned the St. Ignatius complex, had in effect given two-thirds of it, vacant for some years, to the local professional theater for a new home. Architect James R. Grieves, working with theater consultant Roger Morgan, conceived a masterful plan for this space; construction of the first half was completed in eleven months.

Using half of the 90,000 square feet of available space, Grieves designed a broad, shallow, five-hundred-seat auditorium with moderate thrust stage, two-level lobby, offices and workrooms, and provision for a café and restaurant off the first and second levels of the lobby.

Grieves's achievement is most noticeable in the theater itself, which is extremely flexible, technically modern, and has a seating plan in which no seat is more than 35 feet from the stage. The extensive use of found space and found materials, less evident to the visitor, was a factor that kept the cost to $1.7 million and the conversion time to less than a year. It is important to note that, according to estimates published at the time of the conversion, if Center Stage had built its own building it would have taken two to three times as long, cost close to $1 million more, and provided less space. In 1978 the conversion received a national American Institute of Architects Honor Award.

In 1991 the second part of the plan was realized with the opening, three floors above the original theater, of the flexible, innovative Head Theater. Using a "found" space that had once been the upper part of the school's auditorium, architects Ziger, Hoopes, and

Snead of Baltimore, working with Theatre Projects Consultants of New York, left the space essentially as it was, painted the walls, included five existing windows so that lighting designers can incorporate natural light if desired, and created a technically modern facility in what still shows its roots as a historic building's interior.

One of the innovations was a series of two-story seating towers that can be moved around to accommodate various stage configurations or removed altogether. One can have, for instance, a thrust stage, a proscenium stage, a theater-in-the-round, or cabaret-type seating, and the seating capacity can range from one hundred to four hundred seats.

Additional construction in the seventeen-month, $5.9 million project included a scene shop, paint deck, prop shop, hoist way, two elevators, two rehearsal halls, dressing rooms, lobby, coatroom, and a lounge inside the former high school chapel.

With the successful completion of this project, Center Stage realized its dream of a complex with two complementary theaters, and the St. Ignatius building is more thoroughly inhabited than it was for many years. ❖

C7 • BROWNSTONE ROW
22–32 East Mount Vernon Place
1853—Louis L. Long

This is the only example of speculative row-house building on the four squares of Mount Vernon and Washington places. Richard E. France, known as the "lottery king," bought six parcels of land from William Key Howard and built these to a design by Louis L. Long. They are contemporary with Long's design of the original St. Ignatius buildings [C6] a block away, and are fronted with the brownstone façades that proliferated in American cities in the second half of the nineteenth century. Mount Vernon Place had become so popular as a residential area by the time these houses were built that they all sold before they were finished. Originally one-family houses, they have long since been divided into apartments. ❖

C8 • ASBURY HOUSE
(NR)
10 East Mount Vernon Place
ca. 1855—Niernsee and Neilson

Now owned by the Mount Vernon Place United Methodist Church, this house is typical of the Renaissance design patterned after houses by the English architect Sir Charles Barry, as at the Travellers' Club in London. The style first appeared in this country in the Philadelphia Atheneum. The richly decorated interior of Asbury House is the result of an 1890s renovation. ❖

C9 • MOUNT VERNON PLACE
UNITED METHODIST CHURCH
(NR)
Mount Vernon Place and Washington Place
1872—Dixon and Carson

"No picture, unless carefully colored, and no mere
description, can give the reader a notion of its appearance," said the author of an 1888 guide to Baltimore
concerning the Victorian Gothic Mount Vernon Place
United Methodist Church. The polychromatic effect
is achieved by gray-green serpentine sandstone from
Baltimore County, complemented by brown sandstone trim. (Neither stone wears well; in 1932, five
thousand individual pieces had to be replaced.) The
main exterior features are the three spires and the
large, caliper-shaped relieving arch that encloses the
rose window.

On the inside, tall, slender, cast-iron columns support the balconies on either side as well as a system of
dark wood arches and trusses whose openings are filled
with scrolled, wrought-iron decoration. A row of small
clerestory windows lights the west side. Benjamin F. Bennett, a well-known contractor who was familiar with metal construction, built the church. In 1989, the roof,
walls, and stained-glass windows were renovated. ❖

C10 • GRAHAM-HUGHES HOUSE

718 Washington Place
ca. 1888 — George Archer

At the corner of Washington Place and Madison Street stands one of the French-chateaulike houses popular among the wealthy toward the close of the last century, although this example is considerably less grand than those found in New York and other major cities. It has been squeezed onto its lot, so that it looks a bit like a folded accordion, as if it's just waiting to take a breath and expand to full size. This is one of Baltimore's curiosities. ❖

C11 • EMMANUEL EPISCOPAL CHURCH

811 Cathedral Street
*1854 — Niernsee and Neilson; 1890 — J. Appleton Wilson
and William T. Wilson; 1914–18 — Ralph Adams Cram;
1919 — Waldemar H. Ritter*

In 1854 Niernsee and Neilson designed a far simpler church here, which has been altered almost beyond

recognition inside and out. The adjacent parish house, to the south, is the work of the Wilsons, 1890.

At the period of the First World War, Cram removed galleries around three sides of the nave and iron trusses supporting the roof and added stone columns and arches and a cantilevered chancel that projects into the alley behind the church.

In 1919 the façade of the church was made over by Waldemar H. Ritter of Boston, who clothed the simple stone tower in Flemish Gothic finery. John Kirchmayer provided the sculpture, which represents the Ephiphany story with shepherds and wise men, but the tower has always been known as the Christmas tower. The parish house was rebuilt in 1923.

Among the church's decorations are the reredos by Kirchmayer, three stained-glass windows by John La Farge and five by Tiffany, and a baptismal font angel by Daniel Chester French, who later created the statue of Lincoln at the Lincoln Memorial in Washington. The east window, made in London, contains five traceried sections devoted to the history of the Christian church. ❖

C12 • TYSON STREET

Off Read Street between Park Avenue
and Howard Street
ca. 1830—architect unknown

Originally built for Irish immigrants, the little houses along Tyson Street are interesting not so much for their architecture as for the fact that this is a highly successful private urban renewal effort. Most of the houses had fallen into disrepair when, one by one, beginning in the early 1950s, they were bought and renovated by people wanting to live near the center of town. Real estate values have risen sharply since then, and Tyson Street is a desirable place to live. ❖

C13 • FIRST AND FRANKLIN STREET PRESBYTERIAN CHURCH

(NR)
210 West Madison Street
1854–75—Norris G. Starkweather

This is the fourth home of the oldest Presbyterian congregation in Baltimore, founded in 1761. A log meeting-house was succeeded by a brick chapel and then a two-steeple church (1791), which stood on the site of the old Post Office Building at Fayette and Calvert streets. The current building, begun in 1855, with its 273-foot tower (the highest church tower in Baltimore), was designed by Starkweather and completed in 1875. It

is notable for the tower incorporating structural iron, and the truss construction of its roof, eliminating the need for interior pillars. The visitor sees the results of this, an interior with elaborate plasterwork that Washington preservationist and architectural consultant C. Dudley Brown has called "the most remarkable plaster interior in America." Its most conspicuous feature is the fan-vaulted ceiling ending in a series of unsupported pendants, as at the Henry VII Chapel at Westminster Abbey in London.

The principal tower was a notable structural accomplishment. Solid stone piers 8 feet thick and 14 feet deep form the base and penetrate the ground to a depth of 8 feet. Atop these are granite blocks 6½ feet square from which 21-inch-thick clusters of cast-iron columns rise 35 feet. Above these are iron shafts 23 feet high reaching to the pediment and formed into a frame by wrought-iron ties. The spire is a core of brick, reinforced with wrought-iron I-beams placed on the iron pillars, and the whole is faced with the same New Brunswick freestone that faces the body of the church. The height of the tower is emphasized by contrast with its smaller companion to the east, 125 feet high. Much of the ironwork was fabricated by Wendell Bollman's Patapsco Bridge and Iron Works.

Starkweather left Baltimore for Washington, D.C., while construction was still under way, leaving supervision of the completion, including the towers, to Edmund G. Lind, best known for the Peabody Institute complex on Mount Vernon Place [C2]. The former manse to the west, now known as Backus House and used for offices and meeting rooms, was also designed by Starkweather. Reid Memorial Chapel to the north of the church, formerly a lecture room, was redesigned in 1940 by Ralph Adams Cram. In the late 1970s and early 1980s the church underwent a major renovation-restoration, involving introduction of steel trusses to augment the wooden roof trusses, which were discovered to have been underdesigned and were collapsing under too much weight. Architects were Kann and Ammon and C. Dudley Brown and Associates, with Robert Giannetti and Associates responsible for restoration of the ornamental plasterwork.

First Presbyterian Church and Franklin Street Presbyterian Church [B11] merged their congregations in 1973, choosing the First Presbyterian site as their home. ❖

C14 • ENOCH PRATT HOUSE
(Maryland Historical Society)

201 West Monument Street
1847—architect unknown; 1868—Edmund G. Lind, renovation architect

Plain despite its Greek Revival porch and mansard roof with iron cresting, the mansion was plainer still when Pratt built it because it lacked those features. The character of the building reflected that of its owner: ample, but unassuming. Pratt was a successful banker and businessman with interests in iron, coal, and railroads who became one of Baltimore's leading philanthropists. The Sheppard and Enoch Pratt Hospital and the Enoch Pratt Free Library were his great gifts to the city.

As first constructed, Pratt's brick house was three stories with basement. Lind, in 1868, added the fourth floor and probably the marble porch, the latter acquired from the Washington mansion of Mathew St. Clair Clarke, a lawyer, author, politician, and failed investor (in iron and coal). The renovations cost ten thousand dollars.

Pratt died in 1896. In 1916, Mrs. H. Irvine Keyser bought the house, renovated and enlarged it, and three years later gave it to the Maryland Historical Society. This work, supervised by architects Wyatt and Nolting, consisted mainly of replacing the verandas and stables at the rear of the mansion with a library building facing Park Avenue.

Pratt's double parlor separated by four Corinthian columns and his Gothic Revival library with its bossed ceiling, spiky chandelier, and Gothic chairs and bookcases can still be seen.

In recent decades the Historical Society has expanded far beyond the confines of the Pratt House, and continues to do so. In 1967 it added the Thomas and Hugg Memorial Building to a design by Richard Ayers, Sr., of Meyer, Ayers, and Saint. The 1982 France–Merrick wing, also by Ayers, incorporates the octagonal counting room of the old Equitable Trust Company offices in the Munsey building at Calvert and Fayette streets.

In 1994 the society was given the former Greyhound bus garage on Park Avenue south of its present complex for renovation as exhibition space. The architect is David Wright of Grieves, Worrall, Wright, and O'Hatnick. ❖

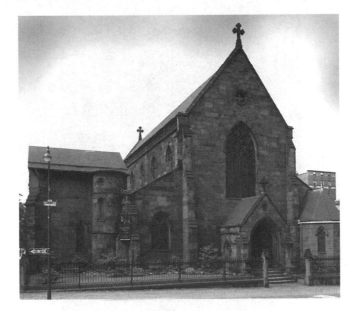

C15 • GRACE AND ST. PETER'S EPISCOPAL CHURCH

707 Park Avenue
1852—Niernsee and Neilson

Grace and St. Peter's is a careful rendition of English rural parish church architecture in the Gothic Revival style, executed in brownstone. A planned tower was never completed above the first story on the west side.

The church consists of nave and clerestory, transepts, chancel, chapel, and sacristy. Seven pointed arches define the nave and side aisles. The attractive interior offers hammer beam–style roof trusses, fine wrought-iron gates on either side of the chancel, stained-glass windows (one of them by Tiffany), and black walnut furniture. ❖

C16 • MOUNT VERNON CLUB OF BALTIMORE

8 West Mount Vernon Place
1842—architect unknown

A fine Greek Revival town house with a plain front and classical portico, the former Tiffany–Fisher house has been a private women's club since 1942. Around the turn of the century, the interior was considerably altered

to give it a Georgian appearance. The ground floor contains a central hall (a feature repeated on the upper floors), a lounge, and double parlor. To the left, a graceful winding staircase ascends to the structure's principal floor, which has a library, music room, dining room, etc. The third floor had six bedrooms; these spaces are now used for offices and storage. Carved marble mantels, leaded-glass windows, and rich architectural detailing evoke the building's life as a private residence occupied by socially prominent families. In back is an enclosed, brick-paved courtyard. ❖

C17 • ENGINEERING SOCIETY OF BALTIMORE

7–11 West Mount Vernon Place
1884–93—McKim, Mead, and White;
1905–16—John Russell Pope

This was once the Garrett–Jacobs mansion, the largest, most expensive residence ever built in Baltimore. It was designed on the baronial scale of a New York town house for the purpose of lavish entertaining, which took place here to a degree that the city had never experienced before and probably never will again.

Mr. and Mrs. Robert Garrett (he became president of the Baltimore and Ohio Railroad in 1884) commissioned Stanford White to design the first part of the house. The western two-thirds of the second Renaissance Revival façade reflect White's work. It almost immediately became a subject of controversy.

Critics felt that the size and style of the house were not in keeping with the conservative character of Mount Vernon Place. A neighbor, Henry P. Janes, objected to the "monstrous vestibule" that he said cut off his light and air and deprived him of his first-floor view of the Washington Monument. He sued, claiming the vestibule extended beyond the building line. The court ruled in his favor, but the decision was reversed on appeal and work continued. (Mrs. Garrett later had her revenge; in 1915, she acquired the offending neighbor's house at 13 West and promptly demolished the back of it for "light and air" for her stairway.)

The three-story carved wood spiral staircase with a Tiffany glass dome and the two-story grand entrance hall, which has windows by Tiffany, are perhaps White's most distinctive contributions. The hall, surrounded by a gallery and wooden balustrade on three sides, also features a fireplace and coffered ceiling. The original family dining room behind it has a wealth of carved wood decoration in its Baroque fireplace and sideboard.

The house was largely the creation of Mrs. Garrett, the former Mary Sloane Frick. She was the undisputed leader of Baltimore society at the time. In 1902, after the death of Mr. Garrett and her marriage to Dr. Henry Barton Jacobs, she acquired and demolished 7 West Mount Vernon Place and hired John Russell Pope to design the last great extension to the house, equal in size to the original.

Pope continued White's brownstone façade, which swells out in front and is embellished with marble columns and stone cartouches. He added a library in the front, a large ballroom with a stage in the back, and, in between, a Caen stone hall and a grand marble staircase leading down to the "supper room," complete with a musicians' gallery, where formal dinners were served. Later on, a gallery was built in the rear on the site of the former stables.

This last addition allowed the creation of the principal architectural feature of the house, which was now shaped like a hollow rectangle: the great central conservatory, originally roofed, that once enclosed doves, palm trees, and a trickling stream. It was later converted into an open court with terraces.

The structure of the mansion is load-bearing brick; the smaller art gallery is of steel and concrete construction. The house contains forty rooms, sixteen fireplaces, and about one hundred windows. It is finished with exotic marbles, oak and mahogany woodwork, mosaics, parquet floors, decorative metalwork, and gold-plated bathroom fixtures. The house cost a reported $1 million to build and another $1.5 million to furnish with tapestries, paintings, and other artwork. When it was the turn-of-the-century scene of elaborate dinners, performances, and social gatherings, a staff of twenty servants was required.

Mrs. Jacobs died in 1936 and her husband in 1939. Since then the mansion has had several owners. The Engineering Society of Baltimore took it over in 1961, has been slowly restoring it, and is now raising funds for modernization. The building is occasionally open to the public. ❖

C18 • HACKERMAN HOUSE
(BCL)
One West Mount Vernon Place
1849–51—Niernsee and Neilson; 1892—Charles A. Platt, renovation architect; 1989–91—James R. Grieves Associates, renovation-restoration architect

This is a happy tale. One of the great town houses of the nineteenth century has remained essentially intact throughout its century-and-a-half history and has now become a splendidly renovated museum building with its beautiful interior permanently open to the public.

Originally built for Dr. John Hanson Thomas and his wife, the former Annie Campbell Gordon, the house encompasses aspects of more than one style. In form it is essentially Greek Revival, like the Mount Vernon Club across the street, but certain details, including the tall casement windows with their surmounting brackets and the heavily modillioned cornice with iron palmettes, suggest the Italianate style then coming into vogue. Originally covered with a gray stucco wash to resemble stone, its bricks were bare in recent decades but have now been painted to resemble the original and proper appearance.

A portico of Beaver Dam marble with fluted columns and a double stairway leads to a marble-floored hall with Corinthian columns, at the rear of which rises a dramatic spiral staircase surmounted by a dome with a Tiffany stained-glass skylight, a later addition. The west side of the house is a double parlor, its two rooms separated by more columns, and to the east are a library in front and the dining room behind, with a porch running the full length of the back of the house.

In the 1880s the Thomases died and in 1892 the house became the property of Mr. and Mrs. Francis M. Jencks, who hired Mrs. Jencks's brother, architect

Charles A. Platt, to modernize the house. He added the bay window in the dining room, enclosed the back porch, widened the staircase, added the Tiffany window, and in general made interior changes in the Italian Renaissance style then fashionable.

The house remained substantially the same through the tenure of the Jenckses and subsequent owner Harry N. Gladding, who maintained it well. In the 1980s, after Mr. Gladding moved out, its future was in doubt until Baltimore businessman Willard Hackerman bought the house and gave it to the city for use by the Walters Art Gallery [C19].

More than one observer has noted that in preparing the house for its new role as the Walters's Museum of Asian Art, architects James R. Grieves and Associates had symbolically the same task as those who much earlier had placed some of the collection's eighteenth- and nineteenth-century Chinese porcelains in European ormolu mounts: to create a Western setting for an Eastern treasure. There was the additional task of making the spaces, especially the magnificent first-floor spaces, suitable for museum use while preserving their architectural integrity, elaborate decoration, and domestic flavor. Minor complaints have been registered, such as that the windows were tinted too dark, and that the house's front door is no longer used as an entrance; but on the whole, the job is a smashing success. The main-floor spaces, retaining their integrity, have become sumptuous repositories of the collection's later, more ornate porcelains and other objects; the second floor's spaces have become quieter backgrounds for the earlier works.

The third floor houses offices, and the former carriage house and backyard have been turned into one enclosed space housing a restaurant and the link between Hackerman House and the Walters's original 1904 building, which faces south Washington Place. ❖

C19 • WALTERS ART GALLERY

Washington Place and Centre Street
1905–9—Delano and Aldrich; 1974—Shepley, Bulfinch, Richardson, and Abbott; Meyer, Ayers, and Saint

From the middle of the nineteenth century until his death in 1894, William Walters amassed a major collection of French academic art and Oriental art. After his

death, his son Henry vastly enlarged the collection, until it encompassed Western civilization from Egyptian times down to 1900. Whether it is Roman sarcophagi, medieval manuscripts, Renaissance painting and sculpture, Sèvres porcelains, or rare jewelry you are looking for, the Walters has it.

In 1905 Henry Walters, who maintained his father's residence at 5 West Mount Vernon Place, commissioned William Delano of the New York firm to design a gallery building which was in effect a private museum opened on occasion to the public. When Mr. Walters died in 1931, he left the gallery and the collection to the city and the people of Baltimore. It ranks with the Johns Hopkins University [L9] and Hospital [G6], the Peabody Institute [C2], and the Enoch Pratt Free Library [B10] as one of the greatest gifts the city has ever received.

The Walters Art Gallery was the first commission for its young architect, and it reflects both his brilliance and his immaturity. Mr. Delano, a relative of the Walters family, later designed the Japanese Embassy in Washington and the U.S. Embassy in Paris.

The interior of the building was modeled on the Palazzo Balbi in Genoa, with a two-story arcade surrounding a square courtyard. At once spirit-lifting and intimate, light and airy, the central space is an appropriate setting for sculpture and small enough to avoid a feeling of monumentality. The stairway leading up to this space, however, is awkwardly placed, so that you run into it the moment you enter the front door, and is too steep to be gracious.

The exterior, if less successful than the court, is a dignified addition to Washington Place, with a rusticated first story surmounted by a second-story wall punctuated by pilasters and smallish windows and topped by a delicate frieze.

Interior gallery spaces surrounding the courtyard on two floors contain the Walters's collections of Renaissance through eighteenth-century art. The galleries are impressive—especially the second-floor paintings galleries—but avoid being daunting. In the mid-1980s the building received a complete renovation-restoration with James R. Grieves Associates as architect. It was highly successful, returning the interiors to pristine condition and installing up-to-date mechanical systems, the effect marred only by the paintings galleries' gaudily bright wall coverings. Mercifully they are fading with time.

In 1974 the gallery added a major wing to the west on Centre Street, which attempted to be at once a completely modern structure and an appropriate partner for the older building. It has some virtues; principally,

that it incorporates almost twice as much gallery space as the original building (50,000 square feet compared to 28,000) and has six floors compared to the original building's three, but stays on the exterior visually compatible in mass and height, with the same cornice line.

In many ways, however, it is flawed aesthetically and as a museum building, from its forbiddingly brutalist exterior façades, its gloomy interior, its thoroughly confusing floor layouts, and its inadequate climate control, down to such off-putting details as its dungeonlike stairwells.

In 1997, however, the Walters expects to start work on a $25 million, several-year project that will include a complete renovation of the building, reinstallation of the collections, and creation of a new family art center as one of its principal attractions. The architect is Kallmann, McKinnell, Wood Architects, Inc., of Boston. ❖

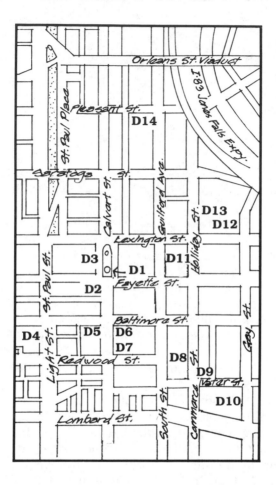

Orleans St. Viaduct

I-83 Jones Falls Expy.

St. Paul Place

Pleasant St.

D14

Saratoga St.

Calvart St.

Guilford Ave.

Holliday St.

D13
D12

Lexington St.

St. Paul St.

D3

D1

D11

Fayette St.

D2

Baltimore St.

Gray St.

Light St.

D4

D5

D6

D7

Redwood St.

D8

Water St.

D9

Commerce St.

South St.

D10

Lombard St.

Tour D: Downtown East (Walking)

Tour D

Downtown East (Walking)

D1 BATTLE MONUMENT
Calvert Street between Fayette and Lexington streets
1815–25—Maximilian Godefroy

D2 EQUITABLE BUILDING
10 North Calvert Street
1894—Carson and Sperry

D3 CLARENCE M. MITCHELL, JR., COURTHOUSE
100 North Calvert Street
1900—Wyatt and Nolting

D4 NATIONSBANK
10 Light Street
1929—Taylor and Fisher; Smith and May

D5 ALEX. BROWN AND SONS BUILDING
135 East Baltimore Street
1901—Parker and Thomas; 1905—Beecher, Friz, and Gregg

D6 ONE CALVERT PLAZA
201 East Baltimore Street
1901—D. H. Burnham and Company

D7 MERCANTILE SAFE DEPOSIT AND TRUST COMPANY BUILDING (former)
Calvert and Redwood streets
1886—Wyatt and Sperry

D8 FURNESS HOUSE
19 South Street
1917—Edward H. Glidden

D9 BALTIMORE INTERNATIONAL CULINARY COLLEGE (former Chamber of Commerce Building)
Water and Commerce streets
1880—John R. Niernsee; 1904—Charles E. Cassell

D10 UNITED STATES CUSTOM HOUSE
Gay and Lombard streets
1907—Hornblower and Marshall

D11 CITY HALL
100 Holliday Street
1875—George A. Frederick; 1975—Architectural
Heritage; Meyers and D'Aleo, renovation architect

D12 ZION CHURCH OF THE CITY OF BALTIMORE
Gay and Lexington streets
1807—Rohrback and Machenheimer, builder

D13 PEALE MUSEUM
225 Holliday Street
1814—Robert Cary Long, Sr.

D14 TERMINAL WAREHOUSE
Pleasant and Davis streets
1893—Benjamin B. Owens; 1912—Owens and Sisco

This has long been the financial and governmental section of the city, as its architecture indicates. The square where the Battle Monument now stands (itself the symbol of Baltimore) has been an important municipal public space for two centuries. Within a few blocks are most of the city's major banks and stock brokerage houses, City Hall, and the city's municipal offices. In 1904 a disastrous fire swept through downtown Baltimore, including some of the area covered by this tour. It was said that many of the then relatively new buildings "burned like torches." In subsequent years Baltimore picked itself up and committed itself to a major rebuilding rivaled only by the post–World War II redevelopment of Charles Center and the Inner Harbor. ❖

D1 • BATTLE MONUMENT
(BCL, NR)
Calvert Street between Fayette and Lexington streets
1815–25—Maximilian Godefroy

The Battle Monument was one of the two structures (the other was the Washington Monument) that prompted President John Quincy Adams in 1827 to toast Baltimore as "the monumental city"; and so it has been called ever since.

The Battle Monument was erected to commemorate the defense of Baltimore and those who died in that

defense in September 1814, during the War of 1812. (Every Baltimorean knows that the bombardment of Fort McHenry during the unsuccessful British attack inspired Francis Scott Key to write "The Star-Spangled Banner.") The monument is unusual for at least two reasons: it is a democratic monument, to all who died, regardless of rank, and its architecture is Egyptian-inspired.

Godefroy, a Frenchman, was influenced by the popularity of Egyptian architecture in France after Napoleon's 1798–99 expedition to Egypt. When he was selected as architect of the monument, he combined Egyptian and other ancient devices in a heavily symbolic plan.

About 39 feet tall and built entirely of marble, the monument has an Egyptian cenotaph base with black stone doors suggesting entrances to a tomb. The eighteen layers of marble used in the base symbolize the

states of the Union at the time the monument was erected.

Griffons, mythical beasts that guarded the doors to ancient tombs, decorate the four corners of the ceno-taph. From the base rises a shaft, its base decorated with friezes representing the two engagements of the de-fense, Fort McHenry and the battle of North Point.

The column is carved in the form of a fasces, or bundle of staves, the Roman symbol of unity. It is bound with cords bearing the names of the thirty-six soldiers who died in the engagements, suggesting the sacrifice of their lives to preserve the nation. Above them, in a band below the statue, are the names of the three officers who lost their lives.

The female statue, in this case symbolic of Balti-more, wears a crown of victory and carries in one hand a laurel wreath, symbol of glory. Her other hand grasps a rudder, symbolizing either stability or navigation, de-pending on which account you read—or perhaps both.

The statue, of Italian marble, was executed by Antonio Capellano (see also his sculptures at First Unitarian [B12] and St. Paul's [B1] churches). The little plaza to the north of the monument was added in the 1960s.

In the early nineteenth century, when the monu-ment was new, this square had a more domestic flavor and scale, and the monument no doubt seemed less diminutive than it does today. But if its immediate neighbors are more massive than their predecessors, it has at least been spared skyscrapers on all sides. ❖

D2 • EQUITABLE BUILDING
10 North Calvert Street
1894—Carson and Sperry

The Equitable, a large and handsome Commercial style building, has Sullivanesque ornamentation. Ten stories high, with an interior frame of cast-iron columns and steel beams, and exterior self-supporting walls, the building was regarded as "thoroughly fire-proof" when built. The walls are of granite on the lower three stories, with buff brick above, and beautiful and elaborate terra-cotta trim. When it first opened, there were Turkish baths in the basement, a top-floor restaurant, and a roof garden. The exterior decoration was produced by Boston's John Evans and Company, architectural sculptors, who did work for H. H. Richardson; McKim, Mead, and White; and other leading American architects. (It is not easily appreciated from street level but is fully revealed from the top floor of the courthouse.)

The Equitable Building's interior was heavily damaged during the Baltimore Fire of 1904, when its three-inch-thick wooden floors burned, the terra-cotta floor arches failed, and heavy safes plummeted from the upper stories to the basement. In the analysis that followed the fire, the architects were criticized for the lightness of the construction and the poor use of materials. Said Sperry: "The Baltimore fire has greatly modified my views regarding the best materials and construction for so-called fire-proof buildings."

The structure was later rebuilt. The original heavy cast-iron window frames and apron panels are intact, as is the barrel-vaulted lobby, clad in marble, offset by mosaic panels, and enlivened by gilded metal decoration. New owners have recently renovated and modernized the interior. ❖

D3 • CLARENCE M. MITCHELL, JR., COURTHOUSE

(BCL)
100 North Calvert Street
1900—Wyatt and Nolting

An imposing building in the Second Renaissance Revival style, the Mitchell Courthouse stands on almost exactly the same site as two previous ones, the first built in 1767. The present building was the result of a design competition in which some of the country's leading architects participated, including McKim, Mead, and White; Burnham and Atwood; and Carrere and Hastings.

The courthouse is a steel-frame structure faced with Woodstock granite on the lower floors and Beaver Dam marble on the upper; it covers an entire city block. There are three main stories, plus a fourth (due to the slope of the land) on the Calvert Street side, which is the main façade. It features a massive loggia with eight marble monoliths (reportedly the largest in the world), each over 31 feet tall and weighing 35 tons.

Inside the Calvert Street entrance, a forest of piers supports a series of groined vaults. Marble stairways on either side lead up to the second-floor Criminal Courts lobby, one of the finest interior spaces, lined with columns, overlooked by landings at either end, and flanked by art glass domes. The floor is laid out with a ring of offices around the perimeter and the courtrooms in the center, separated by a corridor; the upper levels generally follow this plan.

The courthouse was remodeled in the 1950s at a cost greater than the $2,250,000 paid for the entire building in 1900. New elevators, lighting, and mechanical systems were installed. Open light courts were filled in with offices and additional floors were added, making a total of six.

Some of the building's distinctive features were lost during this process; others have been restored in succeeding renovations. The latter include the Criminal Courts lobby and the former Orphan's Court (also on the second floor), which has ornate decor; it is now the Museum of Baltimore Legal History. The ceremonial Courtroom 400 on the fourth floor (located behind the huge exterior loggia) has been refurbished, as have the sixth-floor barrel-vaulted Bar Library and the Supreme Bench Courtroom, which is finished in Siena marble and topped by a coffered dome inspired by the one in the Library of Congress, Washington, D. C.

Yet the Mitchell Courthouse remains antiquated and severely deteriorated; a new $1.5 million roof has been put on, but a $50 million master plan for a complete restoration is unfunded.

Throughout the building are rich marbles, metal railings, oak and mahogany woodwork, and murals by John La Farge and Edwin H. Blashfield, among others. All in all, a "noble pile," as the chief judge described it at the dedication. ❖

D4 • NATIONSBANK
10 Light Street
1929—Taylor and Fisher; Smith and May

Baltimore's only Art Deco skyscraper, this was, at 34 stories and 509 feet, Baltimore's tallest building when it opened as the Baltimore Trust Building in 1929. It is especially notable for the exuberance of its decoration, outside and inside.

The carved granite around the upper-story windows and the elaborately intricate designs in the bronze of doorways and windows on the first floor contain stylized

"modernistic" motifs of the 1920s, such as zigzags, sunbursts, clouds, fountains, and animal heads—here lions and eagles (or perhaps falcons). According to architectural historian Randolph Chalfant, the full-size Art Deco decoration for the building was by Louis Fentner, an Austrian draftsman based in New York; but evidence in the form of drawings was destroyed years later when the Taylor and Fisher firm closed.

The program of decoration is highly symbolic and historical. The entrance arches boast carved figures representing medicine, textiles, shipping, manufacturing, railroads, and other contributors to the city's progress, along with representations of important events, such as the writing of the "The Star-Spangled Banner" and the Baltimore Fire of 1904. These alternate with generic symbols, such as a beehive for industry and a sheaf of wheat for prosperity. The bronze doors reveal symbolic figures, such as the owl and eagle, along with more local references, including the crab. A frieze of carved orna-

ment at the fifth-floor level alternates animals with medallions relating to local activities, such as railroading,
sports, shipping, and banking.

The great feature of the interior is the 50-by-200-
foot main banking room with its rich multiplicity of
adornments. The mosaic floor is by Hildreth Meiere,
who had worked on Radio City Music Hall and St. Bar-
tholomew's Church in New York. Three female figures
represent land, water, and air; the center four figures
stand for vision, courage, industry, and cooperation.

Four 16-by-27-foot murals by Baltimore artist R.
McGill Mackall depict moments in Maryland history:
the 1634 founding of the colony; and views of Baltimore in the eighteenth, nineteenth, and twentieth
centuries. The room's columns are a combination of
marbles, including Levanto, Pyrenees, and Verde Antique, and the ceiling is painted in multicolored pat-
terning. The metalwork, including the entrance grilles
and chandeliers, was by Samuel Yellin of Philadelphia.

When in 1993 NationsBank took over Maryland National Bank (the building's previous owner), it embarked
on a successful $900,000 project of lighting and roof
decoration. The formerly disfiguring "MN" signs were
removed from the mansard roof, whose ribs were completely covered in gold leaf to stand out against the
green oxidized copper background. R. Wayne Reynolds
of Baltimore and Michael Kramer of Olney headed the
team of gilders. Lighting of the upper part of the building and the ground-level entrances was designed by
lighting consultant Douglas Leigh, who earlier was responsible for lighting New York's Chrysler and Empire
State buildings.

As a result of these efforts, the building now stands
out on the Baltimore skyline, bringing an added touch
of much-needed excitement and glamour to downtown. ❖

D5 • ALEX. BROWN AND SONS BUILDING

(BCL, NR)
135 East Baltimore Street
1901—Parker and Thomas; 1905—Beecher, Friz, and Gregg

The Alex. Brown and Sons two-story, Neo-Classical Revival downtown headquarters survived the 1904 Balti-

more Fire (it still bears the scars on the outside), due to its low profile and type of construction: concrete faced with brick and marble trim. Beecher, Friz, and Gregg added the southern two bays facing Calvert Street and probably reconfigured the interior, which now reveals a striking banking room finished in marble, balconies with bronze railings, and a stained-glass dome. ❖

D6 • ONE CALVERT PLAZA
(BCL, NR)
201 East Baltimore Street
1901—D. H. Burnham and Company

The Continental Trust Building, as it was known at first, is the only building in Baltimore by a major practitioner of the Chicago style. Daniel H. Burnham was actually more of an organizer than an original creator of architecture, but he worked with the best designers and, around the turn of the century, his firm produced a large number of buildings throughout the East and Midwest.

Burnham's sixteen-story, steel-frame building in Baltimore is faced with granite, brick, and terra-cotta (the last was also used for the floor arches and partitions). In

the building's design, the architect bowed to local tradition by adding classical pediments over some of the windows and a row of columns at the top under an elaborate terra-cotta frieze and cornice. Burnham confined his use of the Chicago bay (a bay window repeated for several stories) to a single example at the rear. The interior banking spaces were finished in marble, bronze, and mahogany. When it opened, the building presented "a light and almost airy elegance," said a reporter.

The Continental Trust, in a location where the 1904 Baltimore Fire was the hottest (an estimated 2,500 degrees Fahrenheit), was completely burned out. In the aftermath, architects and engineers from several cities came to observe the effects of the first real test of the modern fireproof construction methods developed over the previous twenty years. For the most part, the new methods and materials, especially terra-cotta (used as insulation), were vindicated. Burnham himself arrived to reassure the owners of the Continental Trust, writing them later: "I have minutely examined the steel structure of your building on the corner of Baltimore and Calvert streets from the basement to the roof, and find the same intact and good as the day it was put up. . . . I advise you to at once proceed to repair this building."

They did. However, the decorative terra-cotta frieze and cornice that topped the structure (the single section remaining is missing its crown) was not replaced after being damaged by the fire, and there have been some disfiguring changes above the roofline. New owners made substantial renovations in the mid-1980s that included refurbishing the elevators and installing new fire stairs, energy-saving mechanical systems, and metal window frames that replicated the older, wooden ones. ❖

D7 • MERCANTILE SAFE DEPOSIT AND TRUST COMPANY BUILDING (former)

(BCL, NR)
Calvert and Redwood streets
1886—Wyatt and Sperry

Richardsonian Romanesque architecture was particularly well suited to banks, as exemplified here by the strong, fortresslike appearance, enhanced by dramatic arched windows, fine brickwork, and a wealth of carved stone detail. Although designed by a local firm, the bank building bears comparison with similar works by H. H. Richardson and Stanford White.

It was "the most admirable of the commercial buildings in Baltimore," creating an effect of "classic purity," wrote critic Montgomery Schuyler in his pioneering essay, "The Romanesque Revival in America," that appeared in the October–December 1891 issue of *The Architectural Record.*

The bank's walls, brick with brownstone trim, are load-bearing; there is structural iron in the roof and basement. Generations of Baltimoreans used its "Burglar Proof Money Vault" to store their securities, coins, jewels, and family silver.

The interior was greatly altered after being damaged by the 1904 Baltimore Fire. Although new buildings on all sides of the bank were burned out, the structure itself was not much harmed. The interior would probably have survived also if bricks from the Continental Trust Building to the north had not crashed through the skylight and set fire to the banking room.

After the Mercantile Safe Deposit and Trust Company moved to its new Charles Center headquarters in 1970, a branch opened here, but closed in 1993. ❖

D8 • FURNESS HOUSE
(BCL)
19 South Street
1917—Edward H. Glidden

This little building is in the style of Robert and James Adam, late-eighteenth-century British architects whose use of classical motifs employed in a light, free manner became enormously popular. Here, the double orders of columns, the Palladianesque windows in two interpretations, and the delicate decorative touches, including swags and urns, all add up to a breath of fresh air among the more massive structures of the financial district. The interior was most recently renovated in 1993. ❖

D9 • BALTIMORE INTERNATIONAL CULINARY COLLEGE

(former Chamber of Commerce Building)
(BCL, NR)
Water and Commerce streets
1880—John R. Niernsee; 1904—Charles E. Cassell

Built by members of the Corn and Flour Exchange, with an open hall at the top floor where they did their trading, the original 1880 Chamber of Commerce Building by Niernsee had an exterior derived from Venetian Gothic with white granite ornamentation on red brick. It burned in the Baltimore Fire of 1904, but was speedily rebuilt by Cassell, who gave it a modified Renaissance look in warm ochre brick. It is now part of the Baltimore International Culinary College, which has given it a thorough interior renovation. ❖

D10 • UNITED STATES CUSTOM HOUSE

(BCL, NR)
Gay and Lombard streets
1907—Hornblower and Marshall

The Custom House was constructed on the site of Benjamin H. Latrobe's domed Merchants Exchange, a city

landmark opened in 1820 and demolished about 1900. (Latrobe's building also housed a custom house.)

Perhaps inspired by their predecessor, Hornblower and Marshall, winners of a design competition sponsored by the Treasury Department, produced a landmark of the Second Renaissance Revival style featuring three-story engaged columns, classical pediments over the windows, and a rooftop balustrade. The $1.5 million, six-story, steel-framed building, with load-bearing granite walls, is E-shaped; its rear wings flank a lower pavilion and courtyard.

The building houses government regulatory agencies that monitor the import and export of goods through the Port of Baltimore and the Baltimore-Washington International Airport.

A four-year, $11 million program to renovate and restore the Custom House was completed in 1996. The central atrium, rising through four floors, and the marble and iron stairways, all formerly enclosed, have been reopened. Ornamental ceiling plasterwork and wall stencilling have been restored and painted. New mechanical, plumbing, and electrical systems were installed.

The first-floor Sub-Treasury Room and the large, lofty Call Room (where ship captains once conducted their business and which housed draft boards in recent decades) have also been renovated. D'Aleo, Inc., was the renovation architect. The Call Room's main attraction (restored in the 1970s) is *Entering Port,* a 30-by-63-foot ceiling canvas depicting a fleet of ships and the surrounding smaller paintings illustrating *The History of Navigation.* They are by Francis Davis Millet, reflect the complementary nature of art and architecture at the turn of the century, and are considered by experts to be among "the finest decorative art of any public building in the country." ❖

D11 • CITY HALL
(BCL, NR)
100 Holliday Street
1875—George A. Frederick; 1975—Architectural Heritage;
Meyers and D'Aleo, renovation architect

This building, influenced by the French Second Empire style, was Frederick's first commission. He was under twenty years old when he submitted the winning design.

The four-story building has two connected lateral wings three stories high with mansard roofs. These, the arched windows, bull's eye dormers, and other decorations show French influence applied with a certain dryness that keeps the building, though handsome, from rising to any really exciting level.

The structure of the roof is of iron, and much iron was also used in the interior structure; however, the building has brick bearing walls 5½ feet thick, faced with local Beaver Dam marble. The building is topped by a segmental cast-iron dome.

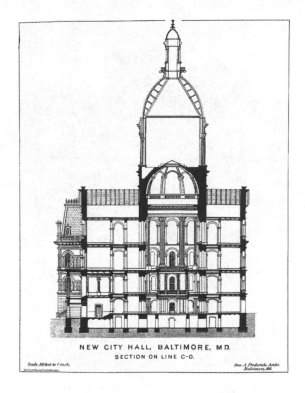

NEW CITY HALL, BALTIMORE, MD.
SECTION ON LINE C-D.

The interior rotunda rises 119 feet through three stories, surrounded by Doric, Ionic, and Corinthian columns, and culminates in an interior dome. The exterior dome rises to 227 feet. The segmental dome design was by Wendel Bollman (see Essays, p.13), with iron by Bartlett, Robbins and Company.

In 1975, the building was successfully renovated, saving the best of the old while making as much use of space as possible. The job involved restoration of the rotunda and ceremonial chambers, repair of the dome, and the opening of two courtyards roofed with glass to make public areas suitable for exhibitions. Two new floors were inserted to make six out of four. The building was rededicated in January 1977.

Its original cost had been $2.3 million ($250,000 less than the appropriation), plus $104,000 for furnishings. The cost of the renovation was $10.5 million, plus $850,000 for furnishings.

The plaza in front of City Hall and the Greek classical War Memorial Building which faces City Hall on the other side of the plaza were both designed by Laurence Hall Fowler in 1925. ❖

D12 • ZION CHURCH OF THE
CITY OF BALTIMORE
(BCL)
Gay and Lexington streets
1807—Rohrback and Machenheimer, builder

The two builders responsible for this church, who were members of its congregation, had worked with Maximilian Godefroy on his St. Mary's Seminary Chapel [J3]. That was probably the inspiration for the pointed windows and crenellations of Zion Church, the older part of which, facing Gay Street and shown here, was built two years later. The parish hall and tower were added in 1913 to a design by Theodore W. Pietsch. ❖

D13 • PEALE MUSEUM
(BCL, NR)
225 Holliday Street
1814—Robert Cary Long, Sr.

This simple Federal building was commissioned by Rembrandt Peale, one of the artist sons of the famous Maryland-born painter Charles Willson Peale, and was the first structure in the United States built specifically as a public museum.

Containing three stories of brick with basement and attic and a square gallery appended to the back, the museum has a façade graced with restrained decoration. An early sketch suggests that the building origi-

nally differed in having an open loggia with four double columns over the first-floor porch.

The interior has been renovated several times to serve the various purposes of the building. From 1830 to 1875 it was the City Hall; later it was a school. In 1930, the front wall was rebuilt and the interior renovated and it became the Municipal Museum of Baltimore City, but has always been popularly known as the Peale Museum.

In the latest renovation, in 1989, the second floor front area was turned into a gallery based on depictions of Charles Willson Peale's long gallery at his museum in Philadelphia. It contains exhibits on Baltimore history and a permanent display of a reproduction of the mastodon skeleton Charles Willson Peale unearthed in New York State. The third floor exhibits paintings by members of the Peale family and other Baltimore artists. ❖

D14 • TERMINAL WAREHOUSE
(NR)
Pleasant and Davis streets
1893—Benjamin B. Owens; 1912—Owens and Sisco

"The external structure of a warehouse should be of the most substantial character," said a turn-of-the-century critic. "It should express immense strength and the greatest security . . . the warehouse should be its own best advertisement." The Terminal Warehouse fulfills these criteria.

Built of brick, with a foundation of Port Deposit granite, it was planned as a "flour house" to handle only that commodity. The ground floor accommodated eight railroad cars and twelve trucks (or horses and wagons). The older section, facing Davis Street, was constructed with pine posts and beams. Steel was used in the newer part, which consists of the three bays at the southern end. The total cost of the two buildings, including the land, was about $200,000.

The architects were careful to match the new work to the old, so that the two structures appear as one. Besides the brick string course, the only other embellishments are strictly functional: steel-covered wooden shutters protecting the windows and a distinctive octagonal redwood water tank standing on the roof. The latter was probably part of the 1912 addition.

In recent years, flour delivered by rail has given way to items for self-storage brought by truck. The Baltimore City Archives is also housed in the building. ❖

Tour E

Downtown West (Walking)

E1   VALU-PLUS (formerly Kresge's)
119 West Lexington Street
1908; 1937—architects unknown

E2   HUTZLER BROTHERS COMPLEX (former)
210–234 North Howard Street
1888—Baldwin and Pennington; 1931–41—
James R. Edmunds, Jr.

E3   PROVIDENT SAVINGS BANK (former)
Howard and Saratoga streets
1903—Joseph E. Sperry; York and Sawyer

E4   BALTIMORE EQUITABLE SOCIETY BUILDING
21 North Eutaw Street
1857—Joseph F. Kemp

E5   EUTAW SAVINGS BANK BUILDING
Eutaw and Fayette streets
1887—Charles L. Carson; 1911—
Baldwin and Pennington

E6   ABELL BUILDING
329–335 West Baltimore Street
ca. 1878—George A. Frederick

E7   BROMO SELTZER TOWER (Baltimore Arts
Tower)
Eutaw and Lombard streets
1911—Joseph E. Sperry

E8   MARLBORO SQUARE
410 West Lombard Street
1890—Charles L. Carson; 1914—Joseph E. Sperry,
addition; 1986—Burns and Geiger, Columbia Design
Collective, renovation architects

E9   PACA-PRATT BUILDING
Paca and Pratt streets
1905—Otto Simonson and Theodore Wells Pietsch,
with Lucius R. White

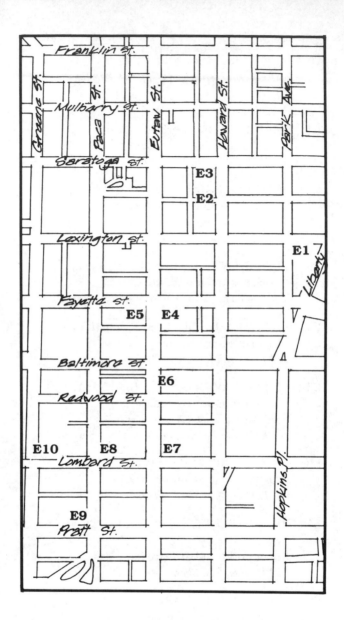

Tour E: Downtown West (Walking)

E10   DAVIDGE HALL
      Lombard and Greene streets
      *1812—Robert Cary Long, Sr.; 1979—Edmunds and
      Hyde, restoration architect*

D own through the first half of the present century,
    this was a lively commercial center, with four of
Baltimore's major department stores clustered near the
corner of Howard and Lexington streets, and nearby
streets alive with smaller stores, movie theaters, and
other elements of a vital downtown. After about 1950,
with the opening of the department stores' suburban
branches, together with changing urban demographics
and the Charles Center and Inner Harbor redevelop-
ments to the east, this area experienced a slow and then
more rapid decline. In the 1970s and 1980s the department stores and movie houses closed, leaving the area
looking somewhat abandoned, although many smaller
retail outlets and the famous food emporium, Lexington
Market, remain.

   In recent years there has been an attempt to rejuvenate the area. Offices now occupy some of the former
department store space, and there has been a proposal
to turn several blocks of Howard Street into an arts
corridor, with a block of buildings turned into artists'
housing and a major cultural center at the northern
end, near the Fifth Regiment Armory. ❖

E 1 • VALU-PLUS (formerly Kresge's)
119 West Lexington Street
1908; 1937—architects unknown

Little is known about this schlocky but amusing building, except the belief that it was first erected in 1908 and
received a thorough face-lifting with the addition of the
current façade in 1937. That was the heyday of the
Moderne style, a successor to the Art Deco style of the
1920s. With the streamlining of airplanes and automobiles, the rounded form supplanted the rectilinear of
classic Art Deco and often resulted in such bulbous
creations as the store windows here. It is fitting that what
can be seen of the building is no more than a façade
pasted onto an older building, for Art Deco and Moderne
were decorative rather than architectural styles.

Although the most recent occupant was Valu-Plus, generations of Baltimoreans will remember this as one of a chain of "five-and-ten-cent" stores called Kresge's. ❖

E2 • HUTZLER BROTHERS COMPLEX (former)

(BCL, NR)
210–234 North Howard Street
1888—Baldwin and Pennington; 1931–41—
James R. Edmunds, Jr.

The oldest department store in Baltimore until its demise in 1989, Hutzler Brothers operated space on the west side of the 200 block of Howard Street from 1858. None of its original buildings remain. They were demolished for the erection in 1888 of the oldest part of the present complex, the five-story, three-bay, largely Romanesque building at 212 to 218. Designed by Baldwin and Pennington, it has two four-story arches filled with thrust polygonal bays flanking a central entrance with a Moorish arch that can still be seen over the altered first-floor entrance. Originally, this building was surmounted by a turret at the north corner, at Clay Street, perhaps part of the reason it has been called the Palace Building. The building was enlarged one bay to the south (Number 210) at the turn of the century; the addition had a similar stone façade, without arch or thrust bay.

The two northernmost buildings of the complex, 228 to 235, were four-story commercial buildings redeveloped as part of the Hutzler's group from 1913 to 1916. In 1931 the first five stories of the central building, including four stories of air rights above Clay Street, were constructed to a design by the firm of James R. Edmunds, Jr. The Art Deco-inspired design was carried across the façade at the first level. Notable aspects of this façade include the brass grillwork over the display windows; the two large vertical windows above the first-floor level; the fluted quarter-columns of the windows and their forestanding urns; the color gradations of the brickwork, growing lighter from bottom to top; and the treatment of the first-level entrances. An additional five stories were added to the central building in 1941. An interesting engineering note is that when the 1931 building went up, the structural steel was welded rather than riveted; it is said to be the first field-welded (i.e., on-site welded) job in Baltimore's business district.

In recent decades, with the decline of Howard Street, parts of the complex closed as public retail space. An effort to rejuvenate the store in the early 1980s included cleaning the front of the 1888 building. Not long after, the store closed. Parts of the complex are now leased out as office space. ❖

E3 • PROVIDENT SAVINGS BANK (former)

(BCL)
Howard and Saratoga streets
1903—Joseph E. Sperry; York and Sawyer

This rusticated mass of granite, with walls seven feet
thick at the base, was designed to simulate an old treasure chest, or so the story goes. It actually looks like one
bay of the ground floor of a Florentine Renaissance
palace, such as the Palazzo Medici-Riccardi.

Originally, the building's interior was an open space
rising 83 feet to a dome at the top, but 1949 and 1953
renovations inserted floors and blocked the view of the
dome. James R. Edmunds, Jr., was the architect of the
1949 and 1953 alterations. His firm was the continu-
ation of Sperry's.

The building no longer belongs to Provident Bank.
It has been bought by a jewelry firm located across Saratoga Street, which intends to use it as a jazz emporium. ❖

E4 • BALTIMORE EQUITABLE
SOCIETY BUILDING

(NR)
21 North Eutaw Street
1857—Joseph F. Kemp

A handsome brick Italian Renaissance Revival building
with a (now painted) brownstone front, this was built as
the headquarters of the Eutaw Savings Bank, which thirty
years later moved across the street. The Baltimore Equitable Society acquired it in 1889.

Except for removal of bars over the windows, the
building remains substantially as it was built. Inside is a
large room with a high coffered ceiling, tile floor, dark
woodwork, and clerks toiling behind the wire mesh above
the old bank counter.

The Baltimore Equitable Society is the fourth oldest
fire insurance firm in the United States, and Maryland's
oldest corporation, founded in 1794. The building features a second-floor museum filled with old fire-fighting
equipment, models, and photographs; but the society's
most prized collection consists of hundreds of old fire
marks (company emblems displayed on buildings to
indicate they were insured) lining the walls of the trea-
surer's office. ❖

E5 • EUTAW SAVINGS BANK BUILDING

Eutaw and Fayette streets
1887—Charles L. Carson; 1911—Baldwin and Pennington

This Renaissance-styled brownstone banking building,
with its wealth of carved material, its pediment, frieze,

Corinthian columns, and other touches, is especially interesting when compared to the Equitable Society Building across the street, which was the bank's first home. In moving to larger quarters, the bank erected a building which, though grander, was in keeping with the style of the older structure. The later building shows more scholastic attention to the correct use of Renaissance elements, while its older neighbor shows a Victorian influence, especially in its window treatment. There is a certain pedantic dryness to the Eutaw building, however, which makes it ultimately less satisfying than the smaller Equitable Society building.

The last three bays on the Fayette Street side of the Eutaw Bank Building, added when it was enlarged in 1911, although of a darker stone, show a careful effort to reproduce elements of the 1887 building.

Inside, there is a two-story banking room with a coved and coffered ceiling. There are twelve Palladianesque windows with pilasters and stained glass in the arches, four on each side and two on each end. A balcony runs around the room, shallow at the sides, deeper at the ends.

The building became a branch of the Maryland National Bank (now NationsBank) in 1974, but closed ten years later. More recently, it has been used for social and musical functions. ❖

E6 • ABELL BUILDING

329–335 West Baltimore Street
ca. 1878—George A. Frederick

The Abell Building's remarkable visual impact is due to a combination of materials and styles. The materials are cast iron and Baltimore brick, with bluestone, white marble, and terra-cotta trim. The styles blend a precise Neo-Grec storefront with an exuberant Italianate façade. The product is Baltimore's finest surviving warehouse from the period.

Its size and corner location also lend prominence to the structure, built as an investment property for A. S. Abell, then owner of the Baltimore *Sun*. It is actually a "double warehouse" with a longitudinal dividing wall creating space for two sets of tenants on each of its six floors. (A variety of tenants, from printers to insurance companies, occupied the building; the clothing industry predominated and some of these firms remain.)

Bartlett, Robbins and Company produced the 276-foot, cast-iron storefront, extending around three sides, most of it now unfortunately covered with metal paneling. However, its Neo-Grec details are exposed on the one and a half stories facing Redwood Street. The rich, polychrome masonry façade above is enhanced by a profusion of crockets, rosettes, and other decorative details.

At Redwood and South Howard streets are twin warehouses in a similar style designed by Jackson C. Gott. One of them, the Rombro Building, owned by the current owners of the Abell Building, has been renovated for federal agencies. ❖

E7 • BROMO SELTZER TOWER
<u>(Baltimore Arts Tower)</u>
(BCL, NR)
Eutaw and Lombard streets
1911—Joseph E. Sperry

One of the most conspicuous ornaments on the Baltimore skyline, especially when seen from the Baltimore-Washington Parkway or Oriole Park at Camden Yards, the Bromo Seltzer Tower is a monument to the well-known cure for headache and hangover developed by local pharmacist Captain Isaac E. Emerson.

Emerson made a grand tour of Europe shortly after 1900 and fell under the spell of the Palazzo Vecchio in Florence. When he returned, he commissioned Sperry to design a building like it. Sperry's tower, when it was built, did not much resemble its model, and does so even less since the six-story Bromo Seltzer factory building that embraced it on two sides was replaced in the 1970s by a two-story firehouse. (The large drug company that acquired the Emerson Drug Company and moved the operation elsewhere donated the tower to the city on the condition that it be saved.)

The Palazzo Vecchio is a thirteenth-century stone structure with a battlemented watchtower 308 feet tall, built of rough stone and with few windows. The Baltimore version is 288 feet high, 30 feet square, and is of steel-frame construction faced with yellow brick. It contains two elevators, office space on most of its sixteen floors, and what was one of the largest four-dial gravity clocks in the world, larger than London's Big Ben. (The clock still operates, but with electricity.)

Yet it was the tower's culmination that made it really memorable: a steel replica of the blue Bromo Seltzer bottle, 51 feet high, 20 feet in diameter, weighing 17 tons, and crowned with 596 lights. The bottle revolved twice every minute and reportedly could be seen at night from the Eastern Shore of Maryland. The revolutions, however, caused serious cracks in the structure, and the bottle was removed and scrapped in 1936. The crenellation was added at the same time.

The tower houses the Mayor's Advisory Commission on Art and Culture. In 1995, it was illuminated with special blue lights in the arches above the battlements and floodlights on the façade as part of the "Brighten Baltimore" program. ❖

E8 • MARLBORO SQUARE
410 West Lombard Street
1890—Charles L. Carson; 1914—Joseph E. Sperry, addition; 1986—Burns and Geiger, Columbia Design Collective, renovation architects

Carson designed the city's earliest Commercial-style warehouse for the Strouse Brothers Company, manufacturers of men's suits and overcoats. It is reminiscent, particularly the fenestration, of H. H. Richardson's massive Marshall Field Wholesale Store in Chicago, completed in 1887 (demolished in 1930). Carson executed his building in brick, red and brown sandstone, terracotta, and cast iron, with a fine sense of proportion and detail. This is particularly notable in the strong, rhythmic arches and use of the cast iron, with stylized decoration, to frame the ground-floor entrances and plate-glass windows. Structural iron was used on the first-floor interior and wooden posts and beams to support the open loft floors above.

In 1914, Sperry (formerly Carson's partner) designed the much plainer addition to the east using structural steel throughout. This section was built for the Marlboro Shirt Company. The Strouse Brothers Company was liq-

uidated in 1920. From that time until the 1970s, the Marlboro firm occupied both sections of the building and became one of the largest shirt manufacturers in the country.

The entire structure (with the exception of ground-floor office space), was converted to apartments in a $7.25 million renovation in 1986. Its main feature is an atrium courtyard finished in stucco and mirrored glass in the post-modern style. ❖

E9 • PACA-PRATT BUILDING
(NR)
Paca and Pratt streets
1905—Otto Simonson and Theodore Wells Pietsch, with Lucius R. White

This is reported to have been one of the earliest steel-and-concrete buildings in the city and the most modern structure of its kind when it was built. Erected as the Henry Sonneborn & Co. clothing factory, it is said to have been the largest men's clothing factory in the world when built, housing more than four thousand workers who could produce more than three thousand men's suits in a day.

The building remained a clothing factory until the 1930s, and then was put to other uses, primarily offices. In 1985 it was completely renovated. Except for the

basic structure of steel piers encased in concrete, the
building was gutted. Even the windows were replaced,
but the new ones replicate the original ones. The renovation has won an award from the National Association
of Industrial and Office Parks. It is now the operations
center for First National Bank. ❖

E10 • DAVIDGE HALL

(BCL, NR)
Lombard and Greene streets
*1812—Robert Cary Long, Sr.; 1979—Edmunds and Hyde,
restoration architect*

One of the earliest buildings of its type in the United
States, predating Jefferson's Rotunda at Charlottesville
by about a decade, Davidge Hall is also the oldest medical school building in the United States. It followed
French examples and the style of a similar though smaller
building by Benjamin H. Latrobe at the University of
Pennsylvania.

The low dome, which sits upon a round drum, is
behind a plain, simple façade with a Doric porch. The
partially rounded side walls are slightly less severe than
the front, each having a fan window.

Of the two major circular spaces, the upper anatomical theater is roofed by a wooden dome. The room

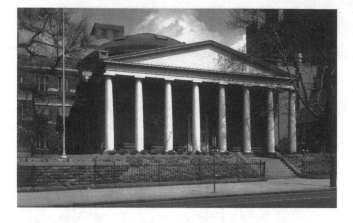

below was a chemistry hall with the same diameter as the theater. The building served its purposes extremely well, both in the use of its main spaces and in the openings and staircases that provided for rapid circulation. It is a tribute to the building that, almost two centuries after it opened, the first-floor main room is still used for teaching medicine. The former anatomical theater is now a museum, and the building also contains offices.

In 1979 the building was completely restored by the firm of Edmunds and Hyde, with Michael F. Trostel the architect-in-charge. Among the restorations were the anatomical hall's original seating, entrances, and railing at the top level of the room. The ceilings of both major rooms were also restored. ❖

Tour F

Downtown East (Driving)

F1   BALTIMORE CITY JAIL GATEHOUSE (old)
Buren and Madison streets
1859—Dixon and Dixon

F2   ST. VINCENT DE PAUL CHURCH
120 North Front Street
*1841—Rev. John B. Gildea?; 1876–95—George A.
Frederick, renovation architect; 1994—Murphy and
Dittenhafer, renovation architect*

F3   SHOT TOWER
Fallsway and Fayette Street
1828—Jacob Wolfe, builder

F4   CARROLL MANSION AND BALTIMORE CITY
LIFE MUSEUMS
800 East Lombard Street
*ca. 1812—architect unknown; 1967—Wrenn, Lewis,
and Jencks; 1985–96—Peterson and Brickbauer,
and others*

F5   SEWAGE PUMPING STATION
701 Eastern Avenue
1912—Henry Brauns

F6   STAR-SPANGLED BANNER FLAG HOUSE
844 East Pratt Street
1793—architect unknown

F7   LLOYD STREET SYNAGOGUE
Lloyd and Watson streets
1845—Robert Cary Long, Jr.

F8   McKIM FREE SCHOOL
1120 East Baltimore Street
1833—William F. Small and William Howard

F9   OLD TOWN MEETINGHOUSE
Fayette and Aisquith streets
1781—George Matthews, builder

F10 EASTERN FEMALE HIGH SCHOOL
Orleans and Aisquith streets
1869—R. Snowden Andrews

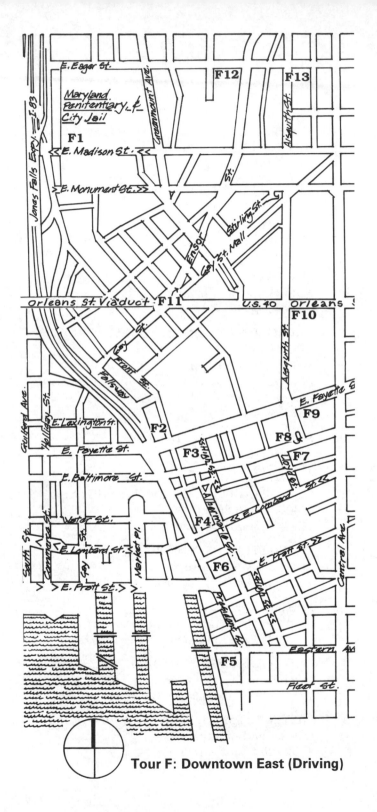

Tour F: Downtown East (Driving)

F11 NUMBER 6 ENGINE HOUSE
Gay and Ensor streets
1853—Reasin and Wetherald

F12 ST. JOHN THE EVANGELIST CHURCH
901 East Eager Street
1856—Niernsee and Neilson; 1892—E. Francis Baldwin

F13 ST. JAMES AND ST. JOHN'S CHURCH
1225 East Eager Street
1867—George A. Frederick

The area covered by this tour includes the section known as Old Town, originally Jones-Town, the oldest part of Baltimore, first surveyed by authority of the Assembly of 1732. The original bounds included Front, High, and Exeter streets between Hillen and Lexington, and early settlers included David Jones, Jonathan Manson, and Edward Fell (not the William Fell who gave his name to nearby Fells Point). Jones-Town was annexed to Baltimore City in 1745, with a bridge across the Jones Falls at Gay Street. Architecturally speaking, there is nothing left from that earliest period, the oldest building here dating from 1781. Nor, on the other hand, is there anything recent of particular note. The buildings included here date primarily from the end of the eighteenth century down to about the period of the Civil War. Styles range from Federal and Greek Revival to Italianate and Tudoresque revival, and most of the buildings are of modest size. ❖

F1• BALTIMORE CITY JAIL GATEHOUSE (old)

(BCL)
Buren and Madison streets
1859—Dixon and Dixon

This Tudor Gothic structure stands on the site where there has been a city jail since 1799. In the 1850s, the Dixons designed a new jail for Baltimore (of which this is a remnant) that is said to have been the most ambitious municipal building project in Baltimore before the Civil War. It stood until it was largely demolished in 1958, with only the gatehouse remaining.

The jail was a fine design for its time, combining security with maximum light and air for the prisoners. It was even criticized as a "palace for felons." The power and dignity of the design are suggested by the five-part stone gatehouse with its octagonal towers and Gothic windows. A drawing in Gobright's *The Monumental City*, a guidebook of 1858, shows a tall cupola atop the gatehouse building; it was either not built or, if built, was subsequently removed. Baltimore's Commission for Historical and Architectural Preservation has called this "one of Baltimore's most picturesque non-ecclesiastical Gothic structures."

The gatehouse is but one part of a penal complex that includes the Maryland Penitentiary and Baltimore City Jail buildings. The most notable feature of the Romanesque penitentiary, designed by Jackson C. Gott and opened in 1899, is the fortresslike administration building at the corner of Forrest and Eager streets with its heavy walls, corner towers, and pyramidal roof. Of the building's two original wings, the south one was recently replaced with a four-story building by Grad Associates. The newest addition to the complex is the 1995 Central Booking and Intake Center, at Madison Street and the Fallsway, by Smeallie, Orrick, and Janka. ❖

F2 • ST. VINCENT DE PAUL CHURCH

(BCL, NR)
120 North Front Street
*1841—Rev. John B. Gildea?; 1876–95—George A.
Frederick, renovation architect; 1994—Murphy and
Dittenhafer, renovation architect*

The Neoclassical St. Vincent de Paul Church is immediately recognizable by its 150-foot, three-tiered tower, topped by a dome and cross. The church and tower are of brick, painted to resemble wood; there is a stone foundation. With the exception of a two-story addition in the rear, the outside of the church remains basically unchanged.

The interior is another matter, having been redesigned several times to reflect changing fashions in architecture and liturgy. The original nave, in the Federal style, was austere. It had a flat ceiling, a balcony supported by cast-iron columns that extended around three sides of the room, and a rear upper gallery for slaves.

Frederick added a two-story structure to the back of the church and gave the interior an ornate, Victorian appearance with the addition of a decorated coved ceiling, plaster frieze and cornice, scagliola pilasters, and painted glass windows. In the 1890s, a baldachino was installed, the upper gallery in the rear and the side galleries were removed, and gilding and frescoes were applied. Much of this Baroque decoration disappeared when the interior was "re-simplified" for the church's

1941 centennial renovation, and new windows with stained-glass medallions replaced the previous ones.

The most recent renovation made the building wheel-chair accessible and adapted the interior to meet the changed liturgy of the Catholic Church. The altar area was redesigned with a reredos, the pulpit area extended, and the pews reconfigured and rearranged in a radiating pattern. The floor was raised to a uniform level and doorways leading into the nave from the narthex were widened. The installation of a glass wall adjoining the cast-iron gallery columns created a large meeting space just inside the entrance to the church.

The neighborhood surrounding St. Vincent de Paul Church has changed drastically since the days when Rev. Gildea served as its founder, first minister, and probable designer. The church, meanwhile, has become a case study in successful adaptation. ❖

F3 • SHOT TOWER
(BCL, NR)
Fallsway and Fayette Street
1829—Jacob Wolfe, builder

This Baltimore landmark is an architectural relic. Once there were three such towers in Baltimore; now there are only a few left in the world. In shot towers, molten lead was poured in drops from the top. It formed into balls as it fell and solidified upon hitting cold water at the bottom, forming shot.

Charles Carroll of Carrollton laid the cornerstone for the 215-foot tower, originally known as the Phoenix Shot Tower, in 1828. Its stone foundation walls are 17 feet deep and rest on rock. The tower's outside diameter is 40½ feet at the base and tapers to 20 feet at the top. The weight on the base is estimated at 6½ tons per square foot.

The circular brick structure's walls are 4½ feet thick from the bottom to about 50 feet up; then they narrow in stages of 4 inches each, until at the top the thickness is 21 inches. The whole is crowned with an 18-inch parapet wall.

Of the fourteen floors inside, the first twelve are of wood construction, the thirteenth and fourteenth of iron. The building has a twentieth-century concrete roof. There are an estimated 1.1 million handmade, wood-burned bricks in the tower.

After a restoration in 1976, the building opened to the public for the first time in eighty-four years. In 1995 it was taken over by the Baltimore City Life Museums, which created a new exhibit and sound and light show explaining how gunshot was made in these structures in the nineteenth century.

The nearby house at Nine North Front Street, built about 1790 and home of the second mayor of Baltimore, Thorowgood Smith, has been restored and is maintained by the Women's Civic League. Visitors can see a colonial kitchen and a docudrama on Mayor Smith. ❖

F4 • CARROLL MANSION AND BALTIMORE CITY LIFE MUSEUMS

(BCL, NR)
800 East Lombard Street
ca. 1812—architect unknown; 1967—Wrenn, Lewis, and Jencks; 1985–96—Peterson and Brickbauer, and others

In recent years the Carroll Mansion, which once stood alone as a house museum, has become part of the burgeoning Baltimore City Life Museums, which has a major complex at this site and buildings at other city sites.

Henry Wilson, Baltimore merchant, originally built a house on this property about 1808. In 1811 he sold it to Christopher Deshon, who is credited with greatly enlarging it. In 1818 it was bought by Richard Caton, son-in-law of Charles Carroll of Carrollton; the latter lived to become the last surviving signer of the Declaration of Independence before his death in 1832. Carroll bought out Caton's interest in the house in 1824 and lived there part of every year.

With its piano nobile (or second floor as the principal reception-room floor), and its decorative plaques between the second- and third-floor windows, the house is somewhat like London houses of the middle to late eighteenth century, and it has excellent Flemish bond brickwork. The first floor of the house was reserved for business and informal family use. A graceful stairway winds to the second floor's formal entertaining rooms.

The house was bought by the city of Baltimore in 1915 and put to a number of uses for the next forty years. Almost demolished in the 1950s, it was restored in the 1960s. It is furnished with Empire or late classical revival decorations of the kind that were in fashion in the 1820s when Charles Carroll of Carrollton lived there.

In the 1980s the expansion of the adjoining complex into what is now the major site of the Baltimore City Life Museums was begun. In 1985, a building dating from the 1790s at the corner of Lombard and Albemarle streets was restored and furnished and decorated to the period of the 1840s. Called the 1840 House, it is a living urban history museum.

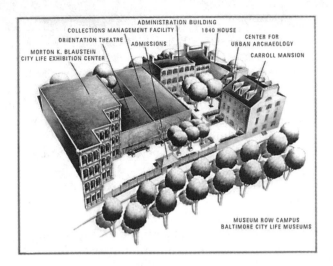

In 1986, the space between the Carroll Mansion and the 1840 House was filled in by the Center for Urban Archaeology, a new building with an exterior inspired by early-nineteenth-century buildings that once stood on the site. The same year saw the creation of the Davis Courtyard behind the archaeology building and 1840 House. Landscape design for the courtyard is by Catherine Mahan & Associates.

In 1987, Peterson and Brickbauer developed the schematic design for a museum administration building next to the 1840 House, with exteriors inspired by early nineteenth-century houses. Design development and construction were carried out by the City of Baltimore.

The Morton K. Blaustein City Life Exhibition Center, opened in 1996, is a four-story urban museum housing exhibits pertaining to life in the city and its history. The façade of this building is the salvaged cast-iron front of the former G. Fava Fruit Company building, one of the city's now largely lost but fondly remembered cast-iron buildings. This one stood on the site of the present Convention Center [A4] on West Pratt Street. The façade has been stepped back to make it appropriate to the site and to prevent overwhelming the Carroll Mansion at the other end of the complex.

The final additions to the complex are an orientation theater next to the Blaustein building and a collections management facility, the latter making use of an existing early-twentieth-century warehouse.

Peterson and Brickbauer are responsible for the conceptual scheme of the Blaustein building's cast-iron façade, and the same firm in association with Ziger, Snead developed the Blaustein building, with Hugh McCormick as supervising architect. The orientation theater and collections management facility are by Ziger, Snead, with Charles Brickbauer as consultant for the theater. Higgins and Lazarus are responsible for design of the long courtyard between the Carroll Mansion and the Blaustein building.

Among the other Baltimore City Life Museums' properties are the Peale Museum [D13], the Shot Tower [F3], and the H. L. Mencken House. The last, at 1524 Hollins Street in West Baltimore, is notable both as the house where the great journalist lived almost all of his life and as a typical nineteenth-century Baltimore row house little changed since it was built in the 1880s. ❖

F5 • SEWAGE PUMPING STATION

701 Eastern Avenue
1912—Henry Brauns

The pumping station is an essay in eclecticism. Brauns designed the body of the building in the Second Renaissance Revival style and crowned it with a Victorian mansard roof bulging with dormers and squat towers, topped by a clerestory monitor. The interior of the station, part of Baltimore's original sewer system, is a single large space where the pumps, on a lower level, go about their business, while brick pilasters and pediments stare down from either end of the room.

The result is a handsome building in spite of its utilitarian function. It is a metal frame building faced with brick; the roof is trimmed in copper. In 1960, electric turbine pumps replaced the original machinery powered by huge Corliss steam engines, and the 205-foot chimney was shortened considerably.

The Baltimore Public Works Museum opened in 1982 in the southwest quadrant of the building. "Street-scape," a life-size outdoor exhibit revealing the under- and above-ground workings of a city street, was added four years later. ❖

F6 • STAR-SPANGLED BANNER FLAG HOUSE
(BCL, NR)
844 East Pratt Street
1793—architect unknown

The Flag House is the best-preserved example of a small Baltimore residence of its period. It is a Federal-style house featuring a hipped roof, dormers, heavily molded cornice, brick laid in Flemish bond, and wooden trim. It was originally part of a group of four. The exterior has been restored to its original appearance, and the interior has been renovated. A museum building has been added to the rear, on the site of the original kitchen. An ongoing restoration program attempts to adapt the building to modern use and simultaneously make it more authentic.

That the Flag House still stands is due primarily to the activities of its famous occupant, Mary Pickersgill, who sewed the huge flag that flew over Fort McHenry during the British bombardment of 1814. The flag, the sight of which inspired Francis Scott Key to write "The Star-Spangled Banner," hangs in the Smithsonian Institution's National Museum of American History in Washington, D. C. ❖

F7 • LLOYD STREET SYNAGOGUE

(BCL, NR)
Lloyd and Watson streets
1845—Robert Cary Long, Jr.

The oldest synagogue in Baltimore and the third-oldest in the United States, the Lloyd Street Synagogue is strongly Greek Revival. It was a style with which Long seems to have been as comfortable as he was with Gothic. One of the later manifestations of Greek Revival architecture locally, this is distinguished by its handsome Doric portico. The interior is a rectangle, lengthened 30 feet in 1860.

A niche in the far wall contained the ark. The ark presently in that position is a relatively modern reconstruction of the ark of 1860, which has not survived. The stained-glass window above the ark is original to the building, though partially restored. It is the first in the United States to show a Star of David design. The other four stained-glass windows were added after 1871 and are greatly restored. The synagogue sanctuary has been painted in the colors used in 1871, based on a paint analysis, and the furnishings are a mix of nineteenth- and early-twentieth-century elements, reflecting the activities of several different congregations.

The Lloyd Street Synagogue was acquired by the Jewish Historical Society of Maryland in 1962 and subsequently restored. It is now on the National Register of Historic Places, as is the B'nai Israel Synagogue at 27 Lloyd Street, also owned by the historical society and open to the public. Designed in 1876 by stonework contractor Henry Berge in a modified Moorish Revival style with Gothic and Vernacular elements, B'nai Israel is the only Maryland example of a synagogue incorporating aspects of an early version of the Moorish style, in which adapted Near Eastern decorative motifs were used as symbols of Jewish identity. Its elaborate brass chandelier of about 1890 is covered with moresque designs, and the Torah ark, carved by John P. Yaeger, is the building's purest example of the use of Moorish Revival style. ❖

F8 • McKIM FREE SCHOOL
(BCL, NR)
1120 East Baltimore Street
1833—William F. Small and William Howard

As a piece of architecture, this is a fine example of Greek Revival Doric architecture, based on ancient models. As a community resource, the school has helped disadvantaged youths in its area of the city for more than one hundred seventy years and continues to do so. The school, in fact, predates the building.

John McKim, son of an Irish immigrant and Quaker cotton manufacturer, before his death in 1819 in-structed his sons Isaac and William to set up a school "for the education of indigent youth, without respect to preference for any religious sect or denomination," and close to the Old Town Meeting House [F9], which still stands just a block north of this building. The school was incorporated in 1821 and first occupied rented quarters. It moved in 1835 to the present building, designed by Small and Howard.

The simple but strongly handsome building, with the pedimented Doric portico its salient feature, is purportedly modeled after the Temple of Haephaestus on the Acropolis in Athens. Howard and Small probably took their inspiration from Stuart and Revett's *Antiquities of Athens*.

The 40-by-60-foot building is of stone, with an original copper roof later covered with tin. The interior has been altered somewhat over the years, including the addition of a wooden floor over the original brick one and of a mezzanine over the rear of the main floor.

The institution has changed, too. In the 1890s, after public education took over the school function, it became a kindergarten and subsequently a community center. Now the McKim Community Association, Inc., it is a private nonprofit organization sponsored by the United Presbyterian Church, Stony Run Friends, and other groups and individuals. It provides tutoring, athletic programs, arts and crafts, and other activities for young people, and a food program for the elderly. ❖

F9 • OLD TOWN MEETINGHOUSE
(BCL, NR)
Fayette and Aisquith streets
1781—George Matthews, builder

The oldest religious building in the city and the second oldest Quaker meetinghouse in the country, this dignified little building recently took a new lease on life. In 1995 it received a $460,000 restoration-renovation for use as an annex by the McKim Free School [F8].

The two-story building was essentially restored to its original state, including the interior balcony and the vertical pocket doors that were lowered to divide the men's part of the congregation from the women's. Windows and shutters replicate original ones, and doors have been reopened.

An addition on the eastern side of the building contains rest rooms and a portion of the new heating system. The building is used for McKim's youth program activities as well as its meal program for the elderly. ❖

F10 • EASTERN FEMALE HIGH SCHOOL

(BCL, NR)
Orleans and Aisquith streets
1869—R. Snowden Andrews

There was a great expansion of secondary public education after the Civil War, and this school is one of the buildings erected as part of it. It is the oldest surviving public school building in Baltimore, and one of the city's surviving relics of the Italianate style of architecture, which flourished here and elsewhere about the middle of the nineteenth century.

The Italianate (or Italian villa) style's happiest use was for country houses, a leading local example of which was the now destroyed Homewood Villa, designed by Richard Upjohn for William Wyman. Asymmetry was one of the style's essential characteristics; the symmetry of this school building is a detriment to it as an example of the Italianate. However, its two low towers, its heavy cornices, and its other ornamental woodwork give some flavor of the style.

After a period of neglect, this, along with several other abandoned school buildings, was converted to apartments. This building is now used as housing for the elderly. ❖

F11 • NUMBER 6 ENGINE HOUSE

(BCL, NR)
Gay and Ensor streets
1853—Reasin and Wetherald

The Italian Gothic bell tower of the Number 6 Engine House is a landmark in Old Town. It was added as a lookout post in 1874 to an existing engine house, there having been one on the site since 1819. The first engine house was operated by the Independent Fire Company, whose volunteer members "ran with the machine" and fought pitched battles with rival companies for the honor of putting out a blaze. These volunteer companies were consolidated in 1858 when the city's fire department was organized.

The wedge-shaped brick firehouse with its six-story tower (a wooden stairway leads up among the distinctive trefoil arches to the bell), is a rare survivor of the old volunteer company firehouses. Except for the rusticated concrete reinforcement at the base and the four-face clock installed near the top sometime before 1900, the tower stands as it was built. (Its three upper stories bear a faint resemblance to those of Giotto's Campanile in Florence, although they are a very simplified and provincial version thereof.)

In 1960, the Fire Board recommended that the tower be razed because it had outlived its usefulness, but the mayor and other citizens acted to save it. The Number 6 Engine House, which had been one of the oldest active firehouses in the nation, was closed in the mid-1970s. In 1979, it became the City of Baltimore Fire Museum operated by the Box 414 Association, a private volunteer group. The building now contains historic fire-fighting equipment and artifacts. ❖

F12 • ST. JOHN THE EVANGELIST CHURCH
(NR)
901 East Eager Street
1856—Niernsee and Neilson; 1892—E. Francis Baldwin

This forlorn-looking Italianate church is of interest for a number of reasons. Its twin-towered style, closely resembling the earlier Calvert Station by Niernsee and Neilson (since destroyed), managed at once to be fashionable in its time and to accommodate a church interior resembling an early Christian basilica. The plan of the church has been called strikingly similar to that of San Apollinare in Classe in Ravenna, Italy.

The five-part façade expresses the components of the interior, which has a high-ceilinged nave separated from lower side aisles by arches supported on cast-iron columns. (It was originally equipped with a marble altar,

oak and walnut furniture, and stained-glass windows.) The roof of the nave reaches almost to the height of the towers, which are capped by pyramidal roofs. In 1882, Baldwin added the apse and two side rooms, or pavilions, at the southern end without violating the original composition. The building is of brick covered with stucco and has a rubble stone foundation. The church closed in 1966. ❖

F13 • ST. JAMES AND ST. JOHN'S CHURCH
(NR)
1225 East Eager Street
1867—George A. Frederick

Like a medieval church in a provincial town in France, the former St. James and St. John's, its rectory, and the adjacent Institute of Notre Dame school buildings dominate East Baltimore's skyline and anchor the surrounding community. (The 256-foot church steeple is one of the tallest in the city.)

In 1841, Redemptorist priests took over the original St. James Church, completed in 1834 on this site, when its Irish parishioners left to worship at the newly established St. Vincent de Paul Church in Old Town [F2], and the German-speaking members remained. The Sisters of Notre Dame bought some of the church property and in 1847 set up a school for young women. The Redemptorists also started a school for training priests. By the 1860s, the growing congregation required a replacement church.

Frederick designed a huge Romanesque Revival building with a high-reaching spire (added 1885) and a variegated façade of brick with stone trim and white marble steps. The interior was a single large space 184 feet long, 65 feet wide, and two stories high, unobstructed by columns, except for cast-iron ones that supported the rear choir loft and galleries. The walnut pews could seat eighteen hundred people (the Redemptorists were dedicated to preaching), and the room was decorated with stained-glass windows, marble altars, railings, statuary, and wall murals. There was a locally built organ in the choir loft, and the four tower bells, weighing 1 to 2½ tons each, were cast by Baltimore's McShane Bell Foundry. The Eager Street rectory is believed to have been built at the same time as the church.

The Institute of Notre Dame gradually expanded to encompass the block bounded by Eager, Aisquith, Ashland, and Somerset streets. The oldest parts date from 1852–53; in the sections added later are striking interior spaces, including the chapel.

In 1966, the church of St. John the Evangelist [F12] (which also began as an Irish parish), closed and merged with the St. James Church. When the combined church closed in 1986, the stained-glass windows, organ, and other decorations were removed and sold or distributed to other churches; the pews and tower bells remain. In 1990, the Urban Bible Fellowship Church bought the church building and now holds services there.

The Institute of Notre Dame, 150 years old, has 440 students, grades 9–12; in 1992, the school added a new gymnasium to the complex. ❖

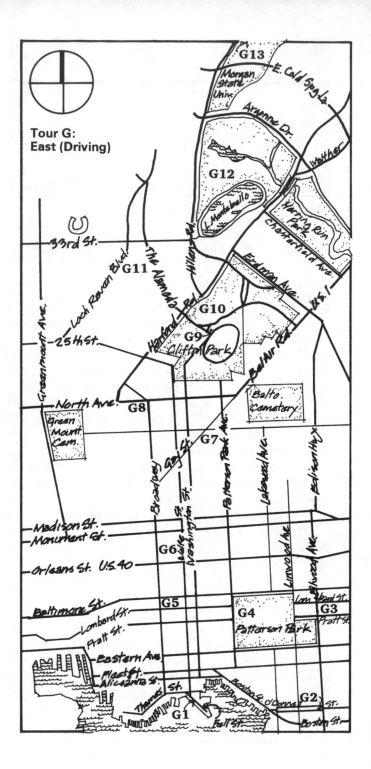

Tour G:
East (Driving)

Tour G

East (Driving)

G1   CAPTAIN STEELE HOUSE
931 Fell Street
ca. 1790—architect unknown

G2   ENOCH PRATT FREE LIBRARY, CANTON
BRANCH
1030 South Ellwood Avenue
1886—Charles L. Carson

G3   HAMPSTEAD HILL JUNIOR HIGH/
HIGHLANDTOWN MIDDLE SCHOOL
Pratt Street and Ellwood Avenue
1933—Wyatt and Nolting

G4   PATTERSON PARK OBSERVATORY
Patterson Park, near Patterson Park Avenue
and Pratt Street
1891—Charles H. Latrobe

G5   CAST-IRON PORCHES
Broadway and Baltimore Street

G6   JOHNS HOPKINS HOSPITAL
601 North Broadway
1877–89—John R. Niernsee; Cabot and Chandler

G7   AMERICAN BREWERY
1700 block Gay Street
1887—Charles Stoll

G8   BAUERNSCHMIDT HOUSE
Broadway and North Avenue
ca. 1889–90—George A. Frederick

G9   VALVE HOUSE
Clifton Park at the bend in St. Lo Drive
1887—architect unknown

G10   CLIFTON
2701 St. Lo Drive, Clifton Park
*ca. 1800—architect unknown; 1852—Niernsee and
Neilson*

G11   CITY COLLEGE
Thirty-third Street and The Alameda
1928—Buckler and Fenhagen

G12 MONTEBELLO FILTRATION PLANT
3401 Hillen Road
1915; 1928—various engineers for the City of Baltimore

G13 CLARENCE M. MITCHELL, JR., ENGINEERING
BUILDING, MORGAN STATE UNIVERSITY
5200 Perring Parkway
1991—Richter, Cornbrooks, Gribble, Inc.

T he harbor was, and still is, one of the main reasons
for the existence of Baltimore as a city. One of the
best places to experience it is in Fells Point, which main-
tains some of the aspects of the seaport community it
became after being founded in the early eighteenth
century by shipbuilder William Fell. It was the birthplace of the Baltimore clipper; the *Constellation*, the first
ship of the U.S. Navy, was launched at nearby Harris
Creek in 1797. A foreign visitor to the area in the early
1800s described an English schooner anchored among
the racier Baltimore-built craft as "a hog amid a herd of
antelopes."

Many of the remaining structures once housed the
shipbuilding trades and places of entertainment for the
sailors. The Broadway Market, at the center of the community, was established in 1783 and is one of the city's
oldest.

Fells Point subsequently became a main disembar-
kation point for thousands of immigrants from Europe;
the area retains its early cosmopolitan flavor. Although
coping with recurrent redevelopment schemes on the
periphery and invading hordes of young suburban weekend revelers, it exists today as one of the few remaining
nineteenth-century downtown waterfront communities.

This tour includes Canton, another early seaport
section, and Highlandtown, the epitome of Baltimore's
row-house neighborhoods; it also takes in some of the
structures associated with Baltimore's water supply. ❖

G1 • CAPTAIN STEELE HOUSE
931 Fell Street
ca. 1790—architect unknown

One of the few virtually intact eighteenth-century town
houses left in Baltimore, this was built for John Steele, a
wealthy shipbuilder.

The late-Georgian, early-Federal-style house has a stone foundation and brick walls laid in Flemish bond. The door, under a fanlight, opens to an entrance hall separated from the stairway by a characteristic archway divider. The two downstairs rooms were originally the captain's counting rooms. (An extension was added to the back of the house in about 1850.) The dining and drawing rooms are on the second floor, the bedrooms on the third, and there are two small attic rooms.

In 1968, new owners acquired the building. Although a rooming house for many years, most of the original mahogany, poplar, and pine woodwork of the staircase, which is suspended from the walls without interior posts, and the baseboards, chair rails, and elaborate mantelpieces were still intact. An intensive restoration program, including replacement decorative plaster fireplace panels acquired from the same London firm that produced those that came with the house, is just about complete. ❖

G2 • ENOCH PRATT FREE LIBRARY, CANTON BRANCH

1030 South Ellwood Avenue
1886—Charles L. Carson

The only one of the first four branches of the municipal library still in use for its intended purpose, the Canton

Branch (Number Four) was designed, as were the others, in the Romanesque Revival style by Carson, who was its leading local exponent. (Carson used the same style for the first central library building at Mulberry and Cathedral streets, built ca. 1883, and razed for the present structure.)

The Canton Branch is brick, with a string course and trim of freestone, terra-cotta decoration, and a multicolored slate roof. (The 1883 plaque on the chimney evidently refers to the beginning of the free library system and not to the construction of this building.) Inside, a high-ceilinged room with an elaborate truss system provides an appropriate atmosphere for the readers and librarians. (The former EPFL Branch Number Two, built the same year at 1401 Hollins Street, once frequented by H. L. Mencken and Russell Baker and closed in 1964, is to be renovated as the headquarters of Baltimore's Neighborhood Design Center.) ❖

G3 • HAMPSTEAD HILL
JUNIOR HIGH/HIGHLANDTOWN
MIDDLE SCHOOL
Pratt Street and Ellwood Avenue
1933—Wyatt and Nolting

Originally built as Patterson Park High School and now housing two other public schools, this is a good Baltimore example of buildings influenced by the Bauhaus style of modern architecture of the 1920s and 1930s. The stone attached columns at the entrances and the

numbering on the cornerstone add a slight Art Deco flavor.

The building's bands of red and brown brickwork and ranks of industrial-sized windows, together with its massing, present a nice balance of horizontals and verticals and create a sense of geometric abstraction. ❖

G4 • PATTERSON PARK OBSERVATORY

(BCL)
Patterson Park, near Patterson Park Avenue
and Pratt Street
1891—Charles H. Latrobe

Known for generations as "The Pagoda," the observatory is a 60-foot octagonal tower with a metal skeleton wrapped in glass and wood. Observation decks both inside and outside are supported on exposed cantilevers. A spiral stairway in the core of the building ascends the four stories to the top. The architect, Charles H. Latrobe, was the son of engineer Benjamin H. Latrobe, Jr.

Light and airy in appearance and one of the more enjoyable Baltimore architectural phenomena, the tower was restored in 1965 and again in 1983. It has since been closed due to deterioration. But recently, the Butcher's Hill Association, a neighborhood group, has been working toward raising the estimated $300,000 needed for a thorough restoration, has hired restoration architect Michael Dowling, and plans to start work on the project in 1997. ❖

G5 • CAST-IRON PORCHES
Broadway and Baltimore Street

The late nineteenth-century cast-iron porches shown here, executed in a grapevine pattern, are particularly fine. During the 1800s, the city's numerous foundries and forges turned out decorative but utilitarian porches, balconies, cornices, window guards, fences, railings, and gates in a variety of styles and designs, sometimes combining both cast and wrought iron. There are several examples of such porches in East Baltimore, and they can be seen in many other sections of the city. ❖

G6 • THE JOHNS HOPKINS HOSPITAL
(NR)
601 North Broadway
1877–89—John R. Niernsee; Cabot and Chandler

When Johns Hopkins died in 1873, he left $3.4 million to create a medical school and hospital "for the indigent sick of this city and its environs, without regard to sex, age or color, who may require surgical or medical treatment." The trustees selected as medical adviser John S. Billings, an expert in hospital design and the control of contagion who had developed his theories regarding public health as a surgeon during the Civil War.

Billings studied the best hospitals in the United States and Europe before submitting to the trustees the overall plan for The Johns Hopkins Hospital, which was drafted by Niernsee. Boston's Cabot and Chandler then designed the buildings in the Queen Anne style.

Construction began in 1877 on a high point of land in East Baltimore. The 14-acre site covered four city blocks. Billings and Niernsee's plan called for three-story buildings fronting on Broadway, a series of lower pavilions linked by covered corridors in the rear, with the whole forming a U shape. In the middle there was to be a "central garden."

Much attention was given to how the wards were heated and ventilated to check the spread of communicable diseases. The pavilions, laid out like rows of barracks, were generally arranged so that it was impossible to pass from one to the other without going outside. There were heated areas in each ward where patients could sit facing the garden. (The plans for the disposal of wastewater, on the other hand, were primitive in a city that lacked sewers—it flowed into open gutters or cesspools.)

The buildings were constructed of Baltimore brick with slate roofs and decorated with copper pinnacles, cast-iron roof cresting and porches, terra-cotta panels, and Cheat River bluestone. When the $2,050,000 hospital opened in 1889, a critic called the Victorian design "not impressive," but that was not the point. The point was that the Johns Hopkins Hospital represented the latest in scientific knowledge and medical planning at the time.

Billings and Niernsee's plan lasted exactly one hundred years. In 1977, the hospital dedicated a new high-rise tower and officially abandoned the low pavilion and corridor scheme, although the original buildings facing Broadway—Billings, with its signature, copper-trimmed dome, and the two wings, Marburg and Wilmer—are to remain. The 1913 former Phipps Psychiatric Clinic on Wolfe Street (now the Frank M. Houck Building), an outstanding older structure, recently won a reprieve as the site of a new cancer center. One of the better new buildings is the Outpatient Center west of Broadway, designed by Boston's Payette Associates, and connected with the eastern campus by an attractive underground concourse linked to the Baltimore Metro. ❖

G7 • AMERICAN BREWERY

(NR)
1700 block Gay Street
1887—Charles Stoll

The American Brewery, a marvel of irregular design, stands high on a hill in East Baltimore, its peculiar silhouette visible for miles. It was the creation of a New York "brewer's architect" who didn't take himself too seriously.

The brewery was founded in 1863 by John Frederick Wiessner, a Bavarian immigrant, who built a three-story brew house on the site in what was then a German neighborhood. By 1887, the business had outgrown the building, and a new five-story brewery was erected with three wooden towers, an assortment of windows (some of them stained glass), and a delightfully dissimilar yet carefully ordered façade. It was designed by Stoll, who also held patents on some of the brewery equipment.

The central tower was functional, housing a 10,000-bushel grain elevator.

A complex of buildings grew up on the site, including an 1892 brownstone wagon house and stable across the street. Next door, separated by a garden, was the former Wiessner house, erected in 1896. The three-story brick residence with brownstone trim was large because, like other brewers, Wiessner adhered to the custom of providing lodging for his workers, mostly German immigrants. Some of the other buildings, added later, have since been demolished. There were numerous changes and additions to the plant in the 1930s when a modern brewery was created behind the old façade.

The American Brewery was the last to occupy the complex, from the 1950s until 1973, when it ceased operations. Since then, the structures have stood vacant while various plans have been proposed for their reuse. The latest calls for the former bottling plant immediately to the north of the brewery building to be renovated as a light manufacturing center, and for the former wagon house and stables and brewmaster's residence across the street to be connected and converted to senior housing units with a new building behind them.

The city-owned American Brewery complex is under long-term lease to the Council for Economical and Business Opportunity, Inc. (CEBO), which hopes to find an eventual use for the brewery building itself. ❖

G8 • BAUERNSCHMIDT HOUSE

Broadway and North Avenue
ca. 1889–90 — George A. Frederick

The architect of Baltimore's City Hall designed this house for a Baltimore beer baron. Although it may look grand by local standards, it is really quite restrained compared with, for instance, Washington's Henried mansion, also built for a beer baron. Still, it can be cited for such elements as the controlled but extensive use of brownstone, the Corinthian pilasters of the entrance and columns elsewhere, and the curious, slightly bowed section of brickwork that rises one and a half stories on the Broadway side. Used for a time as a funeral home, it is now owned by the Great Blacks in Wax Museum. ❖

G9 • VALVE HOUSE

(NR)
Clifton Park at the bend in St. Lo Drive
1887 — architect unknown

This Victorian structure with an interesting alternation of pointed and rounded arches on ground level, decora-

tive dormers above, and a cupola-like crown, was built as part of the city's water system. Now abandoned, it has badly deteriorated. ❖

G10 • CLIFTON

(BCL)
2701 St. Lo Drive, Clifton Park
ca. 1800—architect unknown; 1852—Niernsee and Neilson

Johns Hopkins lived here during the summers, in style. (He also had a mansion on Saratoga Street.) At Clifton, he remodeled an existing farmhouse into an Italian villa and expanded the property to about 500 acres. Much of the acreage was a working farm, with gardens and orchards. Hopkins also added an artificial lake with islands and rustic bridges, an orangery, and one hundred pieces of marble statuary and sculpture. His goal, he said, was to make Clifton a paradise on earth. From the balcony of his six-story "prospect tower," he could survey this estate and much of the city and harbor beyond—proper perspective for one of Baltimore's leading capitalists and philanthropists.

In 1841, Hopkins bought for roughly $16,000 a two-story, ca. 1800 brick farmhouse and 166 acres of land from the estate of Henry Thompson, another Baltimore merchant. Architects Niernsee and Neilson added a third floor to the main block of the house, put an addition on the north side, extended the wings, built a vaulted porte cochere and a tower on the south side, and surrounded the primary façade with a wide, arcaded porch.

The main entrance under the tower led through "an arched way into the principal hall, 23 feet high, paved with marble, lighted by four richly stained arched windows, and wainscoted with black walnut, of which the doors and massive stairway are formed," said the Baltimore *Sun* in a February 5, 1852, article about the completion of the house. A parlor, dining room, salon, and library occupied the ground floor; bedrooms and a billiard room with hand-carved mahogany paneling the second; and servants' quarters the third. The fireplaces had mantels of Italian marble.

At Clifton, Hopkins relaxed, pursued horticulture, and entertained visiting celebrities, including King Edward VII when he was Prince of Wales. When Johns Hopkins died in 1873, the estate declined. Hopkins had wanted the university he established to be located at Clifton, but the trustees decided otherwise. Instead, in 1895 they sold the land and buildings to the city for about $722,000. Today Clifton is a city park with an eighteen-hole golf course, a swimming pool, and clay tennis courts.

For many years, the mansion was used for park offices and also housed a pro shop, locker room, snack bar, etc., for the golfers. In 1993, the city turned Clifton over to Civic Works, Baltimore's youth service corps that is part of the national AmeriCorps program. Besides using it as their headquarters, Civic Works trainees are helping to restore Clifton; so far they have uncovered ornamental plaster niches, cornices, and woodwork dating from the early 1800s. The restoration architect is John Brunett. On the grounds north of the mansion is a picturesque two-story Gothic gardener's cottage, now badly deteriorated. ❖

G11 • CITY COLLEGE
Thirty-third Street and The Alameda
1928—Buckler and Fenhagen

When this edifice was erected in the then-popular Collegiate Gothic style, it cost $2.5 million and was considered wildly extravagant for a school building. Forty years later it was threatened with destruction; fortunately, it was saved and thoroughly renovated according to plans by the Leon Bridges company for $8 million.

Its principal façade is somewhat pedestrian, with its essentially symmetrical composition and dull window tracery. However, the asymmetrical elements of the central tower section rescue it somewhat, and from a distance the tower presents a handsome profile against the sky. ❖

G12 • MONTEBELLO FILTRATION PLANT
3401 Hillen Road
1915; 1928—various engineers for the City of Baltimore

The design of these structures, with their long, low, horizontal planes and projecting eaves, is faintly reminiscent of the work of Frank Lloyd Wright.

The buildings rest on groined vaults that cover reinforced concrete filter tanks beneath the ground. (The lower ones house valves; the towers provide storage space for chemicals used in the filtration process.) The structures themselves are also of reinforced concrete; they are faced with local red brick. The string courses

are buff-colored terra-cotta, and the roofs, carried on steel trusses, are covered with dark green tiles.

The eastern group (shown here), completed in 1915, marked the beginning of Baltimore's modern water-supply system. It is also the more architecturally successful. (The 1911 clarifier basins outside these buildings are currently being replaced, a $30 million project scheduled to be completed in 1997.

The western group was built in 1928. Although the terra-cotta details are attractive, the square towers are overly massive, and the original double-arched windows have recently been replaced with smaller sashes or have been bricked up entirely.

Facing Lake Montebello below the filtration plant is an oddly shaped gatehouse with a high, sloping slate roof, cupola, and fine masonry. It is another of the structures that were part of Baltimore's Victorian-era water-distribution system. ❖

G13 • CLARENCE M. MITCHELL, JR., ENGINEERING BUILDING, MORGAN STATE UNIVERSITY

5200 Perring Parkway
1991 — Richter, Cornbrooks, Gribble, Inc.

Although moderate in size and cost ($9 million), the engineering building has a monumental quality and is a welcome departure from Morgan State's undistinguished institutional architecture. Built of concrete block faced with cast stone and granite trim, it features

a sculptural salient at the south end that houses two instructional television labs. The architects grouped thirty-four offices in the front of the building and twenty-one laboratory spaces in the rear; in between them they placed a two-story meeting place for students and faculty. This consists of a ground-floor hallway overlooked by a balcony and topped by a half-barrel vault lit by a clerestory facing the street. The building is for training civil, industrial, and electrical engineers and represents a major advance for Morgan State's relatively new School of Engineering. ❖

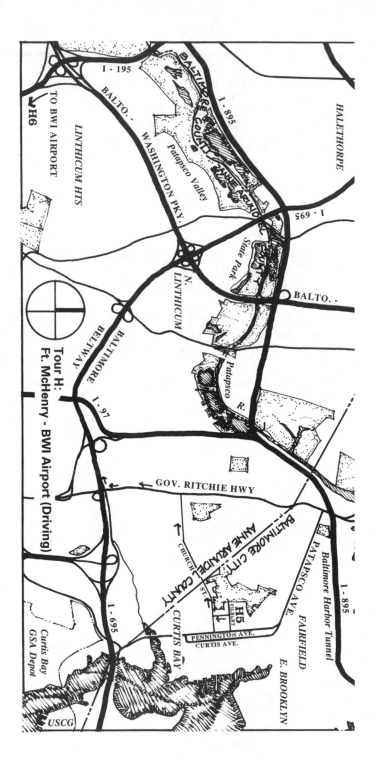

Tour H:
Ft. McHenry - BWI Airport (Driving)

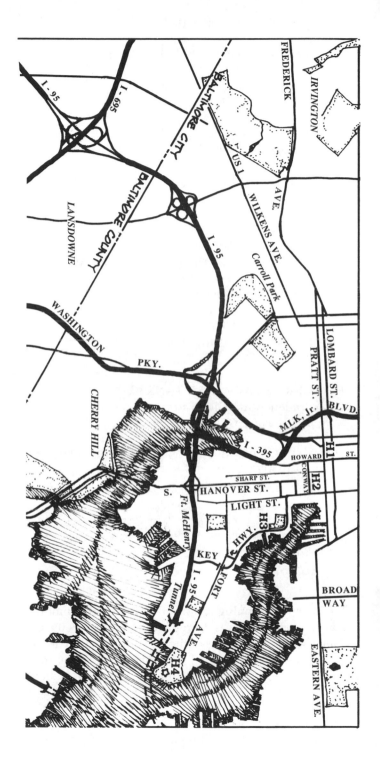

Tour H

Fort McHenry–BWI Airport (Driving)

H1   MARSH AND McLENNAN BUILDING
300 West Pratt Street
*1871—architect unknown; 1989—RTKL Associates,
Inc., renovation architect*

H2   OLD OTTERBEIN UNITED METHODIST
CHURCH
112 West Conway Street
1785—Jacob Small, Sr.

H3   AMERICAN VISIONARY ART MUSEUM
800 Key Highway, at Covington Street
1995—Rebecca Swanston and Alex Castro

H4   FORT McHENRY
Fort Avenue, Locust Point
1799 and after—Jean Foncin and others

H5   CURTIS BAY WATER TANK
Prudence and Filbert streets
1932—Frank O. Heyder, engineer

H6   BALTIMORE–WASHINGTON INTERNATIONAL
AIRPORT (BWI)
Baltimore–Washington Parkway, Anne Arundel
County
*1950—Whitman, Requardt, and Associates, the Greiner
Company, engineers; 1979 expansion—Peterson and
Brickbauer, architect*

The award-winning restoration of one of Baltimore's
few remaining cast-iron-front buildings begins this
tour, which includes one of the city's oldest churches, its
newest museum, dedicated to visionary art, and its most
venerated historic site and finest example of military
architecture and engineering. The tour passes a South
Baltimore landmark designed by a municipal engineer
who had his own idea of what a water tank should look
like, and ends with the ultimate jumping-off place. ❖

H1 • MARSH AND McLENNAN BUILDING
(NR)
300 West Pratt Street
1871 — architect unknown; 1989, RTKL Associates Inc.,
renovation architect

Experts estimate that a century ago more than one hundred cast-iron-front buildings lined Baltimore's downtown streets. The 1904 Baltimore Fire destroyed the majority of them. An actual count in the early 1960s showed that thirty-six of the original iron-front structures were still standing. Inner Harbor redevelopment projects have since claimed most of those. Today, there are just ten original buildings remaining with full cast-iron façades. (The Fava Fruit Company Building's iron front, taken down in 1976 and reerected as part of an addition to the City Life Museums, makes it eleven.) The Marsh and McLennan Building is so far the only original full cast-iron front to be completely restored.

The restoration is a significant if belated recognition of Baltimore's historic importance as a center for the production of architectural cast iron. This role began in 1851 with the construction of the Sun Iron Building at Baltimore and South streets, one of the earliest such structures in the country. (It was destroyed in the 1904 fire.) The Sun Iron Building was a collaboration of three New Yorkers—inventor James Bogardus, architect Robert G. Hatfield, and iron founder Daniel Badger—and Baltimore foundries, which supplied the iron castings.

These foundries were soon producing iron-front buildings for local developers and for shipment to cities nationwide. Bartlett, Robbins and Co. (later Hayward, Bartlett and Co.) became the most prominent Baltimore architectural foundry and probably supplied the iron front for this building. It was built as an office and warehouse for William Wilkens and Company, whose factory on Frederick Road made hair from cattle and horses into upholstery and women's wigs.

The Wilkens Building was built in the Renaissance Revival style four stories high; the fifth story was added sometime in the 1880s. The restrained yet highly detailed decorative scheme incorporates columns and Corinthian capitals, flat and segmental arches, intermediate cornices, quoins, consoles, and a line of rope molding above the top floor. For practical and aesthetic reasons, the floors diminish in height as they ascend. The iron front is filled with glass to admit plenty of light into the offices and workrooms. The building is a double warehouse; for structural purposes, a 22-inch-thick masonry wall runs front to back and top to bottom, halving the interior lengthwise.

Besides being expandable and demountable, such cast-iron fronts were, according to Bogardus, easily ornamented, strong, durable, fireproof, and quickly erected. They also employed modern methods of mass production, standardized components, prefabrication, and modular construction. The iron fronts were the true forerunners of steel-frame highrises.

In 1904, the Wilkens firm consolidated operations at its Frederick Road factory and rented the former headquarters building to a succession of paper companies. The Robins Paper Company bought it in 1940 and remained there until 1972, when the city acquired it. (During the 1940s, the ornamental details were stripped from the façade.) The Wilkens-Robins building then stood vacant and in danger of demolition until 1988 when, after a strong preservation effort, the city awarded the structure to Stone and Associates for redevelopment.

Steven T. Baird, Architect and Associates, of Salt Lake City recast the missing elements and restored the iron front. RTKL Associates, Inc., designed an embracing, five-story curtain wall addition with a prefinished aluminum sunscreen and reorganized the interior of the older building. The setback was a zoning requirement rather than a design decision, but it provides an effective frame for the iron front. The award-winning $10 million project was renamed the Marsh & McLennan Building after its major tenant, an insurance firm. A virtual duplicate of this building stands at 307–309 West Baltimore Street, and there are several examples of iron façades and storefronts nearby. ❖

H2 • OLD OTTERBEIN UNITED METHODIST CHURCH

(BCL, NR)
112 West Conway Street
1785—Jacob Small, Sr.

The second-oldest church building in Baltimore was named for one of its first pastors, Philip Wilhelm Otterbein. It was designed and built for $5,000, according to church records.

The tiny (48 by 65 feet), two-story, Georgian-style building was constructed of brick. Both stories have several semicircular arched windows; the other distinguishing feature is a squat, provincial version of a Wren tower, built in 1789 with the proceeds of a lottery. When Small completed the tower, some of the church members reportedly complained about the incongruous proportions. "Maybe when you see the bill, you will find it high enough," the architect is said to have replied.

Inside, there have been drastic changes over the years. The pulpit, originally on the north wall and reached by a winding staircase, has been moved to the east end, where a modern apse has replaced a large window. The gallery formerly extended around three sides, but only the portion at the west end, containing the organ and choir space, remains. The interior is plain, with painted plaster walls. In 1977, the sagging roof was replaced and the church rededicated. A central air-conditioning system was recently installed.

Although dwarfed and somewhat isolated by the mammoth expansion of the Baltimore Convention Center next door, this very modest church still manages to define its section of the city; the Otterbein homesteading area to the south represents the successful rejuvenation of a historic, inner-city neighborhood. ❖

H3 • AMERICAN VISIONARY ART MUSEUM

800 Key Highway, at Covington Street
1995—Rebecca Swanston and Alex Castro

Visionary art is the art of self-taught individuals working outside the mainstream, often people of extraordinary personal vision who have an overwhelming compulsion to make art. This is unusual art by any standards, and it deserves to be shown in an unusual building—such as this.

The American Visionary Art Museum is the brainchild of Baltimorean Rebecca Hoffberger, who over a ten-year period almost single-handedly raised the $7 million needed to build and open the museum. The first major museum in this country devoted to visionary art, it has been declared the official national museum by resolution of Congress.

The city donated a 1913 former paint company building at the Inner Harbor whose wedge-shaped profile follows the curve of Key Highway. Architects Swanston and Castro worked with this shape by creating an addition that swirls out from the existing building in overlapping concrete curves. The result is a dynamic structure whose exterior raises the spirits and looks non-traditional, non-stodgy, and inviting.

The interior fulfills that promise. A curved ramp leads to the center of the building, where a straight-line "bridge" bisects the interior on each floor, separating the two parts without destroying the unity of the whole. The curved central staircase under a huge skylight carries the eye upward and makes it easy to plan one's progress. Unlike many museum buildings, there's no confusion in this one about where you're going to go and how to find your way, and as a result it's fun to wander.

With their curved walls, most of the six galleries on three levels are unconventional, but they accept art well. There's also a café on the top level with a fine view of the harbor through its eye-shaped window.

Aside from the 35,000-square-foot main building, the museum complex includes a 3,400-square-foot sculpture barn for larger pieces, a walled garden, and a central plaza. This last is occupied by Vollis Simpson's 55-foot-tall, 36-foot-long whirligig, which serves as an appropriate introduction to the happy experience of visiting this museum. ❖

H4 • FORT McHENRY
(BCL, NR)
Fort Avenue, Locust Point
1799 and after—Jean Foncin and others

Fort McHenry was not the first fortification on the site of Baltimore's greatest moment in history—the September 1814 unsuccessful British bombardment commemorated by "The Star-Spangled Banner." Shortly after the Revolutionary War began in 1775, this point of land, known as Whetstone Point, was fortified by a star-shaped

fort later replaced by Fort McHenry. It may be a carry-over from that fortification that has made Fort McHenry known popularly as a "star fort," for in reality the present fort is a pentagon with four-sided bastions at each corner.

Fort McHenry was built as a result of a plan authorized by Congress in 1794 to defend the ports and harbors along the East Coast. It was named for James McHenry, an Irish-born Marylander who was Washington's secretary of war, and according to Scott Sheads, park ranger at the fort and author of three books on the subject, "Fort McHenry at Baltimore and Fort Mifflin at Philadelphia represent the best surviving achievements" of the first system of fortification of the United States. The information for this entry is taken largely from Sheads's 1995 book, *Fort McHenry*.

In the early years of the republic the War Department hired foreign engineers to design forts based on European theories, as especially articulated by Sebastian le Prestre de Vauban (1633–1707), chief engineer to Louis XIV. In 1799 Jean Foncin, a French engineer, was hired to oversee the design and construction of Fort McHenry. It was finished, in basically its present form, by 1805.

The fort was built on a pentagonal plan and enclosed officers' quarters, barracks, and a powder magazine. The salient feature, militarily, was the four-sided bastions at each point of the pentagon. The guns mounted on these bastions could, Sheads writes, "direct enfilading lines of fire along the opposing walls, assuring inter-locking fields of fire. Thus all exterior lines or

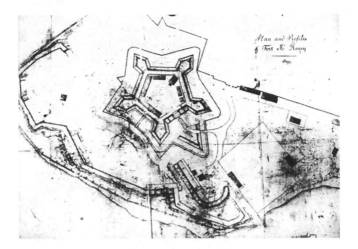

angles of the exterior walls were covered, eliminating any blind spots."

Because Fort McHenry is near the water, the natural assumption is that it was built to defend the land from an attack by water. Its true purpose was to defend double lines of water batteries located on the shoreline from an attack by land. The water batteries defended the harbor. If they were overcome or if there was an attack by land, the fort would be defended by the infantry, stationed in the 5-foot-deep dry moat on the outside of the fort, they in turn supported by the fort's guns. The fort itself, with its 24-pounder guns, was the final point of defense.

There were several later additions to the fort. Originally its gateway, called a sally port, was a passageway through the walls with no roof. In 1813 a ravelin was built in front of the sally port. This was a V-shaped structure to protect the gate from enemy assault.

As many know, the British attacked Baltimore by land and sea on September 12–14, 1814, and were repulsed. The sight of the American flag still flying over Fort McHenry on the morning of September 14, after an all-day-and-night bombardment by British ships, inspired Francis Scott Key to write the song that has become the national anthem.

A month after the assault, in October 1814, two bombproof chambers were added on either side of the sally port. In 1819 these were altered and a covered, vaulted passageway designed by Maximilian Godefroy finally enclosed the sally port. There were further modifications to the adjacent chambers in 1835 and 1857.

Between 1829 and 1839 the fort underwent major construction. Walls were reinforced, an outer gun battery replaced the shore batteries, and the interior buildings were raised to two stories. The fort took on the appearance that, with some modifications, it retains today. ❖

H5 • CURTIS BAY WATER TANK

Prudence and Filbert streets
1932—Frank O. Heyder, engineer

Heyder, a city engineer who designed dams and other facilities for the municipal water-supply system, had a vision of a black metal water tank located high on a hill in a predominantly industrial area, colorfully arrayed with classical masonry.

The tank, supplied by artesian wells, provided the community with water. In 1930, a new metal tank, 120 feet in diameter, 60 feet high, and with a capacity of 4 million gallons, replaced the one erected in 1893. Heyder recognized an opportunity.

He wrapped the tank with a classical colonnade of twenty-four pilasters and blind arches, but the coloration as much as the design creates the effect. Heyder employed more than twenty subtle shades of brick, ranging from orange-tan to reddish brown. The color in the drum (the walls are 2 feet thick) changes from dark to light, bottom to top, while in the blind arches the order is reversed. The belt course, column capitals, round medallions, and architrave are stone, and the zigzag cornice is terra-cotta.

Heyder was a serious student of arches, domes, and bridges; his library reportedly contained some thirty-five hundred books on sixteenth- through eighteenth-century architecture and engineering. He died in 1973, but left the neighborhood's most impressive landmark, which is sometimes mistaken for a synagogue. From the hill there is an outstanding view of the harbor and the Francis Scott Key Bridge. ❖

H6 • BALTIMORE–WASHINGTON INTERNATIONAL AIRPORT (BWI)

Baltimore–Washington Parkway, Anne Arundel County
1950—Whitman, Requardt, and Associates, the Greiner Company, engineers; 1979 expansion—Peterson and Brickbauer, architect

The terminal owes its clean, open appearance and directional and spatial clarity primarily to Peterson and Brickbauer. The architects took a vaguely modernistic 1950 terminal building—a long façade angled at either end—and added a lofty, glass-enclosed steel space frame in front of it to create a new grand concourse. (Little is left of the former structure except the tower, now covered with black metal paneling.) The $52 million concourse doubled the size of the terminal. The black steel space frame was angled at either end, following the original outline and forming a semienclosure for the looping approach roads. It was also cantilevered beyond the large red-tiled support columns and glass front wall to make a covered walkway for people getting into or out of vehicles.

Viewing the new terminal building as a linear event, the designers mounted a line of large-scale, repetitive airline logos over the ticket counters, clearly visible from outside, which simplified finding the right airline. Theatrical lighting of the entrances, columns, and graphics, and the concourse's unobstructed expanse, facilitated movement to the piers. The design team included Ewell, Bomhardt, and Associates, engineers; Howard, Needles, Tammen, and Bergendoff, planners; Architectural Graphics Associates; and William Richardson of Jaros, Baum, and Bolles, lighting consultants.

Under a $30 million renovation program designed by Greiner, Inc., and Cambridge Seven Associates and completed in 1994, new carpeting, graphics, lighting, and an observation gallery with exhibits of airplane parts were installed in the concourse, and landscaping was added outside. The changes moderated the building's austerity, but at the expense of its legibility.

Meanwhile, the piers have been extended several times. A joint venture of STV Group, Baltimore engineers, and William Nicholas Bodouva and Associates, New York architects, designed the new $139 million international pier, scheduled for completion in 1997. The terminal addition will employ a modified space frame and window wall and incorporate a pyramidal glass roof and a Central Light Rail Line station. The parking garage is also being enlarged and the approach roads reconfigured under a six-year, $500 million capital improvement program. ❖

Tour I

Southwest, Railroads (Driving)

Baltimore invented the railroad in America. In 1830, the Baltimore and Ohio was the first long-distance, general-purpose railroad to begin operations in the United States, in fact in the world. Before that there had been only crude, specialized mine or quarry lines or very short intercity routes. To connect its deepwater port with the western rivers and markets, Baltimore announced that it would build a railroad several hundred miles long over a range of mountains—and did.

The Baltimore area, therefore, boasts a number of railroad firsts. Among them are the Carrollton Viaduct, the first railroad bridge in the country, and, just outside the city, the majestic Thomas Viaduct, the nation's first

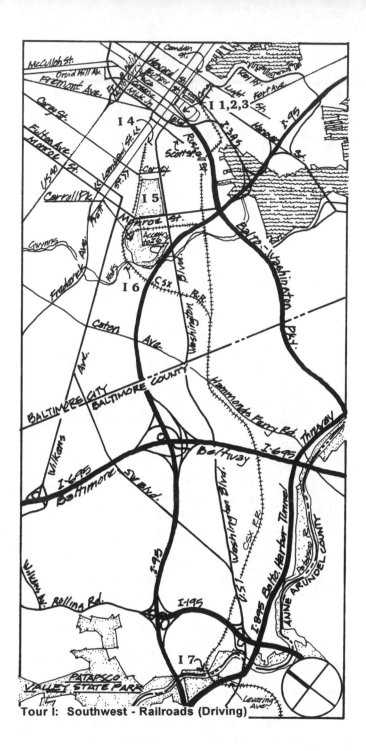

Tour I: Southwest - Railroads (Driving)

multispan railroad bridge. Both of these ancient structures are still in use by the CSX Corporation, of which the former B & O Railroad is a part.

The railroad began its journey to the West on land donated by James Carroll, the then proprietor of Mount Clare. Finally, the restored Camden Station, the backdrop for some of the most dramatic scenes in Baltimore's tumultuous history, now serves as the frontispiece for Oriole Park at Camden Yards, the new emblem of civic pride. ❖

11 • CAMDEN STATION
Howard and Camden streets
1855–67—Niernsee and Neilson, and Joseph F. Kemp

In the nineteenth century this was Baltimore's busiest railroad station and also served as the Baltimore and Ohio Railroad's main office. A 1980 historic structures report cited it as the station in longest continuous use in the United States, but before the decade was out it closed. Now boasting a recently and successfully restored exterior, its situation will be happy again if only a proper use can be found for it.

In 1852, the B & O Railroad purchased the land on which the station stands and construction began. The architects were Niernsee and Neilson, who had at one time worked as engineers for the railroad. Their original design called for a nine-part building in the Italianate style, with a central section topped by a tall tower and flanked on each side by hyphen, wing, porte cochere, and a tower on the end.

In 1856 Niernsee and Neilson parted company for nine years and the first (central) section was apparently carried out by Joseph F. Kemp, cited in the historic structures report as an apprentice in Neilson's office, but referred to in an 1857 newspaper report when the building opened as "attached to the road department of the [B & O] company." His lack of engineering knowledge is cited as the reason the 185-foot tower (which made the building Baltimore's tallest) was unsound and had to be modified only a decade later.

In 1867 the building was completed, essentially according to the original plan, but with some changes: wider wings, no portes cocheres, end towers three stories with one-story cupolas instead of two stories with two-story cupolas. The station remained in this state only briefly before cracks caused the removal of most of the central tower.

The building was renovated and expanded in 1897, giving more emphasis to its eastern end. In 1901 the west tower was removed to create a link to the then newly constructed office and warehouse building [I2]. In 1912, the railroad spent $1 million on additional renovations, more than doubling the size of the waiting area, at least partly in anticipation of the Democratic National Convention held in Baltimore that year.

After World War II the station shrank, most noticeably in 1952 with the removal of the train shed behind the station, as well as the third floor of the east tower, the remainder of the central tower, and a 1912 canopy in front of the east and north façades. The station's baggage building closed in 1971, and by 1988 the station itself was closed and its functions shifted to a railroad car posted in the rear.

With the coming of Oriole Park at Camden Yards, the station was taken over by the Maryland Stadium Authority, which authorized a $2.2 million exterior restoration to its 1867 state, by architects Cho, Wilks, and Benn. Completed in 1992, the job required the imaginative substitution of new materials for old, notably aluminum and fiberglass for the tower and cupolas, fiberglass for cornices and window surrounds, and precast concrete to replace brownstone.

Although it has been much altered over the years, some of the interior's former grandeur remains. The former executive suite on the second floor, the railroad's "seat of power" from the 1860s to the 1880s, retains many of its features and is a significant interior space. The main waiting room on the first floor, which underwent a major renovation in 1912, boasts oak paneling and marble wainscoting.

Current plans for the interior call for reuse of part of the building as a baseball museum to be administered by the Babe Ruth Museum, and the rest as a restaurant and for other uses. ❖

12 • B & O RAILROAD WAREHOUSE

Southwest of Camden Station
*1898–1905—Baldwin and Pennington; 1992—Hellmuth,
Obata, and Kassabaum*

Once the largest freight warehouse in Baltimore and among the largest in the United States, this building stands, both in size and configuration, as a tribute to the heyday of the American railroad. At 1,016 feet long by just 51 feet wide, and with regimented tiers of windows marching down its length, it looks like the opposite of a toy train set: a hugely overscaled freight train, built for some race of giants, and somehow set down here to be a lumbering, majestic presence in the cityscape.

Built in 6 eight-story sections with 22-inch fire walls between each section, the building's first four sections were erected between 1898 and 1901 and the final two in 1904 and 1905. The principal design feature consists of the tiers of third- to sixth-floor windows running the entire length of the building's façade, each tier in a recessed arch.

When used as a warehouse the building stored everything from flour to furniture and had areas for curing and drying goods. Last used as a warehouse in 1974, the building became a model of creative adaptive reuse when it was bought by the Maryland Stadium Authority in 1991 and renovated as part of the Oriole Park at Camden Yards complex. Altogether, $40 million has been spent on the 430,000-square-foot building. The northern two-thirds of the building is occupied for baseball-related purposes, including the Orioles' offices, restaurants, and banquet facilities. The southern part has been recycled for lease as offices and is home to a major printing and publishing firm and one of the city's leading architecture firms. The renovation, by the same firm that designed the stadium, has been lauded by Baltimore *Sun* architecture critic Edward Gunts as "a national examplar of adaptive reuse," its various interior spaces "created with the same attention to detail and respect for tradition that made the ballpark such a success." ❖

13 • ORIOLE PARK AT CAMDEN YARDS
Camden and Eutaw streets
1992—Hellmuth, Obata, and Kassabaum

There was a time when East Coast port cities competed vigorously for the western trade and built their own turnpikes, canals, and railroads to try to capture it. This intercity rivalry is now often represented symbolically by professional sports teams and the competition to have the best and newest stadium. Oriole Park at Camden Yards, adjacent to and incorporating the industrial symbol of Baltimore's entry in the nineteenth-century battle

for commercial dominance—the Baltimore and Ohio
Railroad—expresses the transformation perfectly.

Baltimore's new ballpark has been justly praised for
its siting, urbanity, and retromodern design. The deci
sion of the architects; the Maryland Stadium Authority,
which owns the site; and the Orioles' management to
preserve the B & O Railroad Warehouse and locate the
team offices in it was critical to the ballpark's orientation and appearance.

As initially conceived, it was a typical reinforced
concrete stadium. Retaining the warehouse provided
an opportunity to reorient the structure with a better
view of the skyline at dusk and to clothe it with brick in
keeping with its more traditional neighbor. During the
redesign process, the building's height was also lowered from four levels to three (bringing it below the
warehouse roofline), and the pitch of the upper deck
reduced.

The look of the low-profile steel, reinforced concrete, and brick structure was also a vast improvement
over the earlier version. The new one wrapped the required ramps and portals, formerly expressed in concrete, with walls and towers of brick (with precast
concrete base and trim), interspersed with thirty-two
arched openings, to create a warm and remarkably po-
rous façade. The warehouse, whose exterior was re-
paired and repointed during the construction period,
inspired the ballpark's fenestration and intricate brick
detailing.

Inside, the grass playing field is open to the sky, the
way ballparks used to be. Another nostalgic feature is
the stadium signage by the David Ashton Company.

Some modern features are a vacuum drainage system under the grass field to whisk away rainwater and the seventy-two skyboxes and television screens that line the upper deck. The $105 million stadium seats 46,000 with no obstructed views. It is served by communter (MARC) trains and the Central Light Rail Line. Joseph Spear was the architect-in-charge; and RTKL Associates, Inc., and Wallace, Roberts, and Todd, Philadelphia, the master planners. ❖

14 • B & O RAILROAD MUSEUM
(Roundhouse-Passenger Car Shop)
(BCL, NR)
Pratt and Poppleton streets
1884—Baldwin and Pennington

This site encompasses the story not just of one building but of American railroad history and of a dynamic and growing museum.

Rich in history, the B & O Railroad Museum occupies the site of the oldest continuously operated railroad facility in the world, and, at its height in the first half of the twentieth century, the most complete railroad complex anywhere.

The story begins with the 1829 Mount Clare Station, the first American railroad terminal (the present station building is an 1851 replacement). By the early 1900s it had grown to a sprawling complex of thirty-two buildings including everything from a stables building, left over from the time that horses pulled trains, to a blacksmith shop, passenger car shop, iron foundry and brass foundry, sawmill, paint shop, boiler shop, axle shop, and air-conditioning shop. Altogether, the complex at its height employed three thousand people.

Today the complex is centered on the passenger car shop or "roundhouse," actually a twenty-two-sided structure for building and repairing passenger cars.

The 123-foot-high, 235-foot-diameter roundhouse, including a turntable which still operates, has a structure described by Robert M. Vogel in his 1975 *Some Industrial Buildings of the Monumental City and Environs:*

> Undoubtedly the largest circular . . . industrial building in the world . . . [its] sloping lower roof is supported by radial trusses carried at their outer ends by brick exterior walls and at their inner by 22 wrought-iron columns that also support the lantern and cupola, and surround the 60-foot turntable.

Used as a passenger car shop until 1953, it then became the principal building of the B & O Railroad Museum. It now houses an exhibit of railroad history from locomotives of the 1830s down to a World War II troop sleeper.

The roundhouse, the accompanying annex building, and Mount Clare Station form a complex that has constituted the museum's buildings in the past; but the museum is bigger than that and growing. It now owns the brick car shop south of the roundhouse building and plans to turn it into a working repair shop for locomotives and passenger cars in addition to expanding into two other former Mount Clare buildings. ❖

I5 • MOUNT CLARE
(BCL, NR)
Carroll Park
1753–87, with later alterations—architect unknown

The only surviving colonial plantation house within the city limits, Mount Clare is a fascinating Georgian complex demonstrating the changing styles of the period in which it was built.

Charles Carroll, Barrister (not to be confused with his distant relative, Charles Carroll of Carrollton), returned from England in 1754 upon the death of his younger brother to carry on the family plantation and business. His father had built a modest one-and-a-half-story house on the site of the present bulding. Between 1757 and 1760 the barrister tore down this house and built, partly upon its foundations, a two-and-a-half-story house—the present main block—retained the older kitchen, and constructed a washhouse and orangery on either end of the complex. The two-story pilasters on the garden front are an unusual and interesting feature of the main house.

The next major addition occurred in 1766. The main house was altered by the addition of a Palladian front, including the portico and the chamber above containing a Palladian window. At this time the kitchen was also enlarged and an office wing was built complementary to it on the other side of the main block; both were given polygonal fronts and attached to the main house with hyphens. The rectangular forecourt was replaced by a semicircular one with rectangular wings, an overall shape resembling that of the portico chamber's

Palladian window. An icehouse was added between the laundry and kitchen, matched by a small building, purpose unknown, on the other side between the office and the orangery. Counting the hyphens, the complex now had nine parts and was symmetrical.

The barrister died in 1783. Shortly thereafter, his widow made further alterations and additions. These included a pantry, passages connecting some of the outbuildings, and two more buildings at the far ends of the complex: a greenhouse beyond the orangery and a service building beyond the laundry. At this time, the complex reached its greatest extent, about 360 feet from end to end.

Mrs. Carroll also changed a round window on the southeast façade to a semicircular lunette and installed several new mantelpieces. Before these latest alterations and additions, the house had been in the Georgian style characteristic of Annapolis, the capital of fashion before the Revolution. As architect Michael F. Trostel, author of the book *Mount Clare*, points out, Mrs. Carroll's updatings "are more in the Federal style of which Baltimore was a leader than in the Georgian style of Annapolis, indicating that as early as 1787 Baltimore was supplanting Annapolis as the leader of style."

Over the years all but the main block of the house disappeared at various times. After the Civil War, the original hyphens and wings were removed. The present replacements, by Wyatt and Nolting, date to 1907. The present chimneys are Victorian.

A notable feature of the interior of the house is the stair hall to the left of the entrance, a more sophisticated plan than the center hall, as it permitted a larger drawing room, but rare in colonial country houses. The house was paneled throughout in plaster that imitated wood.

The city purchased the mansion and the land around it for use as a city park in 1890. Mount Clare was designated a National Historic Landmark by the National Park Service in 1970. It has been excellently restored and is operated by the Maryland chapter of the Colonial Dames of America. Among its distinguishing features is that many of the furnishings are original to the house. Mr. Trostel states, "Mount Clare is the only eighteenth century museum house in Maryland to contain so many of the daily artifacts of life belonging to the builder of the house and used by his family in that house."

Recent research includes archaeological discovery of the forecourt configuration, now indicated by a low wall and fence culminating in a gate, and location of the original office and kitchen wings, now indicated by low walls in the grass of the forecourt. The original wings were in front of the present wings, making the main part of the complex a U shape rather than a straight line. ❖

16 • CARROLLTON VIADUCT
(NR)
Carroll Park
1829—Caspar W. Wever, engineer

The Gwynns Falls was the first physical obstacle encountered by the nascent Baltimore and Ohio Railroad as it began its westward journey. The Carrollton Viaduct, now the oldest railroad bridge in the United States, and still in use, was the means to cross the stream. It is a powerful segmental arch with a diameter of 80 feet. The structure is roughly 300 feet long, 26½ feet wide, and 58 feet high from the foundation to the top of the parapet. When it was built it was by far the largest bridge in Baltimore and was praised for being both massive and graceful.

The design was altered a number of times to accommodate the wishes of James Carroll, the proprietor of Mount Clare, who donated the property for the initial segment of the railroad. The changes drove up the expense. The cost of this and other early stone bridges proved controversial within the company and led to a reorganization of its engineering department. The Carrollton Viaduct, named for Charles Carroll of Carroll-ton, who dedicated it, was built of gray granite from Ellicotts Mills and Port Deposit at a cost that was estimated at anywhere from $58,000 to well over $100,000. The bridge includes a smaller 20-foot-diameter arch on the west side for a wagon road, since silted up, but due to be reopened as part of the city's proposed $6 million Gwynns Falls Greenway project. ❖

I7 • THOMAS VIADUCT
Off Maryland Route 1, Relay
1835—Benjamin H. Latrobe, Jr., engineer

When it was completed in July 1835, the B & O Railroad's monumental Thomas Viaduct was the greatest bridge in America and the first built on a curving alignment. Named for the then president of the railroad company, Philip E. Thomas, and designed by the son of the renowned architect, Benjamin Henry Latrobe, the bridge is "an architectural as well as functional masterpiece," according to architectural historian Carl W. Condit. (And yet the young engineer who planned it had never before built a bridge or even taken a formal engineering course.)

The bridge, constructed of Ellicotts Mills granite, consists of eight elliptical arches, each spanning about 58 feet. The piers are faced with engaged columns and capitals, and there are huge stone abutments with battered walls and buttresses at either end. The viaduct is 704 feet long overall, including the approaches, 26 feet wide, and 66 feet above water level. Its west side is finished with an attractive iron railing designed by the engineer. The total cost was about $200,000.

To accommodate the curve, the sharpest on the railroad's Washington Branch, Latrobe laid out the lateral faces of the piers on radial lines, making them wedge-shaped in plan. He thus avoided having to construct the arches on a skew. Several men were killed or injured during the arduous two-year construction period, and so proud was contractor John McCartney of their collective achievement that he paid for the granite obelisk at the north end of the bridge that lists the dates of construction, the principals involved, and the railroad directors.

The Thomas Viaduct gives an impression of great power and dignity. Built when engines and trains together weighed just a few tons, it has proved strong enough to support the 150-ton diesel locomotives used to haul today's freight and passenger trains between Baltimore and Washington. ❖

Tour J

West (Driving)

J1 ORCHARD STREET CHURCH
512 Orchard Street
1882—Frank E. Davis; 1992—Kelly, Clayton, and Mojzisek, and Anthony J. Downs

J2 MOTHER SETON HOUSE
600 North Paca Street
ca. 1805—architect unknown

J3 ST. MARY'S SEMINARY CHAPEL
600 North Paca Street
1808—Maximilian Godefroy

J4 PASCAULT ROW
651–665 West Lexington Street
1819—attributed to William F. Small

J5 WESTERN DISTRICT POLICE STATION (old)
214 North Pine Street
1878—Frank E. Davis

J6 ST. PETER THE APOSTLE CHURCH
Hollins and South Poppleton streets
1842—Robert Cary Long, Jr.

J7 HOLLINS MARKET
Hollins Street and South Carrollton Avenue
1865—architect unknown

J8 WAVERLY TERRACE
100 block North Carey Street
1851—Dixon, Balbirnie, and Dixon

J9 ST. LUKE'S CHURCH
217–219 North Carey Street
1851–58 or later—Niernsee and Neilson; John W. Priest

J10 XAVERIAN BROTHERS RESIDENCE
4430 Frederick Avenue
1864—Walter Kemp

J11 OUR LADY OF THE ANGELS CHAPEL
Charlestown Retirement Community, 711 Maiden Choice Lane
1915—Murphy and Olmsted

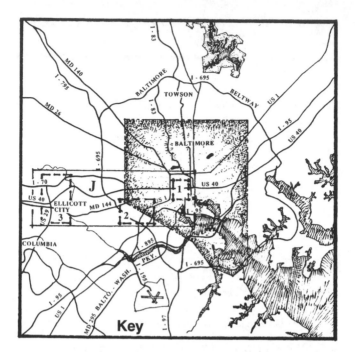

Key

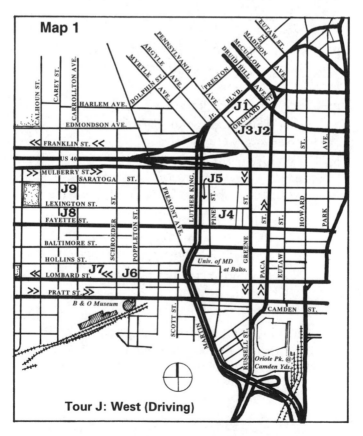

Map 1

Tour J: West (Driving)

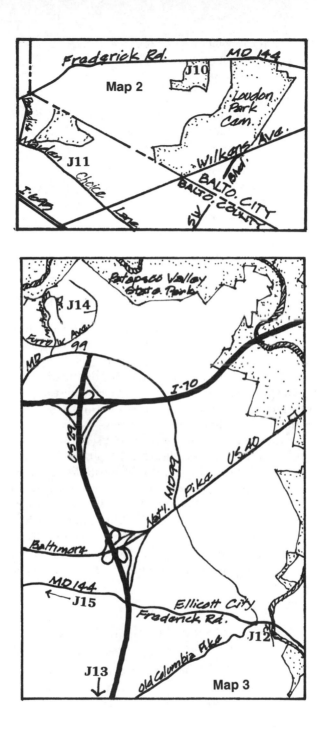

J12   ELLICOTT CITY STATION
      Frederick Road, Ellicott City
      1832—Jacob Small, Jr.

J13   TEMORA
      Columbia Road via St. John's Road, off the Route
      103 West exit from Maryland Route 29
      1857—Norris G. Starkweather

J14   ELMONTE
      Furrow Avenue off Mount Hebron Drive, west of
      the junction of Maryland Routes 29 and 99
      1858—Norris G. Starkweather

J15   DOUGHOREGAN MANOR
      Off Maryland Route 144
      1699 and later—architect unknown

Founded during the French Revolution, St. Mary's Seminary on Seton Hill was also the home of St. Mary's College, which educated many of Baltimore's distinguished citizens. Attracted by the institutions, French-speaking students and refugees from the political turmoil in Haiti settled in the area in the late eighteenth and early nineteenth centuries.

In the mid-twentieth century, the section bounded by Franklin, Eutaw, McCulloh, and Orchard streets became one of the earliest and best examples of private redevelopment in the city. The houses on Jasper and George streets were among the first to be renovated, but the movement spread to other buildings in the district.

This tour includes some of Baltimore's most distinctive rows of houses, public squares, and outlying mansions, and ends at the great eighteenth-century estate, Doughoregan. ❖

J1 • ORCHARD STREET CHURCH

(BCL, NR)
512 Orchard Street
*1882—Frank E. Davis; 1992—Kelly, Clayton, and
Mojzisek, and Anthony J. Downs*

This stands on the site of a church founded in 1837 by slaves and freed slaves that was one of the first African

Methodist Episcopal churches in Baltimore and was long a beacon of the city's African American community. Today, restored to house a museum of African American culture and also the headquarters of the Baltimore Urban League, it again fulfills such a function.

The present church building is the third on the site. In 1837 a group of trustees including ex-slave Truman Pratt, Cato Blake, and Noble Mason began holding services on the site. By 1840 the first church was built, and it was replaced by a second one in 1859. Two successive Sunday school buildings were also erected at the rear of the church, the second in 1879.

The present church building was completed in 1882 to a design by Davis. The existing Sunday school building followed in 1903 to a design by Francis E. Tormey. Services continued until 1970, when the church merged with another, and subsequently the building was vacant and threatened for a time with demolition. In 1972 it was placed on the National Register of Historic Places and efforts toward restoration followed sporadically for two decades.

In 1991 a $4 million restoration was begun and completed the following year, with $2.3 million in city and state funds and the rest raised privately. Architects were Brian Kelly of Kelly, Clayton, and Mojzisek, and

Morgan State University architecture department chairman Anthony Downs.

The Victorian Italian Renaissance-style church was given a loving restoration down to the floral and geometric designs of hand-painted stenciling on the walls and ceiling of the interior.

The façade, with its central round window above an arched loggia and its pedimented flanking windows, assembles a mixture of Renaissance-inspired architectural details. The interior reveals an attractive mélange of colors. Light yellow walls set off dark wood trusses supporting the ceiling and other woodwork, the columns are purple, and the muticolored stenciling outlines the apse opening, ceiling, and walls.

Two sets of columns, Doric below and Corinthian above, support the balcony and the roof trusses. Below the clerestory windows over the balcony runs a band of painted decoration suggesting the triforium of a Gothic cathedral. The "daisy-petal" window facing Orchard Street has been turned into a kaleidoscope of pastel colors. Four square coffers with green medallions punctuate the ceiling, and may have had lights hung from them. The look is restored, but the condition is up-to-date, with new sprinkler, fire alarm, and emergency lighting systems.

In the former Sunday school building, where the Urban League has its offices, a glass-enclosed conference room and a mezzanine were added. The Baltimore Urban League is a part of the 113 service organizations making up the National Urban League. Its activities include job training and placement, consumer and youth services, and a literacy program. ❖

J2 • MOTHER SETON HOUSE
(BCL, NR)
600 North Paca Street
ca. 1805 — architect unknown

This charming Federal-style house is as important historically as it is architecturally, for it was here that Elizabeth Ann Bayley Seton, who in 1975 would become a saint of the Roman Catholic church, started her first school for girls and took her vows as a sister during the single year, 1808–9, that she lived here.

It has been speculated that the house was designed by Maximilian Godefroy, who was working on the nearby St. Mary's Seminary Chapel at about the same time, but there is no proof.

The two-and-a-half-story house has casement windows and a typically Federal entrance to one side of the center. Notice the detailed brickwork around the windows, as well as the way in which the exterior brick curves up under the roofline.

The house is not large, at 26 by 42 feet, but for its size it has an unusually large entrance hall. There are interesting architectural details, such as windows between rooms to increase cross ventilation and the stair rail traversing a window on the steps between the first and second floors.

Restored in 1963 by John H. Scarff and also by William C. Harris of Meyer, Ayers, and Saint, the house is open to the public on weekends and by appointment. Visitors can learn about the architecture and also the story of Mother Seton, founder of the American Sisters of Charity and the first native-born American saint. ❖

J3 • ST. MARY'S SEMINARY CHAPEL
(BCL)
600 North Paca Street
1808—Maximilian Godefroy

Godefroy's elegant, anomalous chapel is one of the earliest Gothic Revival churches in the United States.

The Sulpician Order established St. Mary's Seminary in 1791, and in 1805 Godefroy arrived in Baltimore to teach there. By the following year, he had designed the chapel. However, as a result of the Sulpicians' desire to build economically, his original plans, which included a tower, "suffered drastic alterations," according to Robert L. Alexander, Godefroy's biographer. Brick was substituted for the more appropriate stone, and the height of the nave was reduced. The result was more Gothic scenery than architecture. The church cost about $35,000.

As the chapel stands now, the brick, sandstone, and stucco façade is topped by a parapet wall. Godefroy at first planned this level to contain six rectangular windows, with a rose window in the middle, opening into the church itself. But because the barrel vault was lowered, the windows ended up above the roof; this level of the structure became a parapet wall, with twelve niches replacing the rectangular windows. Statues of the twelve apostles were to occupy the niches, but the statues, a pair of stained-glass windows flanking the main en-

trance, and the tower were all eliminated. Nevertheless, characteristic elements of the Gothic style—pointed arches, flying buttresses, and groined vaults (here suggested in plaster)—are all present. The dramatically proportioned interior is distinguished by rows of columns with tall bases and acanthus-leaf capitals.

The chapel's first major period of change came during the 1830s and 1840s, when Robert Cary Long, Jr., added a tower, spire, and interior decoration. In 1916, Long's tower came down. Some of Godefroy's wooden arches, screens, and plaster vaulting were removed at about the same time, and heavy oak seating with over-head canopies was added, obscuring the bases of the columns.

During a restoration of the chapel by Cochran, Stephenson, and Donkervoet, completed in 1968, this seating was removed and replaced by separate chairs. The floor was relaid and carpeted, a new altar and lighting system were installed, and the interior was painted in white and gold with reddish candy-striping on the arches. The purpose of the alterations was to return the chapel as much as possible to Godefroy's first design and also to make it more amenable to the new liturgy of the Catholic church. ❖

J4 • PASCAULT ROW
651–665 West Lexington Street
1819—attributed to William F. Small

This is the last row of early nineteenth-century town-houses left in Baltimore. In a 1972 nomination form for the National Register of Historic Places the houses were attributed to William F. Small, on the basis that Small was then working in the architectural office of Benjamin H. Latrobe; that the buildings "display the Latrobe influence in their dignity, plain surfaces and bold composition"; and that the doorway treatment and the panels above were copied from a house Latrobe designed for banker William Lorman in 1816. The fact that Lorman also held mortgages on half the houses when they were first built adds another connection.

The houses were built at the southwestern extreme of the property owned by Jean-Charles-Marie-Louis-Felix Pascault, a merchant who had immigrated from Santo Domingo in 1780. During their early history, some of the houses were owned by distinguished citizens, including a general and an Episcopal bishop.

Later in the century the surrounding area changed and they became semicommercial, with first floors converted to shop fronts and apartments above. During the twentieth century they remained substantially the same, but gradually fell into decline until rescued and renovated in the early 1980s by the University of Maryland at

Baltimore. Fortunately one house, number 655, retained its original entrance treatment and from that all the others were copied to return the entrance façades substantially to their original appearance. Inside, they have become apartments for university use. ❖

J5 • WESTERN DISTRICT POLICE STATION (old)
(NR)
214 North Pine Street
1878—Frank E. Davis

Located in an isolated quarter of the city and left derelict for many years, Davis's ebullient high Victorian Gothic station house has gained a new use as a private police station and a well-deserved prominence from the construction of the adjacent Martin Luther King, Jr. Boulevard.

The station house was the headquarters for the Western District until 1951 and then served for another twenty years as a detention center for women and children. Generations of police officers, newspaper reporters, and inmates came to know it as the notoriously antiquated and overcrowded Pine Street Station. The building stood empty from 1971 when the Police Department abandoned it until 1978 when it became a drug abuse rehabilitation center. The center closed in

1980. The structure was vacant again until the University of Maryland acquired it in 1984. The renovated building reopened in 1991 as the headquarters for the downtown campus police force. The renovation architect was Edward A. Masek, Jr.

The exterior of Davis's compact and decorative building has been returned to its early appearance. A granite base supports walls that combine brick with bluestone trim leading up to a hipped, slate roof with a cornice and pinnacles of sheet metal and several monumental chimneys. The multicolored façade and the pointed arches are typical of the Victorian Gothic style.

Part of the rear wing was removed in 1978 to accommodate the construction of the boulevard, and the interior was stripped of its original woodwork during the conversion to the drug rehabilitation center the same year. The University of Maryland installed new wooden window frames and entrance doors and replaced the slate roof and sheet-metal decoration as part of its $1.3 million renovation program.

Two other architecturally noteworthy police buildings are the 1899 Northern District Station at Keswick Road and 34th Street in Hampden, designed in the French Renaissance style by Henry Brauns and executed in granite, brick, and brownstone; and the former Southern District Station located in the first block of East Ostend Street in South Baltimore, a Romanesque Revival structure by Jackson C. Gott built in 1897 of Port Deposit granite. The Police Department plans to vacate the Northern District Station to move to a new headquarters on a different site. When the Police Department left the Southern District Station the building was renovated, with less than total architectural success, as office space for nonprofit groups. ❖

J6 • ST. PETER THE APOSTLE CHURCH
(NR)
Hollins and South Poppleton streets
1842—Robert Cary Long, Jr.

In the early 1840s the versatile Robert Cary Long, Jr., designed (among other things) three major Baltimore churches and a synagogue, all still standing and in use. The Greek temple design of St. Peter's resembles that of his Lloyd Street Synagogue [F7]. Its six-columned por-

tico with pediment introduces a simple brick rectangle, originally painted, with a gently sloping peaked roof. The foundation is of hammered granite from Ellicott City quarries. The interior is an open, unobstructed space, with a basilica-style ceiling bearing on outer walls adorned with Corinthian pilasters. The building and its interior have been altered several times. The eastern end, containing the chancel, originally square, was extended in 1849 and again in 1868, when the present semicircular apse was added. At that time, various windows were added in the west, north, and south walls, though the stained glass in them was installed during alterations carried out between 1898 and 1912. Frescoes added to the walls during those years were covered in a renovation in 1968, when side altars were removed and an altar facing the congregation was installed. The high altar of Vermont marble is from 1914.

The most recent change was a 1989 redecoration of the interior, in which darker colors were replaced with cream walls, white pilasters, and pink trim. One could quarrel with the pink, but on the whole the church looks much brighter and handsomer now.

Long was also responsible for the rectory behind the church on Hollins Street. It is a three-story, three-bay brick town house with a flat roof. Architectural historian Phoebe Stanton has remarked that when the house was built, "The flat roof was clearly the last word in modernity."

Other parts of the church complex are the Convent of the Immaculate Conception at 11 South Poppleton

Street, built from 1865 to 1880 in a style in keeping with the church; the House of Mercy around the corner on Callendar Street, incorporating two houses purchased by Emily MacTavish, granddaughter of Charles Carroll of Carrollton, who presented them to the Sisters of Mercy; and a six-room schoolhouse adjoining the House of Mercy, built in 1868 and used until 1917. The entire complex is on the National Register of Historic Places. ❖

J7 • HOLLINS MARKET

Hollins Street and South Carrollton Avenue
1865—architect unknown

Baltimore has always been a market town. The earliest attempts to establish a public market began in 1751, when there were no more than twenty-five houses in the community. Twelve years later the first public market opened at Gay and Baltimore streets, funded by a lottery. By 1796, when the city was incorporated, there were three market houses. Municipally owned but sometimes privately operated, the markets continued to grow in popularity until at one time there were eleven. There are still half a dozen, of which the Lexington Market is the best known.

A *market* in the Baltimore sense is typically a building (or buildings) and the area around it, filled with stalls of vendors selling meats, fish, produce, and other goods, mostly foods. Here is an early-twentieth-century description of a typical market:

> A large low-roofed open area with a . . . centre aisle running throughout the length, bordered on either side by 8- or 10-foot-front stalls or booths, with crossing aisles at regular intervals for two or three or more city blocks, and in addition stalls known as movable stalls located back against the outer sides of the markets. In addition at either extreme of the market trailing along the curb for several squares . . . may be seen on market days numerous street stalls which the vendors, farmers, truck raisers and Italian fruit dealers carry to and from the markets.

Such is an accurate description of Hollins Market in the late nineteenth and early twentieth centuries, when it consisted of the building now standing, a shedlike building in the rear much like the one there now, and more stalls along the streets.

Most of the Baltimore markets were owned and run by the city, at least at first, with stalls rented to the vendors. Gradually this gave way to a system whereby the vendors bought their stalls, the more ambitious of them buying several stalls and leasing all but their own out to others. The city, which still maintained the buildings, ended up losing money on such a proposition in the long run, and some of the markets fell into disrepair. They were further hurt by the post–World War II era of supermarkets and suburban shopping centers, but in recent years there has been a revival of interest in them, and the city has renovated several old markets. In 1995 management of the markets was privatized, with a corporation that again leases space to vendors, while the city retains the buildings and some responsibility for maintenance.

The history of the Hollins Market is fairly typical. It was organized in 1835, when the city granted the petition of a number of residents, including piano manufacturer Joseph Newman, to erect a market at their own expense on land donated by banker George B. Dunbar. The first market structure must have been flimsy, for it collapsed in a windstorm in 1838. It was rebuilt the following year, and in 1863–64 the City Council appropriated $23,000 to build the present Italianate addition, now the city's oldest market structure still in use. The market was named for the Hollins family, which owned land in the vicinity.

The form of the building, with its low first floor and high hall above, is typical of early markets. They served not only as markets but, above the stalls, as community centers and as theaters for traveling entertainment. Later, when schools, theaters, and other public buildings had taken over the functions of such second stories, market buildings had one story or a low second floor with offices.

Hollins Market's upper story was in use until the 1960s, and there has recently been some neighborhood talk of putting it to use again. The market experienced a period of decline in the 1950s and 1960s, but it was renovated in 1977 and has grown in popularity since. In 1980 it was open on Fridays and Saturdays only; now it is open Tuesdays through Saturdays. ❖

J8 • WAVERLY TERRACE

100 block North Carey Street
1851—Dixon, Balbirnie, and Dixon

What the steel-frame highrise is to Chicago, the lowly row house is to Baltimore. It provides the city's architectural ambiance, its character, and, with the legendary white marble steps, its traditional claim to fame.

Waverly Terrace is an outstanding block of Italianate row houses that defines the eastern border of Franklin Square—among the finest of the public squares in the city (see Essays, p. 21). The façades are rusticated on the ground floors, plain above, and enhanced by their cast-iron balconies.

The Baltimore *Sun*, on September 30, 1851, described what lay within:

> These fine specimens of architectural skill are each provided with vestibuled entrances which communicate with sitting rooms in front and dining rooms in the rear, which are finished in fine parlor style. The ascent to the principal story is by easy rail stair cases conducting to the parlor, which is 40 feet deep, divided by a pair of fluted columns in *antes*, ornamented with finely carved centre pieces and mantels of statuary marble. The stories above are occupied with chambers of a cheerful and handsome

finish, intersected by spacious dressing closets, each house containing six chambers.

In the back were two-and-a-half-story buildings with a kitchen and pantry on the ground floor, bathrooms and servants' quarters on the second, and an attic dormitory.

Rehabilitated in 1979 under a federal program, Waverly Terrace has been turned into cooperative apartments. Canby Place, another excellent group of Italianate row houses with brownstone fronts (and also having cast-iron balconies), borders the square to the south. Some of these have been renovated as apartments and private homes.

Baltimore row houses come in a surprising variety of shapes, ranging from primitive, pitched-roof wooden cottages such as those in the 600 block of South Wolfe Street in Fells Point, to the "band-boxes" or half-houses at Leadenhall and West Montgomery streets in South Baltimore, whose peculiar form has influenced some of the newer domestic architecture in the area. Most, however, have three stories and flat roofs, but within those rather narrow parameters, numerous styles can be discerned: Federal (Pascault Row [J4]); Greek Revival (Monument Street west of Mount Vernon Place); Italianate; Second Empire; Queen Anne (Mount Royal Terrace Houses [K23]); and Neoclassical. A contemporary variation on the theme is the award-winning group of houses designed by Washington architect Hugh Newell Jacobsen in Bolton Hill [K14].

Other Baltimore row houses, notable in themselves and illustrative of the evolution of the genus, are located in the 600 block of Stirling Street in Old Town, where a curving block of homes dating from the 1830s has been vigorously restored under the city's Urban Homesteading Program, which began there in 1974; on Belvidere Terrace [K5], the acme of Victorian design; and in the 2600 block of Wilkens Avenue, the longest row of houses in the city, built around 1910 and emblematic of the local vernacular.

Row houses are found in many other cities, of course, but their proliferation and distinctive styles in Baltimore are largely due to two factors: a system of financing through ground rents that enabled many people to become homeowners who could not otherwise have afforded it, and the availability of marble in quantity from local quarries. The ground rents, by which an owner rented rather than bought the ground under his house, enabled him to reduce his costs by about 20 percent. The marble gave a touch of elegance to otherwise ordinary rows.

Row houses were economical and eminently practical. They saved land for the builder and heating and maintenance costs for the owner. In fact, while modern group homes are advertised in the suburbs today as town houses, they are still row houses and still built with the same economies in mind.

Row houses have many advantages besides those already mentioned. Their exteriors can accommodate a wide range of design treatments and their height, no more than four stories, imparts a human scale to the street; indeed row houses seem to be made for leaning out of. They can house people densely, but without tenement overcrowding.

The row-house interior is infinitely adaptable and capable of enclosing numerous commercial uses. Stores or restaurants often occupy the ground floors, with offices or apartments above. What was suitable for one era can be easily changed in another, as storefronts become artists' studios, for example.

"The houses were not works of art," wrote Phoebe Stanton, "but the rows were. They gave the city its own anonymous, slow visual rhythm."

Some row houses, however, are neighborhood works of art. On a summer evening in the Patterson Park vicinity, for instance, the marble steps have a luminous glow. Window screens present views of waterfalls and forests, and vases line the basement windows of house after house, block after block, row upon row. It is the essence of the city. ❖

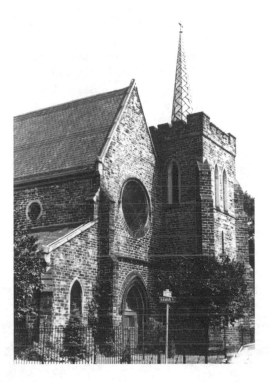

J9 • ST. LUKE'S CHURCH
(NR)
217–219 North Carey Street
1851–58 or later—Niernsee and Neilson; John W. Priest

The curious history of the building of this church, the largest Episcopal church in Baltimore at its completion, involved a number of architects. Organized as a parish in 1847, the church first hired Robert Cary Long, Jr., but the vestry, which seems to have been vacillating and argumentative in the extreme, deferred a decision on the design he submitted until after his death in 1849. They then turned to John Notman, a New York architect, with whom they also couldn't come to terms. Finally they settled on Niernsee and Neilson, but their design was only partly built when the church held services in 1853. At length another New York architect, John

W. Priest, was brought in in 1857 and found the structure unsound and poorly built. After Priest died the following year the work was carried on by H. M. Congdon, his partner, but architectural historian Phoebe Stanton writes, "St. Luke's was in the end the creation of Priest, for he corrected the proportions and converted it from a troublesome 'anomaly' to an adequate ecclesiological church."

She goes on to say, however, that the church "was a composite work by several architects and had little of the vigor, freshness, or power possessed by St. Mark's Philadelphia." It is notable, though, for its lofty nave and especially for its stained-glass windows, most of which were designed by English architect William Butterfield. Those in the side aisles tell the story of Christ, and especially impressive is the north transept window depicting the Last Judgment. The choir screen is a later addition, thought to be of the 1880s, and the visitor should note the unusually large baptismal font, with its elaborate and tall wooden cover, still raised by means of a chain and counterweight. ❖

J10 • XAVERIAN BROTHERS RESIDENCE
4430 Frederick Avenue
1864—Walter Kemp

With its heavy cornices, its commodious porches, its distinctive quoins, and its delightful wooden trim, this Victorian house is a welcome survivor. It would perhaps look more Italianate than it does if it had retained its original tower in the center of the front (above the protruding bay, but rising from the main body of the house).

It was built in 1864 as a wedding present for Henrietta Wilkens Schlens (wife of Gustav), from her father, William Wilkens. It descended in the female line of the same family (one married a Knabe of the piano manufacturing family), until in 1925 it was bought by the Xaverian Brothers, and currently sits on the property of Mount Saint Joseph High School. For a time it was put to the use of the school, then became the headquarters for the head of the Xaverian Brothers for the region stretching from New England to Kentucky. When the headquarters moved to Silver Spring in the 1970s, it became a residence for some of the brothers.

The interior has been altered, but not ruined, and there are indications of an interest in gradually restoring it. Original doors, crown moldings, and ceiling medallions remain, and with the proper attention over a period of time it could become something of a gem. ❖

J11 • OUR LADY OF THE ANGELS CHAPEL
Charlestown Retirement Community, 711 Maiden Choice Lane
1915—Murphy and Olmsted

One of the best unkept secrets of Baltimore, this chapel is the site of cultural events that are frequently open to the public; but it is probable that few aside from residents of Charlestown Retirement Community, on whose

grounds it is located, know of this building and its magnificent interior.

The chapel sits on land that was once the home of St. Charles College. It was run by the Sulpician Fathers, who originally came to Baltimore in the wake of the French Revolution and also founded St. Mary's Seminary. Robert and Elizabeth Jenkins, of the prominent Baltimore Catholic family, endowed the chapel in memory of their parents, Alfred and Elizabeth Jenkins, and all four are buried in a crypt beneath one of the building's small chapels.

Dedicated in 1915 by Cardinal Gibbons, the chapel's completion was held up by World War I, and the last of its stained-glass windows was not installed until the 1950s. A basilica in form, with nave, side aisles, transepts, a dome over the crossing, and an apse with seven small chapels, it has an exterior of rusticated stone, buff brick, limestone, and terra-cotta. It features a stone porch at the entrance, with paired columns above, arched side windows, and rose windows in the west façade and the two transepts. The building is 155 feet long with a nave height of 48 feet and a dome height of 68 feet.

While the exterior is handsome enough, it does not begin to prepare the visitor for the interior. The walls and floor are covered entirely in marble imported from Carrara. The panels are so perfectly matched in their graining that they have been compared in their precision to the decoration of the Library of Congress. The effect is far richer than any other church interior in Baltimore.

Bancel La Farge, son of the noted nineteenth-century artist John La Farge, created the chapel's mosaics, culminating in the mosaic of Our Lady of the Angels in the apse. The elaborate altar was fashioned by John J. Earley and is also inlaid with mosaics, including one representing the seven days of creation. The four evangelists are represented on the front of the altar, and flanking the opening to the sanctuary are statues of Mary and Joseph. The stained-glass windows, which in part tell the story of a young man's progression to the priesthood, are by Charles J. Connick.

The chapel now serves as both a spiritual and cultural center for the Charlestown Community. ❖

J12 • ELLICOTT CITY STATION

Frederick Road, Ellicott City
1832—Jacob Small, Jr.

This is America's oldest railroad station. It was built as a freight depot at what was then known as Ellicotts Mills, founded in 1772. The proprietors built the largest flour mill in the United States and furnished it with the latest equipment. The town was the initial terminus of the Baltimore and Ohio Railroad.

In January 1831, the railroad company hired Colonel Jacob Small, Jr., son of the architect of the Old Otterbein Church, to "furnish plans for improvements at company depots." A few months later, the directors approved his plan for Ellicotts Mills. A stone building "for the reception of produce, and which also includes a car house and office," was completed by 1832, according to the company records.

Contractor John McCartney built the depot of dark gray granite from local quarries and framed the interior with heavy timber. At first, freight was brought in by wagon, hoisted up one floor to track level, and loaded on freight cars. Smoke funnels in the roof indicate that locomotives lay over here in the early days. Passengers got off the trains across the street opposite the Patapsco Hotel, which was a stagecoach stop on the old National Road, now Route 144. In 1856, the railroad considered erecting a separate passenger station at Ellicotts Mills, but decided instead on a "refitting of the warehouse for passenger accommodations."

A turntable was added to the complex in 1863 and the freight house was added in 1885, the latter designed by E. Francis Baldwin. At that time, the station building was again renovated for passengers and given a Victorian appearance, doubtless by Baldwin. Historic Ellicott City, Inc., the current owner, has maintained the depot's Victorian look and plans to reconstruct the turntable.

Oella, located across the Patapsco River, was the site of the Union Manufacturing Company, the second cotton mill to commence operations in Maryland, in 1810. Union Manufacturing owned 1,670 acres of land extending for 3 miles on both sides of the river. In 1825, the town had 700 people, 70 brick and stone houses, a company store, a schoolhouse, and a church. W. J. Dickey and Sons, Inc., acquired the property in 1887 and operated a woolen mill in Oella until 1972, when it closed down. At that time, there were 500 mill employees and 110 company-owned houses.

In 1973, Charles L. Wagandt, a descendant of the Dickeys, bought the village with plans to restore it. Oella today is a preserved nineteenth-century mill town. Nearby is the birthplace of Benjamin Banneker, the first African American astronomer and surveyor.

Remains of the Oliver Viaduct, built contemporaneously with the station to carry the railroad over Tiber Branch and the turnpike; of the 1837 Patapsco Female Institute, designed in Greek Revival style by Robert Cary Long, Jr.; and of the former flour and cotton-milling industries linger in this historic and picturesque area. ❖

J13 • TEMORA
Columbia Road via St. John's Road, off the Route 103
West exit from Maryland Route 29
1857—Norris G. Starkweather

When Thomas B. Dorsey, jurist and descendant of a long line of Howard County landowners, died in 1855, his property was divided among the family members. Four of them hired Starkweather to design Italianate villas. Two are still extant: Temora and Elmonte. (The other two were Wilton, which stood opposite Elmonte and burned in 1939, and Chatham, demolished in the 1950s.) Of the pair remaining, Temora, with its broken pediments and prominent cupola, is the more fanciful and inviting. ❖

J14 • ELMONTE

Furrow Avenue off Mt. Hebron Drive, west of the junction of Maryland routes 29 and 99
1858—Norris G. Starkweather

This is the other of Starkweather's remaining Italianate villas constructed for members of the Dorsey family.

Built of the local gray granite, it is a large and somewhat dour mansion with center halls running the length of each floor, twenty rooms, and seven fireplaces with marble mantels.

Thirty years ago it was the seat of a large estate and dairy farm. When Elmonte was sold, not quite half of the 285 acres went to the Maryland State Highway Administration and most of the remainder to the Patapsco Park Estates development. The house remains surrounded by about 3 acres of land. The owners have done some renovation. ❖

J15 • DOUGHOREGAN MANOR
Off Maryland Route 144
1699 and later—architect unknown

The real interest of the manor, which is never open to the public and which outsiders are emphatically discouraged from visiting, is that it is what remains of a once enormous plantation complex—an eighteenth-century family community.

The estate is still in the hands of the Carroll family, who have owned it since 1689, when it was granted to Charles Carroll, grandfather of Charles Carroll of Carrollton, signer of the Declaration of Independence. It once consisted of between 13,000 and 15,000 acres, on which were situated several houses of other members of the family.

In the 1770s and 1780s, the property had a population of almost 500 slaves and it included a vineyard, a flour mill, a saw mill, a weaving manufactory, and the first sheep barns in Maryland. Gradually, parts of the estate have been sold, but it still comprises about 2,500 acres.

While the Carrolls have steadily modernized the farming operation, there were until relatively recently four brick and stone–base barns dating to the eighteenth century, one of which, built in 1710, was the oldest building on the property. These burned in 1968 in a fire that consumed five barns.

The manor house (though not in its present form) dates back to about 1735. In the eighteenth century there was a one-and-a-half-story brick house with kitchen and chapel dependencies on either side. A visitor in the early nineteenth century described it thus: "The house is an old one or at least the gradual growth of several generations, parts having been from time to time added —some one story, some two—some rough cast, other brick—so that although full of rooms, it is quite an insignificant place." In 1832 Charles Carroll of Doughoregan inherited the property from his grandfather, the signer, and extensively remodeled and enlarged it. The entire central block was raised to a full two stories, the roof of the chapel (shown above) was raised, the dependencies were attached to the main house, a balustrade was added to the roof line, and Greek Revival porticos were added on both entrance and garden façades. The complex then took on essentially the appearance it retains today. ❖

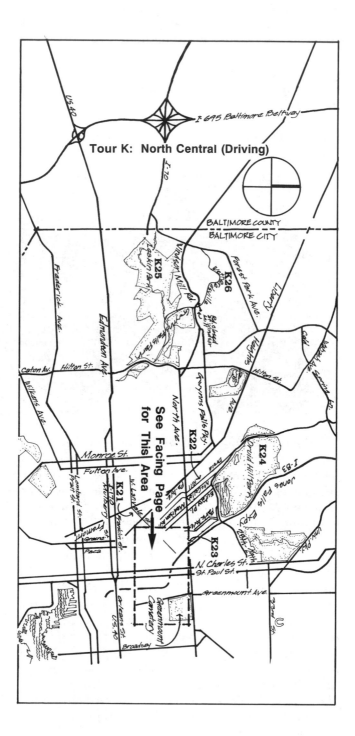

Tour K: North Central (Driving)

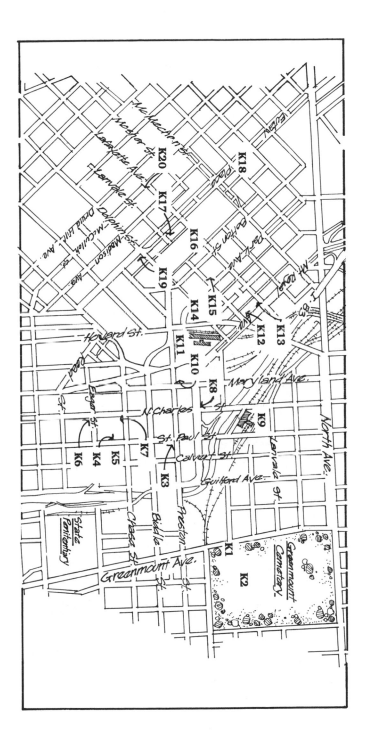

Tour K

North Central (Driving)

K1   GREEN MOUNT CEMETERY GATEHOUSE
     Greenmount Avenue and Oliver Street
     ca. 1846—Robert Cary Long, Jr.

K2   GREEN MOUNT CEMETERY CHAPEL
     1856—Niernsee and Neilson

K3   WINANS HOUSE
     1217 St. Paul Street
     1883—McKim, Mead, and White

K4   1020 ST. PAUL STREET
     1938—Charles Nes, Jr.

K5   BELVIDERE TERRACE
     1000 block North Calvert Street
     *ca. 1882—Wyatt and Sperry; J. Appleton Wilson and
     William T. Wilson*

K6   MARYLAND CLUB
     Charles and Eager streets
     1891—Baldwin and Pennington

K7   BELVEDERE CONDOMINIUM
     1 East Chase Street
     1903—Parker and Thomas

K8   UNIVERSITY OF BALTIMORE ACADEMIC
     CENTER (The Garage)
     Charles Street and Mount Royal Avenue
     *1906—Beecher, Friz, and Gregg; 1971—Fisher, Nes,
     Campbell, and Partners, renovation architect*

K9   PENNSYLVANIA STATION (Amtrak)
     1525 North Charles Street
     1911—Kenneth M. Murchison

K10 GREEK ORTHODOX CATHEDRAL OF THE
     ANNUNCIATION
     Maryland Avenue and Preston Street
     1889—Charles E. Cassell

K11 MOUNT ROYAL STATION
     Mount Royal Avenue and Cathedral Street
     *1896—Baldwin and Pennington;1964—Cochran,
     Stephenson, and Donkervoet*

K12 MARYLAND INSTITUTE, COLLEGE OF ART
1300 Mount Royal Avenue
1908—Pell and Corbett

K13 CORPUS CHRISTI CHURCH
Mount Royal and Lafayette avenues
1891—Patrick Charles Keeley

K14 BOLTON HILL

**K15 FAMILY AND CHILDREN'S SERVICES OF
CENTRAL MARYLAND**
Park Avenue and Lanvale Street
*1848—Robert Cary Long, Jr.; 1862—Edmund G. Lind;
1910–15—Laurence Hall Fowler*

K16 BOLTON COMMON
200 block West Lafayette Avenue, 1400 blocks of
Jordan and Mason streets
1968—Hugh Newell Jacobsen

K17 PRINCE HALL MASONS MASONIC TEMPLE
Eutaw Place and Lanvale Street
1893—Joseph E. Sperry

K18 EUTAW PLACE

K19 CITY TEMPLE OF BALTIMORE BAPTIST
Eutaw Place and Dolphin Street
1871—Thomas U. Walter

K20 BOOKER T. WASHINGTON MIDDLE SCHOOL
Lafayette Avenue and McCulloh Street
1895—Alfred Mason

K21 UPTON
811 West Lanvale Street
1838—architect unknown

K22 DRUID HILL CABLE RAILWAY POWER HOUSE
2500 Druid Hill Avenue and Retreat Street
1891—architect unknown

K23 MOUNT ROYAL TERRACE HOUSES
1900 block Mount Royal Terrace
ca. 1885—architect unknown

K24 DRUID HILL PARK
*1860 and after—Howard Daniels; George A. Frederick;
and others*

K25 CRIMEA
4921 Windsor Mill Road
1857—James Crawford Neilson

K26 DICKEYVILLE
Wetheredsville Road off Forest Park Avenue

This tour embraces more than a century and a half and a wide range of styles and building types. There are the country houses later engulfed by the city, from the Federal period Nicholas Rogers house—some of which still survives within the present Druid Hill Park Mansion House—to the Greek Revival Upton, to the faintly Italianate Crimea. There are the Victorian revivals, such as the Tudor Green Mount Cemetery Gatehouse, the Gothic Green Mount Cemetery Chapel, and Corpus Christi Church. There is late-nineteenth-century eclecticism as represented by Stanford White's Winans House and the Romanesque Revival Maryland Club and Greek Orthodox Cathedral. There is the turn-of-the-century return to classicism, with the Beaux-Arts Belvedere and Pennsylvania Station and the Renaissance Revival Maryland Institute Main Building. And there are more modern touches, such as the Art Deco 1020 St. Paul Street and the vaguely Wrightean University of Baltimore Academic Center.

One can also experience here a variety of types of row-house building, especially in Bolton Hill, but also at Belvidere Terrace and Eutaw Place. There are as well examples of adaptive reuse of buildings, as with Mount Royal Station and the aforementioned University of Baltimore building. And there are examples of what we might now call adaptive reuse of land, in the form of old country estates which have been turned to city park use, as at Druid Hill and Crimea.

In all, this tour offers numerous examples of how a city's survivors—whether individual buildings, neighborhoods, or tracts of open land—survive: some by tenaciously hanging on, some by changing a little or a lot to accommodate changing needs, some through the wisdom of city fathers, some through the wisdom of private preservationists, and some (notably Upton) seemingly through sheer luck more than anything else, at least until recently. ❖

K1 • GREEN MOUNT CEMETERY GATEHOUSE

(BCL, NR)
Greenmount Avenue and Oliver Street
ca. 1846—Robert Cary Long, Jr.

Long's Tudor Gothic gatehouse, with its 80-foot front and 40-foot towers, guards the entrance to the burial grounds of some of the city's most illustrious citizens and some of its most notorious—John Wilkes Booth is buried here. The land was formerly the country estate of merchant Robert Oliver. The first burial took place in 1839. ❖

K2 • GREEN MOUNT CEMETERY CHAPEL

(BCL, NR)
1856—Niernsee and Neilson

The buildings designed by these architects tend to "seize the landscape," according to Baltimore architectural historian Randolph W. Chalfant. Their Gothic Revival chapel, sited on an eminence in Green Mount Cemetery, certainly does; its 102-foot spire is visible for blocks. The chapel's flying buttresses, pinnacles, and tracery are in the decorated English Gothic style, and its strong silhouette is remarkably open. The octagonal structure, with a porch, is built of brownstone. The designers incorporated a stained-glass dome under the tower. ❖

K3 • WINANS HOUSE
1217 St. Paul Street
1883—McKim, Mead, and White

A perfectly integrated example of architecture and once one of Baltimore's finest private residences, the house was built for about $300,000 by Ross R. Winans, member of a family prominent in the construction of railroads in America and Russia. (He was the grandson of Ross Winans, engine-builder for the Baltimore and Ohio Railroad, and the son of Thomas Winans, who equipped the first Russian railroad. See Crimea [K25].)

The exterior of the Winans House is ruggedly compact, with rich surface patterns; inside, the grand entrance hall, intricately carved stairway, and splendid use of materials recommend it to the admirer of good design.

The first story is brownstone; the upper three are of narrow, light red brick, with brownstone trim and panels of carved relief. The solid, carefully proportioned building with its twin towers and dormers, fancy chimneys, and deep-set windows is in the French Chateau style popularized by Richard Morris Hunt.

The oak-paneled entrance hall has an open-beamed ceiling and is surrounded by a frieze of wood mosaic. Sliding doors permit the ground-floor rooms to be used in various combinations. In front, a lavishly ornamented staircase with parquet walls is lit by three grand windows of leaded glass. Plaster ceiling medallions, ornate fireplace mantels, burnished metal decorations, and elegant oak, teak, and mahogany woodwork—all in the grand Stanford White manner—occur throughout the house. Charles Follen McKim, White's partner, probably designed the exterior; Cass Gilbert, on-site superintendent for the firm, contributed some details.

In the rear, the former Winans stable building at 107 East Preston Street was designed by Wyatt and Nolting in the Romanesque Revival style and completed in 1888. Its brick and brownstone front presents a pair of large, highly detailed arches. The west façade had four major arches with semicircular windows and wrought-iron grilles; about 1930, one of these openings was converted into a side entrance. The parking lot was once a garden. Only its fountain remains, standing before a decorated brownstone wall and flanked by small benches.

A private girls' school occupied the Winans complex from 1914 to 1927. From 1928 through 1968, it was a funeral home. After that, doctors had offices in the mansion while the stable housed an architectural firm. In late 1995, the Agora Publishing Company, a publisher of financial newsletters and reports, acquired the Winans House, which it uses as its offices. ❖

K4 • 1020 ST. PAUL STREET
1938—Charles Nes, Jr.

This simple, appealing building was inspired by the International style of Walter Gropius and his followers at the Bauhaus, and was certainly one of the earliest buildings in Baltimore to reflect the style. Young architect Charles Nes created its clean lines and modern feeling for the architectural firm of Palmer and Lamdin, which first occupied the building; Nes later became a partner in a successor to that firm, Nes, Campbell, and Partners. The Art Deco touches of the entrance treatment perhaps compromise the Bauhaus style in theory, but they are restrained enough not to violate the building visually. Originally there was an open driveway under the second-floor south bay; it was later filled in to give the present appearance. The building in recent times has housed a law firm. ❖

K5 • BELVIDERE TERRACE

1000 block of North Calvert Street
ca. 1882—Wyatt and Sperry; J. Appleton Wilson and William T. Wilson

On the site of Belvidere, the John Eager Howard mansion, J. B. Noel Wyatt and others created, on both sides of this block of Calvert Street, terraces of houses with aspects of the then-popular Queen Anne Style, especially in variety of surface materials and large gables. They avoid the monotony found in many blocks of row houses. The false gables on the east row actually mask a mansard roof. The east side was designed by J. Appleton Wilson and William T. Wilson. The west side, pictured here, is by Wyatt and Sperry. ❖

K6 • MARYLAND CLUB

Charles and Eager streets
1891—Baldwin and Pennington

In the 1870s and 1880s Henry Hobson Richardson, based in Boston, created a Romanesque Revival style of

architecture which drew on earlier periods but achieved great originality and strength through Richardson's genius for use of materials, massing, and proportion. The style became wildly popular and was copied by many lesser architects to such a point that it became a cliché and fell from favor. But Richardson's impact on the work of later architects, especially Louis Sullivan and Frank Lloyd Wright, make him one of the most influential and important of American architects.

There is no Richardson building in Baltimore; but this example, probably designed by Pennington, although it fails to achieve the nobility of Richardson, gives some flavor of the style with its horizontality, balanced asymmetry, rough cut gray stone walls, large and low-arched entrance and flanking windows, and other window treatments, including the eyebrow windows in the roof. The generous interior spaces open off of a great hall with a staircase of monumental proportions. The exterior stone is Beaver Dam marble, and the interiors are appointed with mahogany, Tennessee marble, and quartered oak.

A 1995 fire did much interior damage, but the club was restored, with Walter Schamu of Schamu, Machowski, Doo, and Associates as architect in charge. It reopened in 1996. ❖

K7 • BELVEDERE CONDOMINIUM
(BCL, NR)
1 East Chase Street
1903—Parker and Thomas

Once the grandest of Baltimore's hotels, the Belvedere Hotel was designed in the popular turn-of-the-century style known as Beaux-Arts and is fairly typical of the style. Called "pictorial classicism," Beaux-Arts is characterized by elaborately decorated, symmetrical façades, often with advancing and receding fronts, combinations of columns and arches, doubled columns, and sculptural elements; it gives the viewer "plenty to look at," as one observer noted.

Designed by the Boston and Baltimore firm of Parker and Thomas, the Belvedere rises from a two-story rusticated base with a cornice at the third-floor level through a main body of brownish pink brick with quoins and other embellishments to a massive cornice at the eleventh floor. All this is surmounted by a 35-foot-high mansard roof with broad moldings at the hips and ornate dormers on the twelfth-floor level. Much of the decoration is of terra-cotta and metal simulating stone.

The interiors were done mostly in plasterwork described in 1904 as "a free version of Louis XVI." An exception is the lofty barroom with its walls of patterned brickwork and its patterned ceiling.

After a period of decline, the Belvedere was renovated in the late 1970s by Cochran, Stephenson, and Donkervoet. There followed a period of financial difficulties, but by the mid-1990s the building was being run on a complete condominium basis, with retail stores, restaurants, banquet facilities, offices, and eight floors of apartments. ❖

K8 • UNIVERSITY OF BALTIMORE ACADEMIC CENTER (The Garage)

Charles Street and Mount Royal Avenue
1906—Beecher, Friz, and Gregg; 1971—Fisher, Nes, Campbell, and Partners, renovation architect

Built to house the Automobile Club of Maryland and to provide a place for drivers to relax in the pioneering days of highway travel, the Garage originally contained a bowling alley, billiard room, roller-skating rink, gymnasium, and restaurant. It was also an automobile salesroom and was the model for others as the area turned into a center of the new car culture in Baltimore. (The former Monumental Motor Car Company showroom, designed in 1916 by Smith and May, still stands at Mount Royal and Maryland avenues.)

The Garage's wide roof overhang and low horizontality, emphasized by the broad fenestration, are reminiscent of the early work of Frank Lloyd Wright. The comparison was more apt before the second-story balcony was removed during the renovation. The three-story structure is of reinforced concrete faced with brick. Previously owned by an automobile dealer, it stood vacant for a time before being acquired by the University of Baltimore in 1968 and renovated as their academic and administration center. ❖

K9 • PENNSYLVANIA STATION (Amtrak)
(BCL, NR)
1525 North Charles Street
1911—Kenneth M. Murchison

Penn Station was constructed when Beaux-Arts Classicism was segueing into the Neoclassical Revival. The façade incorporates both styles: the coupled columns are emblematic of Beaux-Arts buildings, but the plain decoration is typical of the succeeding fashion.

Murchison was a New York architect. Penn Station is considerably less flamboyant in appearance than his Hoboken Terminal for the Delaware, Lackawanna, and Western Railroad, built in 1907 in true Beaux-Arts style. Rather, it more closely resembles his Scranton D L & W station building constructed the same year, and also McKim, Mead, and White's Neoclassical Pennsylvania Station in New York, completed in 1910 and destroyed in 1963.

Baltimore's Penn Station replaced previous station buildings of 1873 and 1885 on a site where several rail lines converged. Built at a cost of $750,000, it was intended as the Pennsylvania Railroad's response to its traditional and bitter rival, the Baltimore and Ohio Railroad, and the latter's 1896 Mount Royal Station a few blocks away. Penn Station is still, after several cycles of renovation, a very functional and imposing structure.

The steel-frame building is clad in granite and terracotta and has a cast-iron marquee running the length of the front and down the sides. Inside is a two-story lobby (with offices on the balcony level), covered by three domical skylights of leaded glass, each 23 feet in diameter. There are also decorative iron railings, walls of Sicilian marble, mahogany benches, bronze wall sconces, terrazzo floors with mosaic borders, and one of the few remaining intact installations of Rookwood ceramic tiles. These were produced by Cincinnati's Rookwood Pottery Company, the country's foremost art-pottery manufacturer, which developed complete interior decorative schemes for train stations and other buildings. The tiles can be seen around windows, wall sconces, and drinking fountains.

Penn Station is now owned by Amtrak. In the mid-1970s, the federal government undertook a major renovation of the building and finished it about ten years later at a cost of $6.7 million. This included the installation of a new ticket counter, elevator, and escalator, along with new plumbing, mechanical, and electrical systems. The stained-glass skylights, blacked out during World War II, were restored, as were the mahogany benches and tile floors. Missing wall sconces and Rookwood ceramic tiles were replaced. Skidmore, Owings, and Merrill; Robert J. Nash of Washington; and Leon Bridges of Baltimore were the renovation architects.

In 1995, the station was dramatically lit at night and a two-level, reinforced-concrete, underground parking garage beneath a landscaped plaza in front of the building was completed. A new entrance to the plaza from Charles Street and a new exit from the garage to the Jones Falls Expressway are planned as part of an overall $14 million upgrading that will improve traffic circulation and also enhance the visual perception of Baltimore's only operational railroad station. Whitman, Requardt, and Associates is the engineer-architect of the improvements. ❖

K10 • GREEK ORTHODOX CATHEDRAL OF THE ANNUNCIATION

Maryland Avenue and Preston Street
1889—Charles E. Cassell

Although its architectural style seems admirably suited to its present occupants, Cassell's Romanesque Revival building with its strong Byzantine influence was con-

structed as a Presbyterian church and used as one until 1934. The building was about to be destroyed for a gas station when the Greek Orthodox congregation, the oldest and largest in Maryland, acquired it in 1937. The large, semicircular auditorium dictates its unusual form. "The amphitheater is not only completely expressed, but constitutes the building," said critic Montgomery Schuyler in *The Architectural Record*.

The church was built of Port Deposit granite with light sandstone trim at a cost of $137,000. Carved stone decoration, polished marble columns, and four pairs of oak entrance doors, two of them curved, distinguish the exterior. In the 1950s, a new wing was added on the west. The interior of the church contains four Tiffany stained-glass windows. In the 1960s, a flat ceiling was installed, masking the original trusses that support the roof as well as new air-handling equipment and lights. A central icon screen was also added in front and the oak pews were refinished. In the 1980s, the balcony was extended and made curvilinear, a new chandelier was hung, and several new stained-glass windows were put in, considerably brightening the interior. ❖

K11 • MOUNT ROYAL STATION
(BCL, NR)
Mount Royal Avenue and Cathedral Street
1896—Baldwin and Pennington; 1964—Cochran, Stephenson, and Donkervoet

Built for the Baltimore and Ohio Railroad at the height of its power, and as a symbol of that power, Mount Royal

Station has always been striking. It is now additionally interesting as a good example of adaptive reuse: that is, how architecture no longer useful in its original role can be saved and converted to another use by imaginative redesign.

Architecturally, the building stands at a crossroads. The feel of its massing, the heavy granite walls, and the horizontality of the effect of station and shed behind show the influence of Richardsonian Romanesque. However, the windows are Italian Renaissance, like those of the Palazzo Medici-Riccardi and Palazzo Strozzi in Florence, and would be repeated a decade later in the Renaissance design of the Maryland Institute building up the hill [K12].

The largest passenger station ever built to accommodate one line when it opened, Mount Royal Station combined solidity of appearance with such lighter touches as its train shed girders. Built at track level in a hollow, it is thus seen from above. To some this increases its attractiveness, while others think it would be much more impressive if it were approached at eye level or from below.

The original interior was notable for the loftiness of its main waiting room. In 1964, no longer used as a station, it was sold to the Maryland Institute, College of Art, which was seeking to expand from its building a block away. The job of converting the building for maximum Institute use while preserving the interior was accomplished by Cochran, Stephenson, and Donkervoet, Inc., with Alexander Cochran as principal and Richard Donkervoet as project director.

The following is from an article by Cochran in Historic Preservation concerning the conversion: "The exterior was altered only by the enclosure of open roof areas. The interior was high enough to create two ample floors in much of the waiting room with the addition of a grand staircase on axis with a newly opened central space at the porte-cochere. Considerable interior architectural decoration was preserved in toto, such as the central columns, all the waiting room ceiling, much of the decorative floor and most of the exposed iron structure."

The building now houses studios for the Institute's sculpture programs, an auditorium, a major gallery space, the college's library, and offices. In a 1984 renovation the train shed roof was replaced, preserving its long line, and mezzanines were added in the library area. The college now has plans to move the library into another building and may move its interior design department to the station building in its place. ❖

K12 • MARYLAND INSTITUTE, COLLEGE OF ART
1300 Mount Royal Avenue
1908—Pell and Corbett

At the end of the nineteenth century there was a spate of architectural revivals in reaction to the century's me-

dieval throwbacks, Gothic and Romanesque. Almost at once appeared Beaux-Arts classicism, a purer Neoclassical revival, a Georgian revival, and a Renaissance revival. To the last of these categories belongs the Maryland Institute building, with its gleaming white marble façade, Italian Renaissance palazzo window treatment (compare the second-floor windows with those on Mount Royal Station [K11]), barrel-vaulted entry, imposing central court, and grand but too steep stairway.

In 1990–92 the building received a $5 million renovation, which modernized its mechanical and safety systems and some of its interior spaces and rehabilitated the central court. ❖

K13 • CORPUS CHRISTI CHURCH
Mount Royal and Lafayette avenues
1891—Patrick Charles Keeley

Viewed against the western sky on a clear day, Corpus Christi presents a sharply outlined, perfectly proportioned façade. Yet there is much more to the church: a variegated three-dimensional form and a richly decorated interior. Called "a landmark . . . a monument . . . a beautiful work of art," by Cardinal Gibbons when he consecrated it in 1891, Corpus Christi remains, after a

recent renovation, a truly handsome Gothic Revival church.

It was built at a cost of $200,000 in memory of Thomas C. Jenkins by his family and was formerly known as Jenkins Memorial Church. (The Jenkins family also donated the land for the Maryland Institute's main building next door.)

The church was designed by a Brooklyn architect with several hundred churches to his credit. (Corpus Christi closely resembles Keeley's Holy Name Cathedral, 1874, in Chicago.) The proportions were vastly improved in 1912 when the original stumpy, square spire was replaced by a much taller, octagonal one, also paid for by the Jenkins family.

A baptistry, two side chapels, and two sacristies project from the body of the building. Its walls are of Woodstock granite, 2½ feet thick, lined with brick inside. The windows are framed in Kentucky sandstone. The interior contains rare stained-glass windows and mosaics by London's John Hardman and Company, decorative marble from Tennessee and Siena, bronze doors, oak pews, and carved marble altars.

The building had fallen into disrepair when an extensive renovation was done in the 1980s that included a new roof and cleaning and pointing of the church's exterior. The interior was painted and restored and new heating, air-conditioning, electrical, and sound systems installed. ❖

K14 • BOLTON HILL

(NR)

The Bolton Hill neighborhood takes its name from Bolton, the early-nineteenth-century house that stood on the site of the present Fifth Regiment Armory, just south of the neighborhood. Now a historical and architectural preservation district, Bolton Hill is almost exclusively nineteenth century in character.

The earliest surviving houses are the two cottages, or villas: the one at Lanvale Street and Park Avenue dating from 1848 [K15] and the one a block away at Lanvale and Bolton Street from 1850. The semidetached houses in the 1300 block of John Street date to the 1850s, and the row houses primarily date from the 1860s to the 1890s.

What distinguishes Bolton Hill architecture in general is not so much the excellence of individual buildings or rows as the diversity of façades one can see in a walk around the neighborhood. There are groups notable for their unusually handsome proportions, as at the western end of the south side of the 200 block of West Lanvale Street, ending at Bolton Street. There are rows that make more imposing statements, as the one running north down the hill from the northwest corner of Park Avenue and Mosher Street. There are cottagey pairs with front porches in the 1200 block of Bolton Street and the 1300 block of Park Avenue. There are double houses here and there, as at the corner of Park Avenue and Lanvale Street. There are stone façades to contrast with the more usual brick façades, as in the 1200 block of John Street and the 1600 block of Park Avenue. There are individual curiosities, such as the house with the oriel window and Second-Empire style mansard roof at 1409 Park Avenue. There are individual blocks, such as the 1300 block of Bolton Street, where one can see up to half a dozen different types of individual buildings and rows mingling comfortably. There are infills of more modern groups which have attempted to be good neighbors in character and scale. One of the more successful of these is Bolton Place, off the 1100 block of Park Avenue, its houses grouped around an attractively intimate interior court, giving the feel of a quiet refuge from the city's bustle; another is Bolton Common [K16].

All in all, there's plenty to keep the stroller visually interested in this neighborhood, roughly bounded on the south by Dolphin Street, on the west by Eutaw Place, on the north by North Avenue, and on the east by Mount Royal Avenue.

With the exception of Eutaw Place [K18], which may or may not be counted part of Bolton Hill depending on your point of view, this was always a middle- and upper-middle-class area, never the preserve of the rich. It has been maintained down the years by the efforts of countless residents, and has a neighborhood improvement association that dates to World War I. There have been periods of deterioration, such as during and after World War II, when houses sold for as little as $3,000. But the neighborhood has always rebounded and remains a fashionable one, often compared to Washington's Georgetown or Philadelphia's Society Hill as a successful in-town residential area. ❖

K15 • FAMILY AND CHILDREN'S SERVICES OF CENTRAL MARYLAND

Park Avenue and Lanvale Street
1848—Robert Cary Long, Jr.; 1862—Edmund G. Lind;
1910–1915—Laurence Hall Fowler

Three prominent architects have been associated with this building. Robert Cary Long, Jr., designed the original "Gothick Cottage" typical of the type that dotted the eastern United States in the 1840s and 1850s. It is two and a half stories, of brick which has always been painted. The doorway, window, and roof trim are original.

About 1862 Lind added the bay window on the west side and the two "enclosed verandas" flanking the entrance porch and enlarging the two front rooms. Fifty years later Fowler added the side porch, Georgianized the dining room, front hall, and staircase with Annapolis detailing, eased the rise of the stair, enlarged the landing, and tucked a lavatory under it.

Since 1937 the house has been used by the Family and Children's Society, now known as Family and Children's Services of Central Maryland. ❖

K16 • BOLTON COMMON

200 block West Lafayette Avenue, 1400 blocks of Jordan and Mason streets
1968—Hugh Newell Jacobsen

This complex of thirty-five town houses arranged roughly in an omega shape with a private oval-shaped

park in the center has won awards for town house design and land use, including a national American Institute of Architects award in 1969.

The architect created modern houses which achieve a degree of harmony with the nineteenth-century row houses of neighboring Bolton Hill. This involved the use of North Carolina brick and other materials more expensive than, but aesthetically preferable to, local materials.

The houses look similar in size from the front, but there is actually a wide variance, from 18-by-30-foot, two-bedroom ones to 20-by-40-foot, four-bedroom houses with two-story living rooms. Each house has a private walled garden in the rear.

The architect, Jacobsen, and the builder, Stanley I. Panitz, were responsible for touches that usually go unnoticed, such as completely concealed rain gutters and underground telephone and electric wires, which help to enhance this attractive grouping.

Other modern-day Bolton Hill infills include the group across Lafayette Avenue from these and Bolton Place [see K14]. ❖

K17 • PRINCE HALL MASONS
MASONIC TEMPLE
Eutaw Place and Lanvale Street
1893—Joseph E. Sperry

With the sun behind them in the evening, the three domes of the former Eutaw Place Temple (Oheb Sha-

lom Synagogue) form one of the outstanding features of the Baltimore skyline. The style is Byzantine. The heavy, almost fortresslike exterior (the walls are of Beaver Dam marble) is in marked contrast to the light, spacious interior. The latter consists of a single, mosquelike room, roughly 82 feet square, under a series of half-domes, arches, and vaults. The woodwork is of quartered oak. Surrounded by galleries on three sides, the space can accommodate 2,200 people. In 1892, the temple cost about $225,000 to build. In 1961, it was purchased by the Prince Hall Masons, who use it for meetings and concerts. ❖

K18 • EUTAW PLACE

The purpose behind creating boulevards or squares with landscaped parks in the middle, as in Mount Vernon Place, Union Square, Broadway, Park Avenue, and here, was to encourage residential development and enhance property values. It worked on Eutaw Place as well as anywhere, for in the last part of the nineteenth

century this became one of the most fashionable sections of Baltimore in which to live. Some of the grandest town houses of the era were built here, as well as the stately Marlborough Apartments. Residents of Eutaw Place at one time or another included the Hutzlers and Schleissners, both of local department-store fame; Dr. Howard Kelly, one of Johns Hopkins Hospital's "big four" doctors pictured in the well-known painting by John Singer Sargent; the Cone sisters, Claribel and Etta, whose great collection of modern art remains the chief jewel in the crown of the Baltimore Museum of Art; and civil rights activist Lillie Carroll Jackson.

Unfortunately, after World War II, many of the Eutaw Place houses were torn down in the rush of urban renewal and replaced with public housing, a school, and other such standard buildings. But more recently preservation reared its welcome head, and the demolition was stalled. What hadn't been destroyed has remained. ❖

K19 • CITY TEMPLE OF BALTIMORE BAPTIST
Eutaw Place and Dolphin Street
1871 — Thomas U. Walter

Gothic Revival in style, the former Eutaw Place Baptist Church, with walls of white marble, is the only building in Baltimore by Walter, the architect of the dome and extensions of the wings of the U.S. Capitol. The 190-foot

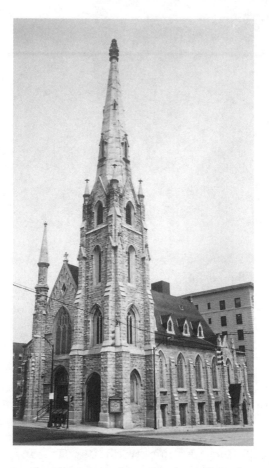

tower predominates, and so condensed is the entire structure on its corner site, that it almost appears fore-shortened. The interior is a single open space free of supporting columns with the exception of two small ones under the balcony; the roof load is borne by wooden trusses. The false ribs, beams, moldings, and ceiling pendants are plaster, and the church furniture is walnut. ❖

K20 • BOOKER T. WASHINGTON MIDDLE SCHOOL
(BCL)
Lafayette Avenue and McCulloh Street
1895—Alfred Mason

Mason's superb Romanesque Revival structure was built of red brick and carved Seneca stone as the Western

High School. Besides classrooms, it contained a gymnasium, assembly rooms, and laboratories. The tower is functional as well as decorative, its windows providing extra light for the corner rooms. Later additions date from 1911 and 1951. Although threatened with destruction fifteen years ago, the building was saved and is once again in use as a school. ❖

K21 • UPTON
(NR)
811 West Lanvale Street
1838—architect unknown

Upton, a Greek Revival country house, is a survivor. Despite several remodelings for various uses, the mansion essentially retains its original form, floor plan, and interior details.

Upton was built for David Stewart, briefly a U.S. senator. With extensive adjacent grounds and situated on an eminence, the two-and-a-half-story brick house had a commanding view of the city and harbor from the garden (south) side, and was admirably suited for entertaining. To the left of the central hall that divides the ground floor in half are two rooms, originally connected, that served as a double parlor. The second floor, similarly divided, contained bedrooms, and the attic, under a hipped roof, also provided living quarters, probably for servants. The original cast-iron porch railings featuring a motif from the Stewart family crest, and interior pilasters, molded cornices, doors, and baseboards remain intact.

Upton was still a private residence when a small service wing was added to the west side in about 1868. After that it became, successively, a radio station, an interracial music conservatory, and a public school for special students. The City of Baltimore acquired Upton in the 1950s, renovated the mansion as a classroom building, and replaced the original two-story porch on the south side with a brick stair tower, but retained the building's architectural integrity. It is now The Upton School. ❖

K22 • DRUID HILL CABLE
RAILWAY POWER HOUSE
2500 Druid Hill Avenue and Retreat Street
1891—architect unknown

Built as the northern terminus of the Baltimore Traction Company, which operated a cable car route between Druid Hill and Patterson parks, the building once housed cars, cable machinery driven by two 500-horsepower Corliss steam engines, and other equipment. Now it serves as a warehouse, but its Romanesque Revival arches, tower, and distinctive roofline make it a still powerful presence on its corner site. ❖

K23 • MOUNT ROYAL TERRACE HOUSES

1900 block Mount Royal Terrace
ca. 1885—architect unknown

The variety of color and texture in surface materials characteristic of the Queen Anne style, and the furniturelike columns and porch spindles of the Eastlake style can be seen in repeated patterns in the nineteen row houses that make up Mount Royal Terrace. Although there is a similar group farther west at North Avenue and Fulton Street, row houses of this style are a relative rarity in the city. Statuary and urns in a small park setting and the gateways of the former entrance to

Druid Hill Park face Mount Royal Terrace, a remnant of nineteenth-century Baltimore, whose new borders are defined by heavily traveled roadways. ❖

K24 • DRUID HILL PARK
(BCL, NR)
1860 and after—Howard Daniels; George A. Frederick; and others

One of Baltimore's great amenities is its collection of public parks, thirty in all, covering more than 6,000 acres. Many of them are small areas under the jurisdiction of the Department of Recreation and Parks, such as the four squares in Mount Vernon and Washington places. But there are ten large parks, and the principal reason Baltimore has them is that a remarkably consistent and forward-looking parks board acquired by gift or purchase seven major estates between 1827 and 1942, as the city moved outward.

The first of these was a portion of the present Patterson Park, given in 1827 by William Patterson (father of Betsy Patterson Bonaparte, famous for having married Napoleon's brother Jerome). Other estates that became parks include Clifton, summer home of Johns Hopkins; Druid Hill; Crimea, summer home of Thomas DeKay Winans and now known as Leakin Park; and Cylburn, bought in 1942 for $42,000. One can only imagine what a 180-acre tract of prime northwest Baltimore land would bring today on the open market.

Another factor to be credited to the parks board is that it retained a number of the imposing estate man-

sions built in the eighteenth and nineteenth centuries and converted them to park use, thus preserving several architecturally important buildings. These include the mansion house in Druid Hill Park; Clifton [G10]; Cylburn [N18]; Crimea [K25]; and Mount Clare [I5] in Carroll Park. Mount Clare is an exception to the parks-use category; it has become a house museum.

Druid Hill, at something over 600 acres, is not the largest of the city parks (that honor goes to Gwynns Falls Park at about 700 acres). Thanks to its creative natural landscaping and the wealth of interesting buildings constructed and preserved there, it is both the most beautiful and the most interesting of Baltimore's parks. It is also a good example of how the parks were developed from estates.

The history of Druid Hill goes back to 1688. By 1716 some of the land was owned by the Rogers family, who would figure so prominently in its story. In the 1780s Colonel Nicholas Rogers raised a house which burned in 1796, and the subsequent house, which is the core of the present mansion house building, dates to about 1801. It was a Federal period structure with tall main-floor windows and some similarity to Homewood. The colonel died in 1822 and the estate passed to his son Lloyd Nicholas Rogers, who married the great-granddaughter of Martha Washington and, after her death, the granddaughter of James Monroe. The property, which had had several names under successive owners, was being called Druid Hill by the first decade of the nineteenth century, but no one knows why.

By the middle of the nineteenth century the expanding city sought to buy the estate for a park, a move which Lloyd Rogers resisted. But two events intervened:

over his objections, the Green Spring Avenue Company was granted a right-of-way for a turnpike to run through the property, and in 1858 Baltimore Mayor Thomas Swann attached a tax on the gross receipts of a new street railway, the proceeds to pay for establishing "one or more large parks." Money accumulated quickly, and in 1860 Rogers sold the property for a little less than $500,000 ($1,000 an acre—the park has since been expanded). He moved out in mid-October 1860 and died less than a month later.

The land had apparently been well landscaped by Colonel Rogers. Joanne Giza and Catharine F. Black, in their book *Great Baltimore Houses* (from which much information about the house has been taken), quote Thomas Scharf's earlier history of Baltimore, stating that Colonel Rogers had the land laid out "in the best tradition of English landscape gardening." Under city ownership, engineer Augustus Faul supervised the landscaping along the property's natural lines; the design was by Howard Daniels, described as "landscape gardener and engineer." Daniels took advantage of the hills and valleys to create lakes, scenic views, picnic groves, pathways, and promenades. George A. Frederick designed a number of fanciful pavilions, most of which still remain and are believed to be among the oldest park buildings in the country. These originally served as stops along a small railway that wound through the park and that has long since been discontinued. Either Frederick or John H. B. Latrobe (both claimed it) designed the imposing Madison Avenue gateway to the park.

The mansion house has undergone a number of changes. In 1863 the most sweeping were executed by John H. B. Latrobe, who removed the entrance, added 20-foot-wide open porches all around the house, tore out the house's middle section, and Victorianized it with Gothic arches and a new staircase leading to a newly installed cupola. This would be thought architectural desecration today, but the building has worked well for the purposes to which it has been put. The surrounding pavilions were enclosed in the 1930s. In the late 1970s the house vastly benefited from an $850,000 restoration under the direction of architect Michael F. Trostel, who preserved both Federal period elements of the original house and Victorian additions. The building now houses administrative offices of the Baltimore Zoo, which in recent years has itself been undergoing a twenty-year plan of major improvements.

In 1888, the conservatory, a large greenhouse of metal and glass construction, possibly by Frederick, was added. It is believed to be the oldest surviving public conservatory building in the country and has been the subject of a recent $800,000 restoration.

A structure which had been the Maryland Building at the Philadelphia Centennial Exposition of 1876 was moved to a knoll near the mansion house after the exposition ended. It was restored in 1978 and reopened as headquarters of the Baltimore (now Maryland) Zoological Society. One other building should be mentioned: the large pool house of 1924 by Josias and Pleasants Pennington.

During the Depression and World War II, and for some years afterward, the park declined somewhat. More recently, some parts have improved, while other parts appear to be neglected. ❖

K25 • CRIMEA
(BCL)
4921 Windsor Mill Road
1857—James Crawford Neilson

Thomas DeKay Winans chose a spectacular setting on the city's west side to build his summer house. Thomas

Winans was a son of Ross Winans, locomotive builder for the Baltimore and Ohio Railroad. In 1843, Thomas and his brother William, with other engineers, won a five-year, $7 million contract from Czar Nicholas I to produce the engines and rolling stock for the first railroad (420 miles long) between Moscow and St. Petersburg. Establishing a plant at Alexandrovsky, near St. Petersburg, they finished the work a year early and returned to America as wealthy men. Crimea and Alexandroffsky, Thomas's fantastic estate on West Baltimore Street (designed by Niernsee and Neilson and razed in 1926), were the local monuments to this exotic and profitable Russian adventure. (Thomas's son, Ross R. Winans, built the Winans House [K3]).

Crimea, a faintly Italianate mansion originally known as Orianda, sits on the high point of Winans's estate, which once encompassed nearly 1,000 acres. It is a three-story building of ashlar stone construction. (The basement creates a fourth story on the south side due to the slope of the land.) Verandas with heavy wooden railings and brackets enclose three of its sides, and large eave pendants and a cupola adorn the roof.

In 1940, the City of Baltimore bought 200 acres of the Crimea property for roughly $108,000 and eight years later incorporated the mansion into the park system. Crimea is now part of Leakin Park, and the mansion is used as offices for the Parks and People Foundation. Also on the grounds and built in the same style are a carriage house and a caretaker's home. (The latter is now the headquarters of an Outward Bound program.)

Near the park entrance is a small wooden Victorian chapel with a steeply sloping roof and bargeboards. Heavily damaged by lightning in 1987, it was restored two years later. ❖

K26 • DICKEYVILLE
(NR)
Wetheredsville Road off Forest Park Avenue

Dickeyville is less important for the design of its individual buildings than for its overall appearance and secluded atmosphere as a historic mill town. It grew up around several mills that once occupied the banks of the Gwynns Falls. In 1762, Wimbert Tschudi, a Swiss, built a stone house and grist mill alongside the stream. Around 1812 the Franklin Company erected a factory and paper mill; some of the village's stone houses date from this period.

The Wethered family bought the factory in 1829 and converted it to a woolen mill. The town (taking the name of Wetheredsville) prospered, and its wool cloth won prizes. Later, a cotton mill was added; at one time it employed 210 hands.

In 1854, the mills burned to the ground and were rebuilt. Three years later, a dam was washed away upstream; the resultant flood caused $100,000 worth of damage to the mills. Another "great freshet" in 1868 demolished a covered bridge at Wetheredsville and carried away part of the schoolhouse. Later, there were more fires in the mills.

In 1871, the Wethereds sold three mills, several stone houses, and 300 acres to William J. Dickey for $82,000. The new owner added several frame mill houses, a warehouse of dark gray rubble stone with red brick trim on Pickwick Road and, in 1885, the white clapboard Dickey Memorial Presbyterian Church on Wetheredsville Road. In the 1880s, four hundred hands worked in the mills and the town entered a period of prosperity that lasted until 1909, when the Dickeys sold out. Dickeyville subsequently went into an economic decline that was aggravated by the Depression.

In 1934, the town was sold at auction to the Maryland Title Guarantee Company, which paid $42,000 for 65 acres of land, eighty-one stone, frame, and brick buildings, a mansion house, and three factories. The Dickeys reacquired the mills in 1954, and they continued to produce everything from kitchen cabinets to gun covers, but by that time a new industry had sprung up: providing housing for people attracted by Dickeyville's bucolic charm. The former Ashland Chapel at Pickwick and Wetheredsville roads, built in 1849, became a private home, as did the old mill office and jail at 2435 Pickwick Road.

Milling operations ended in Dickeyville in 1967 when production was shifted to South Carolina. The former Ballymena Woolen Mill (named for the town in Ireland from which the Dickey family emigrated), a two-story structure with double windows overlooking Wetheredsville Road, dates from 1873 and is now occupied by various commercial and cultural enterprises. ❖

Tour L

North Charles Street and Environs (driving)

L1   LOVELY LANE UNITED METHODIST CHURCH
2200 St. Paul Street
1887—McKim, Mead, and White

L2   GOUCHER HALL AND CAMPUS
2220 St. Paul Street
*1888—McKim, Mead, and White, with Charles L.
Carson*

L3   GOUCHER HOUSE
2313 St. Paul Street
1892—McKim, Mead, and White

L4   ST. JOHN'S EPISCOPAL CHURCH,
      HUNTINGDON
Greenmount Avenue and Thirtieth Street
*1847—Robert Cary Long, Jr.; 1859—John W.
Priest; 1877—Henry M. Congdon*

L5   OAKLAND SPRING HOUSE
Grounds of the Baltimore Museum of Art
ca. 1812—Benjamin H. Latrobe

L6   BALTIMORE MUSEUM OF ART
Art Museum Drive, Wyman Park
*1929—John Russell Pope; 1982 and 1994—Bower,
Lewis, Thrower; 1988—Sasaki Associates*

L7   WOLMAN HOUSE
3213 North Charles Street
1939—Laurence Hall Fowler

L8   HOMEWOOD
Charles and Thirty-fourth streets
*1801 and after—Charles Carroll of Homewood; Robert
and William Edwards, builders*

L9   GILMAN HALL
The Johns Hopkins University
1904—Parker and Thomas

L10   UNIVERSITY BAPTIST CHURCH
Charles and Thirty-fourth streets
1926—John Russell Pope

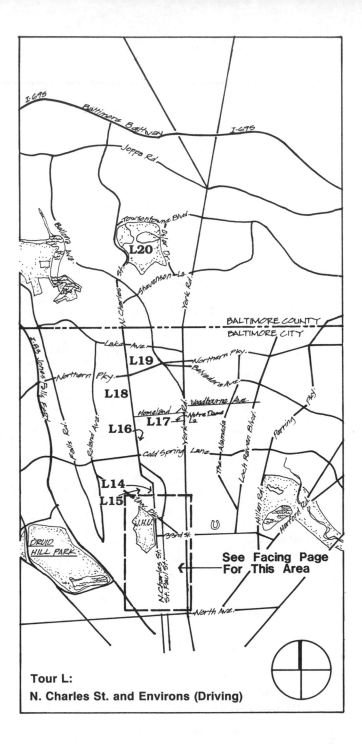

**See Facing Page
For This Area**

**Tour L:
N. Charles St. and Environs (Driving)**

L11 CARNEGIE INSTITUTE EMBRYOLOGY
BUILDING
University Parkway and San Martin Drive
1962—Anderson, Beckwith, and Haible

L12 EPISCOPAL CATHEDRAL OF THE
INCARNATION
University Parkway and St. Paul Street
1909–47—various architects

L13 SCOTTISH RITE TEMPLE OF FREEMASONRY
Charles and Thirty-ninth streets
1930 and after—Clyde N. Friz, with John Russell Pope

L14 HIGHFIELD HOUSE CONDOMINIUM
4000 North Charles Street
1964—Mies van der Rohe

L15 LAURENCE HALL FOWLER RESIDENCE
10 West Highfield Road
1925—Laurence Hall Fowler

L16 EVERGREEN
4545 North Charles Street
*1857–58—architect unknown; 1885—Charles L.
Carson; 1922–41—Laurence Hall Fowler*

L17 GALLAGHER MANSION
431 Notre Dame Lane
*ca. 1855—architect unknown; 1879—Edmund G.
Lind, renovation architect; 1996—Smeallie, Orrick,
and Janka, Ltd., renovation architect*

L18 CATHEDRAL OF MARY OUR QUEEN
5200 North Charles Street
1959—Maginnis and Walsh

L19 CHURCH OF THE REDEEMER
5603 North Charles Street
1958—Pietro Belluschi; RTKL Associates, Inc.

L20 SHEPPARD AND ENOCH PRATT HOSPITAL
6501 North Charles Street
*1858–88—Dixon and Dixon, with D. Tilden Brown,
Calvert Vaux*

Charles Street is Baltimore's north-south axis and its
most important as well as its longest street. Not only
has the city grown up fairly equally on both sides of this
thoroughfare, but some of its finest buildings lie along

or near the street. The city grew toward some of the examples on this tour, such as Homewood and Evergreen; more were built where they were because Charles Street was already there.

Almost a century after Homewood, Stanford White's Lovely Lane Methodist Church, although Romanesque in flavor, was a reflection of the attempt to find an American style through "free eclecticism." Forty years after that, John Russell Pope's Baltimore Museum, University Baptist Church, and Scottish Rite Temple used classical models, even as the Bauhaus style was flowering elsewhere. When the products of the Bauhaus finally arrived in Baltimore in the 1950s and 1960s, as at Highfield House, the style was so familiar that it had attained a kind of classicism of its own. Other buildings are notable for being modern but fitting in with their more traditional surroundings; Belluschi's Church of the Redeemer is an outstanding example.

Baltimore has often been called an ugly city, and some of it certainly is. But it has a trio of extraordinarily well-planned suburbs in Roland Park, Homeland, and Guilford, which lie along and not far from Charles Street, from University Parkway north almost to the city line.

From the downtown shopping district to the northern suburbs, Charles Street has been thought of as something of a showplace; a ride along it will show that with some exceptions those who have built along Charles Street have at least made some attempt to live up to its rich if conservative character. ❖

L1 • LOVELY LANE UNITED METHODIST CHURCH
(BCL, NR)
2200 St. Paul Street
1887—McKim, Mead, and White

The fortress of American Methodism, Lovely Lane defines its neighborhood, the home of Goucher College until the 1950s. Stanford White, designer of the church and several college buildings, wrote in a rare personal description of his work:

> The whole treatment is broad, simple, and natural, without ostentation or ornamentation of any kind. Techni-

cally, from an architectural standpoint, the building belongs to the order of the early churches and basilicas in Ravenna. The exterior is built in undressed ashlar with a natural face, with ample porches and broad flights of steps. . . . The mass of the church, of which the tower is the aspiring point, is carried out by the College which is now being built, and which will balance with the mass of the tower.

The interior consists of the church proper and a large Sunday School, with subsidiary rooms, the Pastor's house connecting with the college. The church proper is a vast auditorium of an elliptical shape, with a light gallery running around the entire auditorium. The detail leans toward a classic treatment. The color scheme, befitting a church of this character of architecture, is both quiet and rich. The vault of the auditorium is treated in blue and gold in exact representation of the heavens at night.

There were about fifty houses in the mostly wooded area beyond the city line at Boundary Avenue (now North Avenue) when construction began in 1884, one hundred years after the Christmas Conference at Lovely Lane Meeting House, Baltimore, that resulted in the formation of the American Methodist Episcopal

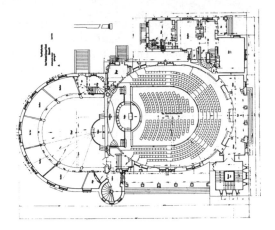

Church. (The meetinghouse was located on what is now
Redwood Street.) John Franklin Goucher, church pastor, donated the adjacent land for the first building of
the Woman's College of Baltimore City, established in
1885. In 1890, he became the second president of the
college, which was later named for him.

Intuitively grasping the symbolic significance of
Lovely Lane, his firm's first church, White fused several
borrowed elements into a bold and forceful Romanesque
Revival composition. The 186-foot, 10-story bell tower, with
its conical roof, built of 6,000 tons of Port Deposit granite,
was modeled on the campanile of the eleventh-century
brick Church of St. Maria of Pomposa, east of Ferrara,
Italy. White regarded his tower as the southern boundary
and focus of the church-college complex, but the building
committee rejected as "too Roman" his idea of putting a
cross on top. They compromised by arranging the tower
windows in a cruciform pattern; when lit up at night, they
are visible for blocks around.

Similarly, White adapted design details from Ravenna churches and mausoleums for his major interior
space, the oval-shaped auditorium, whose theatrical
seating and lighting allow its use for pageants and concerts as well as religious services. The clerestory window
designs are abstractions of the mosaics decorating
Ravenna's tomb of Galla Placidia, built in 450. White's
original lighting scheme—a crown of three hundred forty gas jets below the vaulted ceiling that cast no
shadows—was based on techniques used in Ravenna's
San Vitale.

The cupola of Galla Placidia has a star-decorated ceiling. The Lovely Lane auditorium ceiling mural (now badly deteriorated), containing 719 stars and planets representing the appearance of the heavens on the morning of the dedication, was based on a star chart prepared by Simon Newcomb, the noted American astronomer and professor at The Johns Hopkins University. (The church was dedicated November 6, 1887; more than 5,000 people attended the day-long services.)

The secondary interior space, behind the auditorium, is the chapel, also oval-shaped with a gallery and Tiffany stained-glass windows. The form of the chapel, which features six radiating Sunday school classrooms that can be opened onto the main space (the "Akron plan"), along with that of the auditorium, influenced later church planning.

As part of his total design, White oversaw everything from the window and carpet patterns to the end castings for the auditorium seats, which remain intact, as does the original heating and ventilating system installed by Baltimore's Bartlett, Hayward and Co., with individually controlled registers under the seats. White exercised his usual taste in fine materials: black birch for the auditorium woodwork (including that covering the cast-iron columns supporting the balcony), oak, mahogany, black walnut, and ash in the adjoining parsonage. There is also a handsome, tightly wound wooden staircase in the hallway between the auditorium and chapel and several tiled fireplaces.

Lovely Lane cost $250,000 when it was built. An $8 million fund-raising program has recently been undertaken to restore the building, including the 130-ton tile roof, supported by iron and timber Howe trusses, and the interior of the church. So far, the tower has been repointed and reroofed with terra-cotta roof tiles. The church roof, originally covered with tiles custom-made in Baltimore, has received a temporary shingle roof which will be covered permanently with ceramic tiles (made elsewhere). ❖

L2 • GOUCHER HALL AND CAMPUS

(NR)
2220 St. Paul Street
1888—McKim, Mead, and White, with Charles L. Carson

McKim, Mead, and White provided the site plan for the college and the designs for its first four buildings, the initial one being Goucher Hall. (This effort preceded their plans for New York's Columbia College.) Since Stanford White designed the next three Goucher buildings, it is probable that he also designed this one, although absolute proof is lacking. It is also likely that Charles L. Carson, superintending architect for Lovely Lane, had a hand in this and some of the other buildings.

According to local legend, Carson and Benjamin F. Bennett (contractor for the church and several of the college buildings) gave Goucher Hall the shape of the letter "E" as a memorial to Goucher's daughter Eleanor, who died at a young age. It is built of granite in the Romanesque Revival style and has a red tile roof. Originally, a large, open central hall divided the interior from top to bottom and front to back, with galleries on the upper floors for exhibit cases; the rest of the space was devoted to lecture rooms and laboratories. The rotunda has since been filled in with an elevator and the galleries no longer exist, although some of the original classroom spaces remain. The building is now owned by the Hearing and Speech Agency, which uses it for their school and clinics.

Bennett Hall, to the north at 2300 St. Paul Street, designed by White, again using the same materials and the same style, was constructed in 1889, with a hipped roof and a polygonal tower that was later removed. A swimming pool and bowling alley were located in the basement and a gymnasium on the upper floors. A similarly styled rear annex, connected by a bridge over Lovegrove Street, was added in 1894. Both structures were renovated in 1986 for the current occupant, the Maryland Geological Survey.

The last classroom building added to the campus, whose primary axes are St. Paul and Twenty-third streets, was Catherine Hooper Hall (Girls' Latin School), at 2401 St. Paul Street, in 1893. Designed by White in the same style as the rest, it was used initially as a preparatory school for the college and then to house its physics and chemistry departments. The New Antioch Baptist Church has the building now.

Four dormitory buildings remain from the area's college days, prominent brick structures with stone bases and trim, large arched entrances, and swelled fronts. Their architect is unknown, but they were all built by Benjamin F. Bennett. Alfheim Hall, at 2304 North Calvert Street, built in 1889, served as the model for the other three. It housed fifty students, a kitchen and dining room, laundry, and dispensary. Glitner Hall, at 2300 North Charles Street, was added in 1892. Both are four-story buildings with flat roofs and bracketed cornices and are currently used as private offices.

In 1894, Fensal Hall was built at 2300 Maryland Avenue, and the following year, Vingolf Hall at 101 West Twenty-fourth Street. (The names come from Norse mythology.) They are five-story buildings with mansard roofs and both are occupied by the Mayor's Office of Employment Development. ❖

L3 • GOUCHER HOUSE
(BCL)
2313 St. Paul Street
1892—McKim, Mead, and White

For his sole exercise in domestic architecture in the neighborhood, Stanford White employed Pompeian brick and the Italian Renaissance mode in the house he designed for John Franklin Goucher, church pastor and college president. It is modeled on a Florentine palace. The interior is laid out around a central hall with an oak staircase and incorporates some of

the opulent materials characteristic of the architect's work: Mexican onyx, Siena marble, exotic woods. The building is now the corporate headquarters of a fraternity. ❖

L4 • ST. JOHN'S CHURCH, HUNTINGDON

Greenmount Avenue and Thirtieth Street
*1847—Robert Cary Long, Jr.; 1859—John W. Priest;
1877—Henry M. Congdon*

As originally built, St. John's was one of the early Gothic Revival churches in Baltimore. It was influenced by the Ecclesiological movement in England, which in the 1840s strove to influence the design of churches outside of Britain. Bishop William Whittingham of Maryland was a member of the Ecclesiological Society and, according to a St. John's publication, "through his influence St. John's was built in the Gothic style recommended for American country churches."

The church is supposed to have been one of many influenced by the design of St. Michael's, Long Stanton, in England; and St. James the Less in Philadelphia, closely modeled after St. Michael's. The parish register

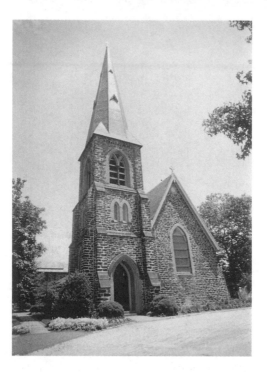

of St. John's mentions for the year 1846 commencement of the church "to plans prepared by R.C. Long, Architect"—obviously Robert Cary Long, Jr.

In 1858 that church was a victim of arson and the present church—or part of it—was erected in 1859. It is thought that the remains of the original foundation and walls were used. The parish register records that a Mr. Priest of New York "was unanimously invited to give plans and superintend the new church." That was John W. Priest, who was at the time also overseeing St. Luke's in Baltimore [J9].

The stone church built in 1859 consisted of the tower and about as much of the present church as the nave of four bays with lancet windows. The south porch and chimney probably closely resemble those of the original church, since they are much like those at St. James the Less. The present transepts and chancel were added in 1877 to a design by Henry M. Congdon, another New York architect and the successor to Priest.

The interior has undergone various decoration changes down the years, so it is probably best to mention only the recent ones which have given the church its present appearance. In 1980 the Reverend Douglas Pitt became rector and during his eleven-year tenure

undertook extensive changes. Among them were the
ashlaring (painting to resemble stone) of the interior
walls; cleaning of the ceiling and cleaning and revarnish-
ing of the panels at the top of the walls; and restoration
of the late-Victorian painted decoration of the east wall
around the window behind the altar. The iron graveyard
fence was also added under Mr. Pitt, after the design of
that at Otterbein Church [H2]. The rectory, shown above,
was built in 1868. Further changes to the interior, including additional painted decoration, have been undertaken
under Mr. Pitt's successor, the Reverend Jesse Parker. ❖

L5 • OAKLAND SPRING HOUSE
(BCL)
Grounds of the Baltimore Museum of Art
ca. 1812—Benjamin H. Latrobe

This small but beautiful building with its fine Ionic
porch is Baltimore's other extant Latrobe building,
aside from the Basilica of the Assumption [B9]. It originally stood on the grounds of Robert Goodloe Harper's
country estate, Oakland, the land of which now forms
part of Roland Park [N10]. The spring house, or probably more accurately the dairy, stood near the present
Spring House Lane, East of Falls Road and across from
Cross Keys. It was one of a number of buildings, including the stables, that Latrobe designed for Oakland. A
Baltimore Museum of Art publication quotes an 1827
letter by Henry Gilpin: "In a fine grove with a turf like
emerald itself is the Dairy, a building built by Genl.

Harper after a design by Latrobe taken I presume from the little temple on the Illipces given by Stuart. . . . " This refers to James Stuart and Nicholas Revett's *The Antiquities of Athens* (1762). The great Baltimore collector Robert Gilmor, Jr., also wrote in his diary in 1827 that "The prettiest building at Oakland is the Dairy in the form of an ancient temple with Ionic Portico of 4 columns."

In 1994, coincidental with completing its New Wing for Modern Art just behind the spring house, the museum had the building restored and lighted. It had been moved to the museum grounds in 1932 as the gift of W. J. O'Brien. ❖

L6 • BALTIMORE MUSEUM OF ART
(BCL)
Art Museum Drive, Wyman Park
1929—John Russell Pope; 1982 and 1994—Bower, Lewis, Thrower; 1988—Sasaki Associates

Over the span of seven decades this now sprawling museum complex has grown to more than four times its original size (or more than six times, counting the sculpture gardens), employing a succession of architects. If the results are, perhaps inevitably, mixed, three positive comments are in order at the outset: the complex works better for the collections it houses than it does as an overall architectural statement; thanks to its axial layout, it is a less difficult museum to become oriented to than it may at first seem; and the dignified classical façade of

John Russell Pope's original building has not been obscured by subsequent additions—although no longer
the main entrance point, it's still the complex's principal visual statement.

Pope, at the time he designed the museum's original building, was the leading American Classical Revival
architect, now known for the original National Gallery
building in Washington. The Baltimore museum building originally consisted of the symmetrical front portion
of the main building complex, with a portico and columned openings facing east and west on the two ends.
The interior consisted of a columned central hall (originally used to exhibit sculpture) flanked by galleries. In a
1991 article on Pope's museums, architectural historian
Steven Bedford wrote, "The Baltimore project set the
standard for Pope's museums. The reserved monumentality of the exterior is relieved by the carefully placed
string courses, niches, and recessed panels. The masonry is graded in size and tone to create an image of
strength and continuous tonality. The same care was
employed in the basilicalike central sculpture hall. . . ."

In 1935 Pope added a courtyard behind this building, which as planned has acted as the core of the entire
complex and the center of the east-west axial plan along
which subsequent parts have been added. Immediately
around the court, forming parts of what from the inside
seems like one central building, are the Jacobs wing to
the east, added by Pope in 1937; and the May wing to
the north and the Cone wing to the West, both by
Wrenn, Lewis, and Jencks in 1950 and 1957, respectively. The smaller Woodward wing to the northwest,

another 1950s addition, is also by Wrenn, Lewis, and Jencks.

In 1982 the museum added a new east wing that was obviously not part of the central complex. Designed by Bower, Lewis, Thrower of Philadelphia, it presented a new appearance, especially with its tiled serpentine exterior wall; but the architects did line up cornices and take other measures to make it as compatible as possible with the existing structure. The Wurtzburger Sculpture Garden outside this wing was added at about the same time.

In 1988 the museum added a far larger sculpture garden, the Levi, to the east of the Wurtzburger. Designed by Sasaki Associates of Boston and taking advantage of a small natural valley, the Levi garden in design is far different from the usual platformlike museum sculpture garden that looks like a large outdoor gallery with greenery. This was planned as a parklike natural setting with sculpture, and in theory it's a great success. In practice, the garden has had serious problems due to dying trees, understaffing, and difficult growing conditions. But in recent years there has been improvement, and it is hoped that one day the garden will fulfill its great potential.

In 1994 the museum opened another major wing, this one to the west and called the New Wing for Modern Art. This, also designed by Bower, Lewis, Thrower, presents a metal-clad mass set at an angle to the earlier structure. While it perhaps succeeds in declaring its function as a home for modern art, the exterior of this building is out of keeping with the classical dignity of the main building and looms too large to balance the

east wing. But the interior consists of a series of hand-some, well-appointed galleries on two levels that work well for the art entrusted to them.

Fortunately, one cannot see the whole building complex from end to end, except perhaps from the air, and Pope's central façade still leaves the major impression. ❖

L7 • WOLMAN HOUSE
3213 North Charles Street
1939—Laurence Hall Fowler

The unusual countenance of the Wolman House and the simplicity of its design are noticeable even though it is recessed between two larger buildings. Built for the late Abel Wolman, who was a Johns Hopkins University professor of sanitary engineering and internationally renowned expert on drinking water and public health, it has several interesting features.

The size of the lot (40 by 156 feet), dictated the shape of the house: a narrow, rectangular box with a singular arrangement of windows, particularly the large oriel set in the middle of the façade. The Wolman House contains structural steel, rarely used in residential construction. The interior is arranged like an English town house with the dining room and kitchen on the first floor, the main living spaces including a living room and master bedroom on the second, and a guest bedroom and study on the third. A basement room opening onto a small garden in the rear constitutes a fourth level.

The Wolman House is now owned by The Johns Hopkins University. The Jewish College Services plans to use it for their offices, meeting rooms, and library. ❖

L8 • HOMEWOOD
(BCL, NR)
Charles and Thirty-fourth streets
1801 and after—Charles Carroll of Homewood; Robert and William Edwards, builders

The latest and most refined of the Federal period country houses built near Baltimore is Homewood. Its owner, Charles Carroll, Jr., son of Charles Carroll of Carrollton, was no doubt responsible for its Adamesque flavor, which he would have known about through the then-popular English pattern books and building guides.

Homewood has a five-part plan typical of the area plantation house massing of the time, the dependencies joined to the main body of the house by hyphens deep enough to contain small rooms in addition to hallways. Made of brick with marble trim, the house is basically a one-story design, but with a high basement and a second story over the central section, the latter indicated by the unusual, unpedimented dormers.

Approaching the building from the Charles Street side, one can appreciate the thought that went into the beautiful entrance façade. The windows are carefully proportioned to the sizes of the various sections. The height of the walls above the windows in the central section, necessitated by the second floor, is minimized by the deep cornices and the marble panels above each window. The vertically oriented formal portico has a pediment with a delicate frieze containing a shield-shaped window in the center. The doorway, with its attached columns, coffered arch, fanlight, and carved cornice, is rich but not ostentatious. The garden entrance on the other side of the house has a handsome but appropriately less formal appearance, with the porch here horizontally oriented and the pediment set back in the main block of the house.

The interior has an eminently practical plan. A cross-hall runs the length of the building, with all rooms opening from it, so that it is never necessary to go through one room to get to another. The large number of closets attests to the fact that the requirements of comfort were not sacrificed to the desire for elegance, and the placement of some of them attests as well to the ingenuity of the designer.

Through its long life the house, now owned by The Johns Hopkins University, has been used for various purposes including offices, a faculty club, and even a boys' school. Miraculously, it remained virtually intact, so that when finally restored in the 1980s to its former glory, its superb interior architectural detailing did not have to be reimagined or conjectured, but merely highlighted. It was all there, from the rooms' elegant crown moldings and the hall's vaulted center section to the

extraordinary mantels, each one given a different treatment. No wonder Charles Carroll of Carrollton, who paid for it all, wrote his son frequent complaining letters, at one point declaring in exasperation, "I . . . shall not advance any more money for *improvements* on your Farm." He did, though, fortunately for us.

Unlike Mount Clare [I5], the house is not filled with Carroll furnishings. Only one piece, an English painted armchair of 1800–20, is thought to have been in the house when the original owner occupied it. It has been decorated with Federal-period furnishings, in some cases replicating objects known to have been in the house, such as a set of New York chairs in the drawing room, a set of engravings of Philadelphia by William Birch, and a portrait of George Washington.

The restoration of the building, as well as the research leading to it, was carried out by the architectural firm of Mendel, Mesick, Cohen, Waite, Hall, with an advisory committee consisting of museum curators, university trustees, and others. ❖

L9 • GILMAN HALL
(BCL)
The Johns Hopkins University
1904—Parker and Thomas

When Parker and Thomas set out to design a campus for The Johns Hopkins University soon after the turn of the century, they decided on the then-popular Neo-Colonial style, with bows in the direction of Homewood [L8]. Gilman Hall, named for Hopkins's first president, Daniel Coit Gilman, was the most important building in

the plan; Homewood can be seen reflected particularly in the handsome portico with shield decoration in the pediment, the unpedimented dormers, and the plaques over the first-floor windows. The colonial look was more or less adhered to in later buildings at the university until the 1950s. ❖

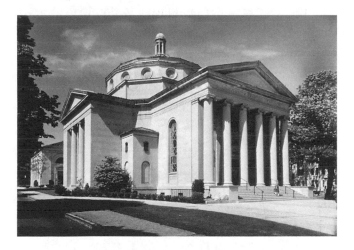

L10 • UNIVERSITY BAPTIST CHURCH

Charles and Thirty-fourth streets
1926—John Russell Pope

Here Pope's Neoclassicism takes on a Renaissance flavor, with the octagonal dome and arcade facing Charles Street. If the building suffers from a somewhat static quality, it nevertheless fits its site well and gives the impression of being larger than it is. ❖

L11 • CARNEGIE INSTITUTE EMBRYOLOGY BUILDING

University Parkway and San Martin Drive
1962—Anderson, Beckwith, and Haible

This design by William E. Haible is one of the more felicitous modern buildings in Baltimore. It presents itself as a pleasant rather than jarring surprise on its woodsy site, it accommodates itself to the slope so that it almost seems to be proceeding out of the ground from east to west, the materials relate to each other well, and the proportions are handsome. The inner courtyard, up a flight of steps from ground level, seems a bit constricted; but that may be because the plant materials are now too large and/or some of the windows to surrounding offices have been closed off, making a wall where an opening ought to be.

Another successful departure from the prevailing Georgian Revival style on the Hopkins campus is Donald L. Sickler's 1974 glass pavilion, an addition to Levering Hall. ❖

L12 • EPISCOPAL CATHEDRAL OF THE INCARNATION

University Parkway and St. Paul Street
1909–47—various architects

This English Gothic church atop a Norman crypt was the subject of much controversy and is actually only a fragment of the church once planned.

In 1909 Henry Vaughn submitted the first plan. Ten years later Bertram G. Goodhue submitted a design for

a huge church similar to the Episcopal cathedrals in New York and Washington. But the Maryland diocese never had the money to carry out such an elaborate project.

Finally this building, representing no more than the guildhall of the grand plan, was built to a design by Frohman, Robb, and Little. Philip Frohman was the principal architect of the Washington Cathedral. ❖

L13 • SCOTTISH RITE TEMPLE OF FREEMASONRY

Charles and Thirty-ninth streets
1930 and after—Clyde N. Friz, with John Russell Pope

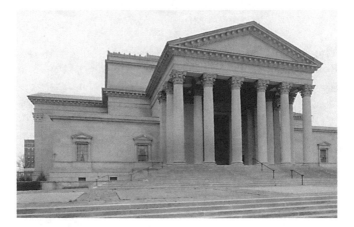

What role John Russell Pope actually played in the design of this building is not on record, according to the temple's current staff, although he is listed in a publication as associated with Friz. The barrel-vaulted, pedimented Corinthian portico has been suggested as his design, and it is certainly the most impressive feature of a building that otherwise, despite its size, stubbornly refuses to rise above the pedestrian, either outside or inside. ❖

L14 • HIGHFIELD HOUSE CONDOMINIUM

4000 North Charles Street
1964—Mies van der Rohe

The second building in Baltimore by Mies van der Rohe, like his first, One Charles Center [A12], is a free-standing tower set on a platform. The glass-enclosed lobby, containing elevators and reception areas, occupies less than a third of the ground level; the rest of the space is mostly open, defined by the columns that raise the building 20 feet above the platform. Below ground level are parking facilities and a glass-walled recreation room. In back is a plaza with a sunken swimming pool-fountain which, seen from above, appears as a Miesian formal garden.

Highfield House is built of reinforced concrete, which the architect arranged in a wide-bayed grid of finely proportioned members. Although the tower has the refined precision and meticulous planning that characterizes his work, Mies van der Rohe made two concessions to the character of the neighborhood. The wide windows and spandrels lend the building a horizontal feeling and help to minimize its height (thirteen residential floors plus a two-story lobby). Secondly, the panels above the spandrels are faced with buff brick, also in keeping with the more traditional surroundings. The extensive use of glass gives the apartments an unequalled combination of light and view. ❖

L15 • LAURENCE HALL FOWLER RESIDENCE

10 West Highfield Road
1925—Laurence Hall Fowler

Fowler, one of the leading Baltimore architects of the first half of the twentieth century (see Biographies), was adept at houses rendered meticulously in a variety of styles, from Jacobean to Spanish Colonial. For his own house he chose no particular style (though a vaguely French flavor may be inferred), but created, as usual, a beautifully proportioned and detailed building. It is not a large house, but its size is nevertheless minimized on the façade; because of the high roof with dormers and the fact that the land falls away from the front, masking the lowest living floor altogether, a four-story house seems to be essentially two stories. The proportions of the façade are admirable, and the alternation between regular and irregular punctuation of windows and doors assures interest.

The interior, little changed in more than seventy years, features an economy of space used for halls and the compact but handsome oval staircase, and the house opens to generous principal rooms. The finest of these are the living room on the main floor (called the library on Fowler's drawings), and the dining room below giving onto the wooded rear grounds.

The house combines up-to-date (for the period) building materials with handsome accents from the past. The construction is hollow tile (a forerunner of cinder block), and the casement windows are metal of standard stock sizes. But the charming glass panes in the front door are obviously much older than the house, some of the hardware is antique, and Fowler introduced architectural elements from older houses. In the living room the entablature and door frame come from a circa-1780 house at 104 North Gay Street; a matching door treatment is at the Baltimore Museum of Art. The black marble fireplace in the living room is from a pre–Civil War Baltimore house, and the wooden fireplace in the dining room below came from a late-eighteenth-, early-nineteenth-century Ridgely farmhouse in Baltimore County that was inundated by Loch Raven reservoir. At the foot of the garden, the granite columns and capitals are from the original Enoch Pratt Free Library building erected on Mulberry Street in the 1880s.

Fowler's carefully kept records at Evergreen [L16] indicate that some compromises were made for the sake of economy, among them that the floors, originally planned to be of oak, ended up of pine.

This is an idiosyncratic house, aesthetically satisfying and eminently livable, but without the grandiosities with which Fowler obliged his rich clients. ❖

L16 • EVERGREEN

(BCL, NR)
4545 North Charles Street
1857–58 — architect unknown; 1885 — Charles L. Carson; 1922–41 — Laurence Hall Fowler

Evergreen isn't your usual house museum, lovingly restored to the period in which it was built; it would be

hard to know to what period to restore a house that was built and enlarged for almost a century, successive occupants adding and remodeling to fit specific needs and tastes.

The original house, Classical Revival with touches of Italianate, including especially the heavy cornice, was finished in 1858; a contemporary account lists John W. Hogg as the builder. Hogg was also an architect, but it has been suggested that the house's design might have been by Niernsee and Neilson, because of its sophistication and specific similarities to their Hackerman House at One West Mount Vernon Place [C18]: the cornice with its row of anthemions and the bracketed cornices above the windows. No record of their participation has been found, however. Since one account has the house modeled after Melville Park, a former country estate east of Old York Road, it may be that Hogg simply took his design from the earlier house.

The house was originally owned by a family named Broadbent, but not for long. The property went through a succession of owners until in 1878, John Work Garrett, president of the Baltimore and Ohio Railroad, bought the house for his son, T. Harrison Garrett. For the next seventy years the house was occupied and enlarged by the Garretts, principally T. Harrison and his son and daughter-in-law, John Work Garrett and Alice Warder Garrett.

In 1885 Carson designed for T. Harrison the north wing, which originally contained a billiard room, a bowling alley, a gymnasium, and study rooms for the Garretts' three sons. Mr. Garrett died in a yachting accident in 1888, at the age of thirty-nine, and his widow, Alice Whitridge Garrett, occupied the house until her death in 1920.

After the John Work Garretts inherited the house, they initiated extensive changes to accommodate the interests of Mr. Garrett, a diplomat and collector, especially of books, and Mrs. Garrett, who took a passionate interest in the arts.

In the early 1920s Fowler made alterations to the north wing; the billiard room and bowling alley on the ground floor became the Far East rooms to exhibit the family collections of Japanese and Chinese art. Upstairs, the gymnasium became a theater, with ceiling and wall designs by Leon Bakst, the Russian artist responsible for costume and set designs for Diaghilev's Ballets Russes.

In 1928 Fowler designed the rare book library, with its slightly domed ceiling, to accommodate eight thousand of Mr. Garrett's books. In the 1930s the area between the double parlor and the library became a reading room, with eight painted wall panels by Miguel Covarrubias depicting Mr. Garrett's diplomatic posts including Berlin, Paris, and Rome. In 1941 the double parlor was turned into a single parlor, and a small book gallery off of this room was added to the south side of the house, the final addition.

On his death in 1942 John Work Garrett left Evergreen and its collections to The Johns Hopkins University, though his widow continued to live there until her death ten years later. Aside from books, coins (which Hopkins subsequently sold), and Asian art, the collections included the modern art amassed by Mrs. Garrett, with works by Vuillard, Bonnard, Modigliani, Dufy, and Picasso, among others.

Between 1986 and 1991 the house underwent an extensive renovation-restoration. Much of it was to modernize the forty-eight-room mansion structurally and mechanically, but the furnishings and decorations were also restored. There was no attempt to give the house the look of any particular period; rather, the effort was to reflect all the living, collecting, and altering that had gone on there.

There is grandeur here, which one senses especially in the approach to the house's magnificent Corinthian portico. But the house is not and probably never was fashionable. It is beyond fashion. It just is. ❖

L17 • GALLAGHER MANSION

(BCL, NR)
431 Notre Dame Lane
*ca. 1855—architect unknown; 1879—Edmund G. Lind,
renovation architect; 1996—Smeallie, Orrick, and Janka,
Ltd., renovation architect*

A derelict for many years, the Gallagher Mansion has been recycled as low-income housing for the elderly. When first constructed for Benjamin Woods, a physician, it was a two-story Italianate mansion with thick stone walls and a rear extension. The surrounding community of Govans was then a suburban village. There were other country estates along the York Road corridor built at about the same time and in the same Italianate style. The survivors include Tivoli (Woodbourne Center, Inc. [M2]), and Anneslie on East Dunkirk Road in Towson, circa 1855, designed by Niernsee and Neilson for civil engineer Frederick Harrison, Jr.

In 1873, Patrick T. Gallagher, an Irish immigrant and successful Govanstown grocer, bought the mansion and hired Lind to redesign it. Lind added a front porch and a slate-covered mansard roof, giving the building a third floor, five additional rooms, and a French appearance. The Gallagher family sold the property in 1972, and the mansion was allowed to deteriorate. The city acquired the house and 2.2 acres of land in the 1980s.

In 1995, the property was turned over to the non-profit Govans Ecumenical Development Corporation, which has restored the mansion to the way it looked after the Lind renovation and added a thirty-five-unit, three-story rear extension. The mansion contains six apartments on the upper two floors and meeting and dining rooms below. Federal and private funds paid for the $3.4 million project, completed in 1996. The restoration architect was James T. Wollon. ❖

L18 • CATHEDRAL OF MARY OUR QUEEN
5200 North Charles Street
1959—Maginnis and Walsh

Funded with money left for the purpose by Baltimore department-store owner Thomas O'Neill, Baltimore's second Roman Catholic cathedral (see also [B9]) was designed by the Boston-based firm which also designed St. Mary's Seminary on Roland Avenue [N11].

An earlier twelfth-century-style design submitted in 1932 and with a huge tower over the crossing was never built. The architects termed the later design "an adaptation of Gothic principles to modern expression." The cathedral is 373 feet long and 239 feet wide at its fullest extensions, with two stone towers, each 128 feet high, on the eastern façade. The building is of brick, with limestone and granite facing. It features Art Deco-like decoration on both the cathedral building and the rectory to the north. There are two independent chapels to the north and south of the nave, but no real transepts. The interior is notable for its extensive stained glass. The cost of the cathedral was about $8,500,000. ❖

L19 • CHURCH OF THE REDEEMER

5603 North Charles Street
1958—Pietro Belluschi; RTKL Associates, Inc.

Pietro Belluschi, the noted contemporary architect, here tackled a difficult commission and created a masterpiece. The problem, as the church committee presented it, was to build a new church several times as large as the original century-old church, which was to remain as a chapel, without dwarfing it; and to build a thoroughly contemporary structure in harmony with its Gothic-style neighbor, designed in 1856 by R. Snowden Andrews (shown on the following page).

Belluschi designed a church which seems almost a natural extension of the ground which supports it. The low walls are of the same local stone used in the old church; most of it was recovered from the original rectory, contemporary with the old church and razed in 1958 from the spot where the new church now stands. The walls are separated from the steeply pitched roof by a row of horizontal windows. The whole church, though massive, is lower than the top of the old church's spire, and the eye travels easily from one to the other.

The interior satisfies the congregation's desire that the church "give expression to the building's function as the link between heaven and earth." The Gothic contours of the huge wooden arches echo those of the old church but are structural here. Though they support the roof, they do not rise to the top of it, "it being felt that separation between arches and rooftop would symbolize the spiritual."

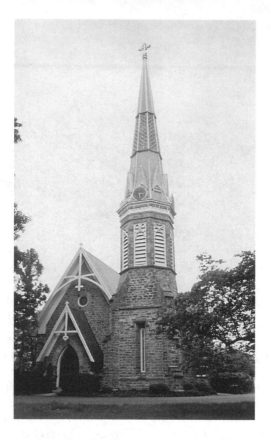

The great wooden arches connote both the power and the aspirations of man, and the effect is enhanced by the band of stained-glass windows separating walls and roof.

The large stained-glass window behind the altar was made at Chartres to a design by Gyorgy Kepes, professor of visual design at the Massachusetts Institute of Technology. It appears at first to be totally abstract, but there is the outline of a cross in the glass.

The church floor was originally carpeted, under the architect's direction. The carpet was removed in 1993 to improve the church's acoustics, which it did, but the present cork tile floor has been criticized as less appropriate.

Overall, the church is an example of successful postmodernism, created long before the term came into vogue to describe an architectural style. It does not merely slap historical decorations on a modern structure but blends elements of the new and the old into an organic unity. ❖

L20 • SHEPPARD AND ENOCH
PRATT HOSPITAL

6501 North Charles Street
1858–88—Dixon and Dixon with D. Tilden Brown,
Calvert Vaux

When Quaker philanthropist Moses Sheppard died, he left a bequest of $571,000 for the building and operation of a hospital for the insane (later augmented with funds from Enoch Pratt, adding his name to the title). Sheppard's principal stipulations were two: having witnessed the inhumane conditions to which the mentally ill were subjected in his time, he directed the trustees to "put first the comfort of the patient," and specifically stated that there should be plenty of light and fresh air everywhere, and he required that only the income from his bequest ever be used to support (or build) the hospital.

It is probable that both these conditions were responsible for the remarkable Victorian buildings which grew over a period of thirty years on the Baltimore County site chosen for the hospital. The two identical original buildings, each 360 feet long, are noted for the spacious, airy, light-filled quality of their interiors, and since the buildings only proceeded as income from the bequest became available, this surely meant that every care could be taken in their construction.

The extended gabled and dormered brick buildings, constructed with iron girders and stairways, slate roofs, and stone foundations—chosen to make the buildings as fireproof as possible—are visually enhanced by the two unequal towers of each, the taller ones six stories high with steep, wedge-shaped roofs. Altogether, in an era when large buildings could be forbidding in appearance, these managed a charming complexity of façade which invites one to enter and explore. No doubt this quality was one reason the Dixons' design was chosen from those submitted in the architectural competition held by the trustees. The amusing gatehouse on Charles Street is also by Dixon and Dixon. Calvert Vaux, a well-known landscape architect who collaborated with Frederick Law Olmsted on the design of Central Park in New York, was named associate architect of Sheppard Pratt.

It is interesting to note that the two principal materials used in the buildings, brick and stone, came from the property, which had been an estate called Mount Airy. The stone was quarried from one portion of the land, and excellent brick clay was used for eleven million bricks, which were fired in kilns constructed at the site.

In the 1960s and early 1970s, a complete renovation of the two main buildings was undertaken by the engineering firm of Fred von Behren, Inc., during which much long-unused space in the original buildings was reclaimed. At the same time the space between them was filled with a new central building designed by Anthony J. Ianniello. ❖

TOUR M

Towson (Driving)

M1 SENATOR THEATER
5904 York Road
1939—John J. Zink

M2 TIVOLI (Woodbourne Center, Inc.)
1301 Woodbourne Avenue, between The Alameda
and Loch Raven Boulevard
ca. 1855—architect unknown

M3 DUMBARTON
300 Dumbarton Road
ca. 1840–41—Robert Cary Long, Jr.?

M4 BALTIMORE COUNTY COURTHOUSE
Washington Avenue, Towson
*1856—Dixon, Balbirnie, and Dixon; 1910 addition—
Baldwin and Pennington*

M5 TRINITY EPISCOPAL CHURCH
120 Allegheny Avenue, Towson
*1860—Norris G. Starkweather; 1869 additions—
Edmund G. Lind*

M6 BALTIMORE COUNTY PUBLIC SAFETY
BUILDING (former Maryland Blue Cross Building)
700 East Joppa Road, Towson
*1972—Peterson and Brickbauer; Brown, Guenther,
Battaglia, and Galvin*

M7 BEST PRODUCTS COMPANY, INC.
1238 Putty Hill Avenue, corner of Goucher
Boulevard, Towson
1978—Site, Inc.

M8 GOUCHER COLLEGE CENTER
Goucher College, Dulaney Valley Road, Towson
1960—Pietro Belluschi; RTKL Associates, Inc.

M9 HAMPTON
Hampton Lane off Dulaney Valley Road at the
Baltimore Beltway, I-695, Towson
1783–90—Jehu Howell, builder

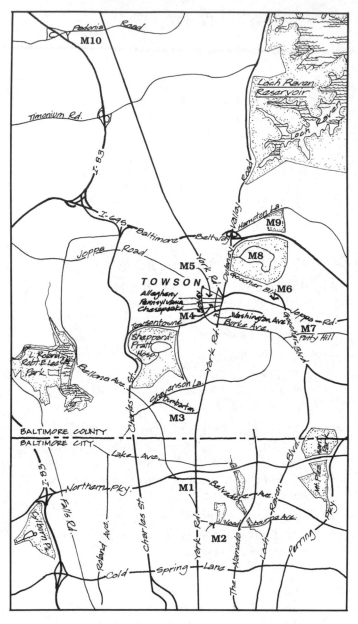

Tour M: Towson (Driving)

M10 PADONIA COMMERCE BUILDING (former
       John Deere Company Warehouse)
       Deereco Road off Padonia Road at the Baltimore–
       Harrisburg Expressway, I-83, Timonium
       1966—RTKL Associates, Inc.

From a former great estate (Hampton) to more modest country houses (Tivoli and Dumbarton); to one
of Baltimore's best examples of Art Deco (the Senator);
to a notable example of modernism (Baltimore County
Public Safety Building); to a zany example of post-mod-
ernism (Best Products Company), this tour includes an
eclectic mix of buildings lying within convenient reach
of the Beltway, the main street of the metropolitan area.
Curiously, this tour is almost completely divided between the quite old and the quite new, with a century's
hiatus between. Five—fully half—of the buildings here
date from before the Civil War; four of the other five
date from 1960 to the present (the Senator Theater is
the lone example in between). The explanation probably lies in that the communities in this part of the
metropolitan area, especially Towson and its environs,
were relatively slow-growing until the postwar era brought
major changes. ❖

M1 • SENATOR THEATER

(NR)
5904 York Road
1939—John J. Zink

Just as Art Deco was dying, what should appear in typically conservative Baltimore but the Senator Theater,
which remains—along with the much grander Nations-
Bank building downtown [D4]—one of the best surviving local examples of the style.

   With its exterior glass-brick upper walls illuminated
by colored lights at night; round lobby with sunburst
panels beneath a lounge balcony; a mural by Paul M.
Roche depicting the "progress of visual entertainment";
its rounded columns and walnut-veneered walls; and the
sunburst effect of the colored lighting display on the
ceiling of the auditorium, echoed in the lighting fixtures of the upper level lounge, the Senator Theater has
become a veritable treasure with the revival of interest

in Art Deco. Some elements, such as the gold leaf on the lobby and auditorium ceilings and the draped female statues on either side of the stage, have disappeared over the years. But enough remains.

John J. Zink was a theater architect of the 1920s and 1930s and a master of Art Deco embellishment. Among his commissions in Baltimore and Washington were several of the Durkee chain of movie theaters, including the Patterson, the Edgewood, and the Ambassador, in addition to the Senator.

The theater is now owned by Thomas Kiefaber, whose mother and grandfather were members of the Durkee family. He has announced plans to erect two new movie auditoriums, one to the north and one to the south of the present one, in order to create a financially viable complex. He promises no encroachment on the interior of the present building.

It's interesting that this has become, by default, Baltimore's most elegant film house. When it opened, and for decades after, in the heyday of the great downtown movie palaces (all of which are long since gone), the Senator was just a neighborhood movie theater. ❖

M2 • TIVOLI
(Woodbourne Center, Inc.)
(NR)
1301 Woodbourne Avenue, between The Alameda and
Loch Raven Boulevard
ca. 1855—architect unknown

One of the summer houses built outside Baltimore in the mid-nineteenth century, Tivoli was purchased by Enoch Pratt in 1870 and he owned it until he died in 1896. The original owner is unknown. The present owners—it is now a home for emotionally disabled adolescents—estimate that it was built about 1855 and shows "an Italian influence popular at the time." This stone structure, however, is rather severe to be called a full-blown Italianate building. ❖

M3 • DUMBARTON
300 Dumbarton Road
ca. 1840–41 — Robert Cary Long, Jr.?

This two-and-a-half-story Greek Revival house with later additions was long thought to have been built in 1853 to a design by Niernsee and Neilson, but more recent research indicates otherwise.

The property was bought by Robert A. Taylor, who had the house erected, in 1840. The next year's assessor's book lists $4,000 worth of improvements, which indicates a house. The original house, without the porches and cupola, closely resembles Mondawmin, a contemporary country house, now razed, thought to be by Long. Mondawmin shared elements such as pilasters and gateposts with other buildings known to be by Long, and both Mondawmin and Dumbarton share features with other buildings known or thought to be by Long, including the indented center bay and the recessed ends.

Niernsee and Neilson added the porches and the cupola and raised the chimneys in 1853. They may also have added some interior architectural decoration, such as ceiling medallions.

The house is three bays wide with a center hall plan. Two full stories are topped by a half-story indicated by square windows punctuating a frieze. There is a wing on each side, that on the east having a bay window. The stair is not in the center hall but on the left (from the front of the house), or west side. The interior is pleasant enough but not prepossessing. As a historic sites inventory says of it, "The house is compact, logically laid out, and not much decorated, a place built for comfort rather than show."

In 1923, Laurence Hall Fowler enlarged the dining room and added bathrooms. The house remained in private hands until 1954, when the Baltimore County Board of Education acquired the property and built a school on the land. At one point the school board proposed demolishing the house, but gave in to protests and used it for offices until 1988. Since 1991 Dumbarton has been the home of the Baltimore Actors' Theatre. ❖

M4 • BALTIMORE COUNTY
COURTHOUSE
Washington Avenue, Towson
*1856—Dixon, Balbirnie, and Dixon; 1910 addition—
Baldwin and Pennington*

The Greek Revival in America was about over when the center portion of this building—the part with two short wings behind the Doric portico—first appeared. But classical architecture was especially appropriate for

courthouses, and Thomas and James Dixon were masters of many styles. (Thomas Balbirnie left the firm soon after the courthouse was finished.)

The fireproof structure was built of limestone with offices on the first floor and a courtroom, library, and lockup on the second. The courthouse tower was much higher and fancier as first constructed; it was cut back to its present form in the 1860s. (The Dixons also designed the simpler Baltimore County Jail at Towsontown Boulevard and Bosley Avenue, built contemporaneously with the courthouse and expanded in 1880, 1940, and 1957.)

Baldwin and Pennington extended both wings of the courthouse, adopting the same style and type of stone. Josias and Pleasants Pennington added another section on the north side in 1925. The remainder of the building was completed in 1958, resulting in the present H-shaped structure. The original courtroom on the second-floor front (directly behind the portico) has been restored. ❖

M5 • TRINITY EPISCOPAL CHURCH

120 Allegheny Avenue, Towson
1860—Norris G. Starkweather; 1869 additions—
Edmund G. Lind

At its 1860 dedication, Starkweather's Romanesque Revival church lacked a spire and vestibule. Lind later added these elements and the results show a Norman (English Romanesque) influence.

Trinity Church and the subsequent additions were built of local limestone donated by John Ridgely of Hampton. The interior, under an open timber ceiling,

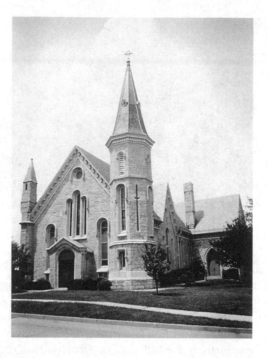

contains some impressive frescoes; four of the stained-glass windows, ca. 1900, are from the studio of Louis Comfort Tiffany.

Baltimore architects J. Appleton Wilson and William T. Wilson added the transepts in 1891, and Laurence Hall Fowler extended the chancel in 1926. In 1989, architects Schamu, Machowski, Doo, and Associates, Inc., and developer Martin Azola completed a $400,000 restoration that included a new HVAC system and interior finishes. ❖

M6 • BALTIMORE COUNTY PUBLIC SAFETY BUILDING
(former Maryland Blue Cross Building)

700 East Joppa Road, Towson
1972—Peterson and Brickbauer; Brown, Guenther, Battaglia, and Galvin

Inside, this is a typical office building, with a lobby on the lower level, ten office floors, and mechanical equipment on the roof, all supported by a structural steel frame. From the exterior, however, it looks like a giant cube of ice etched with black lines, reflecting the sky and the landscape around it. The surface is silver reflec-

tive glass in a black aluminum curtain wall, which emphasizes the cube and square motif of the building itself.

The reflecting glass serves two purposes, according to the architects: an aesthetic one and a functional one. "The site is triangular and is the highest elevation in the area. The neighborhood is essentially residential and the mirrored cube was used to diminish the disparity in scale by becoming merely a reflection of the sky and the constantly changing light formations," the architects state. On the functional side, the reflecting glass considerably reduces air-conditioning costs.

In order to preserve the integrity of the cube, a recessed circular entrance court allows for entrances from below ground level. The nearby flame-red glazed-brick cube houses mechanical apparatus and serves, in the architects' words, to create "in an abstract fashion a gigantic minimal sculpture."

Blue Cross has moved out of the building, and it is now the Baltimore County Public Safety Building. ❖

M7 • BEST PRODUCTS COMPANY, INC.

1238 Putty Hill Avenue, corner of Goucher
Boulevard, Towson
1978—Site, Inc.

Most Best Products Company stores are conventionally bland shopping-mall designs. The Towson "Tilt" proj-

ect, however, has its 14-inch-thick, 450-ton masonry block front wall lifted high in the air at one corner and angled smartly from the rest of the building (the angle is about 20 degrees in each dimension).

The front wall was not easy to construct. (The Whiting-Turner Contracting Company was the builder.) Its left corner rests on a caisson; the remainder of the weight is carried by cantilevered steel beams whose enclosures are visible from underneath. Its bottom edge, which seems to hang by itself, is actually a reinforced masonry beam, connected to the supporting cantilevered steel beams with U-bolts. The masonry beam was fabricated on the ground, raised to the proper angle and tilted, and the rest of the battered block wall laid on top of it.

The store was designed by James Wines, a Towsonite and sculptor, and Emilio Sousa—both principals of Site, Inc., a New York firm. It was the fourth of eight extreme departures from the norm for the country's second-largest catalog-showroom merchandiser. The others, also by Site, Inc., featured crumbling bricks, sliding entrances, and peeling façades, signifying . . . what? Consumer games, apocalyptic visions, commercial gimmickry, de-architecture, and neo-Piranesianism have all been suggested.

"The Best Company founders had a strong interest in contemporary art and architecture," said a spokesman. "This was their attempt to bring interesting architecture to the masses." The company stopped building these bizarre stores in the early 1980s for financial reasons. Four of the experimental designs by Site, Inc., remain, including the one in Towson, but it is scheduled to be razed as part of a $20 million shopping center renovation. ❖

M8 • GOUCHER COLLEGE CENTER

Goucher College, Dulaney Valley Road, Towson
1960—Pietro Belluschi; RTKL Associates, Inc.

In this complex of buildings, Belluschi has combined fieldstone, wood, and concrete in an imaginative way to create congenial spaces without sacrificing functionalism. He has also managed to make a modern architectural statement which is nevertheless in keeping with the campus's older buildings, both because he has chosen sympathetic materials and because he has refrained from making too bold an intrusion on the landscape.

An auditorium, a lecture hall, administrative offices, and a student lounge are accommodated in buildings gathered around an open courtyard. The complex itself presents no unified façade to the visitor, which helps keep a sizable structure from being too imposing. Wide stone stairs separating the auditorium and office buildings mount to the central court. The hexagonal auditorium, its bare concrete walls and floor softened by curved rows of seats sweeping unbroken from wall to wall, is an impressive interior but also a comfortable and functionally successful one. ❖

M9 • HAMPTON
(NR)
Hampton Lane, off Dulaney Valley Road, at the Baltimore Beltway, I-695, Towson
1783–90—Jehu Howell, builder

This imposing mansion, built just after the American Revolution, was one of the largest country houses in the United States before the middle of the nineteenth century. Today the property, a National Historic Site, includes, aside from the house, more than two dozen buildings and landscaped gardens boasting exotic trees.

Colonel Charles Ridgely purchased a tract of land known as Northampton in Baltimore County in 1745, and deeded part of it to his son, Captain Charles Ridgely, in 1760. Captain Ridgely amassed great wealth over the next quarter-century from the family iron business, as a merchant, and from farming lands that eventually totaled more than 24,000 acres. The crowning glory of his great estate was originally called Hampton Hall, built for him between 1783 and 1790.

The house, built on English Georgian models and already old-fashioned when it was begun in the immediate post-Revolutionary Federal era, has a three-story central section surmounted by an oversized cupola, possibly influenced by Castle Howard in England. This is flanked by hyphens and wings in the typical five-part country-house style. The building material is stone, faced with stucco, whose slightly pink tint was originally produced by the iron content of the sand used to mix the stucco. The principal north and south façades of the main block are fronted with two-story porticoes surmounted by pediments with inset Palladian windows. The treatment of entrance doors and flanking windows is elaborate, with pilasters, pediments, and friezes, and decorative urns ornament the roofline. The house is a veritable compendium of design-book motifs, and its own literature refers to its "baronial scale and grandiose design." The design is thought to have been primarily Captain Ridgely's, based both on books and on houses he had seen elsewhere. He was assisted by master carpenter Jehu Howell, who at his death in 1787 was listed as "a very ingenious architect."

The main floor of the central block contains the impressive reception rooms, with a central hall running through the house flanked by two large rooms on either side. Those on the west are the drawing room and the music room, with the dining room and parlor on the east; the latter are separated by the stair hall—for, unlike many houses of its type, the stairs are not in the central hall.

Six generations of Ridgelys were masters of Hampton, until the house was designated a National Historic Site and passed to the National Park Service in 1948. For thirty years it was administered by a private preservation organization, but in 1979 the National Park Service took over the property's administration. Over the years, the rooms of the house have been and continue to be gradually restored to various periods of the Ridgely residence, making use of the many surviving Ridgely furnishings.

In the drawing room, for instance, is the magnificent set of classical revival painted furniture ordered by the Ridgelys from John Finlay, the leading maker of the day. It includes a sofa with arms in the shape of gilt swans and imported slate tabletops painted with scenes. The music room is decorated in Victorian style, and the dining room, parlor, and one upstairs bedroom are furnished in styles reflecting the decades from 1790 to 1820.

There are twenty-seven outbuildings on the grounds of Hampton, some of which date to the period of the house or shortly after. In addition, landscape gardening was an important activity during the Ridgely period, and the present grounds reflect that, with formal parterres, a cutting garden, an herb garden, specimen trees, and other features of interest. Any visit to Hampton should include time spent outside as well as a tour of the house. ❖

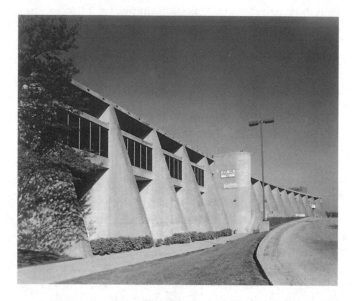

M10 • PADONIA COMMERCE BUILDING
(former John Deere Company Warehouse)
Deereco Road off Padonia Road at the Baltimore–
Harrisburg Expressway, I-83, Timonium
1966—RTKL Associates, Inc.

The architects referred to the roof structure of the warehouse as a "big tent," when the $2 million building won a national AIA design award shortly after it opened. The tent ropes are 1½-inch steel cables tied to concrete anchors buried in the earth on the expressway side. The cables run the length of the building and support, in three 131-foot spans, the precast concrete plank roof. (Dulles Airport in Virginia has a similar roof system.) On the front of the warehouse, facing east, massive concrete counterforts anchor the cables; the bays in between serve as truck loading docks.

There are just two rows of interior steel columns and, as originally built, the warehouse contained about 75 percent open space; the office section in the southeast corner featured an auditorium-showroom on the ground floor, a cafeteria on the second, and offices on the third.

The warehouse is fan-shaped, like its 16-acre site, with the narrower front facing away from the expressway. Enclosing 197,000 square feet, it served its purpose well, yet was also a dramatic departure from the conventional warehouse. The relationship between structure and form is particularly striking, and the concrete counterforts give the façade a Corbusian monumentality.

The John Deere Company sold the building to new owners who have leased it to individual tenants. They include the U.S. Postal Service, insurance and other firms, and even a shooting range. The Timonium Dinner Theater occupies the former company auditorium-showroom, and the building still serves many of its original functions. ❖

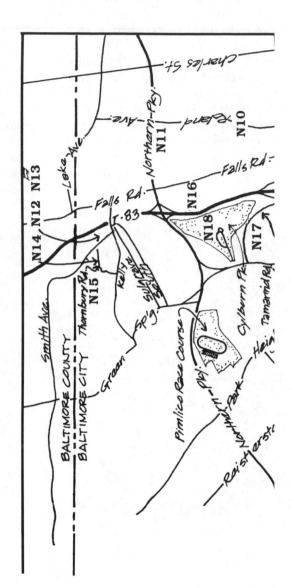

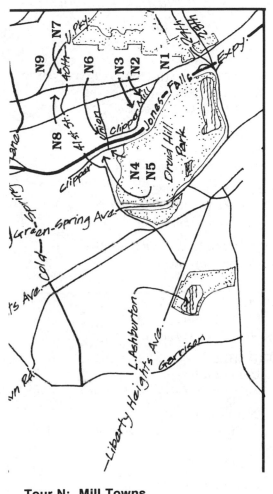

Tour N: Mill Towns and Planned Communities (Driving)

Tour N

Mill Towns and Planned Communities
(driving)

N1   MOUNT VERNON MILL AND COMMUNITY
Falls Road and Chestnut Avenue
ca. 1845–81—architect unknown

N2   EVERGREEN-ON-THE-FALLS
3300 Falls Road
ca. 1860—architect unknown

N3   CLIPPER MILL
3300 Clipper Mill Road
1866—architect unknown

N4   MEADOW MILL AT WOODBERRY
3600 Clipper Mill Road
1877—architect unknown

N5   PARK MILL
1750 Union Avenue
1855—architect unknown

N6   DRUID MILL
1600 Union Avenue
1866; enlarged 1872—architect unknown

N7   GREENWAY COTTAGES
Fortieth Street between Keswick Road and
Roland Avenue
1874—Charles E. Cassell

N8   STICK-STYLE HOUSES
4100 block Roland Avenue
ca. 1888—architect unknown

N9   POURED CONCRETE HOUSES
835–843 West University Parkway
1905—Edward L. Palmer, Jr.

N10   ROLAND PARK
*1891 and later—Edward H. Bouton, Olmsted
Brothers, and other planners and architects*

N11   SAINT MARY'S SEMINARY
5400 Roland Avenue
1927—Maginnis and Walsh

N12 MOUNT WASHINGTON OCTAGON
Near Smith and Greeley avenues, USF&G Mount
Washington Center campus
1855—Thomas Dixon

N13 FIDELITY AND GUARANTY LIFE INSURANCE
COMPANY
6225 Smith Avenue
1990—Peterson and Brickbauer; Emery Roth and Sons

N14 MOUNT WASHINGTON PRESBYTERIAN
CHURCH (The Chimes, Inc.)
1801 Thornbury Road
1878—Dixon and Carson

N15 DIXON'S HILL
Kenway, Maywood, Dixon, and Thornbury roads,
Mount Washington
*1855 and later—Thomas Dixon, Thomas C. Kennedy,
and others*

N16 CROSS KEYS
Falls Road below Northern Parkway
*1964—various architects; 1976—Frank O. Gehry and
Associates*

N17 COLDSPRING
Springarden Drive off Cold Spring Lane
1977—Moshe Safdie

N18 CYLBURN
Cylburn Park, 4915 Greenspring Avenue
1889—George A. Frederick

This tour begins with one of the most unique areas of
a most unique city, the lower Jones Falls valley.
Geographically isolated and largely bypassed by the
twentieth century, it is a living museum of Victorian-era
industrial architecture now given over to modern uses.

Falls Road was an early route through the valley
between the city and the open country to the north.
Railroads followed this route and mills, attracted by the
available water power and transportation, began appear-
ing in the early nineteenth century. By mid-century there
were a number of these in the valley.

The mill owners erected groups of houses for their
workers which grew into full-fledged communities and
remain so today: Hampden, Woodberry, and Mount

Washington are examples. These communities in turn prompted the building of additional transportation facilities. In 1885, the Baltimore Union Passenger Railway Company operated the first commercial electric street railway in the country between Twenty-fifth Street and Hampden.

The cotton industry began in Maryland in 1810 when the Washington Cotton Manufacturing Company at Smith and Kelly avenues started operations. (The complex has been renovated as an office and upscale shopping center.) In 1839, Horatio N. Gambrill and David Carroll purchased an old flour mill and converted it to a cotton factory making yarn and sailcloth. It was on the site of the present Clipper Mill which took its name from the clipper ships that were prime customers. In 1842, Gambrill also purchased and converted the Woodberry Mill. Woodberry was soon the largest manufacturing town in the state. Gambrill and William E. Hooper later erected other mills, including Mount Vernon in 1843 and Clipper and Druid in 1866. The history of these structures is complicated because they frequently burned and were rebuilt. Mill names and ownership also shifted often.

Iron was added to the valley's industries in 1853, when Poole and Hunt's Union Machine Shops were built on Union Avenue. The Poole and Hunt works employed about four hundred men in the 1870s in the manufacture of steam boilers, mining and flour-milling machinery, and other products including the iron columns that support the dome of the U.S. Capitol. In recent years, the buildings housed the Franklin-Balmar Tractor Company, an innovative engineering firm, and, later still, artists. The buildings were destroyed by fire in 1995.

The mills in the nineteenth century were a long way from Baltimore and its labor pool and thus required homes nearby for the workers. The rents in the company-owned houses were low—$5 or $6 a month—but so was the pay. Adult wages ranged from $12 to $75 a month. Most of the work force at the cotton mills was made up of children aged six to twelve; they put in twelve or more hours a day. "Strikes are unheard of," according to the contemporary Scharf's *Chronicles*, "and the only labor demonstration that has taken place in many years was a rejoicing, on February 19, 1874, over the passage by the Maryland Legislature of a law forbidding the employment of children under 16 years of age longer than 10 hours a day."

During their most prosperous and productive period from 1875 to 1890, the mills in the Jones Falls valley employed between four thousand and five thousand people, consumed more than 25 million pounds of cotton a year, and produced much of the world's cotton duck.

The mills declined in this century as owners moved their operations south, to be nearer the sources of cotton and cheap labor. Mechanization took its toll on workers. The last to succumb was the Mount Vernon Mill, which had converted to synthetic yarns and fabrics, and ceased their manufacture in August 1972. Most of the millworkers' houses have been sold. Today, smaller manufacturing firms, offices, and artisans occupy the mill buildings.

To the north along Falls Road are Roland Park, an early planned community, and Coldspring, a more recent one. Farther north and west is Mount Washington, a planned suburb that grew up around a mill village. ❖

N1 • MOUNT VERNON MILL AND COMMUNITY

Falls Road and Chestnut Avenue
ca. 1845–81—architect unknown

The main Mount Vernon Mill building is a three-story brick structure with a tower at the south end (facing the bend in Falls Road), where a stone plaque identifies it as "Mt. Vernon Mills, No. 1." It was built in 1873 after fire destroyed its predecessor, dating from 1843. The mansarded cupola with dormers that once stood atop the

tower and the monitor that ran the length of the roof have been removed, and most of the original window openings bricked up. To the southwest are a pair of gable-roofed picker houses, with datestones showing they were built in 1873 and 1879. Life-Like Products, Inc., a manufacturer of HO-scale model railroad equipment, owns and and uses the former Mount Vernon Mill, No. 1, as a factory and warehouse.

Across from the main entrance at 3000 Falls Road, where a few of the original double-framed windows are still visible, stands the mill's former office building (with a mansard roof and squat tower), and opposite that, on the other side of Chestnut Avenue, is a stone structure that was the company store. Farther up Chestnut Avenue, a large, four-story factory building, also with a tower, was added to the complex circa 1873–81. In 1985, new owners successfully converted it to artisans' studios and small company offices and renamed it the Mill Centre.

A group of twenty-two semidetached stone houses from the mid-nineteenth century, known as Stone Hill, lies east of the Mill Centre, fronting on Pacific Avenue. To the west is Brick Hill, built in the 1870s on Elm Avenue and Darby Street. The company built and owned these mill workers' houses, which featured yards and tangential through streets. Now privately owned, they look southwest across the Jones Falls valley, high above the noise and facing the prevailing summer breezes; it is a site plan that might do credit to a modern developer.

Owner David Carroll's stone house was located on the heights above the mill, overlooking everything. Since 1925, it has been occupied by the Florence Crittenton Services, a youth home. Finally, where the mill complex blends into the larger community at Chestnut

Avenue and Thirty-third Street, the mill owners in 1878 built a church for their employees, now the Mount Vernon Hampden United Methodist Church. ❖

N2 • EVERGREEN-ON-THE-FALLS

(NR)
3300 Falls Road
ca. 1860—architect unknown

The Italianate mansion built for Henry Snyder was occupied for most of the last half of the nineteenth century by members of the Hooper and Carroll families, proprietors of the nearby cotton mills in Hampden and Woodberry. The Carrolls added landscaping and formal boxwood gardens that made the estate a showplace. In 1926, the Maryland SPCA bought it and uses the house for meetings, receptions, and office space.

The brick building has bracketed cornices and canopies. After a bad fire in the 1970s, the SPCA rebuilt the mansion; a few original details, such as the main staircase (restored), marble mantels, and chandeliers, remain.

The restored stone valve house, completed in 1861, adjoined the Hampden Reservoir, since filled in; both were part of the city's early water-supply system. ❖

N3 • CLIPPER MILL

3300 Clipper Mill Road
1866—architect unknown

A handsome, extended, three-story brick building with an unusual stelliform chimney and arched, double-

framed windows, the Clipper Mill faces west and is best viewed from the Jones Falls Expressway; the opposite side, on Clipper Mill Road, is much less attractive. Across the street are some stone mill houses, including two groups of four; a rarity since such houses were usually built as semidetached units. Two earlier mills on the site burned. ❖

N4 • MEADOW MILL AT WOODBERRY
(NR)
3600 Clipper Mill Road
1877—architect unknown

The huge tower of the Meadow Mill, with its distinctive roof, dormers, and wooden cupola, is a familiar land-mark to motorists on the adjacent Jones Falls Expressway. (The cupola is one of the few remaining in the valley, but no longer houses the tower bell that once called the mill hands to work.)

From 1960 to 1989, the imposing, three-story brick mill building was owned by the Londontown Manufacturing Company, Inc., and was used in the production of London Fog rainwear. At that time, the window openings were bricked up to maintain interior temperature control. In 1989, the Londontown Company moved elsewhere and new owners acquired the property, converting it to office and warehouse space. Artisans and light-manufacturing firms moved in, the original window openings were restored, and curtains now appear in them, just as they did during the mill's early days.

Across the old Northern Central Railroad right-of-way (now the Central Light Rail Line) is the site of the

former Poole and Hunt foundry and machine shops whose main building, dating from the mid-nineteenth century, burned to the ground in 1995. ❖

N5 • PARK MILL

1750 Union Avenue
1855—architect unknown

The Park Mill is the site of the old Woodberry mill from which the community takes its name. To the north on Clipper Road are thirty-seven two-and-a-half-story stone mill houses. ❖

N6 • DRUID MILL

1600 Union Avenue
1866; enlarged 1872—architect unknown

In recent years the window openings have been closed in, but other than that the Druid Mill, with its pro-

nounced Italianate tower, has been remarkably well preserved. It is owned and occupied by Life-Like Products, Inc., the same firm that uses the former Mount Vernon Mill, No. 1 [N1]. The wing to the north was added at the later date. ❖

N7 • GREENWAY COTTAGES

(BCL)

Fortieth Street between Keswick Road and Roland Avenue

1874—Charles E. Cassell

Possessing much character and charm, these cottages are notable for their multicolored materials; the integral rather than applied nature of their detailing, such as the red brick arched window heads; their complex, gabled rooflines with prominent stone and brick chimneys; their wraparound porches and bay windows; and their overall substantial appearance.

They were built in the mid-1870s on land purchased by Edward MacDonald Greenway, a prominent Baltimorean who owned a notable town house at the corner of Mount Vernon and Washington places in Baltimore's then premier residential area; the house stood where the Washington Apartments now stand. The cottages are thought to have been built by his son, Edward M. Greeenway, Jr. Originally all three were identical; not long after they were built the easternmost was enlarged. They remained in the Greenway family until the early twentieth century, and then have since been owned, first by Roland Park Country School and now by Roland Park Place. They are occupied by residents of the community. ❖

N8 • STICK-STYLE HOUSES

4100 block Roland Avenue
ca. 1888—architect unknown

The Stick style was a variation on Alexander Jackson Davis and Andrew Jackson Downing's earlier Gothic cottage (see Bare Hills House [O2]). Some of the hallmarks of the Stick style were high, steep roofs, large brackets, and extensive porches with diagonal braces, all of which are seen in the house shown at 4122 Roland Avenue. The jerkinhead roofs and multicolored shingles are also typical. There are several other houses on the block in this style, probably all built at about the same time and perhaps by the same hand. ❖

N9 • POURED CONCRETE HOUSES

835–843 West University Parkway
1905—Edward L. Palmer, Jr.

These houses of exposed poured reinforced concrete were an innovation in their day. Indeed, the late Alexander Cochran, a modern architect and writer on architecture, asserted that the same use of material was not to occur again in Baltimore until sixty years later in the downtown Mechanic Theater [A10]. The houses are a great deal larger than they look from the street, with many rooms of ample size; the middle one, for example, contains eight bedrooms. ❖

N10 • ROLAND PARK

(NR)
1891 and later—Edward H. Bouton, Olmsted Brothers, and other planners and architects

The development of Roland Park and what led from it (see Essays, pp. 24–28 and 37–38) are both less nationally important and more locally important than is commonly known.

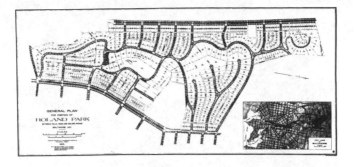

GENERAL PLAN
FOR PORTION OF
ROLAND PARK
BETWEEN FALLS ROAD AND ROLAND AVENUE
BALTIMORE, MD.

As American cities grew in the nineteenth century and methods of transportation advanced, the middle class sought living space away from the inner city. Taking advantage of this development, entrepreneurs, whether individuals or syndicates, bought up land adjacent to the cities (often including the summer estates of the rich) and developed what came to be known as garden suburbs, based more or less on English models. Many of these, here as elsewhere, were humdrum affairs, with interchangeable houses on standard lots laid out in grid-like street patterns. But then there were the more imaginative suburbs; and the best of them in Baltimore—indeed among the best anywhere—were those developed from the 1890s to the 1920s by the Roland Park Company.

Roland Park is often spoken of proudly and loosely by Baltimoreans as the first of the suburban developments, progenitor of all the rest; and sometimes those who speak of it so mean not just locally but nationally. Indeed it was not the first, even locally. Of those which preceded it, the first of architectural merit was Dixon's Hill [N15] of the 1850s to 1870s; this was followed by Sudbrook [O10], laid out by the great landscape architect Frederick Law Olmsted, Sr.—his only project in Baltimore.

But if the developments of the Roland Park Company were not the first of their kind, they were certainly the best in Baltimore, and remain so. Up to a century and more after their development began, they remain among the most successful, sought-after, and stable residential communities in the entire metropolitan area—even though the suburbs long ago pushed far beyond these now relatively close-to-town neighborhoods.

In 1891 a group of investors from Kansas City and London, acting on inquiry from Baltimore, put together a syndicate, amassed about 550 acres north of

Baltimore (including the estates of Woodlawn and Oakland), and began development. The project had several advantages. It was north of the city, the most fashionable, socially acceptable direction in which to move (the direction of the valley fox-hunting elite). It had a number of moneyed, leading citizens as directors, including Douglas H. Thomas and Joseph W. Jenkins, Jr. It had a good site, not flat but sloping and hilly and capable of being developed in interesting ways. It had good planners who developed it well, taking advantage of its natural topography to lay out irregular lots on winding streets; the first of these was George E. Kessler; succeeded by Olmsted, Olmsted, and Eliot; and with the personal involvement of the renowned Olmsted's son Frederick Law Olmsted, Jr. And it had as secretary and manager the inestimable Edward H. Bouton, workaholic and genius at all the complexities of successful suburban development.

It was Bouton who brought public transportation to Roland Park; Bouton who saw the need for a wide thoroughfare connecting the city's main north-south streets (Charles, St. Paul, Calvert), with the suburb, and finally accomplished it with University Parkway; Bouton who saw to architectural control, to see that houses achieved a minimum standard; Bouton who encouraged social amenities such as the Baltimore Country Club; Bouton who saw to every detail down to the smallest, as when he ordered stationery for the Roland Park Company and specified, "We . . . will prefer the matter done in a tasteful script . . . [on] woven linen paper."

And—what many in Baltimore apparently do not know—it was Bouton and the Roland Park Company

that in the decades subsequent to Roland Park's success also developed both Guilford and Homeland, giving Baltimore what many other cities could not and cannot boast: three enviable, carefully planned, and handsomely achieved suburbs, each with its own distinctive flavor, within a few minutes' commuting distance of the city's center.

In terms of landscape and architecture each development is quite different. Roland Park, with its hilly topography and wooded feeling, is the most romantic and countrylike. Guilford, with its substantial mansions on carefully tended lawns and with Sherwood Gardens at its center, is the most formal and the home of the wealthiest. Homeland, with its largely more modest houses lining cheerful streets, is the coziest, most welcoming, and perhaps most American looking of the three.

All three suburbs were fortunate to have—as might be expected from their advantageous locations and well-to-do residents—houses and other buildings designed by some of the city's leading architects of the period. In Roland Park, Wyatt and Nolting designed houses for themselves, as well as the Tudor half-timbered shopping center (shown above) whose variegated façade counteracts its mass; and a shingled Baltimore Country Club which subsequently burned and was replaced by a Colonial Revival building.

The major styles of Roland Park were the shingle cottage, perhaps best suited to the landscape; the Tudor half-timbered, most pretentious and perhaps least suited to the landscape; and the Queen Anne–influenced cottage. Other notable local firms who worked in Roland Park included Ellicott and Emmart; Palmer and Lamdin; and New York architect Charles A. Platt, who designed the block known as Goodwood Gardens, the

most formal and least Roland Park–like block in the complex (but nevertheless handsome).

Before associating with Lamdin, Edward L. Palmer, Jr., had designed in 1911 at the northern end of Roland Park a triangular block of houses with an interior common park. The structures, in singles and doubles, were heavily influenced by the then-popular Arts and Crafts style. In 1917 Palmer also designed a shopping center building (modeled somewhat on the Roland Park one) and a housing development for Dundalk. This development was built for the Bethlehem Steel Company, but the guiding hand was that of Edward Bouton. The houses, more than two hundred of them, were in a modified Arts and Crafts style, somewhat less expensive than their Roland Park predecessors; but they make a harmonious group on their intimate streets and constitute today a considerable part of what is now historic Dundalk. A tour guide to the area states: "Seventy-five years after its conception as a 'working man's Roland Park,' Dundalk continues to be a pleasant community. Few urban areas in the county have the cozy, small town ambiance of historic Dundalk."

In 1925 Palmer entered into partnership with William D. Lamdin, and the firm designed many houses in Guilford and Homeland. Lamdin is generally considered to have been the design genius of the two. Among their felicitous designs are a pair that really aren't a pair, the "gateway" (to Guilford) houses at 3701 St. Paul Street and 3700 Greenway (shown on p. 366). Built for brothers by their parents in 1925, they are notable for their subtle differences, complementary massing, generous though not large-scale rooms, and fine interior and exterior detailing.

Another leading local architect involved with the development of the Roland Park Company's suburbs was Laurence Hall Fowler. Fowler not only advised on the development of Guilford and Roland Park, but designed many houses himself, especially for the well-to-do in Guilford. His work was characterized by wide historical knowledge, attention to detail, and ability to fulfill his clients' needs and wishes. He was equally adept at a baronial Jacobean mansion, a Spanish-style Mediterranean villa, or a modest but well-proportioned town house, such as the Abel Wolman house [L7].

By the time of the Depression, the Roland Park Company was running out of steam, and its plans to develop Northwood were never fully carried out. But in the years between 1890 and 1930, thanks to the combination of forces led by the tireless and resourceful Edward Bouton, a major area was transformed from a group of country estates into what swiftly became—and remains, more than a century after it began—one of the most successful suburban developments in America. ❖

N11 • SAINT MARY'S SEMINARY

5400 Roland Avenue
1927—Maginnis and Walsh

This, the oldest Roman Catholic seminary in the United States, was founded in 1791 by the Sulpician Fathers and was once housed at One Mile Tavern on Market Street downtown. From there it moved to Paca Street, and in 1923 Baltimore's parishes raised $1 million to build a new seminary on 62 acres on the northern edge of Roland Park, bought for $173,000. Four years later

Archbishop Michael Curley officiated at the ground-breaking for the building, designed in a reserved Italian Baroque style by Maginnis and Walsh with Lucien Gaudreau in charge. (The firm subsequently designed the Cathedral of Mary Our Queen [L18].) The Depression and World War II held up completion of the project until 1954.

Five stories high and with a 470-foot-long façade clad in Indiana limestone, the complex is E-shaped, with three legs reaching back perpendicular to the north and south ends and the center of the long corridor that runs along the front of the building. The dining room is in the south leg, the library in the north leg. The middle leg, behind the entrance, contains the somewhat cold but imposing chapel, with its barrel-vaulted ceiling and stone walls. This was the final section, added in the early 1950s, essentially to the original design but with bell towers eliminated and using cast instead of quarried stone to save money. The two end legs are 301 feet long each, the chapel 220 feet long.

Library and other recent renovations have been carried out by Gaudreau Architects (successors to Lucien Gaudreau). They also designed a further addition, a center for continuing studies as an extension of the south leg, which opened in 1996. ❖

N12 • MOUNT WASHINGTON OCTAGON

(BCL)
Near Smith and Greeley avenues, USF&G Mount
Washington Center campus
1855—Thomas Dixon

The octagon was built under the direction of the Reverend Elias Heiner of the German Reformed Church and was used until 1861 as the Mount Washington Female College. The college failed after the Civil War and, in 1867, the Sisters of Mercy bought the building and opened a school called Mount Saint Agnes. It later included 129 acres of land and several more buildings. In 1971, Mount Saint Agnes merged with Loyola College, moved from the Mount Washington campus, and put it up for sale. In 1982, the United States Fidelity and Guaranty Company bought it, retained certain buildings including the octagon, added others, and planned a major future expansion.

The octagon mode, which flourished in the United States in the mid-1850s, was inspired by Orson Squire Fowler, a phrenologist who also wrote on health and marital happiness. The octagon form was credited with a number of advantages: more light-filled, superior ventilation, greater floor space, and more efficient use of space. Other examples were built in the area. This one was of four stories with surrounding wooden verandas or porches on two floors and a wooden cupola above.

Between 1982 and 1984 the octagon received a restoration-renovation by Cochran, Stephenson, and Donkervoet, Inc., with Thomas Spies in charge. The walls and windows were restored as closely as possible to the originals, the cupola was taken apart and restored on the ground, and concrete porches that had replaced the original ones were removed and replaced with new wooden ones. The interior, however, is totally new. A central spiral staircase was removed, leaving an open well straight up to the cupola, and the floors were attractively redesigned as guest rooms and suites. The building is now used as a conference center. ❖

N13 • FIDELITY AND GUARANTY LIFE INSURANCE COMPANY

6225 Smith Avenue
1990—Peterson and Brickbauer; Emery Roth and Sons

Charles Brickbauer, architect-in-charge of this building, has here fused modernist and postmodernist aes-

thetics in the best way: not by slapping classical details on a modern structure, but by creating a thoroughly modern building that uses the most up-to-date technology yet is subtly infused with ideas from the past. These historical references refrain from striking the visitor in the eye, but they serve to make the experience of the building visually and psychologically rich. Brickbauer has called his creation "essential Baroque," and with reason.

Situated on the Mount Washington campus of the United States Fidelity and Guaranty Company, of which F & G Life is a subsidiary, the building is a 250,000-square-foot, three-and-a-half-story office complex over a two-and-a-half-level, mostly underground garage. The visible part of the garage is clad in gray-green Brazilian granite and serves as the base of the building in places. But elsewhere, and especially on the entrance façade, the glass office structure appears to sit directly on the grass, with only a thin band of stainless steel between. The building descends a wooded ravine, fitting into and preserving a large amount of its wooded site.

The architect took advantage of recent technology to create an all glass curtain wall that is in effect "glued" to the metal frame with adhesives to eliminate the need for visible fasteners. The complex is really two office buildings faced in green glass and connected by an atrium walled in clear glass.

The atrium is mildly Piranesian, with a wide staircase under bridges that connect the two buildings at their upper levels. The buildings themselves, unequal in size, are shifted slightly out of alignment to create a dynamic feel so characteristic of the Baroque.

But that dynamism, immediately apparent as one faces the building, serves only as an introduction to a building rich in illusion and allusion. The green glass can be both transparent and reflective, so that at times it mirrors the surrounding landscape, at times it lets the eye travel into and even through the building, and at certain times, and places, you think you're seeing through when you're really seeing a reflection, and vice versa. And at the same time that it's dynamic and transparent, the building is also solid and highly sculptural, its many corners emphasizing the physicality of its presence.

It's difficult if not impossible for the visitor to tell that the glass in the building's recessed rectangular arches is slightly darker green than the rest of the glass, but it nevertheless enhances the effect of these elements. They add life and variety to the façades, and as Baltimore *Sun* architecture critic Edward Gunts noted, "add a sense of Beaux-Arts formality, evoking the work of the French-born architect Paul Philippe Cret." As Gunts also noted, that is not the only allusion here. The atrium staircase refers to that at Washington's National Gallery, by John Russell Pope; and another staircase refers to a Louis Kahn staircase at Yale.

While there are many complexities to this architecture, it is also very much of a piece. Above all, it is both interesting and exhilarating. As Gunts observed, the architects here "have taken the lowly glass box, subject of much derision in recent years, and made it worth our attention again." ❖

N14 • MOUNT WASHINGTON PRESBY-TERIAN CHURCH (The Chimes, Inc.)
1801 Thornbury Road
1878—Dixon and Carson

A good example of the Stick style, the church was built for just $4,200. The initial 30-by-60-foot section consists of the tower and nave; attached to it at right angles is a later addition housing a meeting room and kitchen. The battens covering the wooden joints of the vertical siding, the timber buttresses, and the braces suggesting stone tracery lend the building a definite Gothic flavor. The nave, with dark wood trusses, is a small and intimate space. The walnut altar and pews have been removed because the building is no longer a church. The neighboring Chimes, Inc., bought the building in 1968 and

uses it as a school in their training program for children
with special needs. ❖

N15 • DIXON'S HILL

Kenway, Maywood, Dixon, and Thornbury roads,
Mount Washington
*1855 and later—Thomas Dixon, Thomas C. Kennedy, and
others*

Mount Washington was one of Baltimore's earliest
planned suburbs (see Essays, pp. 23–24). It traces its
origins to Washingtonville, the mill town that grew up
around the Washington Cotton Manufacturing Company, established in 1810. In the 1830s, the Baltimore
and Susquehanna Railroad connected Washingtonville
to the city (and to York, Pennsylvania); in 1854, the
same year the development of Mount Washington was
undertaken, the line was reorganized as the Northern
Central Railroad.

The railroad played an important part in the plans
of the developers of Mount Washington, who offered
rail commuting to the city. George Gelbach and Elias
Heiner, the developers, also helped to found the Mount
Washington Female College. By 1854, they had acquired about 300 acres west of the Northern Central rail
line. First known as the Mount Washington Rural Retreat, it encompassed most of today's Mount Washington, including the town center, the former college
campus, part of Dixon's Hill, and The Terraces, a later

development located on Terrace Road, across Smith Avenue from Dixon's Hill.

According to their 1854 pamphlet, "The design of the enterprise is to furnish to those seeking it, a healthy, retired, and respectable country residence, avoiding the monotony of a village, or the crowding and confinement of the city, yet retaining the advantages of a community; in short, having the convenience of the city with the advantages of the country."

In succeeding years, as what began as a summer resort became a year-round place to live, various entrepreneurs purchased lots and built houses. Among them was Thomas Dixon, architect of the Mount Washington Presbyterian Church, who in 1856 bought land near that building. Eventually, having acquired interest in a lumber company and seeing a ready market for his product, he designed and built a number of houses in what became known as Dixon's Hill. The earliest date from 1855; the one shown in the photograph, at 1808 Thornbury Road, was built about 1870. The homes on The Terraces are grander; some were designed, ca. 1890–1900, by Thomas C. Kennedy, briefly Dixon's architectural partner and Mount Washington resident. The 1856 home of developer George Gelbach, though missing its original Italianate tower, can still be seen at 1705 South Road.

Although annexed to Baltimore in 1919, Mount Washington retains the character of a suburban village with many active shops and restaurants in the town center. The construction of the Jones Falls Expressway divided the original mill buildings (some have been renovated for retail and office use) from the original summer retreat and also effectively ended rail commuting on the Northern Central Railroad. But with the railroad's conversion to the Central Light Rail Line (the stop is located at about where the former station stood), Mount Washington is again connected to Baltimore and the northern suburbs by train. ❖

N16 • CROSS KEYS

Falls Road below Northern Parkway
1964—various architects; 1976—Frank O. Gehry and Associates

Across Falls Road from Roland Park, one of Baltimore's oldest planned communities, is one of the newest, the Village of Cross Keys. Built for about twenty-five hundred residents by The Rouse Company, the developers of Columbia, it predates and is in many ways a miniature version of that much larger new town. Like Columbia, Cross Keys has a variety of types of residences, a town center, pedestrian pathways, and so on.

The site comprises 72 acres of the Baltimore Country Club's original golf course. Cross Keys took its name from an inn that stood near the corner of Falls Road and Cold Spring Lane whose signboard consisted of two large crossed keys. It was a favorite stopping place for travelers to and from the outlying districts.

The inn and stores at the present Cross Keys have similarly become popular destinations for residents and shoppers. The village center was designed by Toronto architects Murray and Fleiss to resemble an old-fash-

ioned village green; the landscaped square can accommodate concerts and art shows. Surrounding it are shops
with offices above.

Richard C. Stauffer, an architect, and James W. Rouse,
the developer of shopping malls and new towns, collaborated on the site plan for Cross Keys. Stauffer and
Collins-Kronstadt and Associates of Silver Spring designed the first town houses. In 1976, Harper House was
built, designed by a not-yet-famous West Coast architect,
Frank O. Gehry and Associates. Since then, other structures and amenities have been added, but preservation
of the larger trees and natural landscape features have
helped to maintain an almost bucolic setting. A $6.8
million renovation of the commercial and public spaces
at Cross Keys was completed in 1996. ❖

N17 • COLDSPRING
Springarden Drive off Cold Spring Lane
1977—Moshe Safdie

Coldspring did not fulfill its considerable potential as a
"new town in town"; neither did it fail. The original
Coldspring—the sole project in Baltimore by the renowned architect of Montreal's Habitat '67—was stark
and self-enclosed. Coldspring was recently expanded in
a more conventional and open fashion.

Planning began in the late 1960s. The site stretched
almost 2 miles on the west side of the Jones Falls Expressway between Cylburn and Woodberry. The 1972
master plan by Safdie and landscape architect Lawrence

Halprin envisioned a $200 million, 375-acre, 3,800-unit new town with 11,000 residents, to be built in ten or so years. It featured a buffer zone on the north, a town center in the middle, and high-rise apartments lining the walls of the quarry near the southern end, with small lakes, parks, and recreation areas throughout.

Factory-produced housing units, like those at Habitat '67, were also projected. However, the first 124 "deckhouses," which faced each other across pedestrian decks over parking areas, were conventionally built by the F. D. Rich Corporation. Construction began in 1975. The exterior materials were mainly precast concrete and brick; the light-filled interiors were arranged in varied configurations. The first units were occupied in 1977, and the average price was $45,000.

By 1985, 128 more "deckhouses" and a 151-unit, seven-story apartment building for the elderly had been added. That year, the city ended the Rich Corporation's exclusive right to build in Coldspring. A 1986 design competition produced a new, more traditional master plan for up to nine hundred residences and a village center. In 1994, the City Council altered the urban renewal plan for Coldspring, officially ending Safdie's grand design. ❖

N18 • CYLBURN

(BCL, NR)
Cylburn Park, 4915 Greenspring Avenue
1889—George A. Frederick

Cylburn is the keystone of the former estates ringing the city that became municipal parks. It functions now as an arboretum and potential house museum.

Jesse Tyson began Cylburn in 1863 as a summer home for his mother, but her death and the Civil War intervened, and the house with its tall central tower (unfortunately now missing its iron roof cresting) was not completed until 1889. Designed in a simplified Second Empire style by Frederick, the architect of City Hall, it was built of gneiss, a stone quarried at nearby Bare Hills.

Jesse Tyson's father, Isaac Tyson, Jr., a Quaker and practical chemist, initiated the processing of chrome in Baltimore. He developed the chrome and copper mines at Bare Hills and Soldiers Delight in Baltimore County and the Baltimore Chrome Works in Fells Point. Jesse Tyson inherited the chrome works from his father. (His brother James, who inherited the chrome mining interests, built the neighboring Ruscombe mansion, ca. 1876, now part of Coldspring.)

Jesse Tyson remained a bachelor until 1888 when, in his sixties, he married nineteen-year-old Edyth Johns, a Baltimore debutante and renowned beauty. The mansion was then completed and she made Cylburn a home, furnishing it with European imports. Tyson reportedly boasted, "I have the fairest wife, the fastest horses, and the finest house in Maryland."

In 1910, four years after he died, his widow married an army lieutenant, Bruce Cotten. They commissioned the Olmsted brothers to landscape the property, and Cylburn became the scene of lavish parties, with guests arriving at the estate's own station on the Northern Central Railroad and strolling among fountains, gardens, and rare trees lit with Japanese lanterns. Edyth Cotten reigned as a society hostess and patron of the arts for many years. When she died in 1942, her husband sold the house and 176 acres to the city for $42,300.

The Cylburn estate is now a nature preserve, and the mansion serves as headquarters for the Parks Department's horticultural division and the Cylburn Arboretum Association, a volunteer group. However, one can still visualize how a wealthy family lived and entertained on a country estate in nineteenth-century Baltimore. The owners and Frederick must have had society gatherings in mind when they laid out the interior as a central hall with four formal rooms opening from it and a grand stairway in back.

Beginning with the vestibule with its mosaics and leaded-glass transom, the architect's use of materials and arrangement of spaces are impressive. The entrance hallway has parquet floors laid in a diamond pattern of oak, maple, and black walnut, opulent mirrors and chandeliers, and Belgian tapestries depicting a mansion in the woods.

The drawing room, to the right of the front door, was furnished in Louis XV style. Its Rococo marble fireplace, carved wood paneling, and floor-to-ceiling French windows with their original heavy brass hardware are vivid reminders of Cylburn's previous life. The stairway (painted white), is also of black walnut. A floor above, in Edyth Cotten's former bedroom, bas relief cherubs pose in a unique curved plaster frieze.

An ell containing a kitchen with servants' rooms above it is located behind the main block of the house and discreetly connected to it so that the help could go about their tasks without disrupting the guests.

Cylburn's exterior was recently renovated at a cost of $200,000; the interior awaits restoration. ❖

Tour O

Northwest, Houses (Driving)

O1   COCHRAN HOUSE
      901 West Lake Avenue
      1975—Alexander S. Cochran

O2   BARE HILLS HOUSE
      6222 Falls Road
      ca. 1857—architect unknown

O3   HOOPER HOUSE
      Address withheld at owner's request
      1959—Marcel Breuer

O4   ROCKLAND MILL, COMMUNITY, AND HOUSE
      Falls and Old Court roads
      1810 and after—architect unknown; 1977 and
      after—Joseph and Martin Azola, Grieves
      Associates, Rockland Village Partnership

O5   RICHTER HOUSE
      2005 Ridgecrest Court
      1963—Charles H. Richter, Jr.

O6   BROOKLANDWOOD (St. Paul's School)
      Falls Road north of the Beltway
      ca. 1790 and after—architect unknown

O7   EUCHTMAN HOUSE
      6807 Cross Country Boulevard
      1940—Frank Lloyd Wright

O8   TEMPLE OHEB SHALOM
      7310 Park Heights Avenue
      1960—Sheldon I. Leavitt, with Walter Gropius,
      consulting architect

O9   STATE POLICE HEADQUARTERS, PIKESVILLE
      1200 block Reisterstown Road and Church Lane
      1816—architect unknown

O10 SUDBROOK PARK
      Sudbrook Lane off Reisterstown Road
      1887—Frederick Law Olmsted, Sr.

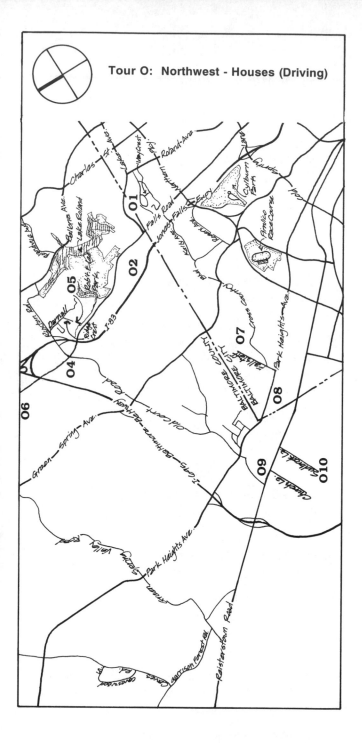

Tour O: Northwest - Houses (Driving)

Essays in domestic design by America's greatest architect and landscape architect—Frank Lloyd Wright and Frederick Law Olmsted respectively—highlight this tour. It also includes works by European immigrants and one-time partners Marcel Breuer and Walter Gropius, and by Baltimore architects, the late Alexander S. Cochran and Charles H. Richter, Jr. Along the way is a delightful nineteenth-century example of a country house based on a plan by Andrew Jackson Downing. ❖

O1 • COCHRAN HOUSE
901 West Lake Avenue
1975—Alexander S. Cochran

The late architect's first house on West Lake Avenue was a modern "split-level" before the term became generic, and created a local sensation when it appeared in 1950 in a neighborhood of more traditional homes. It also won a national American Institute of Architects design award. As his family became smaller in later years, Cochran sold this house and most of the 5-acre lot to the Boys' Latin School (which recently demolished it for expansion purposes) and built a smaller home to the east on the remaining acreage.

In the second house (pictured and described here), he substituted brick for stone plus cypress siding and built on a single level, but retained some of the previous features: living spaces with a southern exposure facing away from the street, a clerestory allowing natural light (augmented by fluorescent lighting) into the north side, and a rear cantilevered roof covering a sunken terrace. Bluestone, brick, and walnut paneling were some of the interior finishes.

In back, Cochran created an atrium effect with a brick wall surrounding a large courtyard, a sculpture garden, and a small pool, or "plunge." The wall has narrow vertical slots at 12-foot intervals, through which light plays in varying patterns.

William H. Potts was the landscape architect. ❖

O2 • BARE HILLS HOUSE
6222 Falls Road
ca. 1857—architect unknown

Set well back from the road on 2½ acres of land, 6222 Falls Road is a picturesque example of the "rural Gothic" cottage popularized in mid-nineteenth-century America by Alexander Jackson Davis and Andrew Jackson Downing. Except for its porch and octagonal cupola, the Bare Hills House closely resembles "A Gate-Lodge in the English style," shown in Downing's *The Architecture of Country Houses*, first published in 1850.

The foundation is of soapstone and serpentine, quarried nearby at Bare Hills (so-called because the underlying rock stunts the growth of trees; copper and chrome were also mined in the vicinity). The remainder of the house is built of wood in the bracketed style with battens covering the joints in the vertical siding, an approach approved by Downing because it expressed "strength and truthfulness." Prominent bay windows at the first and second levels (the upper one covered by a jerkin-head roof), and a large wraparound porch complete the façade.

Inside there are four large rooms downstairs with two fireplaces and a central hall and five bedrooms upstairs. These have odd planes and angles due to the steeply pitched roof and gables. Original wooden mantels and moldings, plaster cornices, ceiling medallions, and hardware remain in the house, which has been remodeled numerous times. Doctors and a U.S. admiral were residents in the 1800s. The current owners won a Baltimore Heritage preservation award in 1979 for their restoration. ❖

O3 • HOOPER HOUSE

address withheld at owner's request
1959—Marcel Breuer

Built to fit the area and not spoil its surroundings, the Hooper house, in a heavily wooded section overlooking Lake Roland, is by the renowned architect Marcel Breuer—contemporary of Gropius, member of the Bauhaus, designer of many architectural masterpieces.

The plan of the house is basically a rectangle, with a mid-court and entryway, open to the sky, between the living and sleeping areas. The house thus follows Breuer's bi-nuclear design, in which, according to the architect, "whole living areas are considered as unities. The result [is] . . . to separate and give privacy to distinct areas of the house."

Rugged Maryland fieldstone taken from the site forms the exterior walls. The stone façade is broken only by the entry, two sliding glass doors permitting a view through the entry court to Lake Roland beyond. The stone provides an effective barrier to the western sun and helps orient the house to privacy and the eastern view.

The interior has stone floors and walls and acoustical tile ceilings. Breuer designed spare furniture for the house, to allow the rooms themselves to speak.

The house is spanned by steel beams resting on stone walls or on Lally columns (concrete-filled steel cylinders), and topped with 2-by-10-inch wood joists. Floors are concrete slabs on grade or reinforced concrete where not supported by the ground.

We made an exception to include this house, even though its address is not given, because of Breuer's importance. ❖

O4 • ROCKLAND MILL, COMMUNITY, AND HOUSE

Falls and Old Court roads
1810 and after—architect unknown; 1977 and after—Joseph and Martin Azola, Grieves Associates, Rockland Village Partnership

Between 1810 and 1813, the mill building at the corner of Falls and Old Court roads was constructed. An entire village sprang up, of which the old stone houses across Old Court Road from the mill remain. Also in the vicinity were a blacksmith shop, a wheelwright shop, and other community amenities. The whole was owned by the Johnson family, who also owned extensive property in the vicinity. In 1836–37, they built a handsome Greek Revival house, subsequently enlarged with porches and an addition to the back, both entirely in keeping with the original structure. The house still stands, but is not visible from the road and is not open to the public. It is still owned by the Johnson family, who sold the mill building and a piece of the property north of Old Court

Road and west of the mill houses to the firm of J. R. Azola and Son, builders. The Azolas have handsomely renovated the mill building, which now serves as their headquarters and other commercial offices. They have also constructed, on the property across the road, a housing community designed by Grieves Associates.

The old stone mill houses on Falls Road north of Old Court Road were owned by the Johnson family and rented out until 1980. In that year Robert H. Johnson, of the Johnson family, Martin Azola of the Azola firm, and David Wright, architect and member of the Grieves firm, formed the Rockland Village Partnership. They bought fifteen of the houses, renovated the exteriors to standards set by the Department of the Interior, which had earlier designated the village a Historic District, and sold them. Individual owners subsequently renovated the interiors. The result is a happy outcome for the houses, the owners, and the village as a whole. In a subsequent article, Mr. Johnson wrote, "Rockland Village may be the only mill village in Maryland which has been rehabilitated in total at one time to one set of standards. More importantly, though, a deteriorating rental situation has been renovated to high standards of excellence and authenticity, the homes have been placed into individual private ownership, and yet the sense of community has been preserved intact." ❖

O5 • RICHTER HOUSE

2005 Ridgecrest Court
1963—Charles H. Richter, Jr.

The architect sited his house near the top of 2 acres of steeply sloping wooded land and built it into the hill-

side, with railroad ties forming the retaining walls. There are two main levels and a series of terraces. The upper story, faced on three sides with redwood siding, is cantilevered over the lower, built of cinder block. Set well back from the street down a winding walk, a wooden footbridge crossing a shallow moat leads to the front door.

The interior spaces are simply and clearly defined. They look out over the woods to the south through a wall of glass, creating the effect of a ski lodge in winter and a vacation cottage in summer. A wooden deck extends out in back among the trees. ❖

O6 • BROOKLANDWOOD
(St. Paul's School)
Falls Road north of the Beltway
ca. 1790 and after—architect unknown

Charles Carroll of Carrollton, also associated with Doughoregan [J15], the Carroll Mansion [F4], and Homewood [L8], provided this house on 1,400 acres of land for his daughter Polly and her husband, Richard Caton. The house, later owned by Alexander D. Brown, broker, and Captain Isaac E. Emerson, famous locally as the inventor of Bromo Seltzer, has undergone many changes in its two-hundred-year history.

Construction of the original, Federal house was begun in 1790, and a tax assessment of 1798 records a 33-by-57-foot house of two stories, the core of the pres-

ent building. It is said to have had an octagonal bay projecting from its north side. East and west wings were added by 1812, at which point the house attained a length of 117 feet, with a south façade portico somewhat enlarged from the original. The Browns bought the property in 1847, and by 1860 the house had acquired a wide porch around the semioctagonal bay on the north.

In the 1890s Mrs. George Brown oversaw major changes, extending the north wall 15 feet to eliminate the octagonal bay and adding a Palladian window, extending the south porch, altering rooms inside, and adding much interior Georgian-style decoration still in evidence. A 1948 article in *Maryland Historical Magazine* by architect Robert Erskine Lewis remarked politely but pointedly about these changes: "The delicacy the house must have originally possessed has gone, but there is still charm."

Emerson bought the property in 1916 and made few changes. St. Paul's School acquired the house and property in 1952, and since then the house has been put to both residential and office uses while preserving the essential flavor of its major rooms. In 1970–71 it received a $450,000 restoration, which updated it for the school's purposes but made minimal structural changes and maintained its integrity. ❖

O7 • EUCHTMAN HOUSE

6807 Cross Country Boulevard
1940—Frank Lloyd Wright

The Euchtman House was one of about twenty-six Usonian houses built in some fourteen states. These houses, which one critic has called "a brilliant galaxy of

small and beautiful homes," are collectively as significant as any of Wright's larger, more famous projects.

Usonia was Wright's acronym for the United States of North America, and the Usonian house, conceived during the Depression, was his attempt to provide well-designed, affordable housing for all Americans. The effort failed, but Wright did establish a part of the vocabulary for the suburban home; the carport, built-in furniture, and indirect lighting were a few of his innovations. The Usonian house contributed to Wright's own concept of a future decentralized America—Broadacre City—an idea that has since become reality but not as the Utopia he envisioned.

Economy, flexibility, and comfort were the main Usonian principles. The houses were organic: their design evolved from the site, the climate, the owner's needs, the budget, and the unique architect-client relationship. They were low-slung, part of the landscape, with flat roofs and wide overhangs to shield against the summer sun. They were linear, articulated, hexagonal, or curved in plan. They had condensed interiors: bedrooms in back, bathroom and kitchen amidships, living and dining areas in front. They were technologically advanced with radiant heating pipes enclosed in the concrete floor slab and composite wall systems of lightweight wood.

The Baltimore version was built for Mr. and Mrs. Joseph Euchtman and supervised by Gordon Chadwick, an apprentice architect from Wright's Taliesin fellowship, who also oversaw the construction of the 1940 Pope-Leighey house in Falls Church, Virginia, another Usonian project.

Both the Baltimore and Virginia houses had in-line plans and two levels due to their sloping sites. Both were built on concrete slabs with embedded heating pipes. Skeptical of Wright's wall system—a sandwich of cypress screwed to a plywood core—the Baltimore building inspectors loaded a 4-foot wall panel with twenty-three 100-pound bags of cement, about four times the required load. Unpersuaded by this practical demonstration of strength, they were finally convinced by an engineering calculation.

The interiors of both houses were zoned for use; the spaces flowed into one another, defined less by doors and walls than by subtle shifts in level and ceiling height. Clerestory windows, fireplaces, and built-in bookshelves were included.

The Baltimore Usonian house was a very modest, 900-square-foot dwelling on a ¾-acre wooded lot, but its careful siting and Wright's genius for design and attention to detail lent it a special grandeur. The diagonal carport was constructed around an existing tree; the tree was later removed.

Inside, a narrow hallway led from the rear bedrooms past the bathroom and down to the compact kitchen (Wright's "work-space"), located in the center of the house, "an alcove of the living room," as he dictated. The passageway then opened out into the combined living and dining areas. Natural brick, cypress, and floor-to-ceiling glass were the original interior finishes.

There have been many changes over the years. Wright's custom furniture was disposed of, and a small storage room was added on to the back of the house. In 1976, a family that includes an architect and a landscape architect among its members acquired the building; in 1981, they partially rebuilt it. The floor slab was replaced and heating and air-conditioning ducts substituted for the radiant heating pipes. (The original heating system had broken down.) The termite-damaged wooden walls were reconstructed, insulated, and recovered with cypress siding. Interior walls were removed to make a single large space from two small bedrooms, eliminating the hallway. Skylights were added over the bedroom, bathroom, and kitchen. The grounds were landscaped and a small pool and redwood deck and fence put in.

Wright's basic Usonian design, however, remains intact. The house cost just $16,000 when it was built. ❖

O8 · TEMPLE OHEB SHALOM

7310 Park Heights Avenue
*1960—Sheldon I. Leavitt, with Walter Gropius,
consulting architect*

Most distinctive among this building's features are the
four great vaults designed by Gropius, which give both
the façade and the interior of the sanctuary their character. Of continuously poured concrete, a process new
at the time, the arches taper from an 8-inch thickness at
the bottom to a 3½-inch thickness at the top. The vaults
carry through the sanctuary, creating a large open rectangle 83 feet by 90 feet, seating 1,100 people.

The front part of the temple complex, of brick
masonry construction, also includes a wide entrance
hall and a rectangular auditorium on the same axis as
the sanctuary. On major religious occasions the walls
between the three areas slide back, creating a space
capable of seating twenty-four hundred.

From this area the corridor or spine of the complex
passes an enclosed garden and an office and boardroom

area and continues in a covered walkway to the school beyond. The twenty-three classrooms of the school have a reinforced concrete roof and floor construction, with curtain walls of glass and concrcte. ❖

O9• STATE POLICE HEADQUARTERS
1200 block Reisterstown Road and Church Lane,
Pikcsville
1816—architect unknown

Since 1949, when the State Police took over the former arsenal and Confederate veterans' home, they have added a major complex of buildings housing everything from an accident records bureau to an aviation division. The principal architectural interest remains the pleasing proportions and solid integrity of the 1816 building on the left facing Reisterstown Road. The porch railings arc cast iron.

Built just after the War of 1812, the arsenal was seized by local Confederates at the outbreak of the Civil War, but soon retaken by federal forces. Maybe some of these Confederates returned after 1888, when it became a home for Confederate veterans, a role it continued to play until 1932. Subsequently it served a number of groups until the State Police took it over. ❖

O10 • SUDBROOK PARK
(NR)
Sudbrook Lane, off Reisterstown Road
1889—Frederick Law Olmsted, Sr.

Olmsted, America's first great landscape architect and the codesigner of New York's Central Park, was responsi-

ble for only three residential designs that survive: River-side, in Illinois; Druid Hills, in Atlanta; and Sudbrook (the original name, later changed to Sudbrook Park). On 204 acres of what had been the estate of James Howard McHenry, Olmsted created a plan of curvilinear streets with generous use of trees and other plantings and with open green spaces for the use of the community. He also suggested deed restrictions covering lot size and other aspects of ownership that influenced similar restrictions in the later development of Roland Park, according to Sudbrook researcher Melanie Anson.

Sudbrook was ahead of its time. Located eight miles

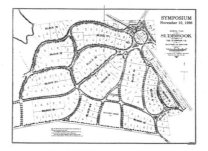

from the city when it was created, it was planned for year-round residents but became primarily a community of summer renters in its early years. The Sudbrook Company was out of business by 1910, and later developers somewhat compromised Olmsted's plan. But not enough to destroy it, for Sudbrook retains a sense of community more than a century after it was designed. In the 1990s, portions of Sudbrook have become a Baltimore County Historic District. ❖

Brief Biographies of Architects (Deceased) Who Lived and Practiced in Baltimore

Andrews, Richard Snowden (1830–1903). Born and educated in Washington, D.C., Andrews began his career in architecture as an apprentice carpenter. After his family moved to Baltimore in 1849, he interned with Niernsee and Neilson, then formed a partnership in 1852 with Eben Faxon. Andrews fought for the Confederacy during the Civil War, was horribly wounded by a shell fragment near Winchester, Virginia, and was not expected to survive, but did. Embittered by the war's outcome, he moved to Mexico, where he worked on railroads and swore never to return to the United States. He did, however, in 1867, and went on the lecture circuit carrying the bloodstained jacket he had worn when he was wounded. (It now belongs to the Maryland Historical Society.)

Andrews's extant works in Baltimore include the Franklin Street Presbyterian Church parsonage (1859) [B11], the Eastern Female High School [F10], and the original Church of the Redeemer (1856) [L19]. He also designed the governor's mansion in Annapolis, later radically altered, and the south wing of the Treasury Department in Washington, D.C. Eben Faxon, Andrews's partner, is chiefly known for his work on the portico of the Basilica of the Assumption [B9].

Archer, George (1848–1920). Archer, a Harford County native, graduated from Princeton in 1870, then went to work for George A. Frederick. He established his own office in 1875 and about 1904 took in Raymond Allen; the firm became Archer and Allen. Archer practiced a variety of styles, culminating in the overdrawn forms of the Neo-Classical Revival, an example being the Schloss Building, 5 East Lexington Street (1904). Still standing among his many other designs are the former Denny and Mitchell Building on the northwest corner of North Avenue and Howard Street (1885), the Graham-Hughes House [C10], and the Brady wing of the Johns Hopkins Hospital (1913).

Baldwin, Ephraim Francis (1837–1916). Born in Troy, New York, the son of a civil engineer, Baldwin was raised in Baltimore. He attended Mount St. Mary's College in Emmitsburg before joining John R. Niernsee's office as an apprentice draftsman. In 1867, he left Niernsee to practice architecture on his own, and in 1869 he formed a partnership with Bruce Price, which lasted until 1873. Baldwin again practiced by himself until joining forces with Josias Pennington in 1883, an association that continued until Baldwin's death.

Baldwin and Pennington succeeded Niernsee and Neilson as the house architects for the Baltimore and Ohio Railroad, and they designed numerous warehouses and other railroad structures in the city and stations along its main and branch lines. Many of the station buildings remain, those at Point of Rocks and Oakland, Maryland, being particularly well known. In addition to their B & O Railroad buildings in Baltimore [I2, I4, K11], Baldwin and Pennington designed the Fidelity Building [A15], the Hutzler's Palace Building [E2], the 1911 addition to the Eutaw Savings Bank [E5], the Maryland Club [K6], the 1910 addition to the Baltimore County Courthouse [M4], the 1895 City College building at Howard and Centre streets, and the former Maryland Trust Building at Calvert and Redwood streets, a survivor of the 1904 Baltimore Fire.

Carson, Charles L. (1847–91). One of Baltimore's most important native architects, Carson was a natural and prolific designer. He was a major practitioner of the Romanesque Revival, but was equally adept in a variety of commercial styles, including the then popular Neo-Grec. In his twenty-two-year professional career, he designed and supervised the construction of more than 150 projects including houses, banks, hotels, synagogues and churches, factories and warehouses. Those that survive are almost all of high quality, the more surprising since Carson had almost no formal training in architecture.

He was the son of builder David Carson and began work as a carpenter with his father. About 1870, he joined architect Thomas Dixon and simultaneously enrolled in architectural drawing courses at the Maryland Institute. The following year, Carson became Dixon's partner and, in 1880, opened his own office. About

1888, he brought in Joseph E. Sperry as his chief assistant. Two of Carson's best local buildings appeared in 1890: the former Central Savings Bank [A14] and the former Strouse Brothers Company Building [E8]. Montgomery Schuyler's 1891 essay, "The Romanesque Revival in America," in the second issue of *The Architectural Record*, prominently featured Carson's designs. Carson died that year, aged forty-four, and Sperry carried on the firm's work.

In addition to his work on the Masonic Temple [A16] and the Equitable Building [D2] (both by Carson and Sperry), the Mount Vernon Place United Methodist Church [C9] (Dixon and Carson), and the Pratt Library's Canton Branch [G2], Carson designed the Eutaw Savings Bank Building [E5] and was the supervising architect for Stanford White's Lovely Lane Church and Goucher Hall [L1 and L2]. He also designed the 1887 Marburg Brothers Tobacco Warehouse on South Charles Street (demolished ca. 1990), and notable cast-iron structures: the 1871 Wilmington Opera House, recently restored, and the 1875 Baltimore American Building, destroyed in the 1904 Fire (both with Thomas Dixon).

Cassell, Charles E. (ca. 1838–1916). Cassell's family emigrated from Genoa, Italy, to Norfolk in the 1820s; the family name was originally Casselli. Cassell was born at Portsmouth, graduated from the University of Virginia with a degree in engineering, and served in the Confederate Army. Charged with treason after the Civil War, he fled to Chile where he became an admiral in the Chilean navy. The charges were later dropped and Cassell returned to Virginia. He then practiced architecture in St. Louis for a time before moving to Baltimore in about 1868. Cassell was a founding member of the Baltimore Chapter of the American Institute of Architects. From about 1905 to 1909 he practiced with his son John (Charles E. Cassell and Son), and was also sometimes associated with his nephew (Cassell and Cassell).

A prolific and competent designer, Cassell contributed to the city many churches, warehouses, commercial structures, hotels, apartment buildings, and houses, including the Greek Orthodox Cathedral of the Annunciation [K10], the Greenway Cottages [N7], the Stafford Hotel and the Severn Apartments on Mount Vernon Place, the Brexton Apartments on Park Avenue, Stewart's Department Store on Howard Street, and the former Hotel Junker on East Fayette Street, the last recently restored.

Cochran, Alexander S. (1913–89). A native Baltimorean, Cochran attended Princeton, the Yale School of Architecture, and the Harvard Graduate School of Design. He returned to Baltimore in 1947 and established Alexander Cochran and Associates. In 1963, the firm became Cochran, Stephenson, and Donkervoet, Inc.; Richard C. Donkervoet is the surviving partner.

Cochran helped to bring modern architecture (and modern architects) to Baltimore. He wrote and lectured on these subjects at several schools and universities and served on the boards of numerous civic associations, including the Greater Baltimore Committee, the Citizens Planning and Housing Association, the Baltimore Fine Arts Commission, and the Baltimore Planning Commission. His firm designed the Baltimore Convention Center [A4] and numerous churches, schools, institutional buildings, and houses in the city, but Cochran is probably best known for his own house [O1].

Davis, Francis (Frank) E. (1839–1921). Born in Ellicott City, Maryland, Davis apprenticed with Lind and Murdoch in the late 1850s and then worked for a time with Thomas Dixon. He practiced by himself in the 1870s and after about 1880 with his brother Henry. Davis designed the old Western District Police Station [J5] and several other police stations, schools, and municipal buildings in Baltimore. He also designed the Orchard Street Church [J1]. Davis retired about 1915, moved to Los Angeles where two of his sons were practicing architects, and died there.

Dixon, Thomas (1819–86). Dixon, originally from Wilmington, Delaware, arrived in Baltimore in the late 1840s and began practicing architecture about 1850. Soon thereafter, with his brother, James M., and Thomas Balbirnie, a Scotsman, he designed Waverly Terrace [J8] and the Baltimore County Courthouse [M4]. After that, until 1870, he practiced with his brother, then by himself, and later with Frank E. Davis. Projects during this period included the Mount Washington Octagon [N12] and Dixon's Hill [N15], the Sheppard and Enoch Pratt Hospital [L20], and the old Baltimore City Jail Gatehouse [F1]. From 1871 to 1879, Dixon's partner was Charles L.

Carson; the Mount Vernon Place United Methodist Church [C9] and the Mount Washington Presbyterian Church [N14] resulted from their collaboration. In 1880–81, Dixon practiced with Thomas C. Kennedy and then worked by himself again until a year before he died.

Faxon, Eben. See Andrews, Richard Snowden.

Fowler, Laurence Hall (1877–1971). Fowler executed a few large commissions, but the private home was his true métier. He designed some eighty houses in the mid-Atlantic states, most of them in his native Maryland where he was the architect of choice for families of means.

Fowler was born in Catonsville, the son of a judge. He graduated from The Johns Hopkins University in 1898, did graduate work at Columbia University, and although admitted to the Ecole des Beaux-Arts in Paris, chose to return to Baltimore to practice architecture. He worked briefly with Wyatt and Nolting, then opened his own office in 1906. The Wolman House [L7], his own home [L15], and a 1941 house for Owen Lattimore in Ruxton are some of his designs which are characterized by subtle refinement, elegant proportions, and careful attention to landscaping.

Fowler advised the Roland Park Company on its development of Guilford and Homeland and was one of the organizers of the Baltimore Museum of Art. He left his large collection of drawings and rare books on architecture to The Johns Hopkins University. Fowler also published articles and made extensive notes for a history of local architecture.

Frederick, George A. (1842–1924). Frederick practiced a variety of styles and produced some of Baltimore's major municipal and commercial buildings. He also designed churches and park structures. In the 1870s he was responsible for extensive renovations to the State Capitol in Annapolis.

Born in Baltimore, Frederick began his architectural career at the age of sixteen with Lind and Murdoch; he also worked for a time with Niernsee and Neilson before establishing his own practice in 1862. One of his first projects, as architect for the Baltimore city park commission, was the design of the pavilions in Druid Hill Park [K24]. The commission for City Hall

[D11] soon followed. In 1867, Frederick designed the huge St. James and Saint John's Church [F13] and in 1878, a colorful warehouse for A. S. Abell [E6]. Later he turned to residences, among which were Cylburn [N18] and the Bauernschmidt House [G8].

In his 1912 "Recollections," recounted to J. B. Noel Wyatt, Frederick credited Wendel Bollman, the engineer and bridge builder who designed the City Hall dome, as the source of much of his knowledge concerning structure and the strength of materials. Although it is a valuable source of information on nineteenth-century Baltimore architecture and architects, the "Recollections" (on file at the Maryland Historical Society) must be read with care because Frederick tended to extol his own accomplishments at others' expense. Frederick served on the national board of the American Institute of Architects; a public dispute between Frederick and E. Francis Baldwin (see p. 395) led to the latter's resignation from the AIA in 1888.

Friz, Clyde N. (1867–1942). The Enoch Pratt Free Library [B10], the Garage [K8], and the Scottish Rite Temple of Freemasonry [L13] are the major buildings in Baltimore by this Michigan-born architect. Friz studied architecture at the Massachusetts Institute of Technology and worked for various architectural firms in St. Louis before moving to Baltimore in 1900. He first joined Wyatt and Nolting, then was associated with the firm of Beecher, Friz, and Gregg. Friz opened his own office in 1925.

Ghequier, Thomas Buckler (1854–ca.1910–12). Ghequier was the grandson of Robert Cary Long, Sr. He worked for five years in the office of J. Crawford Neilson. Later, on his own, he specialized in church architecture in Maryland, Virginia, and the Midwest. Ghequier also designed a number of local houses. The Baltimore building for which he is chiefly known is St. Paul's House, 309 Cathedral Street, long believed to have been the work of Frank Furness [see B4].

Glidden, Edward H. (1873–1924). Glidden, one of the sons of the founder of the Glidden Paint Company, was born in Cleveland, Ohio, studied architecture in Paris for four years, and came to Baltimore in 1912. Shortly thereafter he established his firm and designed several apartment houses, including the Washington Apartments on Mount Vernon Place. Glidden is chiefly known as the architect of the Furness House [D8].

Godefroy, Maximilian (1765–ca. 1838). After Latrobe (see p. 403), Godefroy was the most important architect to practice in Baltimore during the first half of the nineteenth century. Widely read and classically educated, he worked for a time as a civil engineer in his native France until he was arrested, imprisoned, and then exiled for his opposition to the Napoleonic regime. Godefroy arrived in America in 1805 and at the end of that year came to Baltimore to teach drawing, architecture, and fortification at St. Mary's College. He also began a friendship with Latrobe. In 1808, he married the socially prominent Eliza Crawford Anderson and through her met many of Baltimore's leading families, some of whom later became his clients.

By the time of his marriage, he had completed the Gothic Revival St. Mary's Seminary Chapel [J3]. A few years later, Godefroy contributed designs for the Washington Monument. His Commercial and Farmers Bank at Howard and German (now Redwood) streets was built about 1810. In his design for a Masonic Hall, ca. 1812 (built by Jacob Small and William Steuart), he began to develop the sense of three-dimensional geometric form that he was to perfect in his masterpiece of Romantic Classicism, the First Unitarian Church [B12]. Godefroy designed the sally port at Fort McHenry [H4] and the Egyptian Revival–style cemetery gates for the First Presbyterian (later Westminster) churchyard (1815), one of which remains, facing Greene Street. Several vaults in the Westminster Burying Ground, one of them a pyramid, are by Godefroy. (Edgar Allan Poe and many other well-known Baltimore figures are buried there.) Also in 1815, he designed the Battle Monument [D1], the first great civic monument built in the United States. That same year, he began work on the Merchants Exchange with Latrobe. However, they quarrelled irreconcilably over the design, Latrobe's being adopted, and the brief collaboration ended in great bitterness on Godefroy's part.

A proud, impulsive, and vindictive man, Godefroy sailed with his family for Europe about 1819, blaming Latrobe for his inability to find more work in America. His daughter died of yellow fever as they were leaving the Chesapeake Bay and customs officials seized his books and drawings on his arrival in England.

Godefroy lived for a time in London but later returned to France. His architectural career continued to decline. In 1838, at age seventy-three, he was working in the mud and cold laying out new streets in Laval, France, where he was the municipal architect. The time, place, and circumstances of his death are unknown.

Godefroy designed structures in Richmond and other American cities, but his major architectural legacy is in Baltimore. Robert L. Alexander's *The Architecture of Maximilian Godefroy* is a thorough account of his life and work.

Gott, Jackson C. (1829–1909). A native Baltimorean, Gott learned carpentry as a young man and worked in the building trades. He also served as an apprentice for several local architects before establishing his own highly successful architectural firm in 1863. In his long career, Gott designed numerous residences, offices, warehouses, and factories, railroad stations, college buildings, and Masonic temples throughout Maryland and beyond. He employed many styles, perhaps most effectively the Neo-Grec. Gott was a prominent Mason and an active Democrat, which may have accounted for his many public commissions. A bachelor, he lived in downtown hotels for most of his life and was "a well known figure about town," according to the Baltimore *Sun*. Gott's extant works include the Johnston and Rombro buildings on South Howard Street, 1880–81; the Maryland Penitentiary, 1899 [see F1]; and the former Southern District Police Station, 1897 [see J5] all in Baltimore; the library and other structures for Western Maryland College in Westminster, Maryland, 1909; and the Masonic Temple in Richmond, Virginia.

Howard, William (1793–1834). Member of a Baltimore family prominent in state and national politics and military affairs, William was the fourth son of John Eager Howard. The father was a Revolutionary War hero, governor of Maryland, and U.S. senator. One of his sons was governor of Maryland, another was a congressman, and both father and sons (including William) were active in the War of 1812. William was a civil engineer (he participated in the first canal and railroad surveys in Maryland) and amateur architect with a large library of books on the subject. He was also known as doctor, perhaps due to the experiments he conducted with a chemist. His only surviving building in Baltimore is the McKim Free School, with William F. Small [F8].

Kemp, Joseph F. A somewhat elusive figure, Kemp is known to have been associated in the mid-1850s with both the Baltimore and Ohio Railroad and James Crawford Neilson. He is credited with the design of the central section of Camden Station [I1] and was the architect of the Baltimore Equitable Society Building [E4]. He also supervised the construction of both phases of the Peabody Institute [C2].

Kennedy, Thomas C. (ca. 1854–1914). British by birth, Kennedy worked in architectural offices in London and Dublin before emigrating to the United States. In 1880, he formed a partnership in Baltimore with Thomas Dixon, but it lasted only about a year, after which they each maintained separate offices. Kennedy had an extensive residential practice and designed several churches and institutional buildings for Catholic colleges, such as Mount St. Agnes, Loyola, and Notre Dame. Some of the houses on The Terraces in Mount Washington [see N15] are his work. While riding his bicycle, Kennedy was killed in a collision with an automobile.

Latrobe, Benjamin Henry (1764–1820). Benjamin Henry Latrobe was described by his son, John H. B. Latrobe, as "an artist as well as an architect, botanist, geologist, entomologist, mathematician, poet, musician, and composer." To this list might be added surveyor, engineer, author, and linguist; Latrobe was fluent in four modern languages and could read and write Latin and Greek. He was also an astute and talented observer whose letters, journals, and watercolors constitute a unique landscape of the United States during the Federal period. (Latrobe's papers and drawings, many of which are held by the Maryland Historical Society, have been published by the Yale University Press.)

Latrobe, of French ancestry, was born in Yorkshire, England. He was educated at the University of Leipzig, Germany, served a term in the Prussian army, and returned to England where he studied architecture under S. P. Cockerell and engineering with John Smeaton, the first modern civil engineer. In 1789, Latrobe became surveyor of public office and engineer of London. Following the death of his wife, infant child, and mother, he emigrated to the United States in 1796.

Latrobe was this country's first trained architect and engineer. After working in Norfolk and Richmond, he designed Philadelphia's Bank of Pennsylvania in 1800, the earliest Greek Revival structure in America. In partnership with Nicholas Roosevelt, he built that city's first waterworks, powered by steam engines. Later he surveyed canals, wrote the first report on railroads received by the Congress in 1808, and built steamboats in Pittsburgh with Robert Fulton.

During these years, Latrobe produced Baltimore's Catholic Cathedral [B9], his finest remaining building. He also made significant architectural contributions to the Capitol in Washington, D.C. Having been appointed surveyor of public buildings by Thomas Jefferson in 1803, Latrobe designed the Capitol's most distinguished spaces, including the original domed and vaulted Supreme Court and the House and Senate chambers, with their famous tobacco leaf and cornstalk column capitals. He rebuilt the Capitol after the British burned it in 1814, but his work has been somewhat obscured by that of his successors.

In 1815, in partnership with his colleague Maximilian Godefroy, Latrobe began work on Baltimore's Merchants Exchange. It was designed in the shape of the letter H, and the wing facing Gay Street, built by Jacob Small, Jr., was completed in 1820. The main feature of the Exchange was its coffered dome, 115 feet high and 53 feet in diameter. The building was razed in 1904 to make way for the United States Custom House [D10]. Latrobe's only other building in Baltimore is the Oakland Spring House [L5].

The partnership between Latrobe and Godefroy ended badly. Godefroy was to have made the working drawings and supervised the construction of the Exchange, but instead attempted to substitute his own designs and to undercut Latrobe's relationship with the trustees, according to Talbot Hamlin, whose *Benjamin Henry Latrobe* is the standard biography. Godefroy withdrew from the work and later blamed Latrobe for the subsequent failure of his career in America. For his part, Latrobe gave his old friend credit for the main front of the Exchange and refused to compete against him for the design of the First Unitarian Church [B12], Godefroy's major structure in Baltimore.

Latrobe's own career suffered from the intrigues of political enemies, poor pay, and lack of recognition, but he never lost his intellectual curiosity and enthusiasm. Scholars in many fields are indebted to him for his acute observations of early America. Some of the young nation's most prominent architects, such as Robert Mills and William Strickland, received their initial training in Latrobe's office. His influence is clearly discernible in the lives and careers of two of his sons, John H. B., and Benjamin H., Jr. Latrobe died of yellow fever in New Orleans while at work on that city's municipal waterworks.

Latrobe, Benjamin H., Jr. (1806–78). Benjamin H. Latrobe, Jr., started out as a lawyer but switched careers to become one of the country's foremost civil engineers and bridge designers. He spent most of his professional life with the Baltimore and Ohio Railroad and became its chief engineer. He had a major role in laying out and supervising the construction of the B & O Railroad line between Harpers Ferry and Wheeling, West Virginia. He also surveyed the B & O line from Baltimore to Washington and designed the masterful Thomas Viaduct at Relay [I7]. Latrobe was later a consultant on the Hoosac Tunnel in Massachusetts and to the Roeblings on the Brooklyn Bridge.

Born in Philadelphia, he attended Georgetown College in Washington and St. Mary's College in Baltimore before he started to study law. Having discovered that he was more interested in surveying, he got a job on the B & O Railroad with the help of his brother, John H. B. Latrobe, who was the company lawyer. Although he had never designed a bridge nor taken a formal course in engineering, Benjamin H. Latrobe, Jr., was given the task of designing the Thomas Viaduct. His journals show that he was reading Perronet's books on bridges in French and other borrowed works as construction began. Nothing inspires the acquisition of knowledge like the need to impart it to others, he told a friend. His son, Charles H. Latrobe, also a civil engineer, designed the Patterson Park Observatory [G4] and several of the early iron bridges over the Jones Falls. Charles H. Latrobe was consulting engineer for Lovely Lane United Methodist Church [L1].

Latrobe, John H. B. (1803–91). A sometime architect, John H. B. Latrobe worked on his father's drawings for St. John's Church and the Capitol in Washington, D.C., and had a hand in the design of the portico of Baltimore's Basilica of the Assumption [B9] and the entrance to Druid Hill Park [K24]. He was also an artist, writer of poetry and fiction (one of the first to recognize the literary talents of Edgar Allan Poe), inventor (of the Latrobe stove), and civic organizer (of the Maryland Institute and the Maryland Historical Society).

Born in Philadelphia, he attended the same prep schools as his brother Benjamin and was about to graduate at the head of his class at West Point, where he was studying engineering, when his father died. John H. B. Latrobe left college, took up law, and served as general counsel for the Baltimore and Ohio Railroad from its inception in 1828 until near the time of his death.

He spent several months in Russia during 1857 and 1858 as the emissary of the Winanses' railroad interests to the imperial court. His work for the B & O Railroad brought him into contact with many of the fascinating figures of nineteenth-century America, from Daniel Webster to Samuel F. B. Morse. John H. B. Latrobe's son, Ferdinand C. Latrobe, served seven terms as mayor of Baltimore between 1875 and 1893.

Lind, Edmund G. (1829–1909). Lind was most notably the architect of the Peabody Institute [C2], but according to his meticulous record book (now at the Maryland Historical Society), he provided original or renovation designs for more than nine hundred other projects, mostly in Maryland but also in several mid-Atlantic and southern states. He was one of the founders and the first president of the Baltimore chapter of the American Institute of Architects.

Lind, the son of an engraver, was born at Islington, near London, and showed an early interest in art. He studied architecture at the London School of Design and worked as a draftsman for various British architects before emigrating to the United States in 1855. Arriving in New York, he soon took a job with Norris G. Starkweather, architect of Baltimore's First Presbyterian Church [C13]. Lind helped draw the plans for the church and, when he came to Baltimore around 1856, supervised its erection, particularly the towers. From 1856 to 1860, he was in partnership with former Starkweather draftsman

William T. Murdoch; Lind then went into practice by himself.

He was the original architect for the Masonic Temple [A16] and the renovation architect for the Enoch Pratt House (Maryland Historical Society) [C14], the Family and Children's Services building [K15], the Gallagher Mansion [L17], and Towson's Trinity Episcopal Church [M5]. He also designed the Brown Memorial Church parsonage on Bolton Hill (1881) and numerous cast-iron storefronts. In subsequent years, Lind designed many structures in Atlanta, Georgia. Interested in the relationship between music and color, he applied his acoustical theories to his buildings.

Long, Louis L. Little of a personal nature is known of Louis L. Long, who practiced architecture in Baltimore in the mid-nineteenth century. His extant works are the 1855 spire of St. Alphonsus' Church [B5], the initial section of the St. Ignatius complex [C6], and the 1858 Mount De Sales Academy of the Visitation, 700 Academy Lane, Catonsville (quite similar in form to St. Ignatius).

Long, Robert Cary, Sr. (1770–1833). A Marylander, Long was a carpenter's apprentice before taking up architecture. His extant buildings are Davidge Hall [E10] and the Peale Museum [D13]. Long is thought to have been responsible for the Hamilton Street row houses [B13] as well. He also designed the third St. Paul's Church, with a central tower; the Holliday Street Theater which stood across from City Hall; the Greek Revival Union Bank at Charles and Fayette streets; and a house for merchant Robert Oliver on Gay Street. Long was one of the founders in 1816 of the Gas Light Company of Baltimore, the first in the country to manufacture gas for street lighting.

Long, Robert Cary, Jr. (1810–1849). Robert Cary Long, Jr., was born in Baltimore, attended St. Mary's College, and trained in the New York office of architect Martin Thompson. He returned to his hometown in the early 1830s and became an outstanding Greek Revival architect. In 1835, he designed the Record Office, Baltimore (demolished 1895), and two years later, the Patapsco Female Institute at Ellicotts Mills [see J12]. In the mid-1840s, Long designed several Baltimore churches and other structures, some in the Tudor Gothic style, including St. Alphonsus' Church [B5], Franklin Street Presbyterian Church [B11], Lloyd Street Synagogue [F7], St. Peter the Apostle Church [J6], and the Green Mount Cemetery Gatehouse [K1]. Long was a student of architectural history, wrote well about architecture, and lectured on art. His life was cut short by cholera at age thirty-nine after he had gone back to New York to continue his career.

Mason, Alfred (1844–1912). Mason was born in Burton-on-Trent, England, studied architecture, and designed several buildings in London before emigrating to America in 1880. He opened an office in Baltimore in 1885 and specialized in school buildings; by the time he retired in 1904, Mason was credited with having built forty-five schools in Maryland. Besides schools, Mason designed numerous firehouses and other types of structures in Baltimore. He was active in fraternal organizations, especially the Elks and Masons. His Western Female High School is still in use as the Booker T. Washington Middle School [K20].

Mills, Robert (1781–1855). Mills considered himself to be America's first native-born, professionally trained architect. A classical revivalist best known for his monumental architecture, he was also a talented designer of churches and government buildings and an engineer who built bridges, surveyed canals, and published far-sighted schemes for a monorail and a transcontinental railroad and telegraph system. He was an early advocate of fireproof construction and central heating.

Mills was born in Charleston, South Carolina. His father, a tailor, was a Scotsman; his mother, American. He attended the College of Charleston and at age nineteen moved to Washington to work for James Hoban, designer of the President's House (the White House), who was then supervising the construction of the U.S. Capitol. Mills came to know Thomas Jefferson, who opened his architectural library to him and introduced him to Benjamin Henry Latrobe.

Beginning in 1803, Mills worked with Latrobe for about twelve years and from him learned the vocabulary of Classical Revival architecture, professional standards, and engineering and surveying skills. Latrobe thought Mills an excellent designer of houses, but more industrious than inspired as an architect.

Mills designed buildings in Charleston and Richmond before opening an office in 1808 in Philadelphia. There, he added two wings to Independence Hall. In 1812, Mills collaborated with Lewis Wernwag, early builder of wooden bridges, on the design of the Colossus, a 340-foot, single-span, arched truss bridge over the Schuylkill River, longer than any such bridge then known.

By 1814, Mills had moved to Baltimore and was soon at work on the Washington Monument [C1]. He devised a pair of timber shears (a rudimentary crane) to hoist Causici's 30-ton statue of Washington to the top, and accomplished the job under the watchful eyes of several thousand spectators in the square. He was appointed the city's engineer of waterworks and also did street surveys. Mills designed in 1815 the block of houses on Calvert Street east of the Monument known as Waterloo Row (demolished in the 1960s), and in 1817 the Pantheonesque First Baptist Church at Sharp and Lombard streets with a circular, domed auditorium (demolished in 1877). (Of his several round or octagonal auditorium churches, only the one in Richmond remains.)

Mills moved back to Charleston in 1820 and mainly produced churches and municipal buildings. In 1830, he returned to Washington where Andrew Jackson appointed him architect of public buildings. In that capacity, Mills designed and supervised the construction of the Treasury Building in 1836, the General Post Office, and the south wing of the Patent Office, both begun in 1839. The General Post Office, now the U.S. Tariff Commission Building, and the Patent Office, now the National Portrait Gallery and the National Museum of American Art, are among the best of Washington's many Neoclassical structures. (The latter building has a fine projecting stairway and third-floor vaulted gallery.) Mills's Washington Monument for that city was begun in 1848 and finally completed in 1884. *Robert Mills, Architect of the Washington Monument, 1781–1855*, by H. M. Pierce Gallagher, and "The Papers of Robert Mills," published by the Smithsonian Institution, describe his life and work.

Mottu, Howard M. See White, Henry S. Taylor.

Murdoch, William T. See Lind, Edmund G.

Neilson, James Crawford (1816–1900). Born in Baltimore, Neilson moved with his British mother to England in 1822 after his father died, and then to Brussels, before returning to Baltimore in 1833. Two years later, he was working as a surveyor for the Baltimore and Port Deposit Railroad under Benjamin H. Latrobe, Jr. Also under Latrobe, he helped to survey the line between Harpers Ferry and Wheeling, West Virginia, for the Baltimore and Ohio Railroad; in 1842, Neilson was listed in the company records as a $3-a-day resident engineer. In 1843–44, he participated in the U.S. Coastal Survey for Maryland's Eastern Shore, and in 1848 formed an architectural firm with John Rudolph Niernsee. In 1856, Niernsee left Maryland and Neilson practiced alone until Niernsee returned to Baltimore in 1865 and they resumed their partnership. This lasted until 1874 when the firm finally disbanded. After that, Neilson designed a railroad station and houses for members of the Latrobe family in Baltimore and several buildings for Washington and Lee University in Lexington, Virginia.

Nes, Charles M., Jr. (1907–89). Born in York, Pennsylvania, Nes graduated from Princeton University in 1928, then attended Princeton's Graduate School of Architecture for two years before joining the Baltimore architectural firm of Palmer and Lamdin, which designed many private homes in Roland Park, Guilford, and Homeland. Stationed in England during World War II as a photographic interpreter for the U.S. Army Air Force, Nes helped to plan the bombing for the D-Day invasion of Europe, attained the rank of lieutenant colonel, and was awarded the Bronze Star and the Croix de Guerre. He became a partner in the successor firm to Palmer and Lamdin—Fisher, Nes, Campbell and Partners—and helped to design banks, schools, residences, clubhouses, university buildings, and major structures in Baltimore's State Office Complex. In 1966, he was elected president of the American Institute of Architects; he also served on state architectural advisory and examining boards. Nes was a preservationist who argued eloquently for the retention of Baltimore's row house architecture. Fisher, Nes, Campbell and Partners designed the addition to the Baltimore Gas and Electric Company Building [A13] and renovated the Garage [K8]. Nes himself designed 1020 St. Paul Street [K4].

Niernsee, John Rudolph (1814–84). An Austrian, Niernsee was trained as an engineer at the Polytechnic Institute of Vienna and continued his studies in Prague;
from there he emigrated to America in 1838. Niernsee
spent six months surveying a projected southern railroad, but the scheme went no further and he wound up
in New York, broke and unemployed. A job offer brought
him to Washington, and when his employment there
ended, Benjamin H. Latrobe, Jr., hired him as office
draftsman for the B & O Railroad in August 1839. Later
that year, Latrobe, Niernsee, and resident engineer
James Crawford Neilson toured the railroad line then
being built between Harpers Ferry, West Virginia, and
Cumberland, Maryland. The trip may have been the
first meeting between the future architectural partners.
(The Maryland Historical Society has Niernsee's very
colorful diary concerning this period.) Niernsee designed a series of prefabricated iron roofs for B & O
Railroad freight houses, engine sheds, and stations.
These designs are the earliest known instances of composite iron roofs in this country; he described their
construction in a series of articles for an Austrian
engineering publication.

Niernsee and Neilson left the B & O Railroad to
open their office in 1848 and their significant early work
was for railroad interests: the Italianate Calvert Station
for the Baltimore and Susquehanna Railroad (1848),
Alexandroffsky (the Thomas Winans mansion, 1852),
and stations for the B & O Railroad in Washington (1852),
Wheeling (1853), and Baltimore's Camden Station [I1].
During this period, theirs was the largest and most successful architectural firm in Baltimore.

In 1855, Niernsee was named architect for the Capitol of South Carolina. He moved to Columbia, South
Carolina, and worked on it until the start of the Civil
War, in which he served as an engineer for the Confederacy. Sherman spared his partially built Capitol building, but Union troops destroyed his house and scattered
his library and papers. After the war, Niernsee returned
to Baltimore and continued his architectural work with
Neilson until their association ended in 1874. Niernsee
then did design work on his own until 1883 when he
moved back to Columbia, South Carolina, to continue
work on the Capitol building; he died there.

Although many of Niernsee and Neilson's local buildings have disappeared, the list of those remaining is

impressive both in extent and quality: the YMCA Building (former) [B3], Asbury House [C8], Emmanuel Episcopal Church [C11], Grace and St. Peter's Episcopal Church [C15], Hackerman House [C18], Chamber of Commerce Building [D9], St. John the Evangelist Church [F12], Johns Hopkins Hospital [G6], Clifton [G10], St. Luke's Church [J9], Green Mount Cemetery Chapel [K2], and Crimea [K25].

Nolting, William G. (1866–1940). Born in Baltimore and educated in Richmond, Virginia, Nolting aspired early to be a chemist and spent time as a young man planning buildings to house his imaginary future companies. He began his architectural career in Richmond, continued it in Washington, D.C., and finally returned to Baltimore where he joined the office of J. B. Noel Wyatt, who later made him a partner. Wyatt and Nolting designed the Baltimore Courthouse [D3], the Patterson Park High School [G3], the 1888 stable for the Winans House [K3], the Fifth Regiment Armory, the Warrington Apartments in the 3900 block of North Charles Street, the nearby St. Paul Garage, and buildings for The Johns Hopkins University, The Johns Hopkins Hospital, and the Sheppard and Enoch Pratt Hospital.

Owens, Benjamin Buck (1841–1918). A Baltimorean, Owens apprenticed himself to various architects before striking out on his own in 1875. He designed the Terminal Warehouse [D14] and for seven years was the architect for the Pennsylvania Steel Company's plant at Sparrows Point. In the mid-1890s, Owens was briefly in partnership with Alphonsus H. Bieler. He was appointed inspector of buildings for Baltimore City in 1896, and from 1900 to 1910, he served as the city's supervisor of school buildings. During this period, he formed a partnership with Spencer E. Sisco; the Owens and Sisco firm continued after Owens's death. Owens was one of several Baltimore architects who talked to a Baltimore Sunday *Herald* reporter about their profession in 1893. Said Owens: "One peculiar characteristic that I have noticed about architects is that they can shine forth, make a bigger flare-up and die out quicker than any other class of professional men."

Parker, J. Harleston (1873–1930). Parker was the senior member of Parker, Thomas, and Rice, a leading East

Coast architectural firm of the early twentieth century. He was born in Boston, graduated from Harvard University in 1893, and completed four years of study at the Ecole des Beaux-Arts in Paris in 1900. That year, with Baltimore's Douglas H. Thomas, Jr., he formed Parker and Thomas. They opened offices in Boston and Baltimore and soon had a number of large corporate commissions. In 1907, Arthur W. Rice of Boston joined the firm which became Parker, Thomas, and Rice.

In Baltimore, Parker and Thomas designed the Savings Bank of Baltimore [A9], the B & O Railroad office building (1906), the Alex. Brown and Sons Building [D5], the Belvedere Hotel [K7], and Gilman Hall [L9]. Extant local works of Parker, Thomas, and Rice include the Hansa Haus [A8], the Baltimore Gas and Electric Company Building [A13], the Gilman School, and the former office building of the Pennsylvania Railroad Company on the northeast corner of Baltimore and Calvert streets.

Pennington, Josias (1854–1929). Pennington, a Baltimorean, attended St. John's College in Annapolis and interned with E. Francis Baldwin in the 1870s before becoming his partner in 1883. After their association ended with Baldwin's death in 1916, Pennington's son, Hall Pleasants Pennington, joined the practice, which continued as Pennington and Pennington until the early 1920s, when the elder Pennington retired. Josias Pennington is buried in Greenmount Cemetery. (For the buildings of Baldwin and Pennington, see Baldwin, E. Francis.)

Pietsch, Theodore Wells (1868–1930). A Chicagoan by birth, Pietsch studied architecture at the Massachusetts Institute of Technology and at the Ecole des Beaux-Arts in Paris. In 1904, he opened an architectural office in Baltimore. He was associated with Otto Simonson (1862–1922) in the design of several local buildings. They include the Paca–Pratt Building [E9], the Broadway Recreation Pier (1914), the former Southern Hotel at Light and Redwood streets, a commercial building in the 400 block of North Charles Street, Saints Philip and James Church and rectory in the 2800 block of North Charles Street, and the Maryland Casualty Company on West Fortieth Street, now the Rotunda.

Price, Bruce (1845–1903). Price was born in Cumberland, Maryland, learned to be an architect in Baltimore, and made a name for himself in New York. Not the least part of his claim to fame is that he was the father of Emily Post, the author and expert on etiquette.

Price moved to Baltimore in the early 1850s with his family. He attended Princeton University and then worked as an apprentice in the office of Niernsee and Neilson in Baltimore from 1864 to 1868. E. Francis Baldwin was working in the same office at the time and, after Price spent a year abroad, they established the firm of Baldwin and Price in 1869, remaining partners until 1873 when Price moved to Wilkes-Barre, Pennsylvania, where his wife's family resided. From there, he went to New York in 1877. During the next twenty-five years, Price designed more than 150 projects, including clubhouses and private homes for the rich and socially prominent, as well as banks, railroad stations, apartment buildings, and hotels mainly in New York, New England, and Canada. The massing and axial plans of the Shingle style homes he built at Tuxedo Park, New York (1885–90), an exclusive vacation community developed by Pierre Lorillard IV, directly influenced the early domestic designs of Frank Lloyd Wright.

The extant works of Baldwin and Price in Baltimore include the Albion Hotel, Cathedral and Read streets (1869), the former Christ Protestant Episcopal Church at St. Paul and Chase streets (1870), and the houses at 12–16 East Chase Street (1871). These, including Number 14 where Price himself lived and his daughter Emily was born, were probably his own work. A bank, a parish house, and a private home by Price still stand in Cumberland.

Reasin, William H. (1816–67). Reasin was a Baltimore pioneer of cast-iron architecture who also designed city houses and country villas. He was born in Harford County near what is now Aberdeen. Little is known of his early training in architecture, but by 1850 he was practicing in Baltimore, because A. S. Abell chose him to work with James Bogardus and R. G. Hatfield on the interior of the Sun Iron Building. Bogardus was the inventor of the cast-iron front for American buildings, Hatfield was a New York architect, and the Sun Iron Building was the first major commercial application of

Bogardus's new principles of all-iron construction. When the Sun Iron Building was completed in 1851, Reasin had his office on the second floor. He went on to design two more cast-iron-front buildings in Baltimore for Bogardus. He also designed (with a cast-iron library) the Market Place headquarters for the Maryland Institute, where he was a teacher. All of these buildings were destroyed in the 1904 Baltimore Fire. In the 1850s, Reasin was partners with Samuel B. Wetherald (Wetherall), a combination that produced the Number 6 Engine House [F11].

Rice, Arthur Wallace (1869–1938). Rice, a Bostonian, followed a similar career trajectory as his future architectural partners, J. Harleston Parker and Douglas H. Thomas, Jr. Following his 1891 graduation from the Massachusetts Institute of Technology, where he studied architecture, Rice continued his design studies in the ateliers of Paris. He then worked as a draftsman in various Boston offices until about 1896 when he formed a partnership. In 1907, Rice joined Parker and Thomas to form the Boston and Baltimore architectural firm of Parker, Thomas, and Rice. Their Boston work included bank, utility, and insurance company buildings as well as large suburban homes in Massachusetts and other New England states.

Simonson, Otto (1862–1922). See Pietsch, Theodore W.

Small, Jacob, Sr. (1746–94). Small was a self-taught designer and builder. In 1786, a year after he completed the old Otterbein United Methodist Church [H2], Small built a wooden bridge that spanned the Jones Falls at Baltimore Street with a single, 90-foot segmental arch. He is also credited with finishing, from a design by Maximilian Godefroy, the old Masonic Hall that stood until 1895 on the site of the present city courthouse. For the competition for the Capitol at Washington, Small submitted three designs in 1792.

Small, Jacob, Jr. (1772–1851). An 1833 guide to Baltimore listed Jacob Small, Jr., as an "architect and practical builder." He was also listed that year in the newspaper as one of the master carpenters who supported improved conditions for their trade, including a stipulated twelve-hour workday. Known as Colonel Small (having served in the War of 1812), he had other careers as a lumber merchant and politician. Small was the builder of the Merchants Exchange and a consultant to Benjamin Henry Latrobe on the Capitol building in Washington. He served as mayor of Baltimore from 1826 to 1831, during which time he was a political ally of the nascent Baltimore and Ohio Railroad; when he resigned as mayor, he became the B & O's superintendent of depots. During the one year he was with the railroad, Small designed the Ellicott City Station [J12], his sole remaining building.

Small, William F. (1798–1832). William F. Small, the son of Jacob Small, Jr., was Baltimore's first professionally trained architect. In 1817, he began working with Benjamin Henry Latrobe in Washington, came to Baltimore with Latrobe the following year, and after Latrobe moved to New Orleans in 1819, remained at work on the Catholic Cathedral and the Merchants Exchange. Small designed several buildings in Baltimore: the Athenaeum at St. Paul and Lexington streets (burned 1835), the City Hotel on Monument Square (built 1827, demolished 1889), and a Seamen's Bethel in Fells Point (demolished, year unknown). His major remaining buildings are the Archbishop's Residence [B8] and (with William Howard) the McKim Free School [F8].

Sperry, Joseph Evans (1854–1930). Sperry's sixty-year professional career (he never retired) and his architectural partners contributed to a long list of significant Baltimore buildings; he was involved in the design of some of the finest structures of the late nineteenth century. A South Carolinian, Sperry moved to Baltimore in 1868 and two years later, at age sixteen, advertised his services as an architect. From 1872 to 1876 he was apparently a draftsman for E. Francis Baldwin and in 1877 reestablished his own office. The next year he entered a partnership with J. B. Noel Wyatt; this lasted until 1887 when Sperry moved to Kansas City. He came back a year later and worked with Charles L. Carson; they were about to formalize the partnership when Carson died in 1891. Sperry continued to practice architecture alone. He was associated with Edward York and Philip Sawyer of New York on several projects early in this century. Sperry's extant works include the Church of St. Michael and All Angels at St. Paul and Twentieth streets (Wyatt and Sperry, 1878), Belvidere Terrace [K5], the Mercantile Safe Deposit and Trust Company Building[D7], the Oheb Shalom Synagogue [K17], the Masonic Temple (renovations) [A16], the First Unitarian Church (renovations) [B12], the Equitable Building [D2], the Brewers' Exchange at 20 Park Avenue (1896), the Provident Savings Bank [E3], the old YMCA Building (renovations) [B3], the new YMCA and YWCA buildings on Franklin Street (1908, 1916), the Bromo Seltzer Tower [E7], and the Strouse Brothers Company warehouse (addition) [E8].

Starkweather, Norris Gibson (1818–85). As was true of many of his contemporaries, Starkweather's knowledge of construction was practical rather than schooled, and he learned to design buildings by doing it. Starkweather was born in Vermont. At age twelve he was apprenticed to a master builder for seven years and worked the next six as a foreman. During the 1840s he was a builder in Massachusetts. By 1850, Starkweather had established himself as an architect in Philadelphia. From there he came to Baltimore around 1854 to work on the First Presbyterian Church [C13]. He spent the next twenty-five years in the area; during the 1870s he had an office in Washington, D.C. Starkweather's Baltimore projects include the addition of floors, cast-iron balconies, and an Italianate look to William F. Small's City Hotel, and the plans for Towson's Trinity Episcopal Church [M5]. Starkweather also designed a wing for the Patapsco Female Institute in Ellicott City and four nearby Italianate villas, of which Temora [J13] and Elmonte [J14] remain. In the 1880s, Starkweather worked as an architect in New York.

Thomas, Douglas H., Jr. (1872–1915). Born in Baltimore, Thomas graduated from The Johns Hopkins University in 1893 and studied architecture at the Massachusetts Institute of Technology for the next two years. After a brief period with a Boston architectural firm, he spent two more years studying architecture in Italy and Paris. In 1900, with J. Harleston Parker of Boston, he formed the firm of Parker and Thomas (later Parker, Thomas, and Rice). Thomas was well-connected socially in Baltimore and was a member of numerous clubs. He died at age forty-three when the Pierce-Arrow automobile that he was driving overturned in an early morning accident on Bellona Avenue near Charles Street.

White, Henry S. Taylor (1879–1943). White was born in Baltimore, studied architecture at the Maryland Institute, and became a draftsman in the office of Baldwin and Pennington. In 1904 he formed a partnership with Howard M. Mottu. Over the next fifty years the firm of Mottu and White designed churches, schools, residences, and office buildings, most notably the one for the Baltimore Life Insurance Company [B2]. White later practiced with his son, Henry S. Taylor White, Jr.

Wilson, John Appleton (1851–1927). The architectural team of John Appleton and William Thomas Wilson (John's second cousin) was extremely active in the Baltimore region during the final decades of the nineteenth century, particularly on the railroad and domestic fronts. As J. A. and W. T. Wilson, or Wilson and Wilson, they designed stations, churches, and clubhouses, but the private home was their forte. They lined the developing blocks of Calvert and St. Paul streets between Mount Vernon Place and Mount Royal Avenue with examples of their work. These were in the Victorian Gothic or Neo-Classical Revival styles or the Wilsons' own occasionally startling variations thereon. Many of them, including the east side of the 1000 block North Calvert Street, known as Belvidere Terrace [K5], survive. The Wilsons also added the transepts to Towson's Trinity Episcopal Church [M5].

John Appleton Wilson, a member of a wealthy and well-connected Baltimore family, was raised at "Oakley," an Italianate villa on 13 acres of land at the present intersection of Fulton and Edmondson avenues. After attending college in Washington, he studied architecture for a year at the Massachusetts Institute of Technology, then took a job in 1874 in the office of E. Francis Baldwin. By 1877 he had his own practice and shortly thereafter was associated with his second cousin. He was the secretary of the Fire Proof Building Company of Baltimore and was active in the Municipal Art Society and the Maryland Historical Society. The latter institution holds his extensive office diaries and photographs of his work. During the last two decades of his life, he traveled often to Europe.

Wyatt, James Boswell Noel (1847–1926). J. B. Noel Wyatt came from a socially prominent family in Baltimore, received the best architectural education, and turned both to good advantage. Wyatt's grandfather was for fifty years rector of St. Paul's Church; his father was a civil engineer. In 1865, the family moved to Cambridge, Massachusetts. Wyatt graduated from Harvard in 1870, studied architecture at the Massachusetts Institute of Technology the following year, and spent three years after that in Paris at the Ecole des Beaux-Arts. He returned to Baltimore in 1874 and worked briefly for E. Francis Baldwin where he probably met his future partner, Joseph E. Sperry. In 1876 he was practicing on his own and in 1877 or 1878 entered a partnership with Sperry that lasted until 1887. (For their buildings, see Sperry.) By 1889, Wyatt had taken in William G. Nolting as a partner; their association continued until Wyatt's death. (For their buildings, see Nolting.) Wyatt was a founder or official of numerous clubs and organizations, lectured on architecture and architectural history at colleges and universities, and from about 1878 to 1890 was the Baltimore correspondent for the *American Architect and Building News*; he also wrote for other publications. Among the local architects of note who trained in his office were Edward Glidden, Clyde Friz, William Lamdin, John Zink, James R. Edmunds, Jr., and Laurence Hall Fowler.

Glossary

apse a projection at the eastern (altar) end of a church, often semicircular and vaulted with a half dome.

arcade a series of columns and arches; a covered passageway, open on one side, that is alongside or under a building.

arch a method of bridging an opening, usually in masonry, with individual units which transfer the load to successive units and finally to the piers and abutments, or columns and walls. Some common types of arches are semicircular (round), segmental (an arc), elliptical (two-centered), ogee (sharply pointed), lancet (bullet-nosed), Tudor (four-centered), flat (horizontal), trefoil (three-leaved), and rampant (one pier higher than the other).

architrave the lowest of the three main parts of the classical entablature (see drawing, p. 425); also the molding surrounding a door or window.

Art Deco a 1960s term coined to describe a geometric design style of the 1920s that attempted to render visually the chic precision of modern technology; zigzags and sunbursts were common motifs. The name was taken from the 1925 Exposition International des Arts Decoratifs et Industriels Modernes in Paris which summed up the movement. In the 1930s, sleek streamlining became popular and was applied to everything from furniture to locomotives to commercial buildings; this evolution of the earlier Art Deco style is known as Art Moderne or modernistic.

Art Nouveau a style that began with William Morris and the English Arts and Crafts Movement of the 1880s and spread to Europe and America in the 1890s. Its symbolic, dreamlike shapes appeared in lamps, interiors, and entire buildings. Flowers and other organic forms and the female figure, often used erotically, were its emblems, and flowing, undulating images its trademark. The name itself came from a Paris shop that opened in 1895 to sell articles of modern design. Art Nouveau's great American exponents were Louis Sullivan and Louis Comfort Tiffany.

ashlar masonry of smoothly cut square or rectangular stones laid in regular courses, as opposed to rubble masonry (rough, unhewn stones loosely laid in irregular courses) and cyclopean masonry (huge blocks of stone, roughly dressed, but carefully fitted together without mortar).

attic a low story above the cornice and below the roof; garret.

baldachino a canopy over an altar.

balustrade a handrail supported by balusters, often used decoratively along the roofline.

bargeboard (vergeboard) a face board under the roof edge of a gable (hiding the ends of the roof timbers), often decorated with scrollwork (gingerbread).

Baroque a style of architecture prevalent during the seventeenth and eighteenth centuries, characterized by elaborate decoration, including figural sculpture, curved forms, and subtle spatial effects.

basilica a church with nave and side aisles, the nave being higher than the aisles and usually lit with a clerestory; a form often used for market buildings.

battlement a parapet broken by vertical slots.

Bauhaus an evolving school of art, architecture, and industrial design that was founded in Germany in 1906 and was closed by the Nazis in 1933. Architects Marcel Breuer, Walter Gropius, and Ludwig Mies van der Rohe were faculty members during this period and brought their design theories to the United States when they emigrated. The early expressionism of the Bauhaus school later shifted to severe geometry and stark functionalism.

bay the portion of a building or a bridge between two adjacent columns or piers.

Beaux-Arts Classicism academic, neoclassical design on the grand scale popular during the last quarter of the nineteenth century. It was named for the Ecole des Beaux-Arts in Paris where many American architects went to study. Beaux-Arts-style buildings are richly decorated, often with sculpture; coupled columns and monumental flights of steps are generic features.

bond the joints in successive courses in a masonry wall (see drawings). Some well-known ones are:

    common bond courses of stretchers (bricks faced lengthwise) with each sixth course made of headers (bricks faced crosswise);

English bond alternate courses of stretchers and headers;

Flemish bond alternate stretchers and headers in the same course (with bricks centered over each other vertically).

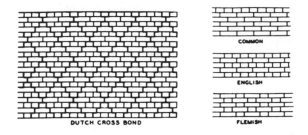

brace a diagonal member, usually used as a roof support.

bracket a triangular unit of wood, stone, or metal, used to support a cornice or overhanging roof; decorative as well as structural.

Brutalism A British term coined about 1954 to describe the monumental rough concrete buildings of Peter Smithson and Le Corbusier; Paul Rudolph was associated with the style in America, which was in vogue ca. 1950–80. Its massive, heavy masonry forms were often overbearing.

buttress an exterior pier that strengthens a wall, sometimes absorbing the thrust of an inner arch.

cantilever a beam or other structural member whose unsupported projection beyond a pier or wall (which acts as the fulcrum) is counterbalanced at the opposite end.

capital the crowning element, often decorated, of a column, pier, or pilaster (see drawing, page 425).

casement a window hinged at the side.

chancel the east end of a church where the altar is located; often the whole east end beyond the crossing.

Chateauesque a style based on sixteenth-century French Renaissance chateaux and popular in America during the final decades of the nineteenth century; masonry Chateau-style buildings featured towers, large gables, and tall, highly decorated chimneys.

Classical Revival see Beaux-Arts, Neo-classical Revival, Neo-Grec.

clerestory the upper part of a church nave, with windows above the roofline of the side aisles.

coffer a recessed panel, usually square or octagonal, in a flat, domed, or vaulted ceiling.

Colonial refers less to a style than to a period of imperial domination, which in the United States occurred circa 1607–1781. In Maryland and farther south, colonial architecture followed English Georgian lines which were descended from sixteenth-century Palladian models. The more important houses usually had a central hall, dormer windows, chimneys at the gable ends, and often a one- or two-story pedimented portico. Country estate houses frequently had a five-part plan. The nineteenth-century Colonial Revival or Neo-Colonial style popular for churches and college buildings began in the 1860s and continues today.

column an upright support, round and slightly tapering, that may be of wood, stone, or metal. It is sometimes fluted, i.e., lined vertically with shallow, concave grooves. Its three parts in classical architecture were base, shaft, and capital.

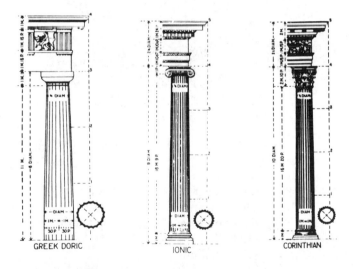

GREEK DORIC   IONIC   CORINTHIAN

Commercial (Chicago) style a type of high-rise, metal-frame construction that evolved from the Richardsonian Romanesque. Perfected by Chicago architects such as William Le Barron Jenney, Dankmar Adler, Louis Sullivan, Daniel Burnham, and John Wellborn Root between 1885 and 1900, it remains the structural basis of today's modern commercial high-rise office building. Its main principle is the support of the entire structure, including the exterior surface (sometimes all glass), by the steel skeleton.

console ornamental scrolled bracket higher than it is deep.

corbel a structural support system each of whose individual wooden or masonry units projects successively slightly beyond the one below, for example at the top of the front wall of a building to form a cornice; the principle is that of the cantilever.

Corinthian one of the classical orders; its capitals are decorated with acanthus leaves (see drawing, page 423).

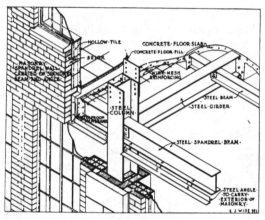

CUTAWAY DIAGRAM SHOWING THE CONSTRUCTIONAL ELEMENTS OF A TYPICAL STEEL SKELETON-FRAMED STRUCTURE. (Drawn by G. J. Wise.)

cornice the crowning piece of an entablature (see drawing, page 425).

counterfort buttress.

course a horizontal layer of masonry making up part of a wall. (A belt, or string, course is a narrow, slightly projecting band of masonry marking a horizontal division in a wall.)

crenellation see battlement.

crocket small, foliate ornament used at regular intervals, primarily on Gothic gables, pinnacles, and spires.

crossing the intersection of nave, transepts, and chancel in a church of cruciform (crosslike) plan.

cupola a small, often domed structure crowning a main roof, steeple, or tower.

curtain wall usually a combination of masonry, metal, and glass hung from the structural framework, most commonly in modern, high-rise buildings of steel-frame construction (cf. load-bearing wall; see drawing, page 424).

dome a major structural element consisting of an arch brought full circle and supported by a round, square, or polygonal base; usually semicircular, segmental, or pointed in profile.

Doric one of the classical orders, with plain capitals (see drawing, page 423).

dormer a small gable in a pitched roof usually fronted by a window.

drum a wall, usually cylindrical, supporting a dome, lantern, or cupola; also the individual circular components of a column.

Eastlake A nineteenth-century style named for Charles Lock Eastlake (1836–1906), British architect, furniture designer, and author whose books advocated the use of Gothic principles of design and construction. The style featured curved brackets and elaborately turned porch posts and spindles that resembled furniture legs (cf. Queen Anne).

elevation a graphic projection of a vertical plane or face of a building (cf. plan).

engaged column a decorative half-round column attached to a wall or pier.

entablature in classical architecture, the horizontal members above the column capitals, consisting of architrave, frieze, and cornice (see drawing).

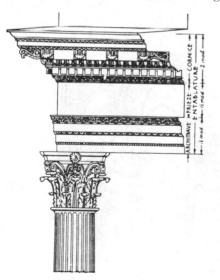

eyebrow window a small, arched dormer shaped like an eyebrow.

façade the face or front of a building.

fanlight a semicircular or elliptical window over a doorway whose radiating mullions suggest the ribs of a fan.

Federal an Americanized neoclassical style concurrent with the early days of the republic, ca. 1790–1820. It was based on the designs of the Adam brothers, Robert and James, eighteenth-century British architects whose work lightly and delicately interpreted Greek and Roman models. Federal-style town houses often had pitched roofs, dormers, and fanlight doorways; their interiors featured niches, spiral stairways, and elaborate carved decoration. A Federal Revival style flourished in the United States during the late nineteenth and early twentieth centuries.

fenestration the proportional arrangement of windows and doors in a building.

freestone a stone, particularly sandstone or limestone, whose fine grain makes it easier to cut and shape for use in building.

frieze the intermediate section of an entablature, often decorated with sculptural relief (see drawing, page 425).

gable the end of a pitched roof and the portion of wall under it, generally with straight sides, but sometimes stepped or curved.

gambrel a ridged barn-style roof with two pitches, the lower steeper and the upper flatter.

TRANSVERSE SECTION of a TYPICAL GOTHIC CATHEDRAL (AMIENS)

Georgian a style of classical revival architecture that takes its name from England during the reign of the Georges, ca. 1714–1830. Neo-Palladian at the outset, then turning Baroque, it is typically characterized by the five-part plan consisting of a main building and two wings joined to the central portion by hyphens. Georgian was a popular American colonial style.

Gothic Revival perhaps the most common Victorian style, it began in this country about 1800, flourished

GATEWAY
S. JOHN'S COLLEGE : CAMBS

at mid-century, and lasted up to the early 1900s. There were many variations: country parish Gothic; Tudor Gothic (see drawing, opposite); the polychrome and embellished High Victorian Gothic; the wooden Stick style; and the simpler, more monochromatic Collegiate Gothic. The hallmarks of Gothic architecture—the pointed arch, the ribbed vault, and the flying buttress—were often suggested rather than stated, or symbolized (the stone tracery of European Gothic cathedrals, for example, by the gingerbread on American "Gothic cottages" of the 1850s).

half-timber a method of heavy timber frame construction used in England and France in the 1500s and 1600s in which the spaces between the beams were filled with masonry or plaster, leaving the wood exposed.

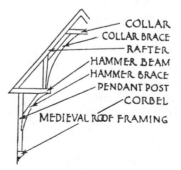

COLLAR
COLLAR BRACE
RAFTER
HAMMER BEAM
HAMMER BRACE
PENDANT POST
CORBEL
MEDIEVAL ROOF FRAMING

hammer beam a short, cantilevered beam that projects from the wall and supports an arched roof truss (see drawing).

header the top, horizontal member of a system of vertical beams or studs; a stone or brick faced endwise
rather than lengthwise in a wall.

hipped a pitched roof whose ends are sloped rather
than vertical, forming a joint called a hip.

hood a projecting molding or pediment over a door or
window that both decorates and protects from sun
and rain.

hyphen a lesser connection, usually one story, between
the main building and the wings or dependencies of
a Georgian-style house.

International a style that began in Europe in the 1920s,
became universal, and has continued almost up to the
present. It offered no ornamentation, but its smooth
surfaces, ribbon windows, and flat roofs resulted in
less mass, greater volume, and the frank expression
of structure and building materials. Steel-frame or
reinforced-concrete construction incorporating plenty
of glass were typical for high-rise commercial buildings.
Henry-Russell Hitchcock and Philip Johnson defined
it in their book *The International Style: Architecture Since
1922,* which accompanied the Museum of Modern
Art's 1932 exhibit. Breuer, Gropius, Le Corbusier, and
Mies van der Rohe were some of its leaders.

Ionic one of the classical orders, with scrolled capitals
(see drawing, page 423).

Italianate the Italian Villa style was popular in the mid-
nineteenth century primarily for domestic buildings
which usually featured short, heavy towers, wide, bracketed cornices, an asymmetrical plan, round-headed
and bay windows, and a veranda or loggia. Italianate
commercial structures often had bowed or peaked
cornices and hood moldings.

jerkinhead a dormer with a hipped roof.

lancet window a slender window with bullet-shaped arch.

lantern a turret crowning a roof or dome, usually with
windows in its side walls.

lintel a horizontal support beam resting on two posts,
for example over a doorway or window (see drawing,
page 435).

load-bearing a pier, column, or wall that carries the
load of the building to the foundation. Load-bearing
walls are inefficient for high-rise construction, hence
the development of the metal frame, which supports
both the floor load and the exterior curtain wall (cf.
curtain wall; and see drawing, page 424).

loggia an open-air gallery set into the building, usually fronted by an arcade.

mansard a hipped roof with the hips near the corners of the building, the top almost flat, and the sides steeply pitched and sometimes flaring out. The roof customarily includes windows because it normally encloses the building's top floor. Second Empire–style structures have high mansard roofs, named for François Mansart (1598–1666), the French architect who introduced them.

modillion a small, scrolled, horizontal bracket used to support and decorate a classical cornice of the Corinthian or Composite order.

molding a continuous decorative band composed of flat and curved surfaces, used mostly around openings on the inside and outside of a building; also between wall and ceiling on the interior and to effect a transition between plane surfaces on the exterior.

mullion the vertical division between the glass panes (lights) of a window; the horizontal division is called a muntin.

narthex the entrance vestibule of a church.

nave the main body of a church extending from the entrance to the crossing and between the side aisles (not including the transepts).

Neo-Classical Revival inspired by the World's Columbian Exposition at Chicago in 1893, Neo-Classical Revival became the required style for railroad, commercial, institutional, and government buildings during the first two decades of the twentieth century. Sculpture and decoration were customarily incorporated as they were in Beaux-Arts Classicism, but were more stylized and grandiose. McKim, Mead, and White and John Russell Pope were major practitioners of the Neo-Classical Revival and official Washington one of its great beneficiaries.

Neo-Grec a High Victorian style that was considered au courant for both residential and commercial buildings in the 1860–90 period and is recognizable by its flattened segmental arches, incised ornament, and stylized classical and geometric details, usually rendered in brick or cast iron. Neo-Grec emerged from the Ecole des Beaux-Arts in Paris in the 1840s, but its inspiration was as much structural as decorative. As defined and exercised by Labrouste, Viollet-le-Duc, and other French architects, it argued for a return to the pure architectural logic of the Greeks.

order in classical architecture, the column, capital, and entablature. There were three Greek orders: Doric, Ionic, and Corinthian; and two Roman: Tuscan and Composite.

oriel a projecting window on an upper floor.

Palladian motif an arched opening supported by minor columns and flanked by narrow, rectilinear openings the same height as the columns. In series, pilasters or engaged columns appear between the openings (see drawing of Palladio's basilica in Vicenza, below). The motif is named for Andrea Palladio (1508–80), one of the greatest and most influential Renaissance architects, who lived and worked in Vicenza and the Venice area. After a careful study of ancient architecture, Palladio fused classical and Renaissance forms into a style suited to local conditions. His most important contribution was the five-part country villa, with a central block joined by straight or curved hyphens to wings on either end. Palladio's buildings and principles, described in his *The Four Books of Architecture* and introduced to England in the seventeenth century by architect Inigo Jones, became the basis for Georgian and later for much American colonial architecture, including that of Thomas Jefferson.

THE BASILICA : VICENZA

parapet a low wall at the edge of a bridge, roof, balcony, porch, or terrace.

parterre ornamental garden with paths between the beds.

pavilion a projecting, subsidiary part of a larger building, often domed; a temporary structure for an exposition or fair; a small, ornamental building used as a summer- or garden house (gazebo).

pediment in classical architecture, a low-pitched gable over a portico. In classical revival styles, decorative pediments may occur over windows and entrances.

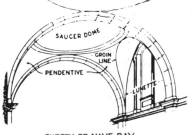

SKETCH OF NAVE BAY

pendentive a triangular section of curved vaulting (a spherical triangle or concave spandrel), employed to effect a structural transition between the corners of a square or polygonal base and a round dome overhead (see drawing, above).

Perpendicular an English Gothic style, post-1350, which emphasized vertical lines.

picturesque a term applied to architecture and natural landscapes that resembled the scenes of landscape painters, especially those of the seventeenth-century artists Claude Lorrain and Gaspard Poussin, which evoked age and the passage of time. Contrast, irregularity, and rough textures were prized qualities. Picturesque buildings were asymmetrical and eclectic; their landscaped gardens sometimes included manufactured ruin or follies.

pier a pillar of solid masonry.

pilaster an engaged shallow pier or rectangular column used decoratively.

Piranesian reminiscent of the work of Giovanni Battista Piranesi (1720–78), Italian engraver and architectural theorist whose accurate renderings of Roman ruins and dreamlike images of prisons were noted for their drama and grandeur.

plan a graphic representation of a building and its component parts and systems in outline form as seen from above, for example a floor plan showing the walls and openings.

porte cochere a covered area to accommodate vehicles at the entrance to a building.

portico an entrance porch with columns and pediment.

post-tensioned a method of reinforcing concrete beams by embedding steel cables that are tightened after the concrete has hardened.

precast building components made of concrete or imitation stone, such as beams or panels (usually reinforced), that are cast in a form before being used in construction.

pre-stressed concrete that has been strengthened by the use of steel cables under tension.

Queen Anne a customarily residential style popularized by British architect Richard Norman Shaw (1831–1912), featuring irregular plans, a variety of colors and surface materials, and prominent gables, turrets, and chimneys. Half-timbered effects and Tudor arches were also common. The Queen Anne style was enthusiastically embraced by American architects during the latter half of the nineteenth century. The name refers to the reign of England's Queen Anne, 1702–14, preceding the Georges.

quoins interlocking bricks or stones used to tie the walls together at the corners of a building and emphasized by special size, dressing, or joints; sometimes solely decorative (see drawing, page 433).

Regency English architectural style of the late eighteenth and early nineteenth centuries characterized by a refined classicism.

Renaissance a style of architecture originating in Italy in the fifteenth century that fell between the Gothic and the Baroque and represented a rebirth of classical forms and a revolt against medieval ones. Florence and Rome were its great centers and Brunelleschi, Alberti, Ammanati, Bramante, Michelozzi, Michelangelo, Sangallo, Vasari, and Palladio some of its greatest names. Renaissance architecture is a generic term covering widely different styles and revivals found throughout Europe and the Americas up through the nineteenth century.

repoint to replace the old mortar in masonry joints.

reredos a decorated screen or wall behind an altar.

Richardsonian Romanesque a style of about 1870–90 named for Henry Hobson Richardson (1838–86), considered the first American architect to attempt a truly American style. His 1872 Trinity Church in

Boston ushered in the new manner, which drew mainly on Romanesque models as inspiration for buildings with rough-surfaced masonry, huge Syrian arches (often of a different stone than the walls), and deep-

N.E. PORTAL : BAMBERC.

STONE QUOINS IN BRICKWORK

RUSTICATED STONE JOINTING WITH QUOINS

set windows. Richardson's massive and powerful buildings communicated strength, simplicity, and substance. His 1887 Marshall Field Wholesale Store in Chicago inspired Louis Sullivan and Frank Lloyd Wright and provided the link between the Victorian Romanesque and the Commercial styles.

Romanesque European pre-Gothic style of the eleventh and twelfth centuries based on Roman forms, particularly the round arch, the barrel vault, and massive masonry (see drawing above, left).

rustication large blocks of finished stone separated by pronounced joints that form a pattern (see drawing above, right).

sacristy a church room where sacred vessels and vestments for the liturgy are kept.

scagliola cement or plaster ornament imitating colored marble.

Second Empire a style named for the French Second Empire, 1852–70, and fashionable in the United States for residential, institutional, and municipal architecture circa 1860–80. Visconti and Lefuel's 1857 New Louvre in Paris provided the prototype. Its defining characteristics were high mansard roofs, dormers, prominent chimneys, pavilions, and exuberant decoration.

Shingle style an American and almost exclusively residential style current ca. 1870–90. Its integrated interiors, rounded exterior forms covered with wooden shingles, and broad, sweeping roofs encompassing secluded verandas were a reaction to the angular, more articulated, Gothic-inspired Stick style. The Shingle style emerged from the work of Richard Norman Shaw and the Queen Anne style, but it was more horizontal and more uniform in color and texture. H. H. Richardson and McKim, Mead, and White set the pattern for the Shingle style in the 1870s with homes and clubhouses for their wealthy clients at Newport, Rhode Island.

side aisle the aisles of a church, parallel to the nave, that lie between the support columns and the exterior walls.

soffit the exposed, finished underside of an architectural element such as an arch, beam, lintel, or cornice.

spandrel the surface between two arches or between the adjacent ribs of a vault; also the beam between the structural columns of a building and by extension the exterior panel that serves as a horizontal separation between the windows.

Stick style name applied by architectural historian Vincent Scully—he also named the Shingle style—to the largely domestic architecture of the 1850–80 period, which was based on the Gothic-flavored designs of Andrew Jackson Downing and Alexander Jackson Davis. Stick style buildings expressed their wooden structural framework through the use of vertical board and batten siding and diagonal bracing. They had high, steeply pitched roofs with bracketed eaves and extensive porches.

Sullivanesque a style named for architect Louis Sullivan (1856–1924) and employed by others around the turn of the century in imitation of his classically inspired high-rise buildings. Sullivanesque buildings were tripartite: a pronounced base with arched openings, tall body, and strong, projecting cornice. The piers separating the windows were usually joined at the top by arches, and the spandrels, doorways, and entablature (and often the entire exterior) were covered with a profusion of the quasi–Art Nouveau relief decoration, customarily executed in terra-cotta, that was devised by Sullivan.

terra-cotta fired clay, of ancient origin, enjoyed widespread use in the United States from about 1890 to 1940 as a structural and decorative material. Terracotta formed the floor arches and fire-proofed the metal framework of early high-rise buildings. It was later employed as exterior cladding, but its prime purpose was decorative since it could be modeled or cast in molds.

tracery in Gothic architecture, the interior decoration, usually in stone or metal, of a screen, vault, or window. In the last, the curving stonework encloses the leaded stained glass.

transept the lateral arms of a church with a cruciform plan.

triforium an arcade above the nave arches and below the clerestory windows in a Gothic cathedral. (It seldom appears in the various American Gothic revivals.)

truss an arrangement, frequently triangular, of straight timber or metal members (or a combination of both), some in tension, others in compression, that acts as a rigid unit. The top and bottom elements are chords; the intermediate structure the web. Trusses are used to span long distances, for example between walls to support a roof, or between piers to support a bridge.

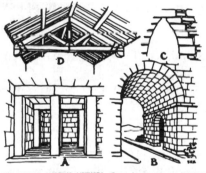

FOUR TYPICAL BUILDING METHODS. (Drawn by the author.) A. POST-AND LINTEL. B. ARCH AND VAULT. C. CORBEL OR CANTILEVER. D. TRUSS.

vault an arched roof or ceiling, usually of masonry, but sometimes (interior) of timber and plaster (see drawings, page 436).

    barrel (tunnel) vault a semicircular vault that resembles a continuous arch.

    fan vault a feature of English Perpendicular Gothic style in which the ribs spring from a single column or corbel and then diverge.

    groin (cross) vault two barrel vaults that intersect at a ninety-degree angle; their lines of intersection are groin lines.

Victorian a vague term that is often substituted for a more specific one. It can apply to numerous revival styles that took place during the reign of England's Queen Victoria, 1837–1901, including Gothic, Romanesque, and Italianate. The High Victorian period in the United States occurred ca. 1860–90 and Victorian Gothic and Romanesque buildings from this period were generally taller and more extroverted than their counterparts from other revival periods, with a variety of polychrome effects and surface textures. The Victorian Italianate style, to some extent domestic but mostly commercial, resembled the Neo-Grec, particularly in the window treatments.

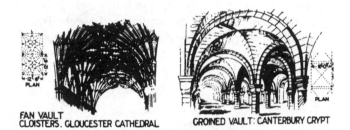

FAN VAULT
CLOISTERS. GLOUCESTER CATHEDRAL   GROINED VAULT: CANTERBURY CRYPT

volute a spiral scroll such as that used on an Ionic capital.

voussoir a wedge-shaped stone, or brick, functioning as one unit of an arch, and lying between the impost block (from which the arch springs) and the keystone.

wainscoting decorative protective covering for the lower portion of an interior wall, usually of wood paneling, although a variety of natural and synthetic materials can be used.

water table a projecting base course, sloping outward, serving to protect the foundation from rainwater.

Index of Buildings, Architects, Architectural Firms, Engineers, Planners

Note: Letters in brackets refer to the Tour (Tour A, Tour B, etc.) and the numbers following letters refer to the stop on the tour (1 for first, 2 for second, etc. [D6] would indicate Tour D, sixth stop on the tour list).

Architects are indexed only if (1) they have existing works in Baltimore *and* (2) their lives and/or work are discussed within the text.

Kallmann, McKinnell, Wood Architects, Inc., 141

Kann and Ammon, 131

Keeley, Patrick Charles, 284–85

Kelly, Brian, 243

Kelly, Clayton, and Mojzisek, 242–44

Kemp, Joseph F., 119, 168–69, 227–29, 403

Kemp, Walter, 258–59

Kennedy, Thomas C., 374–76, 397, 403

Kessler, George E., 25, 365

Kresge's. See Valu-Plus

Lamdin, William D., 368, 419

Latrobe, Benjamin Henry, 5, 7, 8, 9, 40, 90, 98, 99–104, 115, 156, 157, 175, 237, 248, 315–16, 401, 403–5, 408, 410, 416

Latrobe, Benjamin H., Jr., 202, 237–38, 405, 411

Latrobe, Charles II., 201–2, 405

Latrobe, John H. B., 101, 102, 299, 405, 406

Laurence Hall Fowler Residence, [L15], 327–28, 399

Leavitt, Sheldon I., 392–93

Leslie E. Robertson Associates. See Robertson, Leslie E. Associates

Lind, Edmund G., 16, 28, 85–86, 113, 117–19, 131–32, 288, 331–32, 343–44, 406, 407

Lind and Murdoch, 117–19, 398, 399

Lloyd Street Synagogue, [F7], 11, 12, 107, 188–89, 250, 408

Loggia Stores, [B7], 98

Long, Louis L., 122–24, 124–25, 407

Long, Robert Cary, Jr., 9, 10, 11, 12, 17, 90, 95–96, 106–7, 147, 188–89, 250–52, 257, 262, 271, 288, 313–15, 341–42, 407–8

Long, Robert Cary, Sr., 8, 9, 19, 91, 94, 108–9, 160–61, 175–76, 400, 407

Loschky, Marquardt, and Nesholm, 69–72

Lovely Lane United Methodist Church, [L1], 29, 30, 307–10, 397, 405

Lusby House. See Xaverian Brothers Residence

Maginnis and Walsh, 369–70

Mahan, Catherine and Associates, 185

Mansion House, Druid Hill Park. See Druid Hill Park

Markets. See Hollins Market

Marlboro Square, [F8], 82, 173–74, 397, 417

Marsh and McLennan Building, [H1], 52, 215–17

Marshall, John R. See Hornblower and Marshall

Maryland Blue Cross Building. See Baltimore County Public Safety Building

Maryland Club [K6], 29, 270, 275–76, 396

Maryland Institute College of Art, Main Building, [K12], 270, 282, 283–84, 285

Maryland National Bank Building. See NationsBank

Maryland Penitentiary, 180, 402

Masek, Edward A., Jr., 250

Mason, Alfred, 292–93, 408

Masonic Temple (former), [A16], 85–86, 397, 407, 417

Matthai, H. Parker, 65

Matthews, George, 190–91

341, 342, 395, 396, 399, 411, 414

Nine North Front Street, 183

Nolting, William G., 412, 419

Northern District Police Station, 250

Notman, John, 257

Number 6 Engine House, [F11], 19, 192–93, 415

Oakland Spring House, [L5], 315–16, 404

Observatory, Patterson Park. *See* Patterson Park Observatory

O'Connor, James W. and James F. Delaney, 122–24

Oheb Shalom, Temple (new). *See* Temple Oheb Shalom

Oheb Shalom, Temple (old). *See* Prince Hall Masons Masonic Temple

Old Baltimore City Jail Gatehouse. *See* Baltimore City Jail Gatehouse (old)

Old Catholic Cathedral. *See* Basilica of the Assumption

Old Mercantile Safe Deposit and Trust Company. *See* Mercantile Safe Deposit and Trust Company (old)

Old Otterbein United Methodist Church, [H2], 4, 62, 217–18, 315, 415

Old Patterson Park High School. *See* Hampstead Hill Junior High/Highlandtown Middle School

Old Town Meeting House, [F9], 4, 190–91

Old Western High School. *See* Booker T. Washington Middle School

Olmsted Brohters. *See* Olmsted, Olmsted, and Eliot

Olmsted, Frederick Law, Jr., 25, 365

Olmsted, Frederick Law, Sr., 24, 336, 365, 383, 393–94

Olmsted, Olmsted, and Eliot, 25, 37, 38, 364–69, 379

One Calvert Plaza, [D6], 152–54

One Charles Center, [A12], 45, 46, 47, 63, 80–81, 326

One East Lexington Street, [A14], 82–83, 397

One South Calvert Building. *See* One Calvert Plaza

One West Mount Vernon Place. *See* Hackerman House

Orchard Street Church, [J1], 242–44, 398

Oriole Park at Camden Yards, [I3], 51, 228, 230–32

Otterbein United Methodist Church. *See* Old Otterbein United Methodist Church

Our Lady of the Angels Chapel, [J11], 259–61

Owens, Benjamin B., 161–62, 412

Owens and Sisco, 161–62

Paca-Pratt Building, [E9], 174–75, 413

Padonia Commerce Building, [M10], 350–51

Pagoda, Patterson Park. *See* Patterson Park Observatory

Palmer, Edward L., Jr., 364, 368

Palmer and Lamdin, 27, 274, 367, 410

Park Mill, [N5], 361

Parker, J. Harleston, 412, 413, 415, 417

Index of Buildings by Type

Note: The letter after an entry refers to the tour and the number refers to the stop on a tour. So, G6 would indicate Tour G, sixth stop on the tour. For page numbers and cross references, refer to the previous index.

Residential

Emmanuel Episcopal
Church, C11
Episcopal Cathedral of the
Incarnation, L12
First and Franklin Street
Presbyterian Church, C13
First Unitarian Church, B12
Franklin Street Presbyterian
Church (former), B11
Grace and St. Peter's Episco-
pal Church, C15
Greek Orthodox Cathedral
of the Annunciation, K10
Green Mount Cemetery
Chapel, K2
Lloyd Street Synagogue, F7
Lovely Lane Methodist
Church, L1
Mount Vernon Place
United Methodist
Church, C9
Mount Washington Presbyte-
rian Church, N14
Old Otterbein United Meth-
odist Church, H2
Old Town Meeting House,
F9
Orchard Street Church, J1
Our Lady of the Angels
Chapel, J11
Prince Hall Masons Ma-
sonic Temple, K17
St. Alphonsus' Church, B5
St. Ignatius-Center Stage
Building, C6
St. James and St. John's
Church, F13
St. John the Evangelist
Church, F12
St. John's Church, Hunting-
don, L4
St. Luke's Church, J9
St. Mary's Seminary Chapel,
J3
St. Paul's Episcopal Church,
B1
St. Peter the Apostle
Church, J6
St. Vincent de Paul, F2
Temple Oheb Shalom, O8

Trinity Episcopal Church,
M5
University Baptist Church,
L10
Zion Church of the City of
Baltimore, D12

**Civic and Public (includes
hospitals and museums)**

American Visionary Art Mu-
seum, H3
Baltimore City Jail Gate-
house (old), F1
Baltimore Convention Cen-
ter, A4
Baltimore County Court-
house, M4
Baltimore Museum of Art,
L6
Baltimore-Washington Inter-
national Airport, H6
City Hall, D11
Clarence M. Mitchell, Jr.
Courthouse, D3
Curtis Bay Water Tank, H5
Druid Hill Park, K24
Enoch Pratt Free Library,
B10
Enoch Pratt Free Library,
Canton Branch, G2
Fort McHenry, H4
Johns Hopkins Hospital, G6
Montebello Filtration Plant,
G12
National Aquarium at Balti-
more, A2
Number 6 Engine House,
F11
Oriole Park at Camden
Yards, I3
Patterson Park Observatory,
G4
Peale Museum, D13
Sewage Pumping Station, F5
Sheppard and Enoch Pratt
Hospital, L20
State Police Headquarters,
O9

United States Custom House, D10
Valve House, G9
Walters Art Gallery, C19
Western District Police Station (former), J5

Education and Related Use

Booker T. Washington Middle School, K20
Carnegie Institute Embryology Building, L11
City College, G11
Clarence M Mitchell, Jr. Engineering Building, Morgan State University, G13
Columbus Center, A3
Davidge Hall, E10
Eastern Female High School, F10
Gilman Hall, L9
Goucher College Center, M8
Goucher Hall and Campus, L2
Hampstead Hill Junior High/Highlandtown Middle School, G3

Maryland Institute, College of Art, Main Building, K12
McKim Free School, F8
Peabody Dormitory, C5
Peabody Institute, C2
St. Mary's Seminary, N11
YMCA Building (former), B3

Bridges

Carrollton Viaduct, I6
Thomas Viaduct, I7

Monuments

Battle Monument, D1
Washington Monument, C1

Miscellaneous

Green Mount Cemetery Gatehouse, K1
Maryland Club, K6
Masonic Temple (former), A16
Oakland Spring House, L5
Scottish Rite Temple of Freemasonry, L13

Picture Credits

Archdiocese of Baltimore, Archives, 102

B & O Railroad Museum, 264, 265

Baltimore City Life Museums, 185

Basilica of the Assumption, 100, 101

Bodine, A. Aubrey Collection, The Peale Museum, 116, 129, 146, 176, 180, 237, 247, 271 (bottom), 323 (bottom), 326, 332, 360, 392 (top)

Dilts, James D., 71, 191 (top), 331, 361 (bottom)

Eaton, Jon-Eric, 74, 145, 298, 335, 341 (top), 348

Fort McHenry National Monument and Historic Shrine, 220, 221

Gilbert, Alan, 218

Hamilton, William C., 272, 273

Inglehart, Susan, 209, 292, 294, 295, 359, 364, 375, 377, 378

Levin, Aaron, 97, 104, 107, 117, 118, 119 (top), 121, 122, 124–126, 128, 134, 135, 137, 139, 140, 152–54, 156–58, 160–62, 166–68, 171, 172, 175, 181, 246, 248, 249, 251, 252, 255, 258, 261, 263 (bottom), 274–78, 325 (bottom), 340, 345–47, 350, 361 (top), 362, 363 (top), 371

McElhinney, Susan T., 95, 148, 384, 386, 392 (bottom), 394

National Aquarium in Baltimore, 65

Peale Museum, 108, 133

Raedeke, Paul T., 199, 257, 357

Redden, Gretchen, 106, 109, 170, 188, 189, 192, 271 (top), 288, 301, 313, 325 (top), 329, 363 (bottom)

Reikin, Dawn, 132, 243, 263 (top), 327, 366, 369

Savadow, Bruce, 64, 67, 69, 76–86, 91–94, 98, 99, 119 (bottom), 127, 130, 141, 147, 150, 155, 169, 173, 182, 184, 186, 187, 194, 195, 200–203, 205–7, 210, 211, 215, 217, 222–24, 227, 229–34, 245, 259, 260, 279, 281–83, 285, 286, 289, 290, 291, 293, 296, 297, 300, 308, 311, 314–23 (top), 324, 333, 334, 341 (bottom), 343, 344, 358, 367, 368, 372, 374, 376, 379, 383, 385, 387, 388, 390, 393

Schamp, J. Brough, 73

Solomon, Ron, 284

Glossary Illustrations

Fletcher, Sir Banister. *A History of Architecture on the Comparative Method.* New York: Scribners, 1963, pp. 423, 426, 427 (top), 430, 431, 433 (left), 436

Hamlin, Talbot. *Architecture Through the Ages.* New York: Putnam's, 1953, pp. 424, 435

Morrison, Hugh S. *Early American Architecture; from the First Colonial Settlements to the National Period.* New York: Oxford University Press, 1952, p. 422

Saylor, Henry H. *Dictionary of Architecture.* New York: Wiley, 1965, pp. 425, 427 (bottom), 433 (right)